FORMING HUMANITY

Forming Humanity

Redeeming the German Bildung *Tradition*

JENNIFER A. HERDT

THE UNIVERSITY OF CHICAGO PRESS   CHICAGO AND LONDON

The University of Chicago Press, Chicago 60637
The University of Chicago Press, Ltd., London
© 2019 by The University of Chicago
All rights reserved. No part of this book may be used or reproduced in any manner whatsoever without written permission, except in the case of brief quotations in critical articles and reviews. For more information, contact the University of Chicago Press, 1427 E. 60th St., Chicago, IL 60637.
Published 2019
Paperback edition 2024

33 32 31 30 29 28 27 26 25 24   1 2 3 4 5

ISBN-13: 978-0-226-61848-7 (cloth)
ISBN-13: 978-0-226-83690-4 (paper)
ISBN-13: 978-0-226-61851-7 (e-book)
DOI: https://doi.org/10.7208/chicago/9780226618517.001.0001

Published with the assistance of the Frederick W. Hilles Publication Fund of Yale University.

Library of Congress Cataloging-in-Publication Data

Names: Herdt, Jennifer A., 1967– author.
Title: Forming humanity : redeeming the German Bildung tradition / Jennifer A. Herdt.
Description: Chicago ; London : The University of Chicago Press, 2019. | Includes bibliographical references and index.
Identifiers: LCCN 2019013312 | ISBN 9780226618487 (cloth : alk. paper) | ISBN 9780226618517 (e-book)
Subjects: LCSH: Philosophy, German—18th century. | Philosophy, German—19th century. | Humanism—Germany—History—18th century. | Humanism—Germany—History—19th century. | Moral development—Germany. | Bildungsromans—History and criticism. | Philosophy and religion—Germany—History—18th century. | Philosophy and religion—Germany—History—19th century. | Religion and culture.
Classification: LCC B2743 .H47 2019 | DDC 170.943—dc23
LC record available at https://lccn.loc.gov/2019013312

For Cora and Adam

An diesem Tage, dem vergnügtesten seines Lebens, schien auch seine eigne Bildung erst anzufangen; er fühlte die Notwendigkeit, sich zu belehren, indem er zu lehren aufgefordert ward.

Goethe

CONTENTS

Introduction | 1
1 From Paideia to Humanism | 27
2 Pietism and the Problem of Human Craft (*Menschen-Kunst*) | 56
3 The Harmonious Harp-Playing of Humanity: J. G. Herder | 82
4 Ethical Formation and the Invention of the Religion of Art | 112
5 The Rise of the Bildungsroman and the Commodification of Literature | 133
6 Authorship and Its Resignation in Goethe's *Wilhelm Meister* | 156
7 "The *Bildung* of Self-Consciousness Itself towards Science": Hegel | 188
Conclusion | 237

Acknowledgments | 253
Notes | 257
Index | 313

INTRODUCTION

Once upon a time, we awoke to discover humanity as task. We were already human, to be sure. But we were not yet fully or perfectly human. We discovered ourselves internally riven, divided, torn by opposing forces. We found ourselves unformed, immature, not yet capable of taking responsibility for ourselves. Nor could we simply await our full humanity, like the ripening of a fruit. No, it was something we had to take into our own hands. We had to become our own parents, our own teachers. At the same time, in taking up the task of forming humanity, we were conscious of participating in something greater than ourselves, something somehow transcendent. And we were keenly aware of the conditioned character of our self-forming agency, of human beings as always already formed formers, inheritors of language and culture and historical memory.

It was late eighteenth-century Germany. Kant was among those sounding the trumpet, proclaiming "man's emergence from his self-incurred immaturity . . . the inability to use one's understanding without the guidance of another."[1] Humankind was entering into adulthood, and it was time to put away childish things. Now we were capable of autonomy, of free self-determination. And in fact, Kant insisted, we had always been capable of this; our immaturity was "self-incurred." We were not emerging out of a natural childhood but releasing ourselves from a kind of self-imprisonment, from chains of tradition and authority with which we had bound ourselves. The key to release was precisely recognition that we were in fact self-incarcerated.

Kant regarded reason, Enlightenment, as the key to emergence into maturity. For those who followed in his wake, however, reason alone was insufficient; the aspiration to a fully self-realized humanity was integrally linked to a more holistic ideal, that of *Bildung*, understood both as a process of education, cultivation, and development, and as its result. In the person of Bildung, all faculties and drives were developed and balanced harmoniously with one another. And the collective task of forming humanity could be achieved only through the fashioning of self-forming individuals. Clearly this was a vision rooted in a broadly Aristotelian understanding of the flourishing of each natural kind in the realization of its *ergon*, with human beings flourishing as they live lives of virtue, governed well by practical reason. It was thoroughly teleological and normative. It was not merely a matter of the pursuit of self-interest, maximal desire-satisfaction, or mere negative liberty. Thomas Pfau has written of how Romantic and post-Romantic writers show how "Aristotelian praxis and its underlying, public and normative sense of a telos have been supplanted by modernity's autistic notion of a self defined via its exclusive dominium or 'right' to access the fantasized, virtual realm of economic and erotic fulfillment."[2] The project of forming humanity, however, was not this; it was not the displacement of Aristotelian praxis and teleology but the pursuit of a good at once personal and communal, the assumption of living well as task. And those embarked on this post-Kantian project could have agreed with Alasdair MacIntyre that "to live well is to act so as to move toward achieving the best goods of which one is capable and so as to become the kind of agent capable of achieving those goods."[3] To be devoted to Bildung was to be devoted to goods beyond one's self. The ideal of Bildung, however, emphasized not common virtues but individuality, not instruction from without but unfolding from within — ethical formation as self-realization. The person of Bildung was not just educated but was capable of sound judgment and self-direction. She could take responsibility for her own character and life rather than leaving this in the hands of paternalistic authorities. She was often conceived of in terms of broadly aesthetic categories, as cultured, refined, civilized.[4]

Bildung was not just an aesthetic, spiritual, and ethical but also a political ideal. Benedict Anderson has written influentially of the nation as an imagined political community that arose in the context of the decline of religion and dynasty as bases for community. The nation provided an alternative way of transforming "fatality into continuity, contingency into meaning," made possible by print capitalism, by the novel and the newspaper, and the ways in which these created the possibility of a homogeneous, horizontal comradeship.[5] In the eighteenth century Germany did not exist as a political entity; it comprised a set of principalities (Prussia and Austria most prominent among them) loosely united by language, culture (although *not* religious confession), and the memory of having belonged to the Holy Roman Empire. In a modern world dominated by centralized nation-states and their outstretched colonial arms, "Germany" lacked both political unity and economic power. That it was this context that nurtured the meteoric rise of German philosophy and literature has been narrated since the early nineteenth century as a form of compensation. The Germans, Madame de Staël fatefully pronounced, "join the greatest boldness in thought to the most obedient character."[6] But we must be cautious about retrojecting nationalism in Anderson's sense back into eighteenth-century Germany; in those lands it is a phenomenon essentially of the 1820s forward, gaining momentum in the wake of the Napoleonic occupation. What preceded nationalism in Germany was something quite different: the project of Bildung, of forming humanity.

It was not that there was in this earlier period no awareness of nation, of communal ties linked with shared customs, place, and most especially language. On the contrary, both Johann Gottfried Herder and Wilhelm von Humboldt were pioneering philosophers of language and made major contributions to the formation of the modern concepts of culture and nation. But reflection on nation was part and parcel of the project of forming humanity well before it was appropriated by nationalism. The Bildung ideal was cosmopolitan at heart; it imagined a form of identity based on shared humanity, not on shared nation or language or culture or religion or history.[7] Yet it did so in a way that cherished and championed particularity, at both the individual and the communal level. The humanity to be realized was not a homogeneous uniformity. It was thus quite unlike a cosmopolitanism of naked basic human rights.

Martha Nussbaum has argued that nationalism "substitutes a colorful idol for the substantive universal values of justice and right."[8] Cosmopolitanism, she acknowledges, appears by contrast "boringly flat," demanding that "we should give our first allegiance to no mere form of government, no temporal power, but to the moral community made up by the humanity of all human beings." The problem she poses, in effect, is how the moral community of human beings can be imagined in brilliant, diverse color. But the Bildung generation anticipated not only this question but also the answer she offers—to turn quite self-consciously to the tools of the imagination.[9] Anthony Appiah echoes this insight in his account of cosmopolitan reading: "it is not 'reason' but a different human capacity that grounds our sharing: namely, the grasp of a narrative logic that allows us to construct the world to which our imaginations respond."[10] Before the novel and the newspaper became enablers of nationalism, they were seized upon as resources for Bildung.

The Bildung generation, then, did not flee from politics into the compensatory joys of poetry and philosophy. Rather, they took up the politically vital task of forming persons capable of taking an active role in shaping and governing their collective existence, understanding this as part and parcel of the formation of humanity.[11] This set of political concerns is clearly evident in Kant's "What Is Enlightenment?" Writing in 1784, just two years before the end of the reign of Frederick the Great in Prussia, Kant praises this exemplar of "enlightened absolutism" for having prepared the ground for the dismantling of absolutism. In a sentence that appeared particularly prescient in the aftermath of the bloody Reign of Terror in France, Kant insisted that "a revolution may well put an end to autocratic despotism and to rapacious or power-seeking oppression, but it will never produce a true reform in ways of thinking. Instead, new prejudices, like the ones they replaced, will serve as a leash to control the great unthinking mass."[12] What is required is not violent revolution but rather the kinds of reforms instituted by Frederick: religious tolerance, freedom of the press and literature, judicial reform, greater openings for social mobility based on individual aptitude. The heart of the matter, Kant here asserts, is the freedom to *argue* to and before the public: all that is required for enlightenment is freedom, he writes, "and the freedom in question is the most innocuous form of all—freedom to make public use of one's reason in all matters. But I hear on all sides the cry: Don't argue!"[13] Only when the people have by virtue of having accustomed themselves to freedom of argument (worked out in an exemplary way, he thinks, with respect to religious doctrine) do they become equipped for freedom of action, for civic freedom: "Eventually, it even influences the principles of governments, which find that they can themselves profit by treating man, who is *more than a machine*, in a manner appropriate to his dignity."[14]

As it happened, Frederick had reservations about the emergence of a critical public. An edict of the same year proclaimed that

> a private person has no right to pass public and perhaps even disapproving judgment on the actions, procedures, laws, regulations, and ordinances of sovereigns and courts, their officials, assemblies, and courts of law, or to promulgate or publish in print pertinent reports that he manages to obtain. For a private person is not at all capable of making such judgment, because he lacks complete knowledge of circumstances and motives.[15]

Under his successor, censorship accelerated, and with it resistance to the public monitoring of state power.

The same conviction that freedom is essential to the kind of ethical formation necessary for political reform is present in Friedrich Schiller's *Letters on Aesthetic Education*. Schiller's epistles, addressed to the public by way of a new literary journal launched for the purpose, appeared in 1795, the year following the end of the Reign of Terror. All of Europe was reeling; hopes raised high for a new era of liberty and equality had ended in horror and disillusionment. Schiller, developing an argument made earlier by Humboldt, argued that genuine political progress and emancipation require harmony between the "sense drive," our receptivity to experienced particulars, and the "form drive," the active imposition of form by way of reason. Kantian reason alone cannot overcome the gap between theory and practice, reason and feeling.[16] Aesthetic education cultivates just such a harmoniously active receptivity, transforming desire and imagination so that they are directed at what is truly good. It is thus a necessary precondition for responsible moral autonomy and a political liberty worthy of the name. Aesthetic education created, in the words of Jürgen Habermas, "a forum in which the private people, come together to form a public, readied themselves to compel public authority to legitimate itself before public opinion. The *publicum* developed into the public, the *subjectum* into the [reasoning] subject, the receiver of regulations from above into the ruling authorities' adversary."[17] The freely self-realizing subject is thus at the same time the human being who has become capable of being a public reasoner, claiming a right to issue judgments on public affairs and to be the recipient of justifications in terms of reason and the common good: "The principle of control that the bourgeois public opposed to [existing rule] — namely, publicity — was intended to change domination as such."[18]

Bildung is one of those German loanwords, like *Zeitgeist* and *Schadenfreude*, for which no economical translation is available. Moreover, because the term has been significant in different periods and contexts, any translation will tend to privilege one out of a number of ways in which *Bildung* has been used. I will for the most part simply speak of *Bildung*. I will at times use "ethical formation" as a translation of *Bildung*, since this indicates most concisely the particular angle of analysis being undertaken here. I am not attempting to trace an unfolding conversation about education or pedagogy in general, though as the term is used in contemporary German, that might be the expectation. As *Bildung* has entered into English, it has retained a more focused meaning that is fairly well rendered as "ethical formation." While the term *Bildung* never fully entered the English language, *Bildungsroman* — the novel of ethical formation — did, and I shall also retain that term in the original.

For convenience's sake, I am framing my object of study as "the Bildung tradition." This neologism offers a convenient shorthand. It does not imply a uniformity among the thinkers and ideas being considered, beyond a common concern with the ethical formation of individuals and of humankind as such, for which the complex and flexible concept of Bildung provided a unifying thread. Nearly every major thinker and artist working in the German context from the 1770s through the 1830s and beyond might well fall within the scope of a study of the Bildung tradition so understood. This is true despite the fact that it was an effervescent time, spanning in the course of less than half a century a host of movements: the Enlightenment, *Sturm und Drang*, Weimar Classicism, Romanticism, and Idealism. My study will be sharply limited in scope, confining itself to the seminal texts of a small subset of thinkers. Those on whom the study is focused are thinkers whose reflections on aesthetic and ethical formation, and on "humanity" as its telos, have a strong claim to be significant and broadly influential: Johann Gottfried Herder, Wilhelm von Humboldt, Johann Wolfgang von Goethe, Friedrich Schiller, and Georg Wilhelm Friedrich Hegel. Kant, Karl Philipp Moritz, and others come in for cameo appearances. Bildung retains focal, if constantly changing, significance amidst the shift from the calm aspirations of the Enlightenment, through the turbulent emotionalism of Sturm und Drang and the Neohumanism of Weimar Classicism, and into German Romanticism and Idealism. Concentrating on a handful of thinkers allows me to look closely at the place of Bildung in this rapidly evolving cultural scene. Studying the Bildung tradition requires moving across disciplinary boundaries in much the same way as did those who comprise that tradition: Herder was a philosopher, theologian, poet, and literary critic; Schiller styled himself a poet-philosopher but was also a physician and historian; Hegel did not just start out, like many intellectuals of his day, studying theology but was himself a theologian as well as a philosopher. Political, aesthetic, religious, and philosophical concerns were all seen as bound up with one another, and with the task of forming humanity. My particular focus, further, is on texts and thinkers who are not part of the theological canon, despite the theological resonances of their thought.

In the drama of Bildung, Christianity was sometimes cast into the role of the retrograde; it was seen as fostering submission to authority, passive acceptance of tradition, and failure to take responsibility for directing one's own life. Art, literature, philosophy, in contrast, were heralded as bringers of salvation, as capable of forming a "public" equipped for mature self-government, and a humanity worthy of the name. However, the relationship was complex. Clearly the task of forming humanity took shape against the backdrop of Christian conceptions of humankind not merely as immature but as fallen, sinful, and rebellious. Here psychic and social harmony was located not just in a future ideal but in a past now beyond reach, or at least human reach. The concept of Bildung initially took shape in a specifically theological context. Meister Eckhart and other Rhineland mystics, employing for the first time the German vernacular to discuss such matters, took up the term *Bildung*, and its many variants formed through the addition of a wealth of nominal and verbal prefixes, to speak of *divine* formative and re-formative agency: of God's formation of human beings in the divine image, of the fall as the destruction or defacing of that image, and of the re-formation of fallen humanity after the image of God in Christ.

One might, then, tell the story of Bildung as a tale of secularization, and so it has indeed often been narrated: human beings took responsibility for something they had earlier left in the hands of God.

They sought not to become members of the body of Christ, restored bearers of the image of God, formed in Christ's image, but to discover and become themselves. Thus *Bildung* ceased to mean passive formation or re-formation at the hands of an external power, and came to mean active and autonomous self-realization. But this secularization narrative is oversimplified, and the story, as we shall explore in the chapters that follow, is more interestingly complex. What is undoubtedly the case is that we can understand this tradition well only in relation to theological reflection on humankind as created in the image of God and called, by virtue of that fact, to play a special role in the *reditus* of creation to God. More tendentiously, modern reflection on Bildung is as much an inheritor as a critic of this tradition, which we can broadly construe as Christian humanism.[19] If Humboldt, Goethe, and Schiller understood themselves to be crafting a Religion of Art as an aesthetic successor to Christian theology, the same cannot be said of Herder and Hegel. They took themselves to be interpreting and furthering, not displacing, this understanding of the theological vocation of humanity.[20]

While there are a range of Christian understandings of the imago Dei, some of which I will tease out in chapters 1 and 2, a central strand running through medieval and Renaissance humanism conceives of human beings as created in the image of God insofar as they are moral agents, principles of their own actions and therefore capable of being providential for themselves. As moral agents, human beings are called to participate in the end of creation—creaturely participation in the self-giving friendship that constitutes the inner life of God. This friendship is expressed in lives of love and service to others, including strangers and enemies. The imago Dei is thus both gift and task. Hence the Neoplatonic *exitus-reditus* is interpreted not as necessary emanation but as free creation, and the return of creation to God not as ascent out of material reality via contemplation but as the invitation of strangers and enemies into the self-giving friendship of the divine life.

Reflection on Bildung was a site for working out the radical social and political implications of this doctrine of creation in the image of God and its affirmation of human dignity—as a condemnation of social, economic, and political arrangements that fail to treat human beings as principles of their own actions but instead regard the masses as instruments through which the whims and desires of the wealthy and powerful few can be indulged, or as cogs in the machinery of the market economy. It was a locus for affirming the value and importance of diverse individual and collective expressions of humanity, even while insisting that individual and collective self-realization are good only insofar as they take forms capable of mutual recognition, and beyond recognition, friendship—of flourishing life in community. While we do have to do in the Bildung tradition with growing affirmation of human diversity, agency, and self-definition at both individual and social levels, this involved no simple repudiation of divine formative agency. These were thinkers intent on overcoming impoverished notions of God as contrastively transcendent to the world, of divine agency as competing with human agency, and so of finding more adequate ways of characterizing not just human self-realization but also the divine activity within which this self-creation was unfolding. They fell short in a variety of ways: Herder embraces a naive Enlightenment providentialism; Humboldt, Schiller, and Goethe take refuge in the ontological indeterminacy of a Religion of Art; Hegel takes the overcoming of evil up into the unfolding, self-realizing life of God. Their understandings of Bildung and the formation of humanity are nevertheless open to being critically reappropriated by a renovated Christian humanism that accepts the task of the formation of humanity through projects of individual and collective human self-realization as participation in the *reditus* of creation to a radically transcendent God whose life is overflowing self-gift and invitation into friendship.[21]

Habermas has argued that what was being forged in the notion of humanity as telos of Bildung was a kind of immanent transcendence. The original site of this conception of humanity, he suggests, was the bourgeois family. For the family was seen as offering a space par excellence for Bildung—that is, for the "non-instrumental development of all faculties that marks the cultivated personality."[22] It was an illusion to think of the family as free from the constraints of the market economy and its commodity exchanges. Yet it was not *mere* illusion:

> In the form of this specific notion of humanity a conception of what existed was promulgated within the bourgeois world which promised redemption from the constraint of what existed without escaping into a transcendental realm. This conception's transcendence of what was immanent was the element of truth that

raised bourgeois ideology above ideology itself, most fundamentally in that area where the experience of "humanity" originated: in the humanity of the intimate relationships between human beings who, under the aegis of the family, were nothing more than human.[23]

Habermas's reference point here is Max Horkheimer, who argued that despite the reification of the human being in the economic realm, within which the family is embedded,

> nonetheless, since relations inside the family are not mediated by the market and individuals do not oppose one another to be competitors, human beings have always also had the opportunity for acting not merely as determined by a function but as human beings. Whereas in bourgeois life the communal interest has an essentially negative character, concerning itself only with the defense against danger, it assumes a positive character in sexual love and, above all, in maternal care. Within this unity . . . the development and happiness of the other is desired. To this extent, the bourgeois family leads not only to bourgeois authority but to a premonition of a better human condition.[24]

This is a stunningly naive idealization of the realities of family life. What is additionally striking here, however, is the way in which both Habermas and Horkheimer regard humanity as realized only where others are loved for their own sake. The project of Bildung, of self-realization, is here thus seen not in terms of grasping after a mere negative freedom for idiosyncratic projects of self-shaping, nor even solely as freedom for public reasoning and political participation, important as this is: it is freedom for loving relationships. The mutual recognition that characterizes the public sphere of critical judgment and responsibility-holding is glimpsed as serving something fuller, more perfect: a shared life in which persons are cherished for their own sake, a life of friendship. This gesture toward the "transcendence of ideology" and "the premonition of a better human condition" in relationships of love should not be read as a mere diversion from Habermas's driving concern, the possibility of revitalizing the public sphere. On the contrary, it is a most telling gesture, one that points to the ways in which modern reflection on the cultivation of humanity is rooted in and nourished in an ongoing way by a Christian narrative logic—of humankind as created in the image of God and called to a friendship with God expressed in loving recognition of others as similarly called.

We see something akin to Habermas's groping after a form of immanent transcendence also in Martha Nussbaum. "Human life," she writes, "is something mysterious and extremely complicated. . . . In the name of science, the wonder that illuminates and prompts the deepest science has been jettisoned."[25] In trying to capture the mystery of human life, she finds it quite appropriate to speak of having a "soul."[26] "All of human life," she adds, "is a going beyond the facts, an acceptance of generous fancies, a projection of our own sentiments and inner activities onto the forms we perceive about us."[27] Yet she insists that "transcendent extrahistorical standards" are unnecessary; "as concerned readers we search for a human good that we are trying to bring about in and for the human community."[28] She does acknowledge that the problematic aspiration to transcend the human condition and become like God is fundamentally transformed when God is understood as one who "has actually lived out the nontranscendent life and understands it in the only way it can be understood, by suffering and death."[29] She sees in Augustine's account of Christian love, with its christologically rooted anti-Stoicism, an important advance over earlier accounts of the ascent of love "because it situates ascent within humanity and renounces the wish to depart from our human condition."[30] Yet she concludes that what can appear as an affirmation of internal transcendence on the part of Christian thinkers such as Augustine or Dante is marred by an outlook that finally denies the significance of worldly losses and injustices. These Christian conceptions of transcendence are in her eyes finally irreconcilable "with the idea of ongoing compassion for human life."[31] So she fights a two-front battle, against "religious" affirmations of external transcendence on the one hand and scientistic, crudely utilitarian blindness to mystery and wonder on the other.

Is Nussbaum right about the irreconcilability of divine transcendence and compassion? Or is it precisely loving God that makes it possible for persons of faith to be most fully alive to that intrinsic value the loss of which represents a horror or outrage, which cannot be outweighed by some other gain, that makes it possible for them to sustain commitment to universal human solidarity in the face of all the "myriad ways in which real, concrete, human beings fall short of, ignore, parody and betray this magnificent potential"? For they love finite others "not [as] something that can be characterized just by reference to this being alone" but as made in the image of God.[32]

Charles Taylor has drawn attention to the ways in which Romantic thinkers turned to art and the aesthetic in response to the felt inadequacies of Kantian moralism and in search of a higher goal, fulfillment, and harmony. One of the distinctive characteristics of these aesthetic languages is the indeterminacy of their ontic commitments, which therefore remain open for theological reappropriation as well as for purely immanent readings: "If we reach our highest goal through art and the aesthetic, then this goal, it would appear, must be immanent. It would represent an alternative to the love of God as a way of transcending moralism. But things are not so simple. God is not excluded."[33] Immanent transcendence can open up space for noncontrastive radical transcendence. For it is possible for defenders of internal transcendence, as of radical transcendence, to agree that there are things whose "value can neither be measured exhaustively in quantitative terms, nor reduced to utility, nor subjected at someone's whim to trade-offs of the sorts that markets are designed to facilitate."[34] They can insist together on the importance of properly affirming and protecting the significance of life in the world *and* agree that we are capable of doing so only inasmuch as we see the world "as revelatory of more than its immediate, and superficial, self-presentation."[35] And some may move beyond an insistence on immanence to invoke "sacred value" or the "transcendent Good," even if they resist God-talk.[36]

The late-eighteenth-century project of forming humanity was, however, Janus-faced. Even as it represented a commitment to cultivating persons capable of public judgment and public reasoning, of holding those in power responsible to care and concern for all for their own sake, and an aspiration to fostering harmonious friendship-in-diversity, in reality democratic political aspirations were again and again deferred. The project of Bildung could fail altogether as persons allowed themselves to be defined merely as producers and consumers. Or it could be reduced to a mere license for private projects of self-cultivation, or ways of reinscribing social and class status in terms of cultural literacy and polish.[37] Perhaps most insidious of all is the way in which "the public" could again and again be defined in ways that purported to include all voices but in fact failed to do so and indeed policed boundaries that effectively excluded those framed as incapable of or resistant to Bildung. Since humanity was not a given but something that had to be *cultivated*, one could at one and the same time affirm and deny others' humanity. Some were framed as merely vestigially human, or as immature, perhaps permanently so.

Conceptions of Bildung were—in ways that can be traced back to Kant—often bound up with developing theories of race, in such a way that only whites were seen as fully capable of realizing humanity, while other races, representing the species on its way to human maturity, were fated to decay and die out.[38] Only whites—and even more particularly Germans, Kant thought (although Herder resisted strenuously, as we shall see)—were destined fully to realize humanity. Kant's commitment to dialogical encounter thus reveals itself to reach only as far as the boundaries of whiteness; other races stand in no need of the freedom to argue before a public, for they are incapable of the kind of autonomous self-direction that renders civic freedom boon rather than bane. Kant's normative conception of the human species weighed "like a theoretical imposition on the individual human being—overdetermining, extinguishing, and erasing human difference—excluding those human beings who, it turns out, had never belonged to this universal future of humanity."[39] Hence the project of Bildung is bound up with racism, justifications of slavery, colonialism, imperialism, and the origins of National Socialism. Even among those, such as Herder, who sharply rejected race, Eurocentrism, and imperialism, some theorists have seen in the very notion of Bildung "a teleological view of the providential and progressive unfolding of nature and history that is wrapped up with how we think about race."[40]

What, then, are we to make of this project of forming a self-forming humanity? It is tempting either to dismiss it as naively optimistic or to demonize it as irredeemably tainted. Both responses, I would suggest, would be too hasty. For it is not someone else but we ourselves who in the time of modernity became aware of our individuality and our collective self-formative powers, and the story of Bildung is the tale of this coming to awareness. While it may go by other names, the question of how we come to terms with our collective moral responsibility for our norms, practices, and identities is not one that we can simply evade. The project of forming humanity can be revised and reinterpreted, but it cannot easily be laid aside. As

Thomas McCarthy argues with the respect to the idea of "human development," "It is inherently ambivalent in character, both indispensable and dangerous. Thus, . . . there is no alternative to its ongoing deconstruction and reconstruction."[41] To engage in its immanent critique is to further, not to defeat, it. But this is in fact what we should do. Or so I shall argue.

This study turns to an unlikely source of assistance in this project of the immanent critique and retrieval of the project of forming humanity. We would hardly expect Karl Barth, staunch theological critic of liberalism, to be a champion of the Bildung tradition with its emphasis on human self-realizing powers. Nor is he. On Barth's account, modern theology is inaugurated by a retrieval of humanism, the core idea of which "was that the perfect life consisted in the complete autarchy of rational man in a rational world on the basis of the existence and dominion of a Deity guaranteeing this association and thus too man's complete autarchy."[42] A God admitted only as guarantee of human autarchy can eventually be dismissed by a self-authorizing human autarchy, however, and this is for Barth the story of modern theology. Yet in a certain sense Barth himself stands within the Bildung tradition. We see this particularly clearly in his 1926 lecture "Church and Culture," in which he declares that "culture is the task set through the Word of God for achieving the destined condition of man in unity of soul and body."[43] The problem of humanity, he goes on to say, is the problem of culture. "But men exist as soul and body, spirit and nature, subject and object, inwardly and outwardly, judged on the synthesis of both these elements. But also it is just this synthesis which man lacks."[44] Barth here echoes the Bildung tradition quite distinctly: culture is a task, the task of the realization of humanity, conceived of in part as the synthesis of a series of oppositions. It is a task that is sensed through awareness of a missing unity, a unity that is felt as something that ought to be. This missing unity is keenly recognized in encountering God: "when, set before God, he comes to himself, he faces the rift which goes through his whole existence; and he is confronted with the problem of synthesis."[45] The problem of culture is not to be dismissed or refused; indeed Christian preaching "has always legitimately been simultaneously a summons to cultural activity."[46] At the same time, he insists, "Christian preaching, unless it became untrue to itself, has met every culture, however supposedly rich and mature, with ultimate, sharp scepticism."[47] This is because Christian preaching listens for the Word of God. This is a Word of judgment, which calls into question all attempts at synthesis, at resolving the problem of humanity. But it is also at the same time a (prior) Word of grace. For culture confronts humankind not simply as task but also as promise, "the promise originally given to man of what he is to become."[48] This is a promise of "divine friendship" and "an "affirmation of man as his creature and his image," "God's affirmation of man's life in communion with himself, a life to which the desperately sought unity of existence is not denied."[49] For to be created according to the image of God is to be created by God "as a partner who is capable of entering into covenant relationship with [God]."[50] Or, as Barth develops this theme christologically in his massive *Church Dogmatics*, human beings are called to correspond to what has been already accomplished in Jesus Christ's covenant partnership with the God who has willed from all eternity to be for humanity. The fall has not utterly destroyed this capacity for covenant partnership; humankind still remains the addressee of the divine invitation to friendship. So "culture connotes exactly that promise to man: fulfilment, unity, wholeness within his sphere as creature, as man."[51] And this promise is restored through reconciliation in Christ, which "gives man again insight into the meaning of his activity. It gives him the courage to understand even the broken relation in which he stands and acts towards God as still a relation and to take it seriously."[52] The task of the church, for Barth, is to seek to illuminate the meaning of cultural activity, not by way of a "general sanctifying" of cultural activity but by considering culture as always potentially revelatory, as "filled with the promise," of "signs which, perhaps in many cultural achievements, announce that the kingdom approaches" even as no visible sanctification appears.[53] The task of culture, grasped as promise, is also grasped as law, as what God demands from humanity: "to become men, not more than men; but also not less."[54] This is commanded, however, not as an attainable goal but as that to which human being are called to hold themselves responsible. In Christ and in the new creation, not in the world, is found true humanity.[55] This is critical because it rules out participation in "the building of the tower of Babel whose top is to touch heaven"; the church's task is to confront cultural activity with "the comfort and warning of eternity," with "God as the limit," the reminder not to rest content with any ersatz realization of humanity, any false or premature wholeness or unity, but to proclaim unfailingly and at once the task of and the failure and the promise of culture.⁵⁶ Barth thus sets an eschatological limit to the project of Bildung: a limit against which all of our efforts to form humanity must be judged to fall short, but against which these efforts can also be forgiven for having fallen short. Indeed, it is only in the context of this gift that relieves us of the burden of our failures that the task can be taken up again and again.

Barth's critique of the Bildung tradition hence comes from within, not from without; it is a summons to this tradition to be awake to all that is involved in this search for unity and wholeness, and to be unfailingly skeptical of claims to have achieved the task—achieved the telos of humanity. If we understand Barth's critique of modern theology and culture through this lens, it points the way not to an utter dismissal of the Bildung tradition but rather to a subtle discernment of what is worth appropriating from that tradition—on the part of Christians, to be sure, but not solely, I shall suggest, by those who claim that name.

Barth's critical summons to the Bildung tradition, and in particular his *Protestant Theology in the Nineteenth Century*, thus serves as ongoing point of reference for this project. Barth enters in not as part of the narrative of the Bildung tradition, nor as its authoritative judge, but as interlocutor and counterpoint. I have also allowed *Protestant Theology in the Nineteenth Century* to define the scope of the present project. Barth divides his study into two parts: eighteenth-century "background" and nineteenth-century "history." Part I ends with Hegel (1770–1831), and part II runs from Friedrich Schleiermacher (1768–1834) through Albrecht Ritschl (1822–99). Given that Hegel's dates nearly coincide with those of Schleiermacher, this is no neat division of eighteenth- from nineteenth-century thought. Still, the division was significant for Barth. In certain respects he found the philosophical thinkers treated in part I to be more worthy of engagement than the theologians treated in part II. At the conclusion of part I's discussion of Hegel, he noted:

> Theology had, and still has, no occasion to throw stones at Hegel, as if it had not trodden the same path as he, only not in so firm or so logical a manner as he did. When we come to consider Schleiermacher we shall have to ask very seriously whether his secret is a different one from that of Hegel, only that with Hegel it might

be a secret which was to a great extent more respectable and at all events more instructive than that of Schleiermacher.[57]

The liberal theological tradition launched by Schleiermacher refused the "*genuinely* theological element in Hegel" in the course of rejecting the aspects of Hegel's thought that made him "unacceptable to modern cultural awareness."[58] Barth credits Hegel with a concern for theological truth, for knowledge of God, as opposed to Schleiermacher's tendency to make the theme of theology merely human religious consciousness.[59] In this sense part II is of secondary import. Of course Barth does not have the last word on Schleiermacher any more than on the thinkers treated here. Schleiermacher deserves a full hearing, and his own placement within the Bildung tradition. I do not, though, undertake that task here. It would take another book entirely, and a shift to the theological lineage proper, to connect the dots between Schleiermacher, Albrecht Ritschl, Wilhelm Hermann, and Barth, Hermann's student, who saw in his teacher a kind of existentialized Schleiermacher.[60] When it comes to dialogical humanism, moreover, there are other significant trajectories to trace, notably the hermeneutical tradition that runs through Dilthey and Gadamer.[61] My narrative, however, concludes with Hegel as a culminating figure in the Bildung tradition's retrieval of a dialogical Christian humanism. For about the "*genuinely* theological" element in Hegel, Barth is correct. And as far as the uncompleted theological task of Bildung is concerned, today we remain essentially where Hegel left us.

Pietism, Barth argues in *Protestant Theology in the Nineteenth Century*, is key to understanding the entire sweep of modern theology: "in its basic form, Pietism is identical with the pure form of what had later so many modes of expression in Christianity."[62] While Pietism may appear in its focus on religious experience to be a rejection of human autarchy, Barth argued that it was in fact just a particular expression of that grasping after autarchy. Pietism's core aspiration, and core error, is to seek to assimilate and absorb all that is external to or other than the self, an aspiration that is realized when "all that is not one's own as such is dissolved and made one's own." Pietism absorbed all aspects of Christianity that represented this otherness by way of interiorization—of the incarnation, of the "fellow man," of external authority, of divine command, of sacrament.[63] Much could be said about each of these elements and how they relate to one another. For the present context, what I wish to underscore is the significance of the second of these elements, that Pietism sought "the removal or at least the neutralization of the alien character of one's fellow man. . . . He is now to be my own: in other words, in the first place he is no longer to disturb me by his otherness, and in the second place, where possible he is to be the sort of man that I can find again in myself."[64] To grasp why this is so significant to Barth is to understand both Barth's theology and his politics. It also points toward the possibility of a positive appropriation of the tradition of Bildung, as groping towards an understanding of human self-formation *not* as assertion of Promethean autarchy but rather as ongoing dialogical encounter, an encounter whose prerequisite is the willingness to listen to the other, to be open to hearing something new, to something or someone that calls our concerns and commitments—and hence our very selves—into question. What is finally at stake here for Barth is hearing God, and God's Word that declares that the good has been fulfilled and accomplished in our place and hence we are not the agents of our own salvation. God's Word, he consistently emphasizes, confronts us as something that we have not created or originated, something that we cannot generate on our own but for which we must listen. As Barth's account of revelation makes clear, we listen for this Word neither in visions nor in inner voices. It is neither immediate nor transparent.[65] Indeed, while it is only the divine decision on our actions that can determine their worth, this remains secret, hidden to us. This secrecy of the divine decision, as Gerald McKenny has noted, points us back to our fellow finite reason-givers: "the divine secrecy entails that everyone is subject to being held morally accountable by his or her neighbor."[66] Indeed Barth goes even further: "God may speak to us through Russian Communism, a flute concerto, a blossoming shrub, or a dead dog. We do well to listen to Him if He really does."[67] Since God's command and self-revelation, for Barth, always come to us through our fellow creatures, there is here not just a radical theological claim but also a radical political claim. This political claim, moreover, is one that might be compelling to secular hearers (who might not take themselves to have reason to listen to Barth), as well as to Christians.[68]

Dipesh Chakrabarty has argued that postcolonial studies confronts the challenge of holding "in a state of permanent tension a dialogue between two contradictory points of view," "the Enlightenment promise of an abstract, universal but never-to-be realized humanity" and "the diverse ways of being human, the infinite incommensurabilities through which we struggle—perennially, precariously, but unavoidably—to 'world the earth' in order to live within our different senses of ontic belonging."[69] The Bildung tradition is an effort—or constellation of efforts—not just to hold these contradictory points of view in permanent tension but so to understand humanity and the process of its formation that these "infinite incommensurabilities" do not contradict but rather embody the fully human. Ethical formation as a dialogical human activity of mutual accountability becomes corrupted when it takes the form of promethean autarchy, whether this comes in the form of raw self-assertion or of cultural imperialism. Yet in grappling with the Bildung tradition, we can grasp human self-formative agency precisely as mediated through critically self-conscious dialogically developing carriers of social practices. Humanity can take infinitely many individual and cultural forms, but these count as realizations of the ideal of humanity only insofar as they are capable of mutual recognition and affirmation. As Luke Bretherton has said, "The word humanity is a place-holder for the commitment to discover a shared way of being alive with outsiders."[70] The humanity of each is bound up with the humanity of all: none of us has become fully human as long as any of us is not able to speak or be heard.[71]

We can hear an echo of this concern in contemporary critical theory, which carries on the Bildung tradition in asking precisely, "Who can I become in such a world where the meanings and limits of the subject are set out in advance for me?"[72] Think, for instance, of Adorno's understanding of the task of critique as casting light on our very frameworks of evaluation in a way that "strives solely to help the things themselves to that articulation from which they are otherwise cut off by the prevailing language," and of Foucault's and Butler's further articulations of critique precisely as ethics.[73] Yet critical theory can slip into a kind of idolatry of critique, which so dwells in the revelatory tears in the fabric of our epistemological webs that it abandons the constructive task of forming humanity, that is, of reweaving those webs in ways that better support mutual recognition and shared life.[74] Better, then, simply to carry on under the sign of the eschatological reservation—that is, to recognize that the task of construction as well as deconstruction falls to us still, no matter how aware we become—indeed, precisely insofar as we become aware—

of the ways in which our formation as subjects has always already been a sort of de-formation. We should not succumb to the temptation to claim definitive historical progress in forming humanity—but our work, albeit broken, can nonetheless point to divine eschatological consummation.

The first two chapters of this project are devoted to tracing the main tributaries that flowed into the Bildung tradition. Modern thinkers seeking to take responsibility for the formation of humanity took inspiration from the Greek notion of *paideia* and the Roman virtue of *humanitas*, finding here conceptions of a holistic education that linked art with politics and honored emotion as well as reason. If paideia was an elite education for democratic citizenship, humanitas was the virtue of conquerors, of those who could afford to indulge in the *studia humanitatis* and rule with the mildness appropriate to the properly civilized. These ideas were transmitted in part by medieval and Renaissance humanism but were also retrieved directly from pagan thinkers in the eighteenth century and appropriated for the project of forming a politically mature public capable of challenging political domination.

Significant as the classical inheritance was for forging the Bildung tradition, the term itself is rooted, as already noted, in Christian reflection on the doctrine of creation in the image of God. Chapter 1 therefore also considers the ways in which this doctrine was foregrounded within medieval and Renaissance humanism in ways that regarded creation in God's image as attended by a special dignity tarnished but not lost with the fall. It is to this thought-world that the Bildung tradition owes its sense of the formation of humanity as a collective task of cosmic, even divine, significance; dignity comes bundled with responsibility, even as the capacities of ever finite and fallen human beings to accomplish this task are limited. Importantly, human recognition and assumption of this task does not in itself constitute autocratic humanism, with its twin refusal to heed the disturbing otherness of one's fellows and to listen for the Word of God.

It was the philosophical mystic Meister Eckhart who first employed the German vernacular in order to speak of creation, fall, and restoration of the image of God. In so doing he forged the vocabulary that would later be taken up by the Bildung tradition. Eckhart's mystical conception of the importance of freeing oneself from humanly constituted images in order to make room within the soul for the birth of the true image, the Son, with its radical suggestion of the erasure of the ontological distinction between human and divine, was of course only one way of understanding the doctrine of the imago Dei. There were others, and chapter 1 thus also considers two of the most influential. Luther conceived of Christians as through faith becoming "living pictures" of Christ, the essential image of God. Paracelsus, meanwhile, developed an epigenetic conception of Bildung as an unfolding process of development, with human beings as microcosm of creation tasked with revealing the mysteries of God's creation.

If the doctrine of the incarnation underscored the dignity of common humanity over against aristocratic and imperial notions of paideia and humanitas, Christian thinkers lacked pagan confidence in human formative powers. Independent human agency cannot restore the lost imago; it is divine formation (Bildung) that is required, not human imagination (*Einbildung*). Human image-making gets in the way, or imagines God in devilish form. These various strands of Christian reflection on Bildung and the imago Dei became sites for wrestling with the nature and limits of human agency and in particular with the power but also the perils of human imagination.

Chapter 2 turns to the more historically immediate context for the development of the Bildung tradition in seventeenth-century thought, examining the Pietist movement and two mystical thinkers who significantly influenced that movement: Johann Arndt, author of the hugely popular devotional work *True Christianity*, and the mysterious Jakob Boehme, who absorbed and transmitted Paracelsian and Hermetic thought. Pietism was a revival movement that largely remained within the Lutheran Church, even as it gave rise to more radical splinter movements and can be seen as continuous with other movements for practical piety across England, the Netherlands, and Germany. Pietism's primary orientation toward an active, practical Christianity rendered it vulnerable to charges of works-righteousness, which it countered by emphasizing a foundational passivity to divine agency and rejecting *Menschen-kunst*, human imagination and formative agency. The Pietist cultivation of personal religious experience, often blamed for incubating subjectivism and individualism, grew out of efforts to create a site of pure transparency to the transformative work of the Spirit and so to certify the Christian's works of love as works of the Spirit. The embrace of passivity became increasingly unstable as it was deployed as a weapon against the rising tides of rationalism. It was Pietism's fall into a contrastive understanding of divine and human agency that nurtured autocratic humanism. The Pietist evacuation of human agency elicited in Weimar humanism a reactive insistence on Bildung as an expression of autonomous human self-formative agency, even as Pietist practices of introspection and its new language of feeling and inner experience were adopted into secular literature and the project of aesthetic education.

Boehme played a subversive role within Pietist thought. His highly unconventional understanding of God's self-birthing and of the generation of material and spiritual reality through the dynamic interaction of opposing forces was to be deeply influential for German Romanticism; Hegel was to call him "the first German philosopher."[75] It was by way of Paracelsus and Boehme in particular that Bildung came to be understood not simply as spiritual or ethical renewal, nor simply as individual self-realization, but as a process involving all of nature, and nature conceived not as a static backdrop for salvation history but as alive with the divine and caught up in the ongoing realization of the divine will. Together with this appreciation for the generative dynamism of conflict came difficult questions concerning evil and its place in the formation of humanity: Were conflict, opposition, evil *necessary* to the process of Bildung? Was evil, then, part and parcel of the divine life itself? Or was conflict not truly evil? These questions would continue to haunt the coming centuries.

Chapter 3 turns to the Bildung tradition proper, with its focus on human self-forming agency oriented toward individual and communal self-realization and the realization of humanity itself. For Johann Gottfried Herder, individuals and cultures grow into their particularity while constituting increasingly rich webs of interrelation with one another in a process Herder understood as the realization of divine purposes via the finite expression of the image of God. For Herder, Bildung is a process begun at creation, playing out through natural and cultural evolution and taken up into reflective human agency insofar as humans grasp and align themselves and their societies with God's creative purposes at work in the world. It was others, starting with the philosopher-pedagogue-diplomat Wilhelm von Humboldt (taken up in chapter 4), who were to reduce Bildung to a merely human project. Both Herder and Humboldt conceive of Bildung as a process in which innate human potential is developed through a selective, conflictual engagement with the natural and social environments. Both conceive of the telos of this process as "humanity" and regard this telos as enabling rather than excluding individuality and variety, and yet as realized via social interaction, not by isolated individuals. But where Herder's political vision is communitarian and consociationist, envisioning a harmonious web of diverse nations and peoples, Humboldt's is liberal and individualistic: social and political life should maximize individual freedom and thereby foster individual self-realization.

As chapter 4 shows, for Humboldt it is *Kunstreligion*, the Religion of Art, not the dead hand of an authoritarian Christianity, that can best foster the self-formation of humanity. Even as this project aimed at the crafting of an expansive, open public sphere, and hence at a democratized paideia and humanitas, it was not after all clear that this Bildung was for everyone. Yet it was Humboldt's understanding of Bildung, rather than Herder's, that became institutionalized within the pedagogical and cultural institutions of later nineteenth-century bourgeois culture (the *Bildungsbürgertum*). Within this later context, Bildung came to be equated with a classical liberal education, regarded as a badge of bourgeois nobility and taken an excuse for political passivity. In the tumultuous atmosphere surrounding the French Revolution, however, it was not yet evident how easily liberal individualist Bildung could be politically domesticated. Schiller enthusiastically embraced Kunstreligion. Art, it seemed to him, as to Goethe and others, had inherited the mantle of a Christianity grown old and brittle, and was destined to serve as the main vehicle for Bildung and the source of a thoroughgoing social and political transformation. Aesthetic education would generate harmony among the opposing forces of the human spirit, effectively resist the instrumentalizing reduction of human persons, fit them for stable self-government, and preclude the revolutionary excesses of the French Revolution.

Within this project of ethical formation, the new genre of the novel, focused on the experienced particularities of ordinary lives, assumed special importance. Drawing on models provided by Pietist autobiographies, with their searching of inner experience for the signs of providential direction, the novel was conceived both as representing and fostering Bildung and as capable of taking over the formative role played by scripture in Pietist circles. This is the story of the rise of the Bildungsroman as would-be "secular scripture," told in chapter 5. But these high hopes for cultural and political transformation via the novel soon began to ring hollow. Audiences sought entertainment and escape, not ethical formation. Who was the human author to claim the authority to form humanity? Where are exemplars to be found when what we aspire to is autonomy and individuality and authenticity? And if even the most sublime work of art could reach only an elite, where was the hope of broad cultural transformation?

One novel more than any other served to define that elusive creature, the Bildungsroman—Goethe's *Wilhelm Meister's Apprenticeship*. Chapter 6 is thus devoted to a close reading of *Wilhelm Meister* and to its engagement with the challenge of narrating Bildung in the absence of authoritative exemplars and an articulated telos. Goethe sought to narrate the experiences of an ordinary individual seeking to find a form or order for his life, one that brought the individual into harmony with his natural and social environments while also being a genuine form of self-realization. From Pietism's turn toward the analysis of inward experience, Goethe borrowed tools for the exploration of what was authentic and what was foreign to the self. But he hoped thereby to display an immanent teleology, one subject in human beings to conscious adoption and pursuit. In a context in which Humboldtian notions of independent self-formation were in the ascendancy, Goethe brought to life a hero who is not so much active and self-assertive as sensitive and responsive, and who relies on Fate instead of taking his life into his own hands. Wilhelm learns that instead of becoming the consummate human being he must become something specific, that the path to self-realization comes via self-forgetful service to others, and that resistance to the dominance of technical rationality and commerce is effective only through collective action in service of the common good. He finds that the process of Bildung is inherently social and relational, that his own narrative cannot be written in the absence of other narrations and narrators. Goethe's understanding of immanent teleology and organic Bildung clearly inform the novel. Yet the novel is also permeated with an irony that points not just beyond Wilhelm Meister's happy reliance on Fate but beyond Goethe's own theory of Bildung and immanent teleology.[76] It is finally this resignation of providential authority that saves *Wilhelm Meister* from its own grasping after autarchic humanism and allows it to become indeed a kind of secular scripture.

Hegel gently satirized *Wilhelm Meister*, and with it not just the Bildungsroman but the project of Bildung via the Religion of Art. Yet he characterizes his own philosophical project in the *Phenomenology of Spirit* in ways that have licensed generations of interpreters to describe it as a kind of Bildungsroman. Chapter 7 takes this as an entry point into Hegel's thought. Hegel's critique of the novel and of Kunstreligion are not a renunciation of the project of Bildung. Against the notion that modernity involves constructing a substitute for religion in general and Christianity in particular, Hegel insists on the truth of Christianity and the ongoing necessity of religious cult and ritual in the formation of humanity. Bildung, for Hegel, is not a merely human project but a cosmic adventure of divine becoming in which human beings participate. It is Hegel, more fully even than Herder, who (drawing on Boehme) resituates Bildung within the Neoplatonic *exitus* and *reditus* of creation. Aquinas argued that the image of God in humankind is perfected insofar as finite rational agents, following the Way of Jesus Christ, come to know and love God and all of creation in relation to God, and enter into the friendship of the divine life. For Hegel, all things unfold as dynamic expressions of the Concept; self-conscious life can come to be at home in the world by grasping its conceptual structure and the inadequacy of all forms of dualistic or oppositional thinking. Grasping the reciprocal relatedness of all things, human beings grasp themselves as moments in the infinitely reconciling life of God; in humankind this process of infinite reconciliation comes to self-awareness. Genuine Bildung allows human beings to be at home in the world not because it returns them to an unreflective *Sittlichkeit* but rather because it equips them for ongoing critical negotiation with social and political reality, for the never-ending task of articulating the norms intrinsic to the practices by which they have been formed, and of critiquing and correcting them in accordance with the Concept and its reconciling logic.

I regard Hegel as having adopted and furthered the creative reappropriation of Neoplatonic *exitus* and *reditus* characteristic of medieval and Renaissance humanism. But Hegel is often seen as having parted ways in a decisive respect from this tradition. According to that logic, even as human fulfillment of the task of knowing and loving God and all creation in relation to God is made possible by grace and fulfills divine purposes, God remains radically transcendent with respect to creation. It is by virtue of this radical transcendence that divine and human agency do not compete with or exclude one another; a radically transcendent God can be intimately present to creatures.[77] Hegel, like Boehme, has been seen as closer to Plotinus's understanding of the emanation of finite beings from the undifferentiated unity of the One, who thus share in the same univocal being, even as they suffer according to their relative distance from the One.[78] And Hegel, again following Boehme, and rightly seeing differentiation as enrichment rather than impoverishment, draws the process of Bildung into the divine life itself. The eternal Concept (Plotinus's One) is divine only in a relative sense; fully divine is the process itself, perfected in its self-knowledge as such.

The critical question that hovers here is the question of evil. Do conflict, opposition, evil itself, thereby become immanent to the divine life, necessary to its unfolding? It is this, not the insistence, correct in itself, that God be conceived of as beyond the contrast between transcendence and immanence, that would legitimate Barth's charge of autocratic humanism. If conflict and evil are necessary to the divine life, they are authorized, however loud the insistence that we are to move *through* conflict to reconciliation, *through* evil to goodness.[79]

It is a delicate question to adjudicate. I shall argue that Hegel finally thinks only the *possibility* of evil, not its actuality, to be necessary to divine self-gift into finitude. God endures evil in order to work reconciliation. Yet even if Hegel does not regard the actuality of evil as necessary to divine self-realization, he does, in regarding history as necessary to divine self-realization, take evil into the divine process in a way that cannot but legitimize it.

Evil is not to be legitimated but to be confessed. This is how to take up the task of Bildung. We are to seek harmony and reconciliation beyond conflict, to grasp the inadequacy of the unmediated oppositions according to which we live and categorize ourselves and others. And we are to resist our own longing to declare any reconciliation complete and accomplished. For that way lies the failure to be discomfited by the interruption of our fellow creatures. Autocratic humanism confidently certifies the fully human, and just as confidently diagnoses the not-quite and never-to-be-fully human, designating those incapable of Bildung. Authentic humanism recognizes that none of us is fully human until all are recognized as human. And this recognition involves the willingness to be disturbed by the other, what Barth names as listening for the Word of God.

From *Paideia* to Humanism 1

The Bildung tradition conceived of humanity not as a given but as a telos to be realized by human beings, both at an individual and at a collective level. But why? Why not think of "human" simply as what we are? Why conceive of it as a task, and as a task that can be completed only through the accomplishment of a particular process, one for which we are responsible? Three particular features of this complex are noteworthy, easy as it still is to take them for granted. First, the assumption that we, or some of us, are not (yet) fully human, in a sense that is analogous to, yet distinct from, the sense in which all of us begin as infants and mature gradually into adults. Second, the conviction that we do not become human simply as a matter of course; the process is not automatic. Third, the notion that we are *ourselves* in some sense responsible for making ourselves human; it is not something that merely happens to us or is done for us. If this is so, then at least some human beings are only imperfectly or vestigially human. How are they to be regarded and treated by the perfectly or fully human? Are they responsible for their own failure to realize their own humanity? What are the social and political ramifications of erecting these distinctions? The next two chapters are devoted to unpacking various tributaries that fed into forging this constellation of assumptions and their associated problematics. Very broadly speaking, these are twofold: from the ancient world, by way of the classical revival, came Greek understandings of paideia and Roman conceptions of the virtue of humanitas, while from Christianity came an understanding of humankind as created in the image of God, fallen, redeemed, and destined for eschatological consummation through the work of

Christ and the Holy Spirit. Of course, not only is each of these traditions internally complex, but they cannot be neatly separated: the Christian tradition took shape in relation to ancient pagan thought, while eighteenth- and nineteenth-century thinkers often retrieved pagan thought in conscious contradistinction to Christianity. Nevertheless, we can arrive at a satisfactory understanding of the distinctive character of the Bildung tradition, and its conception of the task of forming humanity, only by considering some of the conceptions of ethical formation that flowed into it.

Bildung, as noted in the introduction, is a complex term with no direct equivalent in English. The noun today most commonly means education (particularly in the sense of a holistic *liberal* education), but it can also mean formation, fashioning, shaping, or even simply form, as well as cultivation, culture, or civilization. It can refer either to the process of formation or to the endpoint or culmination of this process. The verb *bilden* means to form, fashion, shape, mold, educate, or to improve/broaden the mind. The ubiquity of prefixes in the German language introduces an even broader range of meaning, for one can speak of *aus-*, *um-*, *über-*, *an-*, and *ein-bilden*, that is, of cultivating a given capacity, of reorganizing a structure, of elevating or "forming-above," of adding onto, or of forming an image (*Bild*) within, that is, of imagining something.

The German term Bildung was used to express the Latin *formatio*, with its associated terms *conformatio* and *reformatio*. In both Latin and German, the oldest sense—and one that remains in active use—is the craftsperson's formation of a material: it is the baker, the potter, the sculptor who are engaged in *bilden* or *formatio*. But even in old high German, there are other meanings for *bildari* and *bildunga*, the antecedents of *bilden* and *Bildung*. Most importantly, these can refer also to imitation or copying of a model and to the conception of mere images lacking in reality.[1] Interestingly, while in the Latin Vulgate God forms (*formavit*) the first human creature out of earth, Luther's translation simply states that God made (*machte*) the human. But in Genesis 1, where the Vulgate uses *imago* rather than *forma*, noting that human beings were created "ad imaginem Dei," Luther instead uses *Bild*: "God made human beings to his image [*Bilde*]."[2] This highlights an important lack of parallelism between the Latin and German terms; while *forma* in Latin can certainly be used to mean image or likeness, *imago* or *pictura* would be the more usual term for a visual representation. *Forma* carries less the sense of a picture than of a material shape that serves as a model. In German, though, *Bildung* always retains an association with *Bild* as picture or image, with significant implications for ways in which the concept is employed.

Theologically, the Latin terms *reformatio* and *conformatio* are perhaps even more central than *formatio* itself.[3] *Conformatio* is used from early on to speak of the Christian's alignment of will and being with Christ. In the Middle Ages the term *reformatio* took over from *renovatio* as the favored expression for speaking of the salvific transformation of fallen human nature.[4] Both are used in connection with the restoration through Christ and the Holy Spirit of the imago Dei, damaged or destroyed in the fall. A variety of nominal and verbal prefixes allow the German language to replicate and extend this range of meaning. Standard accounts note that the German term first becomes prominent in the writings of the German Rhineland mystics of the fourteenth century and is taken up from them by the Pietists, but that the meaning of the term is transformed and secularized in the eighteenth century, arriving at its most culturally influential meaning—and the one to which the *Bildung* in Bildungsroman refers—in the humanistic philosophy of Herder and Humboldt and the German classicism of Goethe and Schiller.[5] Instead of referring to the divine creation of humanity in God's own image, and to the divine restoration of this image through Christ, it comes to refer to the active human cultivation of innate potential through selective engagement with elements in the natural and social environments. In the process, human beings become active agents, not simply passive recipients, of *Bildung*; nature is understood not as fallen but as neutral or good; and the telos of *Bildung* is conceived not as resemblance to God but as achievement of a harmonious unity unique to each individual.

While *Bildung* undoubtedly undergoes significant transformations of meaning before taking up its decisive role in late eighteenth- and early nineteenth-century German thought and culture, this story is in need of revision in a number of respects. Most importantly, in its exclusive focus on the term *Bildung* and its theological significance, it overlooks the fact that the valorization of Bildung in the eighteenth century involved not simply a reworking of certain aspects of received theological understandings of the creation, fall, and reformation of humankind toward the divine image, but also a retrieval and reimagining of classical notions of the virtue of humanitas and of education as *paideia*, with each of these ideals being used to critique aspects of the other. To paint in the broadest strokes: Christian conceptions of the renewal and perfection of the image of God shifted the ideals of paideia and humanitas in a more inclusive, egalitarian direction, even as classical retrievals served to authorize a more confident embrace of human agency.

From the Christian tradition came a complex, dynamic notion of all humankind as corporately formed in the image of God, corporately fallen in Adam, and nonetheless individually precious and worthy of redemption. According to this tradition, a certain lofty dignity accrues to all, regardless of ability, moral achievement, or placement within social hierarchies, and all are summoned to the high calling of participating through grace, as free principles of their own actions, in the *reditus* of creation to God—the realization of God's purposes for creation. This tradition, however, was not immediately seen as holding democratic social and political implications. Christian thought was, moreover, ambivalent about the role of human agency in the formation of persons for this calling, and this ambivalence mounted through the Renaissance and Reformation, as growing assertions of the independence of human agency were countered by ever-louder affirmations of the exclusive character of divine formative and reformative agency. Something like paideia should be accessible to all, eighteenth-century thinkers proclaimed, and only when it is will humankind as such achieve maturity and be capable of taking part in reasonable public deliberations directed toward the common good. However, eighteenth-century theorists of Bildung also inherited from Roman humanitas an association with imperial ambition, justified in terms of spreading civilization. Bringers of Bildung-as-civilization elevated themselves above the not-yet-fully-human, even while proclaiming the ideal of universal humanity.

I thus take a brief look at the Greek ideal of paideia and the Roman virtue of humanitas before considering how aspects of both are preserved in later European conceptions of nobility and flow into Renaissance humanism. I then turn my attention to the concept of Bildung as this developed in relation to Christian understandings of the imago Dei. The doctrine of the imago Dei was highly fluid and thus also immensely fecund. I will structure my discussion by focusing on three thinkers who employ the German vernacular and thus cement the conceptual connections between Bildung and the imago

Dei, albeit in strikingly different ways: Meister Eckhart (1260–1328), Martin Luther (1483–1546), and Paracelsus (1493–1541). The following chapter will attend to thinkers more proximate to the Bildung tradition—Johann Arndt (1555–1621) and Jakob Boehme (1575–1624), and the Pietist movement—and trace an intensifying ambivalence concerning human agency. Renewal of the image of God is possible only by way of an evacuation of human will and agency that opens up space for God to work within, yet there is some sense that human imagination (*Einbildung*) has an active role to play, whether for good or for ill. In Pietism the balance tilted toward suspicion of human art or invention, *Menschen-kunst*, and became bound up with a rejection of worldly art and literature. Scripture assumed a new role in certifying that the practical orientation of the Pietist movement, expressed through the foundation of orphanages, schools, and missions, was in no way to be understood as a form of works-righteousness but rather as the transformative activity of the Holy Spirit. The task of ascertaining whether it was God's formative power or human imagination (*Einbildung*) at work in one's soul gave rise to practices of introspection, self-examination, and spiritual life-writing that fed directly into eighteenth-century understandings of the role of literature and aesthetic education in ethical formation, even where the suspicion of human agency was decisively left behind.

Paideia and the Polis

The Greek ideal of paideia, "the process of educating man into his true form, the real and genuine human nature," was bound up with the notion of the polis as the ideal form of political organization, suitable to free and rational human beings.[6] The citizen must be formed or educated in order to be capable of playing an appropriate role within the life of the polis. The laws of the state are themselves formative and play an important role in the process of paideia. Paideia is directed toward *aretê*, virtue or excellence, which as the perfection of intrinsically social creatures is realizable only within political life. While in some sense the ideal of paideia can be traced all the way back to Homeric notions of excellence, it is with the fifth-century Sophists that the term *paideia* takes on special significance.[7] Paideia was holistic: it involved not just instruction in the liberal arts and sciences but also athletic training and moral education through music, poetry, and philosophy. The aspiration was to a harmonious and proportionate development of all human capacities, such that the citizen will be both beautiful and good—*kalos kagathos*.[8] It was, then, an aesthetic, ethical, and intellectual ideal. It was also aristocratic. Not all occupants of the polis were citizens, and paideia was reserved for the elites.[9] It is they who, freed from degrading manual labor, properly took part in public deliberation and governed the polis.[10] While both *paiedeia* and *Bildung* may be translated "culture," neither is "culture" in a descriptive sense; both point to an ideal of human perfection and a process of formation that realizes that ideal.[11]

So much for a thumbnail sketch of paideia as articulated by its two most influential interpreters, Werner Jaeger and Henry Marrou. Both were refracting the aspirations and anxieties of their own historical moment—of the Weimar Republic, the Third Reich, and their aftermath—as much as giving access to those of a long distant one. The first volume of Jaeger's three-part work offered up in effect a paean to the Prussian educational system created by Wilhelm von Humboldt, with its adulation of all things Greek and its near-identification of culture with virtue. Paideia held out hope for a European self-confidence deeply shaken by the First World War. Jaeger understood himself, and indeed his generation, to be engaged in a "quest for a new humanism that would restore their true significance to school, university and all education by helping to understand their beginnings."[12] In the aftermath of the fall of the Weimar Republic and in exile from Germany, paideia in Jaeger's second and third volumes "metamorphosed into a nostalgia for what was lost, an apology for the Hellenic past whose excellence had failed in the very project of education."[13] Jaeger's original (and in retrospect, chilling) intention of tracing in the later volumes of his work how paideia funded world domination on the part of the Greeks evaporated, but without any thoroughgoing taking of stock in the face of evidence that "the elitism of the Humboldtian university was no moral protection against anything."[14]

Meanwhile for Marrou, a left-wing Catholic intellectual writing under the Vichy regime, paideia came fully into its own only in the context of the cosmopolitanism of the Hellenistic period. Marrou, no less than Jaeger, was searching in the ancient world for a viable humanism for his own day. "In the deep confusion caused by the sudden collapse of ancient beliefs, it was the one true unshakable value to which the mind of man could cling," writes Marrou revealingly; Jaś Elsner comments that "here, finally, scripted as if it were an historical claim about the ancient past, is Marrou's commentary on the immediate past."[15] Neither Jaeger nor Marrou was able to confront the ways in which paideia's elitism poisoned its capacity to offer the kind of cultural salvation for which they yearned.

Humanitas and the Roman Empire

What did become of Greek paideia in the context of the Roman Empire? Aulus Gellius, Latin grammarian of the second half of the second century CE, wrote that "Latin purists give *humanitas* approximately the force of the Greek *paideia*, which we know as education and training in the liberal arts. Those who pursue these goals are essentially human, for the cultivation of this kind of knowledge and training has been given to man alone, therefore it is called *humanitas*."[16] A modern scholar complains that Gellius here confuses means and ends; paideia is the practice of formation that led to the end of humanitas, which thus is closer to the Greek *philanthropia*, love of humanity.[17] In fact, though, what is significant in Gellius's statement here is that it reflects a deeper ambiguity that is visible even in the eighteenth- and nineteenth-century Bildung tradition. For Bildung, as understood by Herder and Humboldt, Goethe and Schiller, refers both to the process of formation and to its product. And while these thinkers speak at times of Bildung as both means and end, they also conceive of Bildung as directed toward the end of Humanity (*Humanität* or *Menschheit*). Just as paideia was understood as "the process of educating man into his true form," so humanitas carried with it something of this same sense.

Roman thinkers, then, carried on the notion that there is an ideal form of humanity realizable only through a process of education and shaping of a particular sort. It is *essentially* human, that which distinguishes human beings from other animals, but it is not *universally* human. Humanitas, like paideia, was invoked to distinguish the fully human from the vestigially human.

Humanitas was not one of the ancient Roman virtues. The Stoic philosopher Panaetius of Rhodes (185–110 BCE) appears, by way of his friendship with Scipio Africanus, his time in Rome, and his influential treatise *On Duties* (the model for Cicero's *De officiis*), to have been responsible for forging the concept of Roman humanitas as a virtue closely akin to clemency and moderating traditional Roman *severitas*. The Romans should not forsake *virtus*, with its manly strength, but should complement it with the softer humanitas.[18] Tellingly, humanity was praised precisely as a virtue of rulers; "of course some men were meant to be ruled and benefited from it; but this imposed a duty on rulers to consult their subjects' welfare."[19] Humanitas, in other words, was deployed expressly for the purpose of justifying Roman rule. Humanity did not preclude conquest. Rather, it dictated the appropriate way to rule the conquered. Once firmly in control, conquerors could afford a bit of mildness. Indeed, a dash of humanitas was likely to strengthen Roman rule. As the anonymous *Ad herennium*, formerly attributed to Cicero, notes, "The victor in war looks on the vanquished as fellow men, and his *humanitas* advances peace."[20]

It was Cicero above all who cemented the Roman understanding of humanitas; the term crops up hundreds of times across his varied writings. Cicero reinforces the notion that humanitas complements the more severe traditional Roman virtues; he praises Atticus for having achieved "the most difficult combination of *gravitas* and *humanitas*, both in his life and in his language. Avidius has such a well-balanced character that it combines the most rigid *severitas* with the highest degree of *humanitas*."[21] He emphasizes the importance of humanitas for improving the Roman image and rendering Roman rule palatable, while being explicit that mildness and clemency are justified only when required by interests of state; Cicero regarded the destruction of cities and the enslaving of whole populations as justifiable, and indeed compatible with humanitas in ruling.[22] And he strengthens the connection between humanitas and paideia; Greek literature and philosophy hold the key, he argues, to true greatness, and thus he devoted himself to what he called the *studia humanitatis*, the sort of studies that "correspond to the being and nature of human beings and at the same time provide the proper nutrition for the human spirit."[23] The words that Cicero in *De re publica* places in the mouth of Scipio eloquently express this conviction: "What power, moreover, what office, what kingdom can be preferable to the state of one who despises all human possessions, considers them inferior to wisdom, and never meditates on any subject that is not eternal and divine; who believes that, though others may be called men [*homines*], only those are men who are perfected in the arts appropriate to humanity [*humanitatis artibus*]?"²⁴ Treating the conquered with mildness and humanitas was a way of displaying that one was civilized, cultured. Those on top could afford to indulge in a little softness, as they could afford to indulge in the *studia humanitatis*. Only the life of leisure could make this possible. Humanitas was thus at one and the same time the badge of perfected humanness, approaching divinity, and the mark of the vanquisher. The fact that human beings possess reason and thus can reflect on divine things proves, in Cicero's eyes, that there is a common ancestry or origin between humankind and the celestial beings: the "seed of the human race" was granted "the divine gift of the soul."²⁵ Thus humanitas is not merely human but also divine: "virtue exists in man and God alike, but in no other creature besides; virtue, however, is nothing else than Nature perfected and developed to its highest point; therefore there is a likeness between man and God."²⁶

Treating others with humanitas was for the Romans not something owed to those others, to their humanity. Rather humanitas was owed to *oneself*, as befitting one's own cultured character. There is, to be sure, a kind of universalism in Cicero, and evident particularly in his philosophical writings. Insofar as all human beings possess reason and speech, there is a kind of natural association that unites them: "We must trace back to their ultimate sources the principles of fellowship and society that Nature has established among men. The first principle is that which is found in the connection subsisting between all the members of the human race; and that bond of connection is reason and speech, which by the processes of teaching and learning, of communicating, discussing, and reasoning associate men together and unite them in a sort of natural fraternity."²⁷ But this universal bond is trumped by the closer associations of clan, nation, language, citizenship, and family. Moreover, the failure of some peoples to cultivate their humanity provides justification for failing to treat them with humanitas. Discussing the treacherousness of the Sardinians, Cicero comments that "in that race it may well be that some individuals have by their own characters and human qualities [*moribus et humanitate*] risen superior to the vices of their stock and their tribe; but that the large majority of them are devoid of honour, devoid of any fellowship or bond with our race, is patently proved by the facts."²⁸

It was thus easy to equate *humanitas* with *Romanitas*; the Romans provided the measure of truly civilized character, and this was the character of rulers, made possible by the very fact of rule.²⁹ The Roman historian Tacitus (58–120 CE), writing with remarkable candor, commented that the Britons who adopted the toga, lounge, and banquet gave the name *humanitas* to these means of their further enslavement.³⁰ Tacitus was inclined to see these accoutrements of Roman culture not simply as tools of empire but also as forces of corruption among the Romans themselves. In a twist that was to prove fateful many centuries later, he praised the relative "freedom, fortitude, morality, and simplicity" of the Germanic tribes that had successfully resisted Roman rule.³¹ It was these northern barbarians who came closest to preserving the rough but sturdy virtues of ancient Rome. Even if Tacitus himself by no means elevated Germanic simplicity over cultivated Roman humanity, his *Germania* planted a myth of tribal purity and traditional virtue that was later to be watered by German nationalists and Nazi ideologues.

Dignity and the Gentleman

Something of the notions of paideia and humanitas as proper to an elite ruling class survived both the disappearance of Athenian democracy and the downfall of the Roman Empire to animate ideals of medieval courtliness and knighthood, as well as later conceptions of the "gentleman." A "gentle" or "noble" man inherits a special dignity, while requiring in turn a particular form of education so that his manners will accord with that dignity; the nobility thus take the place of the citizen in the Greek polis. A gentleman is one who comes from a gentle *family*, "gentle" deriving from the Latin *gentis*, of a race or people. The understanding of "gentility" or "nobility" as properly confined to the hereditary ruling classes began to be questioned as early as the fourteenth century, however. Chaucer, for instance, suggests at multiple points that the true "gentilman" is one whose deeds are gentle.³² Gentle deeds, however, were in effect out of reach of all but the hereditary nobility, since a nobleman was understood to be one who did not engage in manual labor, was learned, and was engaged in military service (a coat of arms serving as badge of gentility).³³ By the sixteenth century, nobility had to do with a right to bear arms primarily in the heraldic sense: only the nobility, from gentlemen at the lowest end of the scale, up through esquires and knights, to lords at the upper end, had the right to display a coat of arms, and many of those who had this right did not possess the wealth that could support a life of knighthood. "Genuine genealogy was cultivated by the older gentry to reassure themselves of their innate superiority over the upstarts: bogus genealogy was cultivated by the new gentry in an effort to clothe their social nakedness."[34] Arms bearing was by this time essentially a display of pedigree and a demand for social recognition. Unlike the terms *knight* and *esquire*, *gentleman* was not a name that itself implied a military occupation: ultimately a gentleman was one who was *recognized* as a gentleman. Nicholas Upton, a fifteenth-century authority on heraldry, wrote that "he ys countyd now a days as noble whych by the comen use and voyce is so taken and calde."[35]

A gentleman upheld the chivalric code—but the chivalric code made little sense outside of the chivalric order. Ideals of noble conduct adapted to the military life had to be transformed for the more domesticated context of courtly society, with military valor taking a backseat to skill in polite, persuasive speech. This was remote from the ancient valorization of oratory—rhetorical skill exercised in public debate. But early modern critiques of false civility appealed back to that ancient ideal in advancing a civic republican vision of true nobility as service to the common good rather than skilled speech in service of private interests.[36] The rise of the bourgeoisie, with its elevation of commercial life, spelled a further challenge to inherited conceptions of gentility, and it is in this context that Bildung comes to the fore.

Humanism

Early Italian humanists revived the Ciceronian notion of humanitas in introducing a new name for the medieval *trivium*—the *studia humanitatis*. These "humane studies," the humanities, no longer included logic but expanded to include, in addition to grammar and rhetoric, history, Greek, moral philosophy, and poetry. Indeed they "made poetry, once a sequel of grammar and rhetoric, the most important member of the whole group."[37] It was thence that Renaissance humanism derived its name, not from some vague emphasis on human values. Yet there was nevertheless the notion, reaching back to Cicero and behind him to Greek paideia, that there was "only one means through which . . . human values and ideals could be attained: through classical and literary—that is, through humanistic—studies."[38] Humanistic studies were prized because through them humanity could be realized.

Given the direct influence of Cicero on eighteenth-century neoclassicism, it is not surprising that Cicero's humanitas directly informs neoclassical understandings both of Bildung and its end, *Humanität* or *Menschheit*. The context of the Roman Empire is of course absent, and the austere Roman virtues are only a shadowy recollection. Yet Bildung too was understood as essentially a matter of achieving a properly balanced and harmonious character by way of a process that essentially involved the arts and culture; the acquisition of virtue was tightly associated with a certain sort of cultural formation. As with humanitas, Bildung-toward-humanity was seen both as the perfecting of human nature and as participation in something vaguely divine or transcendent. Bildung retained, too, something of the ambiguous character of Roman humanitas. On the one hand, Bildung became the watchword for a republican political movement that thus reached back behind imperial Roman humanitas to Greek paideia, a movement that regarded an expanding reading public as the cultivating ground for a decisive challenge to political domination. The arena of Bildung is the arena within which the public sphere is forged, within which it is reason and the best argument that reign, rather than hereditary dignity. In this sense Bildung can be seen as a radical transformation of Roman humanitas. On the other hand, not everyone agreed that the capacity for Bildung was equally distributed among humankind; Kant, for instance, as we have seen, thought that only the white race was capable of autonomous self-government. And Bildung easily became a ground for claims to a new form of nobility, as those of the bourgeoisie who could afford a "liberal" education distinguished themselves from the uncultured masses. So there was a danger that full humanity could once again come to be the possession of the fortunate and placed out of reach for the many.

Medieval Humanism and the Imago Dei

An older, more diffuse form of humanism also helped to shape the Bildung tradition in significant and distinctive ways. This medieval humanism, which flowered from the twelfth through the early fourteenth century, was not, like Renaissance humanism, focused on the retrieval and imitation of ancient Greek and Latin letters, even though it was deeply shaped by the classical inheritance. It was animated by a keen sense of the intelligible character of nature and of the dignity of human nature, signaled in part through a growing confidence in the human capacity to grasp the ordered splendor of the world.[39] No longer was the world, as in earlier medieval thought, seen as essentially threatening or chaotic; rather, nature reflected the goodness and wisdom of its Creator.[40] And human beings, despite the ravages of the fall, were seen as still bearing the dignity of their creation in the image of God.

Within medieval humanism, the imago Dei linked human dignity with a special responsibility entrusted to human beings.[41] We can see this particularly clearly in Thomas Aquinas's *Summa theologiae*, in which the doctrine of the imago Dei serves as a linchpin. The overarching structure of Thomas's *Summa* is a Neoplatonic *exitus-reditus*—all of creation has issued forth from God and is being drawn back to God. Human beings play a special role in this *reditus* of creation by virtue of having been created in the image of God as moral agents, principles of their own actions and therefore capable of being providential for themselves.[42]

An "image" in this context, Aquinas explains, involves more than mere similarity. To be an image of something is to stand in a relationship of imitation to an exemplar, as, he suggests, a coin is stamped with an image or a son is begotten by a father.[43] An image is also more than a mere trace, a causal effect, like footprints left in the sand: here there is a kind of relationship, and also a kind of likeness, but not the sort that counts for Aquinas as a "likeness of species." To say that an image possesses a likeness of species is to say that it possesses a likeness that reflects something central and defining about the exemplar. To say that the cookies I have just baked are made in my image is a misuse of the term, since although I have made them and they bear the impression of my thumbprint, this likeness does not count as a likeness of species. To be in the image of God, Aquinas insists, is to be like God in a way that reflects God's "dignity" and "shape" (*figura*).[44] Aquinas argues that this requires that a creature not merely exist, or live; a likeness of species involves knowing and understanding, free will and self-movement or choice. This counts as a likeness of species because it constitutes an image of the trinitarian relations that constitute the divine life—of the procession of the Word from the Speaker, and Love from both of these.[45] Here he draws on, while modifying, Augustine's trinitarian meditations on the imago Dei in *De Trinitate*.

Setting out in search of an image of the Trinity in the human soul, Augustine had hit upon the mind's remembering, understanding, and willing/loving itself, so mirroring, he argued, the trinitarian relationships among begetter, begotten, and the love coupling them together. Through these reflexive relations the soul is capable of discovering not only itself but God, embarking on a contemplative ascent that returns it to God.[46] The image of God in the human soul is realized when it participates in God's knowledge and love. Nor is this merely a matter of contemplative delight; by way of this participation we come to love self and neighbor rightly, grasping how we and they stand in relation to God rather than our own disordered and prideful desires.[47]

Aquinas, too, unites the contemplative and the ethical and regards the imago as a teleologically ordered capacity. Human beings are set apart as creatures capable of participating in divine providence, of ordering their own actions and thereby of ordering the natural world in conformity with God's purposes. Here Aquinas draws on the functional understanding of the imago Dei present in Genesis 1, which similarly focuses on the human being as God's representative in continuing the work of ordering creation.[48] In a critical distinction from pagan Neoplatonism, the *reditus*, the return of creation to God, is accomplished not by monistic reabsorption but insofar as those creatures capable of recognizing God come to participate in the friendship that constitutes the inner life of God. This friendship is expressed in this world in lives that reflect God's generous friendship, a friendship that reaches out to include even strangers and enemies.[49] The imago Dei is thus both gift and task.

Aquinas defines degrees of the image of God in humankind, reflecting its teleological character. Every human being possesses the first degree, a rational nature, with its aptitude to know and love God. The image in the second degree is conformity to God in this life through good actions and virtues. The third and most perfect degree is realized in the beatific vision, with its perfect knowledge and love of God and of all created things in relation to God.[50] Christ as Savior and as perfect image of God (and therefore as perfect human being) plays for Aquinas an indispensable role in the process of healing and perfecting the imago in humankind at large and thus also of the *reditus* of creation to God.⁵¹ Jesus displays human moral agency that is perfectly receptive of and responsive to divine grace. The grace of Christ is in turn received by Christians above all in the form of God-given dispositions (the supernatural virtues of faith, hope, and charity, together with the infused moral virtues) infused through the sacraments. Human agency is thus perfected in becoming perfectly transparent to divine agency and will. It is an understanding of human dignity and agency perfected in receiving grace, rather than in independence.

This humanistic tradition within medieval theology bequeathed to the later Bildung tradition a sense of the project of forming humanity as a momentous collective task, playing out over the scope of human history and even transcending that finite history; it was not just a matter of the formation of fine, harmoniously balanced individuals, nor the production of proper citizens, or of exemplary rulers, but the realization of a cosmic project, a project that offered a key to the meaningfulness of the world and time. It ensured that a certain set of questions would hover over that tradition, however estranged it became from Christian doctrinal commitments: Are human beings capable of independent self-formation? Or is human self-realization a fundamentally receptive process? Are there models or exemplars at hand, and what is our mode of access to these models? Is the human telos contemplative or active, or somehow both? How, in our individual projects of self-realization, are we related to others and participating in a collective project of the formation of humanity? Is it a task at which some fail, and who has the authority to adjudicate that failure? How are we to relate to others who call into question our own humanity (the stranger, the enemy)? This theological tradition, moreover, helped to shape the Bildung tradition at a most constitutive level: that of language. For the word *Bildung* and its various compounds play a significant role in the writings of the Rhineland mystics, who already in the late thirteenth century were using the vernacular in their discussions of the image of God in humankind and its renewal. This theological context, then, shaped the range of reference, the connotations, the implicit assumptions, of the vocabulary of German neohumanism centuries later.

The doctrine of the imago Dei has been generative in part because it is so highly malleable, with a rather slight scriptural basis that left an opening for an extraordinarily wide range of elaborations.[52] Even within pre-seventeenth-century German vernacular thought alone, quite divergent interpretations are easily identifiable.[53] I isolate for discussion here three thinkers who were particularly significant in shaping the Bildung tradition, each with a distinctive understanding of the imago Dei. For Meister Eckhart, humanly conceived images separate the soul from God; turning inward and away from these makes room for the birth of the Son, the true image of God, within the soul. The birth of the Son within is also the realization of our humanity; it makes possible a love that overcomes division, expressed in works of charity. For Luther, we image God insofar as through faith we become "living pictures" of Christ, the essential image of God, thus expressing God's compassion and generosity toward others. And in the hermetic physician Paracelsus we find an epigenetic conception of Bildung as the unfolding development of seeds planted in the natural world by God, together with an understanding of human beings as an extract and microcosm of all creation, entrusted as the image of God with the task of revealing God's secret and invisible works in nature. At issue here were two questions of fundamental importance for the later Bildung tradition. First, who was the agent of Bildung, God or humankind, and how was human agency to be understood in relation to divine agency? And, second, what was the telos of Bildung? The spread of cultured civilization? The revelation of nature's hidden secrets? Or reconciling neighbor love? Most often eighteenth- and early nineteenth-century theorists of Bildung tried to avoid choosing. This allowed the "advance" of Western civilization and science to be framed as progress in Christian charity.

Meister Eckhart: The Birth of the Son Within

The Dominican theologian, philosopher, and Rhineland mystic Meister Eckhart (ca. 1260–ca. 1327), despite being dogged during his lifetime by charges of heresy, exercised considerable influence within the later mystical tradition as well as on Reformation thought (by way of his disciple the Dominican Johannes Tauler and the anonymous *Theologia Germanica*) and was enthusiastically rediscovered in early nineteenth-century Germany.[54] "Image" (*Bild*; *Abbild*) and various verb forms related to it, including "de-form" (*entbilden*), "transform" (*überbilden*) and "in-form" (*einbilden*), lie at the heart of Meister Eckhart's creative appropriation of the Christian Neoplatonist tradition, leaving an indelible mark on the German language and creating vital conceptual resources that would later be exploited in the Bildung tradition. Eckhart's employment of the language of image and form is complex and multilayered. The soul is for Eckhart the natural image (*Bild*) of God.[55] God has made the human soul like himself so that God can inhabit the soul; Eckhart speaks of the soul as a temple in which God can dwell.[56] This natural image is adorned and perfected through the birth of God's Son within the soul; the birth of the Son was not for Eckhart simply a historical birth of Jesus in the first century but rather a birth that takes place again and again within human persons.[57]

According to Eckhart's epistemology, human knowing takes place through the constant creation of images (*Bilder*): "whenever the powers of the soul make contact with a creature, they set to work and make an image [*Bilde*] and likeness of the creature, which they absorb."[58] Ordinary knowledge, then, requires active image creation. However, these images block the activity of God in the soul. Human beings can create no image either of God or of the soul itself, since they construct images only through sensory contact with an object. While the human soul naturally creates images in its efforts to know, Eckhart insists that inwardly, in its "silent middle," the soul is free of images. It is here alone that the birth of the Son in the soul can take place.[59] For here the soul is free of activity and is able to be purely receptive to the activity of God.[60] The soul must thus be collected and turn inward, away from the senses, in order to prepare for the birth of the Son within. When the Son is born in the soul, the temple shines forth with beauty, in a likeness to uncreated divine beauty that serves as its appropriate dwelling place in the soul.[61]

God's knowledge is unlike human knowledge: God does not need to construct images in order to know. God's Son is therefore properly God's knowledge of Godself *un*mediated by images. Eckhart finds this important to assert because he understands images as standing between knower and known and thus preventing their union with one another. God, in contrast, "needs no image and has no image: without any means, likeness, or image God operates in the soul—right in the ground where no image ever got in, but only He Himself with His own being."[62] The language of birth is appropriate because it captures the unmediated relationship between Father and Son: the Son is the Father's "perfect insight into Himself, profound and thorough knowledge of Himself by Himself, and not through any image."[63] It is because the Son as this unmediated divine self-insight can be born in the soul that a real union of the human soul with God is possible; "if any image were present there would be no real union, and in that real union lies the soul's whole beatitude."[64]

Eckhart's account can seem paradoxical at times. So on the one hand he approvingly cites Dionysius's saying that "God has no image or likeness of Himself," in order to underscore that God does not work through images but through birthing the Son in the soul.[65] On the other hand, Eckhart also affirms both that the Son is properly called the image of God and, as we have already seen, that the human soul is the natural image of God.[66] The Son is properly the image of God not in the sense of a mediating picture but in that all of God's nature "pours out into His image while yet remaining intact within itself."[67] The human soul, meanwhile, is the natural image of God in that the birth of the Son is possible only in this sort of creature, in which there is a "silent middle" or temple.

The process of de-forming (*entbilden*), transforming (*überbilden*), and in-forming (*einbilden*) comes to fruition in the realization of humanity. Hence it is Christ who most fully and properly possesses humanity, having assumed it in the incarnation. We, in contrast, are individual men and women who must realize and receive our humanity from without:

> I say humanity [*Menschheit*] and man [*Mensch*] are different. Humanity in itself is so noble that the highest peak of humanity is equal to the angels and akin to God. The closest union that Christ had with the Father, that is possible for me to win, could I but slough off what there is of this and that, and realize my humanity. All that God ever gave His only-begotten Son He has given me as perfectly as him, no less. He has given me more: He gave more of my humanity in Christ than to him, for to him He gave nothing: he had it eternally in the Father.[68]

Humanity is realized, then, insofar as the Son is born within the soul, received as divine gift.

Much as Eckhart stresses the importance of contemplative inwardness, the ethical trajectory of his thought must not be overlooked. In response to an objector who worries that engagement in works of charity will deprive a person of the possibility of mystical union with God, Eckhart is insistent that "God's purpose in the union of contemplation is fruitfulness in works."[69] One in whom Christ is born does not simply rest in contemplation, for this would be merely self-serving, and love seeks to serve others as well. Eckhart refuses to elevate Mary over Martha and cites "Master Thomas" (Aquinas) as saying that "the active life is better than the contemplative, insofar as in action one pours out for love that which one has gained in contemplation."[70] One in whom the Son has been born is capable of engaging in the active practice of charity without being distracted and scattered by many images, despite the fact that "every act must accord with its appropriate image" and hence activity "implies works galore."[71] This is because in such a person the activity of charity is God's own activity: "what the active intellect does for the natural man, that and far more God does for the one with detachment: He takes away the active intellect from him and, installing Himself in its stead, He Himself undertakes all that the active intellect ought to be doing."[72] If Eckhart here puts this in terms of the displacement of human activity, he also at times understands it as a cooperation of human with divine activity. He is able to speak in this way because he understands the birth of the Son to mean that God's activity in us is indeed our own activity: "We can and must work from our own power from within. If then we are to live in him and through him, he must be our own, and we must work from our own: just as God does all things of His own and through Himself, so we must work from our own, which is He, in us."[73]

That the birth of the Son within is realized in acts of charity toward others flows from the centrality of love in Eckhart's theology; the gospel and epistles of John, interpreted with a strong Neoplatonic accent, play a particularly prominent role. In love, division, disunity, and conflict are overcome. In love, two become one, and out of this union of love, love overflows: "It is the nature of love to arise and flow out of two as a one. One as one is not love; two as two is not love; but two as one must produce natural, willing, ardent love."[74] Where two remain two, there is a lack: "one is not the other, for the *not* that makes the difference is nothing but bitterness, because there is no peace."[75] God wishes to be united with each and every human person, as one capable of receiving the birth of the Son; God yearns to realize this union in every human person.⁷⁶ Indeed Eckhart insists that God *must* love, even as he also insists that acts done in love are perfectly free: "to stop God loving my soul would be to deprive Him of His Godhead; for God is as truly love as He is truth; and as truly as He is goodness, He is love."⁷⁷

The distinctly Plotinian note sounded here is the assumption that conflict can be overcome only when all differentiation is annulled; love is understood not as relationship but as merging or melting together. As Bernard McGinn notes, here God becomes one with the human person "no longer through mystical uniting, that is, an intentional union between God and human emphasizing the continuing distinction between the two entities, but in a mystical identity in which God and human become truly indistinct, at least on some level."⁷⁸ This notion of absorption into the One is worlds away from the Christian humanism that regarded the *reditus* of creation to God as realized relationally, through creaturely participation in the self-giving friendship that constitutes the inner life of God. The birth of the Son within, for Eckhart, enables the realization of humanity precisely insofar as it makes possible a love that overcomes conflict not through harmony but through a unison in which all distinctions are lost.

It was radical indeed to claim that the human soul can become one with, not merely similar to, or in intimate relation with, God. Small wonder that Eckhart was accused of heresy and his claims of mystical identity were condemned. His writings continued to circulate, however, with some of his followers interpreting him in less Plotinian, more broadly orthodox, ways. Aiding this hermeneutical project was the fact that when it came to the interhuman social expression of his thought, Eckhart envisioned not a destruction of all distinctions and an indiscriminate merging of identities but rather relationships of equal regard. Eckhart insisted on the essential equality of human persons, rich and poor, powerful and wretched, as equally the objects of yearning divine love.⁷⁹ And he insisted that humanity is realized in us as we "love all men equally, respect and regard them equally."⁸⁰

Eckhart's imprint on the later Bildung tradition is deep. Three things are particularly noteworthy. The first has to do with Eckhart's contribution to the rich metaphorical repertoire of Bildung. On the one hand, clearly Eckhart primarily conceives of image as pictorial representation rather than as a physical impression of an image as in a wax seal. Yet Eckhart plays with the language in ways that introduce notions of dynamic formation and shaping, of being emptied and filled, de-formed (*entbildet*) and in-formed (*eingebildet*).[81] This paves the way for later understandings of Bildung as an activity of shaping or formation. The second has to do with the agent of Bildung. Clearly Eckhart's focus is on divine activity, not on human self-forming activity. Human image-creation is particularly suspect; images block divine activity; far from mediating God's presence, they prevent the birth of the Son in the soul. Yet the soul is not purely passive but is active in collecting itself and turning inward, away from sensory images. And if Eckhart is sometimes tempted to speak of the utter *displacement* of human activity, his Neoplatonic impulses lead him rather to emphasize that God's activity within the soul becomes the soul's own proper activity, since God and the soul are united. Later reflection on Bildung will continue to wrestle with questions of divine and human agency, with the strongest denunciations of *Menschenkunst* eliciting the most emphatic valorizations of the same. Finally, the telos of this divine-human activity is the realization of humanity, but humanity is not here merged with high culture or civilizational polish, as in ancient conceptions of paideia and humanitas. Rather, humanity is conceived incarnationally: the Son's birth in the soul comes to practical expression in an overflowing love that reaches out to all equally. This too leaves a lasting imprint on the Bildung tradition, as the realization of humanity continues to be understood as intrinsically connected with interpersonal respect and regard, with the affirmation of equality, and ultimately with love and friendship.

Martin Luther: Mirroring the Word of God

It is often noted that Luther was influenced by the mystical tradition, particularly via Eckhart's student Johannes Tauler, but it is also clear that with his heightened sense of the radical character of the fall, Luther could hardly accept Eckhart's Neoplatonic characterization of the soul and its contemplative task. The imago Dei has been lost; fallen humanity is enslaved to sin and death and incapable of earning God's grace. Human reason is no longer directed toward the good; human will is perverse and no longer free to pursue the good. In his

Disputatio de homine of 1536, Luther emphasizes that human beings in this life are simply the raw material on which God's transformative power works.[82] Given that the image of God has been lost and is now known only through the lens of justification, Luther is reticent to speculate about it, although after declaring in his *Lectures on Genesis* that he will not do so, he nevertheless goes on in some detail, insisting that it was a divine gift that rendered Adam altogether righteous and perfect, with an uncorrupt intellect, perfect memory, upright will, good conscience, and strength and perfection of body, free of lust, possessing true knowledge of God and not being subject to death.[83] With the loss of the image, memory, intellect, and will (Augustine's trinity in the human soul) have been altogether corrupted and greatly weakened. The purpose of the gospel is to restore the image; by its restoration we are born again to eternal life and gradually renewed in righteousness.[84]

Only through Jesus Christ and Holy Scripture can there be a new formation of the imago Dei in Christian hearts. Unlike God, who is pure spirit, human beings cannot understand without the help of perceptible images, so it is crucial that God's self-revelation to human beings comes as *Bilder*. Properly speaking, only Christ is the true image (*Bild*) of God; human beings were created *after* or *to* this image.[85] To call Christ the true image of God is to emphasize that he is truly God but a distinct Person from the Father. Luther acknowledges that an ordinary image (*Bild*) retains the substance out of which it is made; a sculpture of stone or wood remains stone or wood, even if it is carved to resemble a man. So all creaturely images remain substantially what they always were. Christ, however, is an image of God in a much fuller sense, sharing fully in the being of the Father.[86]

According to Luther, God has painted (*gemalet*) himself in his Word (both Christ and the Gospel), which is thus a picture (*Bild*) in which God can be seen and felt. Human beings are called to grasp this picture (*Bild*) and offer a clear reflection of it, as a good mirror would.[87] The examples set before us in the gospel (*Vorbilder*) will be formed within (*eingebildet*) in our hearts. Only where God's self-portrait is properly mirrored is God rightly grasped. This is how Luther understands the creation of humankind in the image of God; the image of God was in Adam's heart, indeed he *was* God's image, insofar as he mirrored this true self-portrait of God. We are thus called to grasp God as revealed through Christ in the gospel so that our reflection of that image may become clarified. By way of this process, God mirrors or paints himself in our hearts.[88] Luther illustrates this in a sermon on Jesus's healing of the centurion's servant in Matthew 8; the centurion's understanding that Jesus is a "compassionate Savior, eager to help and do good," who expects only that one have faith in him, shows that he rightly mirrors Jesus.[89] Luther thus closely aligns the formation of the understanding with the formation of the heart: to rightly mirror Christ is at once to conceive him correctly and to have one's affections aligned with his affections. Just as an image in a mirror is not a static representation but moves as the person standing before it moves, so those who mirror Christ are transformed to become "living pictures" of Christ, acting with compassion and generosity toward all. Holding on to this image requires effort and work, Luther stresses, since through the fall we have become a shameful and spoiled mirror. Adam fell prey to the devil's wiles: the devil succeeded in convincing him that God is not after all a loving Father who means only good to humanity. Believing this, Adam lost hold of the image that God had painted and instead formed himself after the image that the devil had painted, imagining God as a horrible demon, eager to damn human beings.[90] No longer mirroring God truly, Adam's heart became spoiled accordingly, so that God's Word became for him poison and death.

The image of God is thus for Luther an active reflection of God's loving character. Justification is for Luther forensic: the faithful are "clothed in" Christ, exchanging roles such that Christ takes on the "mask" of sinner and is given up to death, even as God recognizes Christ's "alien righteousness" as properly theirs.[91] This imputed righteousness is passive, received as a gift.[92] But it is also effective, initiating the transformation of the person. Renewal of the image, the reformation of the raw matter of fallen humanity into the imago Dei, is possible only through union with or marriage to Christ. It is not a matter of neatly linear progress and will be perfected only eschatologically. Thus Luther retains from the mystical tradition something like Eckhart's understanding of the ontological presence of Christ in the soul.[93] Given Christ's presence within, the faithful can gradually reflect God's image more clearly.[94] Yet any sense of perfectibility is further chastened by Luther's insistence that the new righteousness begins with the crucifixion of the fallen Adam; the faithful must be conformed to Christ's death as well as to Christ's life and resurrection, and this crucifixion is in this life never accomplished once and for all, but requires a daily return to the cross.⁹⁵

Luther's understanding of the image was particularly indigestible for the later Bildung tradition. It was not just that Luther insisted that human persons are utterly incapable on their own of mirroring God's self-portrait by becoming living pictures of Christ. This emphasis on relational empowerment was creatively appropriated by some later proponents of Bildung, as we shall see. The greater stumbling block for the later Bildung tradition was Luther's *simul justus et peccator*. Even if the presence of Christ within makes halting improvement possible in the lives of individual Christians, their lives remain marked by sin, and Luther is far too Augustinian to countenance collective human progress in realizing the image of God. However, over the long run the temptation to map the realization of humanity onto history proved too enticing to resist.

Paracelsus: Imagination and Epigenesis

A third theologically distinct account of the imago Dei, also critical for the Bildung tradition, is represented by Paracelsus's (1493–1541) philosophy of nature. Paracelsus was a physician, philosopher, and alchemist. Like Eckhart, he was deeply influenced by Neoplatonic thought, but in a Renaissance vein filtered through the Hermetic philosophies of Ficino and Pico della Mirandola and drawing on an Aristotelian understanding of immanent forms. Within this stream of thought, nature is conceived of not negatively in terms of its distance from pure spirit but positively in terms of its ongoing inner relation to spirit. Outer, material, perceptible realities are an expression of immanent form-giving principles, understood as embodying and revealing divine wisdom.⁹⁶

The doctrine of the imago Dei is important to Paracelsus, as it is to Eckhart and Luther. Its meaning and significance, however, are strikingly different. For Paracelsus, human beings are created in the image of God in order that the will of God might be realized. What is this will? To make God's secret and invisible works of nature manifest.⁹⁷ In other words, humankind has been created in order to engage in science and medicine. Nature and the gospel are equally to be understood as God's books and are both to be read by reason in executing this task. The light of nature is divinely given, but it is entrusted to human agency.[98] It carries no actual knowledge of nature with it; we know the world only by actually examining the world, not by looking within or awaiting illumination. Human beings are specially situated in order to carry out this task in that they are a microcosm of the whole of nature; after having created all other creatures, God created humankind out of extracts of all else that had been created, both the heavens and the earth (God is thus depicted as an alchemist). The heavens, and in particular the stars, Paracelsus identifies as the source of wisdom, reason, and the arts, the earthly elements as the source of flesh and blood: "Man is . . . the microcosm and the son of the whole world, because he has been created as an extract of all creation by the hand of God. . . . Thus man beats like the stars and also like the elements, from which he is made."[99] To live according to divine wisdom is to live according to the image of God. This requires attending to nature rather than turning away from it: "man must . . . fulfil the law of the Lord and live in harmony with Nature, and . . . the will of God and . . . the divine spirit."[100] Eckhart's contemplative inwardness is nowhere in sight, nor Luther's emphasis on the image as mirroring God's compassionate forgiveness.

Humanity's special standing as microcosm of heavens and earth situates us to reveal, among other things, the mysteries of nourishment and procreation. Here Paracelsus emphasized epigenesis—processes of sequential differentiation and development—in ways that would be decisive for later understandings of Bildung. For Paracelsus focuses on processes of formation that consist of unfolding or expression from within as opposed to shaping from without. Paracelsus describes seeds as consisting of two elements: a form proper to a given species and a "master-craftsman." Nourishment from the outside is required in order for a seed to grow, and what we take in becomes incorporated into our bodies: "all our nourishment becomes ourselves; we eat ourselves into being."[101] Living things must constantly preserve their form by eating; what we eat the "master-craftsman" cunningly carves up for the use of our various organs. This is possible because "every bite we take contains in itself all our organs, all that is included in the whole man, out of which he is constituted."[102] Paracelsus compares the activity of the "master craftsman" to a sculptor who carves an image (*Schnizlung*; carving) out of wood, dividing nutrients so that they can shape "the man according to his form."[103] Hence Paracelsus's understanding of epigenesis brings together the concepts of image and form in a newly dynamic way focused on natural processes. Epigenesis takes place in human beings as in other living things, with one important exception: since human beings alone are created by God in order to be free, these processes are not determined by instinct but are rather guided by imagination (*fantasei*). Rather than possessing embedded procreative seeds, for instance, seeds are created in man and woman only when the imagination is kindled by a desirable object and a person freely decides to yield to desire: "God has placed the seed in man's speculation, in which his reason lies."[104] Human beings are thus in certain respects free self-formers, even as in other respects they remain dependent on the ceaseless nutritional work of the inner "master-craftsman." In Paracelsus the vertical dimensions of Neoplatonic thought, of emanation and remanation, thus receive instead a horizontal expression.[105] Creation is not returned to God via contemplation but evolves forward in time, determined by inner seeds but evolving via combination into ever new forms. Nor is this horizontal dimension confined to eschatological realization or to salvation history; it encompasses all of nature. Human beings participate in this general formation of nature and are determined by the same immanent laws that guide the expression of natural forms. But human formation is also distinctive, in that it takes place through the human capacity to imagine (*einbilden*) these inner forms and immanent laws and thus to render the forms present as a concrete goal to be realized, as a *Bild* that awakens desire and active striving.[106] Paracelsus conceives of imagination as a magical sunlike force, with a magnetic power to attract the outer world into itself and transform existing things by impressing itself on them.[107]

Paracelsus regards each species-form as a stable entity, reproduced through seeds and preserved in each individual through nourishment. Yet Paracelsus is also cognizant of intraspecies diversity and recognizes that it is made possible through sexual reproduction and the mixing of the seeds of male and female.[108] This fact is significant because it gives a natural shape to the terminus of the created world. For it is God's will that "all colours, forms, types, and fashions" of humankind be realized. Once these are at an end, such that no "new fashion" can be created, "the age of the world is at an end."[109] Human diversity is here regarded as a positive good and a realization of God's creative plan, furthering God's will that in humankind as the microcosm of creation, both heavenly and earthly, God's secret wisdom will be made manifest. Corresponding to this unfolding diversity of human types is an ongoing realization of the various arts; human beings as the microcosm of the world are capable of receiving influences from the stars that allow them to develop the various arts. God "wills that all the arts—music, the mechanical arts, the faculties, and the doctrines of religion—which He created in the firmament, should become real. . . . And this must be realized through man. . . . For the stars need an agent through which to work, and this agent is man and man alone."[110]

Paracelsus's innovations should not be exaggerated. He affirms that earthly, profane things must be ordered below heavenly, sacred things, and stresses that our kingdom is not of this earth and that we should not waste our time with things that we cannot take with us when we die.[111] The study of science and medicine is not mere earthly, profane wisdom, however. Rather, it is a way of serving God and humankind. He insists that "God has created and made a true religion for the benefit of the sick. This is medicine . . . and it is no mean thing but second to the religion of the spirit."[112] Medicine, then, comes from God and fulfills the will of God. For when people are healed of their ailments, they are given time to repent of their sins and to live a blessed life. Yet while Paracelsus understood himself to be engaged in the proper pursuit of heavenly things in accordance with the divine will, his ideas are undeniably novel in many respects. Particularly noteworthy for later conceptions of Bildung are his emphases on natural processes, on development-from-within, and on the positive character of human imagination and natural diversity, and his confidence that human freedom and wisdom can work creatively in harmony with the powers of nature. It is due to Paracelsus that the project of natural science becomes bound up with the project of forming humanity.

Conclusion

The notion that humanity is not a given but a task to be realized through human activity—that human beings are self-formers—has deep historical roots. The Bildung tradition arises at the confluence of various streams of reflection on the formation of humanity, themselves interacting with one another in complex ways. This chapter has explored a number of the most significant of these: the Greek conception of paideia and the process of educating human beings into a capacity for excellent citizenship; the Roman virtue of humanitas, softening and civilizing the edges of imperial rule; the early modern notion of gentility as a matter of acquired character rather than inheritance; and the dignity of human beings as created in the image of God and summoned despite the fall to participate in the *reditus* of creation to God, variously by way of making room for the birth of the Son within; by faithfully mirroring God's love, forgiveness, and compassion; or by revealing God's secret works expressed in nature. If the ancient world was characterized by a sublime confidence in human formative powers, together with an untroubled chauvinism toward those not fully human, the Christian world was characterized by ambivalence concerning human agency, a recognition of loss of innocence and alienation, and a deep longing for reconciliation. On the one hand, human creative powers—human imagination (*Einbildung*)—are not capable of properly forming a perfected humanity; the images we form separate us from God or erect counterfeits that re-create God in the image of the devil. On the other, human beings can nonetheless serve as temples for the birth of the Son, living pictures of Christ, finite embodiments of God's reconciling love. And at the opposite end of the spectrum of interpretation, human imagination becomes a positive conduit for the manifestation of divine wisdom in the unfolding diversity of the natural world.

The next chapter traces this ambivalence concerning human self-forming agency and imagination forward into the seventeenth century, through two thinkers who serve as mediating figures, Johann Arndt (1555–1621) and Jakob Boehme (1574–1624), and on into the Pietist tradition more narrowly defined. Where Eckhart had seen human image-making as distracting the mind and preventing the birth of the Son within, and Luther had regarded human imagination as distorted by fear and guilt, in the seventeenth-century context Pietist critiques of human imagination express anxiety over the hubris of rationalism.

Recall Barth's diagnosis of modern theology as a retrieval of autocratic humanism, and of Pietism as an expression of this impulse, insofar as it sought to absorb everything external or other into the self, so that the self is no longer liable to being called into question, disturbed by otherness. If this is an apt diagnosis, it is hardly one that can be set cleanly over against the Reformation, insofar as Luther too embraced the mystical tradition's teaching of Christ within the soul. In turning to Pietism and its early seventeenth-century precursors, then, we shall need to be cautious in differentiating Pietism from what came before. For if Pietism was an expression of autocratic humanism, it was also an attempt to flee from it, now regarded not as a confident expression of faith but as a deep threat to faith. What no one fully grasped was that the most seductive temptation facing the later Bildung tradition was not that of emancipating human agency and human imagination, for these could always be read in a participatory mode. It was, rather, that of engaging in an easy conflation of humanity as (a) the spread of civilization or high culture, (b) the unfolding of nature's secrets, and (c) patient neighbor-love that reconciles division and conflict, and to regard all three as advancing together in history. This was not simply a matter of valorizing human agency and imagination; it was a matter of being insulated from the otherness that calls into radical question daydreams of cumulative progress.

Pietism and the Problem of Human Craft (*Menschen-kunst*)   2

As Karl Barth saw it, Pietism and rationalism alike were expressions of autocratic humanism, paving the way for a self-authorizing humanity that has no need of God.[1] Pietism's particular expression of this impulse came by way of a radical interiorizing of Christian faith: the incarnation, fellow man, external authority, divine command, and the sacraments. Both Pietists and rationalists critiqued lifeless orthodoxy in the name of lived Christianity, even as Pietists focused in particular on religious experience, not just outward works.[2] "In practice (though they diverged in theory)," argued Barth, "both sides believed that it was within the power of man, man in general or at least converted man, to experience a new and better life and to give it visible experience."[3] They therefore resisted acknowledging any limits to human capacity and human agency, refused to acknowledge anything that "man could not realize . . . [that] was not the object of his willing and his action, material that could not be shaped by his will for form."[4] This meant resisting the Reformers' doctrine of justification, which for Barth was at heart the notion that Christ in responding to God's summons to covenant partnership has already accomplished the good on behalf of all humankind. It meant, too, resisting the notion of human sinfulness and the need for forgiveness, for accepting a good that we cannot accomplish on our own but must receive from outside, from another.[5] The upshot was Pietist and Enlightenment moralism. This, fundamentally, is what Barth found wrong in modern theology as a whole. Within Pietism in particular it takes the form of the effort to translate every aspect of Christianity into an individual inner experience. Pietism seeks "the appropriation of

Christianity, which is regarded as complete when all that is not one's own as such is dissolved and made one's own."[6] So, for instance, Pietism prefers to speak of the birth of Christ in the heart of a Christian rather than of Christ's incarnation in first-century Palestine: "the history of Christ is seen as simply the outward expression, inessential in itself, of the history that takes place today, here and in us."[7] Insofar as Pietists sought community, it was a communion limited to the spiritual elite: "the freely-formed, chosen community is what is left of the community once it has been in effect assaulted and overcome by the individual, King Man."[8] Even while remaining nominally within the broader church, Pietists removed themselves from responsibility to the community at large.

As we have seen in chapter 1, however, talk of Christ's birth within reaches back deep into the Christian mystical tradition; it is richly developed by Meister Eckhart and is preserved in Luther as well; justification by the alien righteousness of Christ did not for Luther involve a rejection of the notion of the ontological presence of Christ in the hearts of the faithful, even if he held forensic grace and the inner transformative gift in tension with one another. Barth is right, however, both to see in Pietism something fundamentally new or "modern" and to see Pietism and rationalism as deeply interconnected phenomena, however dramatic their differences. This has to do not with Pietism's emphasis on inwardness as such, however, but rather with the context within which this was now being expressed: increasingly, and patently by the time of Francke, as a reaction to and rejection of rationalism. Pietism's turn within was not in itself an expression of autocratic humanism but an attempt to foreclose the possibility of such a declaration of human independence.

The mainstream Pietist movement was primarily oriented toward an active, practical Christianity over against what it perceived as lifeless Protestant orthodoxy. This practical orientation left it open to charges of works-righteousness, in response to which the Pietists emphasized that a foundational passivity to divine agency underlay their activism. The works of love that they so eagerly promoted were to be understood as fruits of faith, the proper agent of which was the Holy Spirit. The Pietists, then, drew on the tradition of mystical inwardness in an effort to certify that their active practical Christianity was anything but an expression of human independence. Hence the vital importance of a mode of spirituality in which human agency was understood as needing to be utterly displaced by divine agency. It was this evacuation of human agency that provoked a secularizing assertion of independent human agency in German classicism and Romanticism. At the same time these movements drew positively on Pietism's emphasis on subjectivity and introspection, and on the language of the heart developed within Pietism, no longer in order to trace the supernatural work of God within the soul, but in search of inner harmony and wholeness. They also drew on a radical wing of Pietism that followed Paracelsus in valorizing the creative power of imagination, rather than seeking to rein it in as expressive of human rebelliousness.

In this sense Pietism can be seen as contributing both indirectly (by way of eliciting a counterreaction to its evacuation of human agency) and directly (through radical forms of Pietism) to an autocratic humanism, and as providing a pathway by which Bildung came to be conceived of as autonomous human self-formation rather than divine re-formation of the imago Dei. Yet as we shall see over the course of the chapters to come, it is hardly the case that the Bildung tradition of the eighteenth and early nineteenth centuries is in its entirety aptly characterized as autocratic humanism. Indeed, the most theologically suspect idea passed along from mainstream Pietism was the assumption of a contrastive either-or between divine and human agency, such that utter passivity before divine agency could be seen as the sole path to encounter with God and reception of grace. With this assumption in place, human self-forming activity could not but appear as a rejection of divine formation. As we shall see, some strands of the Bildung tradition (in particular Herder and Hegel) broke free of this assumption. In doing so they recovered a nonautocratic humanism that did not stand in a competitive relation to divine agency but rather understood the formation of humanity as God's reconciling the world to Godself, a reconciliation in which diverse expressions of goodness are woven into harmony rather than stamped out into monotony. Jakob Boehme's influence was even more dangerously subversive than that of mainstream Pietism: rather than policing the boundary between human and divine agency, he collapsed the two together. Lack, desire, suffering, even evil were thereby taken up into the necessary process of divine self-realization. The formation of humanity becomes part and parcel of the formation of the divine life; God's end in creation is no longer the gratuitous invitation of the finite other into a shared life of friendship but the working through of

God's own inner conflicts. It was Hegel who was to take up this radical challenge most thoroughly, maintaining that evil was no necessity but instead was suffered by the divine life in its tenacious pursuit of reconciliation.

Barth rightly saw that what was at stake in autocratic humanism was a refusal to listen for the Word of God in what is other and different from ourselves. For Barth, Pietism's internalization of Christianity went hand in hand with a refusal to encounter one's neighbor; the neighbor "is no longer to disturb me by his otherness," which might call into question the truth and goodness that I claim to have achieved for myself and might expose me as sinful, as having refused to listen to a voice that reveals that my point of view on the universe is not absolute. Pietists listened for the "inner voice," but this, Barth insisted, must not be conflated with listening for God's command, for the latter has essentially, like encountering the neighbor, to do with openness to being disturbed and called into question by the other. The Bildung tradition of the eighteenth and early nineteenth centuries inherited the Pietist preoccupation with inner harmony, while drawing on the radical Hermetic tradition in thematizing a host of corresponding oppositions the overcoming of which was seen as key to arriving at peace and wholeness: between God and world, subject and object, reason and feeling, individual and society, etc. Barth rightly saw that no ostensible unity obtained by blocking the interruptive voice of the Other could be anything but a sham. We shall have to see how the Bildung tradition fared in this respect.

Pietism and Its Boundaries

The beginnings and scope of the Pietist movement continue to be contested by scholars. Some define Pietism very broadly as a movement of practical piety and see it as beginning at the very outset of the seventeenth century with English Puritanism.[9] This definition has the virtue of highlighting commonalities among renewal impulses in England, the Netherlands, and Germany, which reflected a shared sense that true faith is expressed in a transformed life and that in the face of a lack of wholesale regeneration the Reformation was as yet incomplete. Others define Pietism more narrowly, as a renewal movement taking its inspiration and point of departure from Philipp Jakob

Spener's *Pia Desideria* (1675).[10] Spener himself saw Pietism as beginning with Johann Arndt's *Wahres Christentum* (1605–10) and set the boundary there.[11] I will employ the narrow definition, which takes Spener's *Pia Desideria* as the starting point, even while considering Arndt and Jakob Boehme (1575–1628) as earlier tributaries. For it is with Spener that Pietism acquires its defining focus on practical piety rooted in small-group Bible study. The definition offered in the late seventeenth century by Joachim Feller, professor of rhetoric in Leipzig, aptly captures both the Bible-centered focus of Spener's Pietism and its practical orientation: "What is a Pietist? One who studies God's word and accordingly lives a holy life."[12] Arndt was less Bible-centered and more mystical in his piety, a conduit for the ideas of both Eckhart and Paracelsus. Mystical Pietism, which sought experienced union with God, sometimes took on radical forms associated with claims of extra-Biblical inspiration and a neglect of the church and sacraments. This radical Pietism merged with spiritualist impulses outside of the established churches. Jakob Boehme was a significant influence within these circles, and a conduit of Paracelsan, Kabbalistic, and Hermetic thought to radical Pietism and beyond: Schiller and Hegel in particular were both admirers of Boehme, deriving from him their understanding of *Bildung* as the dynamic reconciliation of opposites.[13] This chapter thus begins with Arndt and Boehme before turning to Spener, Francke, and Pietism more narrowly defined.

Johann Arndt

Johann Arndt was a Lutheran theologian who studied at the Universities of Wittenberg and Strasbourg before going on to hold a variety of pastoral positions. An otherwise obscure figure, he was deeply beloved as an author and editor of devotional literature. Arndt helped to define and nourish the mystical tradition, publishing editions of the *Theologia Germanica*, Thomas à Kempis's *Imitation of Christ*, Tauler, and even (discreetly tacked on the end of an edition of other spiritual works) Eckhart.[14] An eclectic thinker, he was a conduit for radical ideas but understood himself as a loyal Lutheran working for the spiritual renewal of the tradition.[15] His own *True Christianity* eclipsed even the *Imitation of Christ* in popularity over the course of several centuries. Its central theme was the renewal of the image of God

(*Bilde Gottes*) in the life of the individual Christian. It offered not just a theory of the renewal of the imago Dei but a guide to the practice of a renewed life; it is "not a book that attempts to deliver a message but rather a guide that aims at recruiting practitioners" of its proffered spiritual exercises.[16]

Like Luther, Arndt understands the created imago Dei (*Bild Gottes*) in a holistic way; the imago is a similarity of shape (*gleichförmigkeit*) with God and the Trinity, a similarity that encompasses "understanding, spirit, mind, will, all inner and outer powers of body and soul, and godly ways, virtues, intentions and qualities.[17] Even if at one point Arndt does place special emphasis on the Augustinian trinity of reason, will, and memory, he makes no attempt to isolate a particular divine attribute or power possessed by the soul.[18] We can speak of the heart in particular as imago Dei, but only because *heart* refers to all powers of the soul, including understanding, will, passions and desires.[19] Even the body is not excluded here; for prior to the fall the body was the image (*Ebenbild*) of the soul and perfectly conformed (*gleichförmig*) to the soul in all virtues.[20]

The image of God is the fullest reflection of divine perfection possible for a created being. The mirror metaphor is thus central for Arndt. Absent, though, is Luther's emphasis on mirroring as properly grasping and hence embodying God's generosity and compassion to sinners. In its place is a stress on becoming a passive vessel of divine will; Arndt emphasizes, for instance, that a mirror simply reflects what is placed before it; it does not produce its own picture. Creation in God's image means not just that humanity was created to be similar to God in some way but also that the soul mirrors God and thus shines forth God's glory by giving itself over to divine agency; "nothing else other than God should live, glow, work, will, love, think, speak, and enjoy within human persons."[21] Where something else is active, it is that active power, rather than God, whose image is reflected in the human person. And this is in fact what took place at the fall: Satan implanted (*eingebildet*) in Eve the same desire through which he himself fell—to rival God. Thus the image of God was lost and the image of Satan (*Bild des Satans*) was imprinted (*eingedrückt*) in humanity. Original sin is this image of Satan. Fallen human beings therefore first encounter the image of God no longer within, but without, in Holy Scripture and in Christ. Scripture describes the image of God, while Jesus Christ actually presents this image to us as a living example of the perfect reflection of God.[22] Jesus allowed God to work fully through him, giving his will wholly over to God. He was thus, like Adam at creation, a perfect image of God (*vollkommen Bild Gottes*). Arndt hastens to add that Christ was, according to his divine nature, God's image in a much higher sense, "namely God himself, and God's essential image [*wesentliches Ebenbild*]."[23] But Arndt's primary focus of attention is on Jesus Christ as a perfectly *human* image of God.

Given the fall, and the image of Satan within, human beings are not able simply to imitate Christ's example of yielding to God's will. The old Adam, together with the image of Satan, must be killed, and the seed of the image of God replanted in the soul by the Holy Spirit. Here Arndt compares God to a sculptor who, in order to create a work of art, needs new material to work with, not something that has been hacked away at by others. In order for God to make something out of a human person, she or he must first be nothing. If we try to make something of ourselves, we are not God's material.[24] We become nothing, kill the old Adam, eradicate the image of Satan, through true repentance. Arndt places heavy emphasis on the importance of repentance as the true worship of God, "through which the flesh is killed and the person is renewed in the image of God."[25] Having through repentance erased the image of Satan, we once again become God's material, a receptive soil for the Word of God. *Bilder*, pictures, are for Arndt also key to the working of Scripture; in Holy Scripture, God teaches through *Bilder*, images that have a deeper and longer-lasting impact on memory and heart than does abstract speech. What is depicted (*abbildet*) or prefigured (*vorbildet*) in these divine pictures serves as a seed that must grow in the soul and bear the spiritual fruit of a beautiful and new image of God (*Bilde Gottes*) within. Through God's Word and the Holy Spirit "faith is sown in us as a seed of God, in which all godly virtues and qualities are hidden and grow into a beautiful new image of God [*Bilde Gottes*].[26] Here, in his discussion of sanctification, Arndt's understanding of *Bildung* acquires an organic dimension; the image of God is not a static endowment but begins as a seed that gradually grows and develops. Only because the seed of faith has been sown in the repentant soil of the soul is it possible to engage in the practical following (*Nachfolge*) of Christ, imitating Christ's love, gentleness, and humility, thus growing into the image of God that is the holistic reflection of divine perfection in human virtues.[27] At the same time, Arndt acknowledges the need for daily repentance and daily renewal in God's image, so Luther's characteristic emphasis on a continual return to the cross is also retained and held together with Arndt's more wholehearted affirmation of progressive development.

While it can sound at times as though we ourselves accomplish the work of repentance and God does the work of renewal, Arndt also insists, taking himself to be rejecting "Papism," that it is by God's grace confronting us in the Word that condemns our fleshly existence that we are led to repentance. At the same time, one of his most significant shifts away from Luther (and one that was to become the norm within Lutheran orthodoxy) is toward an affirmation of human freedom in the acceptance of saving grace.[28] He insists, for instance, that predestination to eternal life contained the codicil that God would offer his grace to all through the gospel and that those who accept it are ordered to eternal life, in contrast to those who do not: "they themselves make it the case that they are not worthy of eternal life."[29] This decisive rejection of God's offer of grace can take the form not just of rejecting Christian doctrine but also of refusing to walk in Christ's footsteps, refusing to imitate Christ. An outward aping of Christ's actions accomplishes nothing, since God looks at the heart. Given the planting of the seed of faith, however, it becomes possible rightly to walk in Christ's footsteps, imitating his love, gentleness, patience, and humility. The seed thereby grows into the renewed image of God, with outward actions a true expression of the inner reality that it is God who works in the Christian. Human agency is thus properly expressed in an act that cedes agency, creating room for the seed.

It has been argued that Arndt has, unlike Luther, a tendency to understand Christ living within the faithful not just as presence but as possession, a new ontological status of the Christian, which all too easily becomes naturalized into something like the light of nature. Arndt is seen as having simultaneously anthropologized Jesus, seeing him only as a perfect human, and cosmologized Christ as immanent imago.[30] But this is not quite on the mark: Arndt clearly affirms that the renewal of the imago Dei is possible only through the work of grace, and there were myriad other sources for the notion of an immanent light of nature. The real tension in his thought, bequeathed to later Pietism, centers on his understandings of divine and human agency, which emerge to the foreground because of his affirmation (in contrast to Luther's more decidedly eschatological outlook) of the progressive renewal of the imago within this life. On

Arndt's understanding, all that occurs must be parsed out between divine and human agency in order to guard against human hubris. He tends as an anticipatory correction to limit human agency by dwelling on repentance as central act of *imitatio Christi* and then insisting that repentance itself is possible only through the grace of the Word. But in affirming human freedom to reject or accept saving grace, he nevertheless reserves a space for independent human agency. Thus Christians are called to yield their agency to Christ within, but their decision to do so is performed in a vacuum of divine agency. There is an underlying sense here that human agency must indeed be autonomous, even if this is immediately smothered in an affirmation of utter passivity. This either-or of passivity and activity, of divine and human agency, is absorbed into Pietist thought as well. As these tensions become more intense, they set the stage for an anti-Pietist reaction that seeks to articulate a more robust account of human autonomy.

Jakob Boehme

It was perhaps Jakob Boehme's lack of formal education that allowed him to so readily absorb and creatively transform the Hermetic, alchemical, and mystical ideas of Paracelsus, Caspar Schwenckfeld (1490–1561), and Valentin Weigel (1533–88), among others.[31] Working not just to mediate the distinction between Neoplatonic emanationism and the Christian doctrine of creation ex nihilo, but also to regain a sense of balance from the disorientation introduced by a heliocentric solar system, Boehme drew on an alchemical fascination with chemical reactions as a window into the power of unseen natural forces to construct a strikingly novel account of the self-generation of all things out of the undifferentiated unity of the *Ungrund* (unground), a term Boehme nominalizes out of the adjective *ungründlich*, "unfathomable" or "incomprehensible."[32] Creation is to be understood neither as ex nihilo nor out of a preexisting matter, but rather as birthed out of God. And while in some sense God preexists creation, he does so as a pure Godhead (*Gottheit*) that is like a nothingness (*ein Nichts*) and is "not yet God."[33] While in its purity this preexistent Godhead is perfect, the divinity is actualized only through the realization of its potentialities, through an eternal self-birthing.[34] A process of becoming, then, is introduced into God. God does not radically transcend creation, but rather creation is in God; processes unfolding within the Godhead correspond to processes happening in nature and individual creatures. Everywhere there is movement, for it is forces rather than substances that are regarded as primary. Envisioning a serial generation of seven "qualities" out of the undifferentiated matrix of being (in *Aurora*, a pure crystalline *Salitter* or nitre), he describes a quality as "the mobility [*Beweglichkeit*], surging [*Quallen*], or driving [*Treiben*] of a thing."[35] The initial contracting quality of the dry (*Herb*) generates the contrary centripetal quality of the bitter, and the opposition between these is conceived of as generating a turning in place, like a wheel (or a spinning planet). This turning wheel emits a flash of fire, and thence the release of water, the softening of love, music, and the entire complex of qualities.[36] These seven qualities are interpreted in light of the three alchemical principles of Sulfur, Mercury, and Salt, broken in Boehme's analysis into syllables (*Sul/Phur/ Mer/Cur/Ri/Us/Sal*).[37] They are also correlated with the seven days of creation, the seven spirits of the Apocalypse, and the seven planets.[38] In later works, the seven qualities are mapped onto three principles and hence onto the Trinity. All things move from the first principle (Father/dark-world) to the Second (Holy Spirit / light-world) by way of the Third (Son/middle-world).

This movement takes place in eternity, within the Immanent Trinity, but also in time, in Creation, and within the individual human soul. It is knowable, in fact, because the human soul in being reborn is enacting this very movement from darkness to light: "to recognize this self-creating self is to know God," the inner being of all being.[39] Indeed Boehme finds the generation of the qualities recapitulated within everyday psychological experience: "Take for example man, when he is enraged, [see] how his spirit contracts, so that he trembles bitterly, and if there is not soon a resisting and extinguishing, the fire of anger is lit within him, so that he burns in anger."[40] All of the moments of salvation history play out within the very life of God: creation, fall, virgin birth, passion of Christ, resurrection.

The movement from darkness to light is a movement from undifferentiated unity to luxuriant plurality. It is also a movement from hiddenness to revelation and knowledge; it is only through being actualized in the seven principles that God becomes knowable. But this is not simply an operation by which God is revealed or made known to others; it is a process by which God becomes known to

Godself. The notion of a revealing mirror of the divine self-creating will plays an important role here. All things bear a mysterious signature, manifesting how each exists in the interplay of tensional qualities. But the visible world as a whole can be regarded as a mirror of the inner world of God: "the inner holds the outer before it as a mirror in which it regards itself in the property of birthing all forms; the outer is its signature."[41] The divine process of self-revelation gets under way because of God's desire for self-knowledge. "Even God," insists Boehme, "would . . . not have been manifest to Himself in the *Ungrund*, but His wisdom has from eternity become His ground, for which the eternal will of the *Ungrund* lusted [*gelüstert*], from which the divine imagination has arisen."[42] The unfathomable nothinglike pure Godhead yearns for the Virgin of Divine Wisdom, identified as the mirror of the divine darkness; all that is created emerges as reflections in her mirror. Imagination thus plays a central role here; God creates by imagining things, but imagination is not a serene contemplation of forms but an erotic longing for self-knowledge and self-revelation.

For Boehme, it is as possessing the power of imagination that human beings do not simply mirror the divine, as do all things in the outer world, but are properly said to be in the image of God. He is fascinated by the power of the mind's eye, to see with closed eyes and in the dark, to travel virtually while rooted on the spot: imagination (*Imagination*) is to him a mysterious, even magical power.[43] Indeed, with its generative power, Boehme, following Paracelsus, conceives of *Imaginieren* as a form of magic, *magia*, as contrasted with evil *Zauber* a power for creation rather than destruction.[44] The inner divine world observes itself giving birth to all forms in the mirror of wisdom; these forms are *Bildnisse* and the process one of *Einbilden*. By virtue of possessing imagination, *Einbildung*, human beings are specially conceived in the image of God.[45] The imagination acts as a kind of medium between the will of the soul and the powers which seek to determine the soul. Böhme goes so far as to say that "everything arises through imagination."[46] The pictures entertained by the imagination stimulate will and desire.

Imagination can, however, be a power either for good for or evil. Adam was a pure image of God because he allowed God's will to be perfectly expressed in him. But fallen humanity asserts its own will over against God and thus can no longer be a clear, undistorted image of God. This self-will seeks to form itself rather than be formed by God ("der peinliche Wille in eigener Bildung"); the fallen human will relies on its own imagination and conceives of godless things, in tension with the divine images according to which the world was created.[47] Even given the fall, however, enough of the imago Dei remains within human beings to allow a renewal of the Adamic resemblance to God. As Boehme explains, "the inner spiritual man is an image [Bilde] of the formed Word of divine power, and the outer is an image of the inner, as a tool of the inner."[48] There is a positive role for the human imagination here, for the *Einbildung* of the spirit of Christ, its formation within us, involves placing our *Imaginieren*, our imaginings and desires, in Christ, and this leads then to a "putting on" of Christ in body, flesh and blood.[49] The inner transforms the outer, and is itself transformed by the living divine Word in Christ. While Christ is indeed a model (*Vorbild* and *Fürbild*) for us, *Bildung* is not an outward imitation of this model but reaches back to the inner creative Spirit expressed in the Word. There are echoes here of the Eckhardtian notion of the inner birth of Christ, but Boehme's conception of this inner birth is intensely dynamic, as is the divine transformative will. The *einbilden* of Christ is more a matter of opening oneself fully to the Spirit and light of God than it is the taking on of a determinate form or character.[50] Each becomes a Christian, a Christ (*ein Christ*), in his or her own way, as the Spirit expresses itself in infinite forms.

This transformation remains a struggle in this world, particularly since there are actually three distinct principles that impress themselves on (*einbilden sich mit*) each human being—not just the image of God but also those of hell and of the spirit of this world. Each of these seeks to control us through our own desires. Despite the fall and the fact that each of the three principles appeals to us, our wills remain free to determine which of the three will reign. We do not form (*bilden*) ourselves, but we do give ourselves over to one of these principles, which then forms the soul in its own image, *bildet die Bildniss*, of the soul. True *Bildung* requires giving oneself over to being made into the image of God (*Bild Gottes*) by the Holy Spirit. With this *Bildung* comes a new will that is no longer tempted by these competing principles.

Boehme constantly wrestles with the problem of evil and its origin. This was not a merely theoretical matter. From 1617 onward, the writings of the shoemaker of Görlitz are imbued with an apocalyptic aura. The informed reader can discern references to the tumult of the Thirty Years' War; a time of tolerance and freedom for Protestants was at an end in Boehme's Lusatia, as in neighboring Bohemia and Moravia.[51] Suppression of Lutheranism in Lusatia became bound up in Boehme's mind with his own denunciation and persecution. Boehme denounces the war as a *Bruder-Mord*, a conflict among Christian brothers, insisting that Antichrist becomes more powerful when Christians quarrel and compete among themselves for domination.[52] He hopes for religious autonomy for Lusatia but also, even more dramatically, envisions a universal family of all peoples, including "Jews, Turks, and heathens." For even as he conceives of himself throughout as a sincere Lutheran, he insists that it is possible to be born of the Spirit even without the name of Christ.[53] "Look, you dear peoples of the world," he entreats, "you are all of one flesh. That you have divided yourselves has been done by the devil in the Antichrist."[54]

Boehme's yearning to penetrate the secrets of divine wisdom is driven, then, by a desire for peace and reconciliation. There is no glorification of conflict or evil here. Boehme is at pains to insist that God is free from evil and does not deliberately initiate evil or introduce it into the world. This, in fact, is what renders a theogonic picture attractive to him, for it makes it possible to say that evil arises out of God's eternal being while also insisting that God does not *choose* evil: "evil arises out of the eternal nature of God; but, in God, this evil nature is eternally overcome and sublimated, so that it cannot be said that there is evil or darkness in God."[55] However, Boehme's protestations ring hollow given that the *Ungrund* of the darkness of God is hardly the fullness of divine perfection; God is not simply *revealed* through the agonistic generation of qualities but is *realized* through this process. Through it God comes to the light of self-knowledge. Evil and conflict are thus necessary to the divine life, not adventitious: if there were no death, there would be no life; if there were no poison and torment, there would be no joy; if there were no fire, there would be no movement.[56]

Boehme senses and occasionally articulates another possibility:

> God did not birth Creation in order thereby to become more perfect, but rather for the sake of his Self-Revelation, to great joy and glory. Not that such joy began with creation; no, it was from eternity in the great mystery, but only as a spiritual play in itself. Cre-

ation is the same playing out of itself [*dasselbe Spiel aus sich selber*], as a model or tool of the Eternal Spirit, on which he plays, and is a great harmony of many lutes, all ordered in one harmony.[57]

Here we glimpse the possibility of movement and development without evil, without violence, and without necessity. Here revelation is distinguished from self-realization; a God already complete in joy does not *need* to birth creation but nevertheless rejoices in sharing the divine harmony. Here there is abundant self-gift, not desirous lack. A God so conceived, however, would not be undifferentiated *Ungrund* but always already harmonious (trinitarian) communion. Creation would not be the self-realization of God's own self but God's self-gift into finitude; God would thus radically transcend creation; the world would not be God's body. Evil would be adventitious and privative, a creaturely failure to correspond to the harmonies of the divine music, not a necessary motor of differentiation and movement within the divine life. But Boehme drifted far away from this traditionally Christian narrative logic.[58]

Boehme acquired an enthusiastic following that seemed to grow in proportion to the censorship of his writings, spreading in particular in German territories, the Netherlands, and England, where they were associated with radical Pietism and played a role in inspiring a host of sectarian movements, from the English Philadelphians to the Herrnhüter, Labadists, the Ephrata Cloister, and others.[59] But while many of these groups were particularly fascinated by Boehme's introduction of the female figure of the Virgin of Divine Wisdom into the life of the divine, and by the suggestion that the return to unity would involve human participation in the reunion of male and female principles, Boehme's significance for the Bildung tradition lay elsewhere.

Boehme's writings circulated among the German Romantics concentrated in Jena at the end of the eighteenth century. Friedrich Schlegel (1772–1829) was particularly taken by Boehme and likely introduced Hegel to Boehme's ideas when Hegel moved to Jena in 1801 at Schelling's invitation.[60] While repeatedly calling Boehme "a barbarian," Hegel honored him by dubbing him the first German philosopher and devoting dozens of pages to discussing his thought in his *Lectures on the History of Philosophy*.[61] Hegel strikingly anticipates Barth's critique of Pietism's absorption of all things into one's inner reality, but takes it as a reason to praise Boehme and Protestantism at large: "What marks him out and makes him noteworthy is the Protestant principle . . . of placing the intellectual world within one's own mind and heart, and of experiencing and knowing and feeling in one's own self-consciousness all that formerly was conceived as a Beyond."[62] He clearly regards Boehme as having anticipated some of his own key ideas. "The fundamental idea in Jacob Boehme," he writes, "is the effort to comprise everything in an absolute unity, for he desires to demonstrate the absolute divine unity and the union of all opposites in God."[63] Hegel did not shrink back from Boehme's placement of evil within the divine self-realizing process: the "fall of Lucifer" involves the inward-fashioning (*Hineinbilden*) and inward-imagining (*Hineinimaginieren*) of the I as the fire that consumes all. "This is very bold and speculative," continues Hegel, "indeed Boehme has really here penetrated into the utmost depths of divine essence; evil, matter, or whatever it has been called, is the I = I, the Being-for-self, the true negativity."[64] Hegel, like Boehme, here identifies evil with the insistence on self that refuses relation, and flirts with the notion that evil is necessary and generative; the creative power of imagination to take everything into oneself.

Was the process of forming humanity, then, a promethean one in which humankind should seize the creative power of imagination and follow the divine in embracing conflict and evil as a necessary path to self-realization? This was the nagging question that Boehme bequeathed to the Bildung tradition. But this is to leap ahead of ourselves. For Pietism on the whole was deeply suspicious of human imagination, and insistent on reining it in.

Pietism and the Vocabulary of Bildung

In sharp contrast to Boehme, the mainstream Pietist movement was not speculative in orientation. Its driving impulse was the conviction, shared with other movements of practical piety, that lived Christianity, understood primarily in terms of a discipleship to Christ expressed in love of neighbor, had given way to academic disputation, mere notional faith, and a misguided reliance on external means of grace. Thus Spener, Pietism's key founding figure, wrote in *Pia Desideria* (1675) that the mark of a Christian was a love expressed in action and not one that is claimed to reside in the heart but remains unfruitful.⁶⁵ August Hermann Francke (1663–1727) gave institutional expression to this practical piety, founding orphanages, schools for the poor, and foreign missions. A particular conception of the transformed life emerged, one characterized by care for orphans and the poor, Sunday observance, education, and critiques of luxury and sexual transgression. Pietist leaders engaged in dogmatic theology only insofar as this was necessary in order to defend themselves against charges of unorthodoxy.

These charges, which persistently hounded the movement, accused Pietist thinkers of detracting from the sufficiency of the salvific work of Christ, of promoting works-righteousness, and of synergism. In response to these charges, Pietists drew on Arndt and the mystical tradition reaching back to Eckhart to insist that the active life of Christian love was made possible by the indwelling presence of Christ in the heart by the power of the Holy Spirit. The Pietist emphasis on *Christus in nobis* rather than the external salvific work of Christ was, though, sharpened in its insistence on human passivity by efforts to respond to the charges of heterodoxy. Practical activism was defended by coupling it with foundational passivism. Spener, for example, insists that works do not contribute to salvation but are only a fruit of faith, which itself is God's work in us, changing us and killing the old Adam.⁶⁶ By nature there is nothing good in human beings (*wir von natur nichts gutes an uns haben*), so anything good must be worked by God in us; it is not at all impossible for Christians to reach some degree of sanctification, since it is the Holy Spirit who works all of these things (*alles gewürcket*).⁶⁷ It is not that works are capable of earning divine grace but that the lack of works demonstrates the absence of true faith and of the indwelling Christ.⁶⁸ For Pietism, then, there is nothing natural about practical Christianity; it is not finally understood as a form of human activity at all but rather as a form of divine activity in and through human beings. Ambivalence about the imagination and its power continued and was now filtered through anxieties regarding the power of worldly literature to harness the subversive power of the imagination. Reading and study of the Bible assumed central importance for Pietists, as we shall see below; for Christians immersed in the Bible, Christian activity could be trusted to be worked by God rather than by human imagination.

Seeing how a heightened emphasis on the sanctified life of love, when faced with accusations of heterodoxy, joined outer activity with inner passivity, helps to make sense of the distinctive vocabulary with which the Pietists spoke about human formation and transformation. It has been noted that Spener, in contrast to the earlier mystical tradition, did not use the terms *einbilden* and *Einbildung* to capture God's work of restoring the divine image in humanity.[69] Instead Spener spoke of God's salvific work as being accomplished by means of *Einpflanzen* (implanting) and *Eindrücken* (imprinting), both of living faith in God's word and of true Christian virtue. This transformative activity of God is contrasted with a purely human activity of *Einbildung* (imagination), a misguided effort of preachers and teachers to instill faith by forming mere images in others.[70] *Einbildung* is thus nearly always equated with imagination in the sense of mere illusion.[71] It is wide of the mark to conclude, however, that "the term originally so fundamental for expressing religious perfection or the new birth of the human person was so destroyed on the stone of Pietism, that it has ever since retained the meaning of something unreal and related only to human fantasy."[72] While Spener typically uses *einbilden* and its compounds in a negative sense, this is not always the case; he also speaks of a positive task on the part of the preacher, that is, "to energetically impress [*einbilden*] on the people that Christianity consists not in knowledge but in praxis."[73] It is nevertheless true that *bilden* and *einbilden* are not used to speak of the primary divine activity of implanting faith in the Word. Pietist thinkers emphasized the importance of practical imitation or following (*Nachfolge*) of Christ, who is for Pietism savior and redeemer and indwelling spiritual power, as well as model for the Christian life, the *Vorbild*. The deepest positive impact one human being could have on another was not through providing any speculative insights but by similarly serving as an exemplar of Christian love.[74] But it is only through God's power that a human being can become an exemplary Christian for another, and only through God's power that that model has its formative impact on the other.

The terms *Bilden* and *Bildung* were used more broadly by the mystical Pietists, including those, like Gerhard Teerstegen, who remained within the established churches. Here God's transformative activity is spoken of precisely as a formation (*bilden*) of humanity "after his heart."[75] God is Creator and Potter, *Schöpfer* and *Töpfer*, who molds those who give themselves over to him wholly.[76] Teerstegen emphasizes that God's work of formation (*bilden*) can take place only when the soul is wholly still and passive: "Lie still in God, like a child in its mother's arms.... God forms [*bildet*] you wonderfully in his lap."⁷⁷ A hymn from one radical Pietist community proclaimed "Jesus a Melter of our souls," that is, capable of reducing the soul to an utterly pliable, receptive state:

> And so this, following the brief suffering
> Which His melting fire will cause,
> Will bring us great and eternal joys
> When His Image in us fully awakes
> Because He is wholly intimate
> With the Bride he has ransomed out of himself.
>
> Jesus! Let your melting proceed
> To my complete purification here
> So that then only in your image I may see,
> Open wide and break out
> Gradually into its complete brilliance
> And be fully united within it with you.⁷⁸

This combination of imago Dei and bridal imagery, together with an emphasis on human passivity, is typical of radical mystical Pietism. A poem by the radical Pietist Johann Friedrich Rock did not shy away even from the language of deification:

> Lord Jesus! Become human in me
> So that I may be deified in you,
> So, you will become man, and I will become God,
> And then the Enemy will be destroyed and mocked.
> So, having been brought back in you
> I am made into God's image.⁷⁹

While Teerstegen, unlike Spener, does not hesitate to use the term *bilden* to describe God's activity, he does, in an echo of Eckhart, regard the soul's *Bilder*, images, with suspicion. Images are contrasted with the true nature or essence (*Wesen*) of reality; they distract or confuse the soul, which is fully open to God's formative activity (*bilden*) only when free of the images it conceives itself (*bilderlos*).⁸⁰ So, like

Spener, Teerstegen regards human imagination (*Einbildung*) as dangerous. The Christian must be passive to God's transformative activity, and human formative activity is suspect.

This is the key point: what mainstream Pietism absorbed from the earlier mystical tradition stemming from Eckhart was a conception of human and divine formative activity as competing with one another, even if more determinedly orthodox thinkers did not follow Eckhart in thinking this competition could be resolved by discovering an inner identity of human and divine. The more activist forms of Pietism, precisely because of their greater (apparent) insistence on expressing Christian love in action, stood in greater need of sharply distinguishing between human and divine, natural and supernatural activity, so that they could repel accusations of works-righteousness and synergism and insist that they were merely vessels for divine activity. Thus it was these strands of Pietism, led by Spener and Francke, that most fully relegated the vocabulary of Bildung to the purely human, natural realm and most emphatically downgraded that realm. Not surprisingly, then, in the face of the tensions between the outer activism and inner passivism of Pietism, a reactive assertion of the capacity and goodness of natural human agency revalorized both Bildung and the creative possibilities inherent in imagination.

Pietist suspicion of human imagination was expressed more generally in a suspicion of human *Kunst*, where *Kunst* means not only art but also trick, an artificial construction that deceives or leads away from reality. So Spener writes explicitly of St. Paul that "he had his wisdom not from human craft [*menschen-kunst*] but from the enlightenment of the Spirit, which are distant as heaven and earth from one another."[81] Spener also quotes from Luther's *Lectures on Romans*, where Luther compares those with true God-given faith with those who make with their own powers a thought in the heart that says "I believe," but this is merely a "human poem" (*ein menschliches gedicht*) which never reaches the foundation of the heart.[82] But in contrast to Luther, for whom all merely worldly phenomena, while sharply differentiated from the spiritual realm of the gospel, could nevertheless be put to work in service of the gospel, Pietism issued in a rejection of "the world." For Pietist leaders were not simply animated by an age-old concern for human sinfulness and need for redemption but were reacting against specific features of their historical moment: an increasing confidence in human reason, together with an embrace of art, poetry, and imagination as realms of creative human expression.

God's Word versus Menschen-Kunst

Central to Spener's program of reform is the insistence that all Christians should read and study the Bible. As we have seen, anything good that a Christian does is worked by God from within. The "powerful means" of this is the Word of God. For faith, Spener notes, must be ignited by the gospel.[83] Only when actions are animated by gospel faith do we have reason to believe that they are worked by God rather than by *menschen-kunst*. God's Word is the "seed" out of which all that is good in us must grow.[84] The Pietist focus on scripture thus served to keep practical Christianity rooted in divine rather than human agency. Since the lectionary of rotating scripture readings excludes substantial portions of scripture, Spener noted that a Christian could faithfully attend worship services lifelong without hearing all of scripture. Hence it is necessary to supplement these services with private and small-group Bible study.[85] Pietists regarded this insistence on Bible reading as stemming from Luther. What, asks Spener, did Luther seek more eagerly than that the people would devote themselves to scripture reading? And he quotes from a passage in which Luther complains that many in the church neglect the study of scripture and have begun to assemble large libraries without discriminating their value. But the Pietists went well beyond anything Luther envisioned, with their insistence that each and every lay Christian ought to be intimately familiar with each and every biblical text; Luther wanted clergy to focus on scripture, but for the laity he wrote catechisms.[86] In Spener's *collegia pietatis* (schools of piety), in contrast, each participant was encouraged to express what the scriptural text meant in terms of his or her own spiritual edification.[87] Scholarly erudition, too, is a suspect form of human *kunst*; trust should instead be placed in the guidance of Holy Scripture in the heart of the individual reader.

The Pietist focus on lay study of scripture is an exceptional—and modern—phenomenon within the history of Christianity.[88] While it is a truism that vernacular translations of the Bible placed scripture in the hands of the laity, in fact the Latin Bible was for a long time to come more widely accessible than Luther's translation, which after all was written in one particular German dialect (Saxon) out of many, and at a time when literacy was very limited.[89] While Luther's translation of the Bible was indeed over the long run largely responsible for stabilizing and defining the German language, the Bible was no more present in homes in the wake of Luther than it had been in the Middle Ages. The popular image of early Protestant laity interpreting the Bible for themselves is misleading, and is indebted instead to seventeenth-century Puritans and eighteenth-century Pietists. The Pietists were also exceptional rather than representative in their rejection of secular literature. Luther's basic assumption was that worldly phenomena, including literature and art, could be put to use in service of the gospel.[90] The mainstream Reformation had gone hand in hand with humanism, and Latin school curricula in both Protestant and Catholic regions centered on classical Latin literature.[91]

The boundary between spiritual and worldly, supernatural and natural, divine and human agency was for Pietism marked objectively by scripture. Through the divine Word, God acts to bring persons into the life of faith and thus into the sacramental life of the church, which nourishes that faith. Subjectively, this boundary is marked by conversion; the individual Christian must be converted from the world to the life of the Spirit. It is through this conversion that sinful independent human agency is set aside (or rather, put to death) and the Christian can become a transparent vessel for the indwelling Christ and the agency of the Holy Spirit. Conversion is not reserved for those who change from one confession to another, nor is it a way of marking an objective spiritual change in the individual which may not be consciously experienced (like infant baptism). Conversion is rather from a taken-for-granted cultural Christianity to a living Christian faith, and its felt, experiential character is front and center. Pietism thus fostered the development of practices of introspection and self-examination and a rich vocabulary for describing spiritual experience.

The Threat of Rationalism

Pietist understandings of conversion as rebirth drew on mystical accounts of the birth of Christ within. Conversion experiences were expected to fall into recognizable stages, moving from a *Busskampf*, or inner struggle with sin, to the "hours of Grace," *Gnadenstunden*, in which grace is divinely offered, and the breakthrough (*Durchbruch*) of the new birth, followed by periodical trials, *Anfechtungen*, which test the strength of faith and devotion to the divine will.

Pietists, however, deployed these ideas in new ways that responded to the perceived threat posed to Christian faith by mounting rationalism, as is evident in Francke's 1692 autobiography. Even if the *Busskampf*, the inner struggle through which Pietists expected Christian faith to be born, was framed in generic terms as a crisis elicited by an ever-deepening awareness of sin and sorrow over sin, Francke articulates his struggle specifically as a contest with doubt. He doubts the truth of Christian doctrine in the face of other religions, worries that his experiences might have a naturalistic explanation, and questions even the existence of God. The experience of doubt becomes normalized as part of the conversion process; doubts that can be identified and named as trials can thereby be overcome.

Engaged in theological studies as a young man prior to his conversion, Francke relates his encounter with doubt:

> Up to this point I was accustomed to convince my reason on good grounds, because I had experienced little of the new being of the Spirit. Therefore I thought I could help myself through such a way, but the more I wished to help myself the greater I fell into unrest and doubt. . . . I thought that I could hold to the Holy Scriptures but as soon as this came into my mind I wondered, who knows if the Holy Scripture is God's Word; the Turks have their Koran and the Jews their Talmud, and who is to say which one of the three is correct. Such thoughts always took the upper hand until finally there remained not the least thing which I believed from my heart, which I had learned throughout my life and particularly through the eight years of theological study concerning God and his revealed will and essence. I no longer believed in a God in Heaven and therefore I could not hold either to God or to man's word, and I found as little strength in the one as in the other. . . . I sought in this way and that to help myself but it did not work.[92]

The use of reason, including in academic theology, is here framed as an effort to help oneself rather than relying on God. Francke must learn to see reason as itself a temptation to rely on human rather than divine agency. His "erring reason" must be "tamed, so as not to move against [God's] power and faithfulness."⁹³ Once he had experienced the breakthrough to faith, "reason stood away; victory was torn from its hands, for the power of God had made it subservient to faith."⁹⁴ Trials return, to be sure, in the form of the thought that his experience of rebirth "could be natural, that one could also experience such great joy naturally, but I was completely and totally convinced that this was false and that all the world with all its joy and glory could not awaken such sweetness in the human heart."⁹⁵ On the contrary, those who make fun of "heavenly machinery" and think that they can rely on human reason and virtue will discover to their chagrin that Enlightenment deism falls woefully short of its pretensions, and that they cannot do without transformative divine grace.⁹⁶

Conversion and Its Literature

Given the Pietist suspicion even of spiritual erudition, it is not surprising that Pietists were thoroughly hostile to all "worldly" literature, which represented a sphere of human creative agency independent of the gracious workings of the Holy Spirit.⁹⁷ In the eighteenth century, in the face of a rapidly expanding literature, the Pietist emphasis on Bible reading took on increasingly countercultural implications. For all their emphasis on the study of scripture, however, adherents of Pietism probably spent as much or more time reading works of devotional literature; Spener himself recommends Johannes Tauler, *The Imitation of Christ* attributed to Thomas à Kempis, and especially Arndt's *Wahres Christentum*; Spener's own writings soon assumed an important place for Pietist readers as well.⁹⁸ Devotional literature, safely anchored in the Word of God, offered a template against which one's own spiritual experience could be measured and tested and one's own erring reason rebuked.

In its focus on spiritual subjectivity the movement drew self-consciously not only on the German mystical tradition but also on the English Puritan tradition. The first volume (1698) of the *Historie der Wiedergebohrnen*, an enormously popular Pietist collection of conversion narratives compiled by Johann Reitz, consisted almost exclusively of examples drawn from English Puritans.⁹⁹ There were significant differences. Lutheran Pietism, notably, was not predestinarian, so Pietist introspection is not directed toward discerning whether one is among the elect or the damned. But the conviction that it was possible through introspection to discern something of one's spiritual state was shared, as was the language of the heart in which this was expressed. So L.P., an English Puritan woman, wrote that "my heart is stretched out [*ausgebreitet*] and enlivened [*erquicket*] when God through the use of [spiritual] means and exercises comes in upon me."[100] Spener similarly writes that it is not enough to hear the Word with the outer ear. Rather, we must allow it to penetrate (*tringen*) the heart; "we must hear the Holy Spirit itself speaking, that is, feel the Spirit's sealing and the power of the Word with living movement and consolation [*mit lebendiger Bewegung und Trost*]."[101] Because of the importance of experiencing the power of the Holy Spirit, of experiencing a *Durchbruch* or "breakthrough" conversion, of being able to trace practical transformation back to an inworking divine power, the practices of recording conversion experiences and of keeping an ongoing diary of spiritual trials and progress were encouraged. Not only did Pietists eagerly read and reread the *Historie der Wiedergebohrnen*, but they embraced the practice of recording their own spiritual narratives, examining their own experiences against those recorded in the various narratives they had read. This was explicitly encouraged by Reitz, who spoke of "the highly specific and individual nature of true faith," which created the need for "an ongoing process of self-examination, differentiation, and individualization that works by making detailed comparison with the different templates for spiritual rebirth."[102]

By way of spiritual autobiographies, the dialogical encounters of the *collegia pietatis* were transferred into a realm of virtual encounter, moving one commentator to suggest that the practice fostered "the atomistic individualism of radical Pietism with its ideal of a supraconfessional impartiality that leaves little room for any kind of collectivity or solidarity that would go beyond the 'virtual community' of the intimate experiential exchange between pious souls."[103] In seeking to characterize their spiritual experiences, Pietists transformed and enriched the resources of the German language in distinctive ways, developing a rich vocabulary for descriptive psychology and subjective experience, especially its affective dimension. Most notably, Pietists made use of a broad array of verbal prefixes (e.g., *durch, ein, hinein, hinauf, hinnab, hinnach, nach*), which lent an intensified and dynamic character to their introspective narratives. This use of prefixes has been analyzed as an attempt to capture the polarity between God and the soul, in which the soul's agency must be crucified, emptied out, and given over to the converting and sanctifying power of the Holy Spirit: "the drama between God and soul, the powerful tension between the two poles, the dynamic of striving after one another culminating in fusion fosters the piled-up use of dynamic verbs."[104]

This emphasis on introspection and affective subjectivity, together with its characteristic linguistic innovations, had a lasting transformative effect not just on later devotional literature but also on secular literature and the development of aesthetics.[105] Ironically, the Pietist movement, which sought to focus reading on *God's* Word (and on works of devotional piety that sprang from true evangelical faith and which thus could themselves be seen as fruits of divine agency), thereby contributed in fundamental ways to a flowering of secular literature that emphasized human agency and creativity. Pietism was an important source of the ideal of poetic authenticity and of the notions of poetic genius and inspiration central to the Sturm und Drang movement, even as the source of inspiration came to be read as forces immanent in Nature, or in the recesses of the soul, rather than a transcendent divinity.[106] Since most of the Sturm und Drang poets came from Pietist backgrounds, the influence was quite direct. As a young man, Goethe, for instance, defended pastors who welcomed the workings of the Holy Spirit, including speaking in tongues: "The most godly sensation streams out of the soul in tongues, and flamingly announces the great deeds of God in a new speech."[107] And he was to conceive of his own poetic genius along strikingly similar lines, as a kind of spiritual possession over which he had only limited control: "The exercise of this gift of poetic speech can certainly be aroused and determined through inducement, but most joyfully and richly it arrived involuntarily, even against my will."[108] Pietist spiritual autobiographies had an important impact on the development of the psychological novel, and in particular on the highly developed inner experience of the protagonist of the Bildungsroman, a topic to which I shall return in chapter 6.

As an attempt to foreclose autocratic humanism, mainstream Pietism backfired; tracing the work of an external Providence in one's life ended up authorizing the human author's self-forming capacities. The repudiation of *Menschen-Kunst* elicited a contrarian *Kunstreligion*, a Religion of Art that fed on a vocabulary of affective subjectivity that had been developed to distinguish the divine from the human.

Where Pietists analyzed subjective experience in order to trace divine activity, Goethe and Schiller focused, as we shall see, on the subject as an end in himself or herself: "the seeking, finding, and self-mirroring of the subject have become autonomous"; the "I" sinks into itself, loses itself in itself, not in God.[109] As one scholar notes, "The Spirit that inspired Goethe and his generation was no longer that of Christ speaking to the heart. When they experienced themselves as new creators, their partaking of the divine nature was no longer theologically or Christologically determined and grounded."[110] What was rejected from mainstream Pietism, even as the language of subjectivity was taken over, was its underlying passivity, its denial of human agency, which as we have seen was itself a rearguard action against charges of works-righteousness and a deflection of Enlightenment rationalism. This did not, however, necessarily translate into a rejection of divine agency or an assertion of human autocracy.[111] That, as we shall see, remained an open question, capable of receiving a range of answers. For what Pietists listened for was a domesticated Providence, understood contrastively as requiring a vacuum of human agency; it was not a listening for a radically transcendent God, a God beyond all of the distinctions that characterize creaturely existence.

The Harmonious Harp-Playing of Humanity: J. G. Herder 3

It was in the closing decades of the eighteenth century that the neo-humanistic ideal of Bildung came into its own. Rooted as it was in the philosophical and theological traditions we have explored in previous chapters, it was also something novel, reflecting a new consciousness concerning human self-forming agency. Individual human beings were envisioned as oriented toward a telos conceived as the harmonious development of all of their various capacities—including, notably, not merely rational but also sensuous and emotional capacities—into a balanced, unified whole. Bildung named both this process of development and its end, which was also conceived of as the collective realization of humanity itself. Human beings are collectively not yet what they ought to be, what they are destined to become. They can become fully human only by way of the process of Bildung, and only insofar as they are themselves actively involved in that process. What they become, further, is not uniform but intimately personal: they become individuals. One cannot become properly human by being poured into a mold. This was seen as a process integrally bound up with creativity, imagination, and art. And it was recognized as holding significant political implications.

The next two chapters explore the development of this understanding of Bildung, focusing on the two thinkers who contributed the most to the lasting definition of this ideal: Johann Gottfried Herder (1744–1803) and Wilhelm von Humboldt (1767–1835). Friedrich Schiller's vision for aesthetic education, too, will come into play, and will continue to be unpacked in chapter 5 as we turn our attention to the rise of the Bildungsroman and to Schiller's and Goethe's understanding of the critical role of literature in ethical formation. While all of these thinkers would be able to agree on what has been said about Bildung in the previous paragraph, there are important differences in the ways in which they conceive of Bildung. Herder understood human Bildung toward the realization of humanity as a way of participating in a cosmic process of diversification and harmonization, the finite expression of the image of God. Not just individuals but peoples and cultures grow into their individuality while also forming increasingly complex webs of relationship with one another: humanity is realized in expanding fellowship and neighbor-love. Humboldt's understanding of Bildung, in contrast, is focused squarely on the individual and the freedom of his or her self-development. Humanity is an abstract ideal to be grasped and realized by each individual. Bildung is not a cosmic process, and human beings are not essentially constituted by culture and tradition, nor are they oriented essentially toward fellowship or community. Christian faith is for the weak; maturity requires clear-sighted recognition that there is no exemplar for one's own individual humanity. Art displaces religion, or rather, becomes a new religion for mature self-formers.

Herder, much more fully than Humboldt, Schiller, or Goethe, preserved the Neoplatonic narrative of Christian humanism: to take up the task of forming humanity is to participate in the *reditus* of creation to God. The challenge, however, was to integrate this with a thorough historicism, with full recognition of the culturally and historically conditioned character of human identity and agency. Here, even as he resisted racism and European chauvinism, Herder nevertheless succumbed to the temptation of a providentialist optimism: history was an arena in which progress was assured, however ragged and halting. Lacking here was an eschatological orientation capable of looking beyond history for the ultimate realization of humanity, and thereby of sustaining hope even while looking squarely at historical evils. Herder instead squinted, insisting that it was possible to make out the shape of historical progress if one only looked from the right angle.

Herder and the Enlightenment

Despite an explosion of recent research, Herder remains a poorly understood and understudied figure, particularly in the Anglo-American world. It is likely the case that most English speakers still perceive Herder through a filter set by Isaiah Berlin's 1976 *Vico and Herder*.[1] In Berlin's study, Herder emerges as a counter-Enlightenment thinker, founder of historicism and advocate of a position remarkably reminiscent of Berlin's own "value pluralism," according to which values held within different cultures may be conflicting yet equally valid, insofar as they are incommensurable with one another. It is indeed important to situate Herder's understanding of Bildung within his historicism, one of the most innovative features of his thought. To speak of a counter-Enlightenment, however, falsely homogenizes the Enlightenment. It also wrongly suggests that Herder is a champion of particularity and difference over against an Enlightenment advocacy of universality and uniformity. It is more adequate to see Herder as wrestling simultaneously with social, historical, and psychological particularity on the one hand and with the universality of truth on the other: "Herder's political thought does not choose between the universal and particular aspects of human life and moral judgment, but presents them as closely interrelated."[2] This kind of wrestling is actually quite characteristic of the period, in ways that contravene any neat Enlightenment–counter-Enlightenment distinction.[3]

Herder certainly anticipates major themes within Romantic thought: an emphasis on history, tradition, and cultural particularity; however, Herder remained a republican thinker and thus a "progressive traditionalist" rather than either a reactionary or a nationalist, like so many of the Romantics.[4] Herder was keenly aware not just that people in disparate times and places had worshiped differently, governed themselves differently, entertained themselves differently, but also that these variations were woven together into distinct, if loosely bounded, cultural wholes. While cultures were hardly static or insulated from one another, the holistic character of cultures called into question the meaningfulness and adequacy of comparative assessments of isolated beliefs and practices. It seemed clear that it was possible for human beings to flourish in a wide variety of incommensurable ways. And so, as Nicholas Boyle notes, "it became more difficult, first to assert that there was any such thing as a universal truth, whether philosophical or religious, valid for all humanity, and second to explain why any one of these discrete systems should be regarded as having articulated it."[5] Herder was no moral relativist, however, nor a champion of freedom and creativity as ends in themselves. He regarded "humanity," understood most centrally in terms of fraternal encounter, neighbor-love, rather than cultural achievement, as the telos of Bildung and the criterion according to which individuals and cultures should be assessed.

Herder on *Bildung*

Bildung, for Herder, is not confined to the human realm but pervades all of nature: he understands Bildung most basically as any process by which the inner capacities of an organism, working together and in selective engagement with outer forces, enable it to develop into a mature whole. In fact, Herder uses the terms *bilden* and *Bildung* freely to discuss the way in which all the various parts of the universe, not just living beings, are organized. So, for instance, "Nature determined the points of space and being, where worlds should be formed [*sich bilden sollen*], and at each of these points she is present with her inseparable power, wisdom and goodness so fully, as if no other points of formation [*Bildung*], no other world-atoms, existed" (SW 13.1.1,12).[6] Leibniz's monadology is lurking in the background here but transformed in dynamic ways.[7] Herder's philosophy of the history of humanity begins with the earth and stars and proceeds to discussing the organization of plants and animals in order to culminate in an account of the formation of the human person. In the case of human beings and, in a lesser way, of plants and animals, an initial constitution (*Bildung*) by Nature/God continues in time through a process of development (*Ausbildung*) which is also a further form of *Bildung*.

Herder emphasizes both the uniqueness of each individual organism and the variety of species and, among human beings, of cultures, "since no point on our diverse globe, no wave in the current of time is like to another" (SW 13.7.1, 254). Struck, for example, by dissection experiments that had revealed that the nerves of each individual are arranged in a unique pattern, Herder insists that we must in the end speak of each person as an organic whole—"each person finally becomes a world" (SW 13.7.1, 253). Yet peoples (*Völker*) and species are no less real for all the variety of which they are made up; species are defined by the limits of fruitful intercourse, and peoples by language and national character (not, Herder explicitly argues, by color or race).

The whole earth, he writes, "sounds like a harmonious harp, in which all tones have been attempted or will be attempted" (SW 13.8.1, 298). Each individual organism, species, culture, world is capable of arriving at its own peculiar form of perfection or completeness, capable of its own happiness or blessedness (*Seligkeit*; SW 13.8.5, 342). It would be an outrage if individuals lived only for the sake of the species, for the sake of "the image [*Bild*] of an abstract name," but "the All-knowing One does not play in this way; he composes no remote shadow-dreams, but loves each of His children, filled with fatherly feeling, as if this creature were the only one in His world" (SW 13.9.1, 350). Yet as much as he stresses that each individual is an end in itself, Herder argues no less emphatically that no creature is simply an end in itself: "All of his means are ends, all his ends are means to greater ends, in which the Infinite, filling all things, reveals itself" (SW 13.9.1, 350). The perfection of each individual, each species, each people is ordered to a perfection that transcends itself. Herder identifies the final telos of Bildung as humanity (*Humanität*); the human species is "the great confluence of lower organic powers," coming together for the sake of the development (*Bildung*) of humanity (SW 17, 137–38). Individuals are links in the chain of Bildung, but it would be a mistake to say that they are *merely* links in a chain; their happiness and perfection lie in being precisely that which they are. "What then man is and can be, must be the end of humankind. And what is that? Humanity and happiness on this spot, in this degree, as this and no other link in the chain of Bildung, which reaches through the whole species" (SW 13.9.1, 350).

This notion of individual and collective development toward the realization of humanity is neither unique nor original to Herder. Indeed we find something like it in Kant, with whom Herder had studied in 1762–64. Whether Herder in some sense owes to Kant his understanding of humanity as the collective telos and task of humankind is difficult to say; it is likely that Kant articulated ideas of this sort in his early lectures, but the two authors' published discussions of the theme overlap with one another, and similar notions were widespread.[8] Kant's mature articulation is found in his *Anthropology from a Pragmatic Point of View*, which was published only in 1798 but based on a quarter century of lectures.[9] Kant begins by proclaiming that "the human being is his own final end."[10] For Kant, being confronted by this task decisively differentiates human beings from other animals: "it must be noted that with all other animals left to themselves, each individual reaches its complete vocation; however, with the human being only the species, at best, reaches it; so that the human race can work its way up to its vocation only through progress in a series of innumerably many generations."[11] Fully human is not something that one simply *is*; it is something one must actively strive to *become*. This task requires many generations in order to be completed because it involves the development of the arts and sciences, of civilization, of culture, and these develop necessarily over long expanses of human activity.[12] Beyond this, it is an inherently social task: "the human being is destined by his reason to live in a society with human beings and in it to cultivate himself, to civilize himself, and to moralize himself by means of the arts and sciences."[13] And yet Kant also sees this task as destiny, as nature's plan, fulfilled not directly through intentional human action but rather accomplished by "a purpose of nature behind this senseless course of human events," which inform the "history of creatures who act without a plan of their own," unfolding through the unsocial sociability of humankind.[14]

The Telos of Humanity

What, then, is this humanity toward which all Bildung (not just human Bildung but that of creation as such) is directed? For Kant it is realized in an "ethical commonwealth" that encompasses the entire species, within which all persons honor the moral law and recognize one another as ends in themselves.[15] The exercise of universal reason is key, while "the particular is seen to be constituted by the domain of individuated, localized human activity, characterized by chaos, childish malice, and destructive drives."[16] Kant never fully resolves the question of how an end realizable only through free human action can at the same time be brought about despite human intentions, an issue sharpened by his noumenal account of human freedom.[17] Even as Kant recognized that civilizational progress could not be neatly identified with the advance of the ethical commonwealth, he found irresistible the notion that only the truly "civilized" would take part in ushering in that kingdom of ends.[18] He played an important role in developing notions of the natural inferiority of the nonwhite races, and he condemned colonialism only from the mid-1790s onward, likely under Herder's influence.

Herder's conception is at once more holistic, more particularistic, and more pluralist: humanity is realized not by way of stadial civilizational progress but by way of ever-expanding webs of mutual recognition and respect. We know the telos only imperfectly, argues Herder, since it is not fully realized in this life. But he argues that we can discern it by examining our basic capacities, our original form (*Gestalt*) or initial constitution (*Bildung*): "our capacity for reason should be formed [*gebildet*] toward reason, our fine senses toward art, our drives to true freedom and beauty, our powers of movement to love of neighbor" (SW 13.5.5, 189). The human end, then is the harmonious development, at the level of both the individual and society, of all human capacities. As Frederick Beiser notes,

> the end of human beings is not the selfish pursuit of pleasure nor the selfless performance of moral duty. Rather, it is self-realization, the perfection of all a human being's characteristic powers, whether they are intellectual, moral, sensitive, or physical. Not only our reason is distinctively human, but all our powers insofar as we are a single living being. Hence, to realize our humanity we must strive to realize all our powers, to become a single harmonious whole.[19]

Charles Taylor has emphasized the novelty of Herder's "expressivist anthropology," his insistence that each individual and each people has its own distinctive way of being human. In this sense, the vocation to humanity is not a vocation to something generic but rather to something unique: "the idea is not just that men are different; this was hardly new; it was rather that the differences define the unique form that each of us is called on to realize."[20] In other words, Herder articulates an ideal of authenticity: the human vocation is to become oneself. "The realization of his essence is a subject's self-realization; so that what he defines himself in relation to is not an ideal order beyond, but rather something which unfolds from himself, is his own realization, and is first made determinate in that realization."[21]

As illuminating as Taylor's articulation of Herder's "expressivist anthropology" is, it is also overstated. For Herder, while stressing the irreducible plurality of valuable expressions of the human, does not regard human nature as infinitely malleable. Humanity is fully realized only when the dignity of each person, precisely as a creature capable of creative self-realization, is recognized and honored in the broader context of a recognition that human beings flourish not as isolated monads, however self-realizing, but in multiple overlapping yet deeply defining communities.[22] So Herder insists that looking at our weakness at birth, our long period of dependent childhood, we can conclude that we are made to cultivate society. Our tender affects fit us for sympathy with or taking the part of others (*teilnehmen*).[23] Our capacity for empathy (*Mitgefühl*), meanwhile, is made to be governed by the rule of justice and truth, as we can conclude from the fact that our bodies are a unity composed of symmetrical parts that we are made to recognize the truth of the golden rule.[24]

Herder in the Tradition of Natural Law

Herder's reasoning is undeniably fast and loose here, but it is not idiosyncratic; it stands recognizably in the natural law tradition. This has not been adequately recognized in Herder scholarship. As articulated by medieval canonists and theologians, the natural law was not an attempt to deduce action-guiding moral principles from empirical study of human nature but was instead a way of affirming the coherence of the eternal law, comprising the intrinsic principles according to which all created things operate, with the revealed divine law and, ideally, also with human law.[25] The natural law, the special way in which human beings as rational creatures participate in the eternal law, directs human beings to fulfill natural inclinations in ways suitable to rational creatures. Without making any effort to offer a comprehensive enumeration of natural human inclinations, Thomas Aquinas echoed the Stoic tradition in identifying three tiers of inclinations: those common to all substances, those common to all animals, and those special to all rational creatures. All are to be pursued in a way suitable to creatures who are rational moral agents, that is, who are capable not simply of acting according to desires but also of conceiving and acting for something grasped precisely as good, as *worthy* of being desired and pursued.[26] This understanding of natural inclination and natural law is bound up in Aquinas's thought with the *exitus* and *reditus* of creation: all things have been created with an immanent tendency to return to God. This "return" is not a Neoplatonic absorption but rather a finite reflection of God's infinite goodness. Inanimate objects' regularity of motion and irrational creatures' capacity to flourish by following their instinctive drives are reflections of this goodness. Rational creatures, however, "return" to God in a fuller way: by understanding what is good and pursuing it as good. This return to God is most fully realized by those creatures made in the image of God, insofar as they come to know and love God and to love creatures precisely as God's beloved creation.[27] The fullest "reflection" is thus not mere mirroring but relational response to the divine invitation in self-gift.

Herder's thought stands in more proximate continuity with modern natural law thinkers such as Hugo Grotius and Samuel Pufendorf. Modern natural law thinkers sought to discern the Creator's intentions for humanity without recourse to divine revelation, simply by examining the characteristic features of human nature.[28] They also flattened the telos of natural law, conceiving of it not in terms of the knowledge and love of God but simply as articulating principles for the construction of stable human societies. We might think that Herder's thought fits rather neatly here, since he could hardly more clearly signal the anthropocentrism of his thought than in naming the telos of Bildung "humanity." Yet in some ways he was closer to the medieval natural lawyers in that he saw humanity as directed toward a kind of self-transcendence. In defending his use of the term *humanity*, he says that "man has no nobler word for his determination, than what he himself is in whom the image of the Creator of our world here becomes visible as a living impression."[29] The humanity toward which we are developing, then, is the imago Dei, in some sense already impressed on human nature but in another sense still to be realized as the perfection of the process of Bildung.

What is new here is indeed the element identified by Charles Taylor as "expressivism." Herder understands Bildung not just with reference back to an original constitution of human nature but also as an ongoing process in which something genuinely new emerges.[30] This process of Bildung is fully determined neither from within nor from without; it is not simply a process of unfolding from within, but neither is it the case that human beings enter the world as blank slates to be shaped wholly by their experiences. Herder's understanding of Bildung has clear affinities with eighteenth-century conceptions of epigenesis indebted to Paracelsus, in which the seed's general tendencies to develop in certain ways unfold in interaction with the specifics of the environment.³¹ Given predispositions (*Anlagen*) come to expression in complex interactions with climate, language, culture, individual experience, and so forth. "The upbringing of our species," Herder writes, "is in a twofold sense genetic and organic: genetic through what is imparted, organic through the taking up and application of what is imparted."³² And while the term *culture* is of nineteenth-century coinage, Herder anticipates it, noting that we can think of this second genesis of human beings either in terms of horticulture, "from the cultivation of a field, culture," or in terms of the image of light, and thus as enlightenment, *Aufklärung*. Herder often speaks of Bildung as a process of assimilation in which each takes up that which is in accord with its own inner nature and rejects that which is alien to itself. There is for Herder not simply one way in which to realize the imago Dei but rather infinitely many, reflecting the boundless goodness and beauty of God. At the same time, not just any form of individual or collective self-realization can count as *Humanität* but only those ways that are capable of recognizing and affirming one another, animated by *Einfühlungsvermögen*, the intentional empathy that cultivates natural capacities for sympathy (*Mitleid*) and participation (*Teilnehmen*), and that lends substance to the golden rule's abstract symmetry.³³

Herder on Nationality, Consociationism, and Race

Herder has sometimes been seen as a major source of nationalist thinking. He was, to be sure, critical of artificial states that sought to impose unity from above on disparate cultures or peoples. This was to ignore what he regarded as the organic unity of language, customs, literature, art, and religion, which must be respected if culture-forming creatures such as ourselves are to flourish. At the same time, Herder was not a theorist of the nation-state: he did not think that state boundaries must match national boundaries. A state might well be composed of distinct peoples—so long as the integrity of nation- or peoplehood was respected, he did not regard a multinational state as problematic.³⁴ For Herder's political thought was republican and consociationist in character: "the nation was envisioned as a composite structure, as a configuration of self-sustaining groups and associations."[35] What holds a nation together is neither coercion by the state from above nor uniformity but organic relationships—the *Zusammenwirken* (working together) of the various parts.[36] It is a pluralistic, participatory vision of society. Indeed while Herder acknowledged the need for the rule of law, he did not believe that a coercive centralized authority was necessary if the composite groups composing the nation were sufficiently bound together by cooperation and shared standards.[37] "The nation did not displace families, clans, tribes, and other historical groupings but was continuous with them and thus, in its way, as natural a growth as the family."[38] Civic participation is essential for both a pluralistically conceived nation and its inhabitants to flourish, and Bildung forms persons fitted for participatory engagement and self-government. "Herder's philosophy of *Humanität* is an eloquent affirmation of the hope that ethical norms could assume the status of meaningful universals in terms of which people might recognize standards of mutuality to which they ought to aspire as human beings everywhere."[39]

Herder was sharply critical of authoritarian regimes, however "enlightened"; they inevitably work to enrich and empower rulers.[40] This critique of authoritarianism went hand in hand with an equally scathing rejection of European imperialism and indeed any form of Eurocentrism: "ours is not the wise, but the overbearing, intrusive, advantage-grabbing part of the earth; it has not cultivated, but destroyed, the seeds of every culture it has found."[41] He was not taken in by the substitution of trade for conquest, recognizing in it European domination in another, milder, but no less pernicious guise.[42] Indeed Herder is increasingly being hailed as a forerunner of contemporary postcolonial theory, in particular in his turn to "the aesthetic as the appropriate realm for opposing not only discourses of imperialism but also imperialist politics."[43] Europeans cannot bring civilization to the rest of the world, since there is no common European culture and "only a misanthrope could regard European culture as the universal condition of our species. The culture of *man* is not the culture of the *European*; it manifests itself according to place and time in *every* people."[44]

Herder equally rejected vacuous cosmopolitanism and a fascistic attachment to corporate identity.[45] In the former's blindness to cultural particularity he spied a cloak for empire, satirizing it with gusto:

> How miserable when there were still nations and national character, what reciprocal *hate, aversion* to foreigners, *fixedness* on one's centre of gravity, ancestral *prejudices*, clinging to the *lump of earth* on which we are born and on which we are destined to rote! *Native* manner of thought! *narrow circle* of ideas—eternal *barbarism*! With us, God be praised!, all *national characters* have been extinguished! We love *all* of us, or rather no one *needs* to love the other. We *socialize with each other*, are completely each other's like—*ethically proper, polite, blissful*!; indeed have no *fatherland*, no *our-people* for whom we live, but are *friends of humanity* and *citizens of the world*. Already now all of Europe's regents do so, and soon we will *all* speak the French language! And then—bliss!-the Golden Age begins again.[46]

If the erasure of particularity conceals the dominance of one form of cultural particularity over others, fervent devotion to national character is not a solution in Herder's eyes; it belies the plural and overlapping character of our corporate identities, and our calling to develop and express these harmoniously rather than setting them against one another in competition.

Herder's hostility to European chauvinism and his appreciation for cultural diversity led him to be sharply critical of emerging theories of race. Kant, for instance, had argued that while the human species was one, it was created with a variety of seeds (*Keime*) or natural predispositions that had developed in different climates, leading to the emergence of distinct races.[47] Whites represent the "perfect mixing" of all of the various bodily juices and form the strongest human stock.[48] Kant speculated that all other races would die out.[49] Only in whites therefore can the process of Bildung be consummated; only whites represent the possibility of a perfected humanity. Count Ewald Friedrich von Hertzberg (1725–95), Frederick the Great's cabinet minister of foreign affairs and one of Herder's correspondents, meanwhile, seized on Tacitus's *Germania* as a vehicle for promoting German exceptionalism and nationalism.[50] In a 1780 speech to the Prussian Academy of Science, von Hertzberg argued that the virtues of the

Germanen had been superior to those of the Romans. No wonder that they alone had not been subjugated under Roman rule. Von Hertzberg threw in for good measure a reference to Montesquieu's *Spirit of the Laws*. Here one could find ancient Germania portrayed as "the blueprint of a free society," for "Montesquieu . . . redefined freedom from foreign rule as freedom from absolute rulers."[51] The conception of Germans as a superior *Volk* within the superior white race was thus bound up with the imagining of rustic valor, rather than cultivated humanity, as prerequisite for republican liberty.

Herder decisively repudiated such notions of race and German exceptionalism.[52] Humankind is a single species in which each member ought to be regarded as a fellow: "you should not oppress him, nor murder him, nor steal from him, for he is a man, as you are."[53] To fail in this regard is to dishonor one's own humanity. Herder recognized the Roman roots of humanitas. He subtly reinterprets the virtue in an anti-imperialist direction, however: a Roman with humanitas is someone who does not insist upon his citizen rights with respect to "children, slaves, the lowly, strangers, and enemies" but rather treats them as fellow human beings.[54] Beyond this, the notion of races ought to be rejected in favor of attending to the multidimensional differences among peoples, natural cultures, and languages. There are no stable characteristics such as those claimed by theories of race: "the colors run into one another, the forms [*Bildungen*] serve the genetic character, and on the whole everything will finally become only the various shadings of one and the same painting, which extends through all spaces and times of the earth."[55] The construct of race distorts and devalues the genuine diversity of human culture. It is particularly ironic, then, that Herder's ideas were seized upon by Nazi ideologues to justify their racist glorification of the German *Volk*.[56] The nuances of Herder's vision of the collective task of forming humanity through the harmonious self-realization of individuals and collectives in all their malleable and overlapping richness were easy to obscure.

Imitation and *Bildenden* Tradition

As we have already seen, for all his appreciation of variety, uniqueness, and individuality, Herder is no individualist; the fulfillment that each individual ought to seek is to contribute to the realization of flourishing in community. Nor does Herder subscribe to a strong notion of autonomy or human freedom; instead he emphasizes formation by both genetic and cultural factors. At the same time, while Herder is aptly termed a communitarian, he regards traditions as essentially dynamic and individuals as formed formers who flourish in self-governance. He thereby unites typical liberal with typical conservative convictions and commitments.

We do not give birth to ourselves; as he memorably puts it, we are not *Selbstgebohrner* (self-birthers; SW 13.9.1, 344). Our inner predispositions are genetically determined, and their development rests on outer contingencies. As much as we would like at times to believe that we are self-creators, bringing forth everything out of ourselves, in the development of our capacities we are dependent on others—parents, teachers, friends, our people, and ultimately the whole species: "the whole shape [*Gebilde*] of humanity in a person coheres through a spiritual genesis, upbringing, with his parents, teachers, friends, with all the circumstances of the course of his life, with his folk and its forefathers, yes, finally with the whole chain of the species, which stirs with its spiritual powers in each of its limbs" (SW 13.9.1, 346). Much more than nonrational animals, we lack instincts and thus must learn nearly everything from others. The history of humanity is thus a chain of formative tradition, *bildenden Tradition* (SW 13.9.1, 345). Neither imagination nor reason represents an arena of free self-determination; the imagination works with inherited images and mythologies, and reason (*Vernunft*) is an "aggregate of the observations and exercises of the soul" (SW 13.9.1, 345). The human person is "simultaneously subject and object, agent as well as instrument. . . . In possessing freedom of choice, they are therefore not only determined but also determining."[57] Human beings are formed formers of character, culture, and tradition.

Imitation and practice (*Übung*; exercise) thus play a central role in Bildung; "all upbringing can only transpire through imitation and practice, that is, through the passing over of model [*Vorbildes*] into its image [*Nachbild*]; and what could we better dub this than transmission?" (SW 13.9.1, 347). Rather than forming ourselves, we are *Nachbilder*, imitations, formed according to the models (*Vorbilder*) that surround us. Appropriating the traditional image of a seal impressed in wax, Herder asks, "What is this for a poor creature, that has nothing out of its own self, but rather has acquired everything through models [*Vorbilder*], teaching, practice, and, like wax, takes shape accordingly!" (SW 13.9.1, 351). Yet while this is a chastening of human agency, it is not a denial of human agency. The process is organic rather than mechanical; the one who imitates must have powers to take up what is communicated from the model into herself, to digest this and to incorporate it or transform it into her own nature. It is these native powers that determine which models attract our attention, from which sources we will drink and how much. The models we imitate are like spiritual foods, which allow our imagination and reason to function and, indeed, to flourish. This is, then, the kind of agency that human beings possess: to digest, to transform (*verwandeln*) a given exemplar, inherited myth or tradition, into something properly our own, which is not mere repetition.

Innovation and the *Erfinder*

Herder also relies on another account of cultural change and progress, which emerges out of his preoccupation with a different but related issue: how is innovation possible in a world of tradition? In this context his answer is that exceptional individuals are capable not just of absorbing traditions and passing them on, but of redirecting them: "in no other way does God work on the earth except through chosen, greater men" (SW 13.9.1, 351). This "in no other way" strikes the reader as exaggerated, given everything else Herder has to say about the process of Bildung. His account of how traditions are actually selectively assimilated and concomitantly transformed by individuals, given their unique combination of genetic tendencies and social context, seems adequately to account for change and innovation. But the more Herder dwells on the power of tradition, the inherited character of speech and thus of mythologies, philosophies, and social practices, the more he is tempted to regard the overwhelming majority of human beings as passive reproducers of culture: "that you have learned some custom, is merely the working of a machine; that you take up the juice of science, is the service of a sponge" (SW 13.9.3, 371). This forms a key part of Herder's critique of the hubris of "enlightened" Europeans who treat the rest of human history merely as a dress rehearsal for their own glory. Against this, Herder argues that they have no reason to pride themselves on that which they have merely inherited; they should recognize themselves to be no greater than any other part of the process of Bildung. Yet the critique tends not simply to undermine modern European exceptionalism but also to introduce a fundamental distinction between the passive conduits of culture and the few "chosen, greater men," these *Erfinder* (inventors) who introduce something new (also SW 13.9.1, 349).

Thus the notion of genius also plays a role in Herder's understanding of history. It is important, though, to distinguish this conception from Sturm und Drang's cult of genius, however indebted this is to Herder. Within the Sturm und Drang movement the genius is seen as wholly self-determining, a kind of interruption of the flow of tradition. Radical innovation is critical.[58] Not so for Herder, for whom "original no longer means radically new with regard to what is known within any given tradition, but rather it means radically individualized, uniquely differentiated, organized, and put together."[59] For the Sturm und Drang movement, moreover, the genius serves only his own purposes; he is not bound to be socially useful. By conceiving of a common good higher than bourgeois utility, Herder is able to recover a measure for the individual, even for the genius, that lies above and beyond the self.[60] Nothing in the innovating genius is denied or demeaned by serving the realization of the ideal of humanity. The innovator does not, like others, "go forward in a dream of reason, thinking in the reason of others." Rather, the Erfinder is one in whose soul "thoughts engender themselves and form [*bilden*] a body, who sees, not with eyes alone, but with his soul. . . . He, who is able to see Nature in her created state, to espy new tokens of her workings and deploy them through artificial tools for human purposes: he is the true man, and since he appears seldom, a god among men" (SW 13.9.3, 369–70).

God and God's Image

It is probably not accidental that Herder, in speaking of the human impulse to imitate models, uses the term *verwandeln*, which means not just to change or transform but also to transubstantiate. In a particularly pregnant passage Herder writes that "reason is . . . a sum of the upbringing of humankind, which perfects itself finally as a foreign artist on given, foreign models" (SW 13.9.1, 345). The word *fremd* (foreign, strange, other), here twice repeated, emphasizes the extent to which we are indeed caught up in a process that is taking place in and through us; we receive our models from without, and they are other to us. In assimilating these models, we are artists, but in some sense alien to ourselves; we participate in a process that transcends us as individuals, the process of perfecting Bildung. The foreign artist is finally God, at work in our own creative transubstantiation.

Herder has been seen as developing from an "orthodox faith" to anti-Christian humanism, with the key turning points being his 1769 Grand Tour, marking the end of his pastoral ministry in Riga, and the Spinoza Controversy, set off by Jacobi's 1780 announcement that Leibniz had confessed to closet Spinozism (i.e., pantheism).[61] By this is meant that Herder ceased to regard Bildung as requiring supernatural aid and saw it instead as a matter of human activity; second, that he ceased to regard Bildung as alignment with the divine image and saw it instead simply as the development of one's own unique talents and capacities; and, third, that he rejected both the divinity of Christ and the conception of Bildung as imitation of Christ. But there are problems with this characterization on all points.[62] Herder treats the imago Dei as a myth that nevertheless is at the same time true. Since we know no higher form than our own, it was necessarily the case that all religions would conceive of God as more or less similar to humans (*Menschen*); that which should move and humanize hearts had to be conceived as human (*menschlich*). Thus in mythologies either the human was elevated to the status of God (here he is probably thinking especially of the Greeks) or the "Father of the world" created human beings after his own likeness (SW 13.4.6, 163). Here Herder distances himself from the religious phenomena he describes; these are "necessary" ways of thinking, to be sure, but they reflect the needs of humanity rather than reality in itself. Yet in the next paragraph Herder speaks in his own voice: "We are children of the eternal, whom we in this life should learn to recognize by imitating [*Nachahmend*] and to love, to whose recognition we are awakened by all things, to whose imitation we are necessitated through love and suffering" (SW 13.4.6, 163). As one recent scholar notes, Herder "transforms the religious problem of anthropomorphism into a virtue."[63] To imitate God is at the same time to worship God; true religion is "a childlike worship, an imitation of the highest and most beautiful in human form [*Bilde*]" (SW 13.4.6, 163).

The insurmountable obstacle to this imitation might seem to be the fact that we cannot properly know God; we certainly cannot know the inner nature of God, since we cannot know the inner power of anything. When we attempt to form an image (*gestalten*) of God, we necessarily err, since God is formless although the first and only cause of all forms (SW 13.4.6, 162). Yet we can come to know God as the "eternal spring of all life, all beings and forms," and in particular, in perceiving the causes and interrelationships of things we arrive at some understanding of God. Herder is often seen as an Aristotelian thinker, but he is more synthetic: here we might see him as uniting a dynamic Leibnizian understanding of *Kraft* or power with an Aristotelian understanding of immanent form, using the transcendent Platonic concept of *Eidos* to mediate.[64] The unfolding interaction of immanent powers is not merely contingent but teleologically oriented; it issues from God as *Urbild* or archetype and is directed toward the finite and embodied reflection of that *Bild* or image.

It is not that human beings must first know God and then decide to imitate the divine perfection; rather, this coming to know is also at the same time an increasing conformity of our being to God; "the more you recognize perfection, goodness, and beauty, the more these living forms will form [*bilden*] you to an image [*Nachbilde*] of God in your earthly life" (SW 13.4.6, 163). To recognize not just the laws of nature but the goodness of these laws is to love them, and thus to obey them freely rather than out of constraint; in this free and loving conformity we come to resemble the God who is the perfection of goodness and love. So reason, religion, and humanity are intertwined for Herder; the exercise of reason is at the same time a kind of religion or worship and engenders a humanity that is at the same time an *imitatio Dei* and a renewal of the *imago Dei*.

At this point Herder can seem quite Stoic in his affirmation of the goodness of conformity to the natural order as expression of the divine. If God is the eternal source of *all* forms, why is it that the imago Dei is to be understood precisely in terms of the ideal of humanity? In some sense, as we have seen, all of nature is for Herder inspired. Yet Herder does conceive of God not simply as a static Reason or Order undergirding existing things, but as an agent with purposes that play out in time: not just nature but history, too, is an expression of God's finite self-expression in creation. Human beings, as creators of language and culture, have a special place within the ongoing natural processes through which God's self-gift into finitude unfolds, and within humankind, certain individuals will grasp more fully, and more fully express, the imago Dei. This results from the fact that the infinite is expressed in the finite no longer as simple but as multiple, no longer as eternal but in process. That all of this variety contributes in one way or another to the ongoing process of the Bildung of humanity does not mean that all human beings are equally perfect expressions of humanity. It is in struggling to account for how the unfolding of tradition can be guided and directed, and how God's purposes are achieved in the face of stagnation, that Herder appeals to individual innovators. These are capable of discerning a divine plan in the midst of creation and its historical unfolding, and of aligning human activity with this plan. They can thus be said to be inspired. It can appear as though Herder cannot resist looking for some point of inbreaking revelation. But Herder does not, even here, regard this inspiration as a *disruption* of nature by the supernatural. The distinction makes no sense to him; nature simply is the finite expression of the infinite power, wisdom, and goodness of God. God is not outside of or cut off from creation.

What of Herder's Christology? Jesus Christ is for Herder the exemplar par excellence of "a god among men" (SW 13.9.3, 370).[65] Jesus was the source of an unexpected revolution in human history, destined to unite all peoples into one (without, again, diluting their cultural particularity), and therefore bringing them into the process of the Bildung of humanity. Jesus proclaimed a heavenly kingdom, one entered not by fulfilling outer requirements but with "pure virtues of spirit and mind"—in other words, a fellowship of the truest humanity (SW 14.17, 290). It is this "truest humanity" which is contained in Jesus's parables, which he expressed in his actions and which sustained him through his death, and which led him to call himself "Son of Man." Jesus's aim was to form people of God (*Menschen Gottes bilden*) who would unite sympathy and justice in seeking to further the well-being of others. In doing so, argues Herder, Jesus was furthering the only conceivable goal Providence could have had for humankind. Christ, then, is at once the purest imago Dei and the most truly human being, whose own reason and will were perfectly aligned with the immanent divine purpose for the world, the perfection of the image of God in all of humankind. Jesus is not just another *Erfinder*; he is uniquely the turning point in human history from the development of individual peoples to the formation of humanity as such, the point at which individuality and universality come together. Jesus as fully human is not identifiable with the infinite ground of the underlying laws of nature, the *Urkraft* that works in all of creation. But he can nevertheless be said to be God incarnate, the realization of the divine will in a single human person.

Herder's understanding of God's relation to the world has been aptly termed "dynamic panentheism" rather than pantheism.[66] God is certainly not wholly identified with the immanent order as in pantheism. Whatever Herder's fascination with Spinoza's pantheism, God is not for Herder an extended (material) being and so is not enclosed within the world. But neither is God merely the external origin of the laws of nature, as in deism. Taking force to be more basic than matter, Herder conceives of God as the immanent origin and driving force of the whole organic system of forces. God is present in the unfolding interaction of these forces. But as self-dependent being, God transcends nature. This transcendence is in no way opposed to or in tension with God's immanence; transcendence is not a way of being "outside." And we might note that this is hardly a wholly novel theological departure; Aquinas too was careful not to oppose divine transcendence to divine immanence but argued that the soul is in the body as God is in the world.[67] As Brian Gerrish suggests, far from undergirding an increased anthropocentrism (as speaking of the telos of nature as "humanity" seems to suggest), Herder is better understood as correcting a defectively anthropocentric Christian piety that sought to place God at human disposal.[68] "Man," writes Herder, "is only a small piece of the whole, and his story, like the story of the worm, is woven together from within the web that he inhabits"—that is, is subject to the same immanent laws (SW 14.15.5, 244). Hence Herder's opening comment in the *Ideen*—he will personify "Nature," not because he believes that Nature is an "independent being" but rather because "God is everything in his works" (SW 13, *Vorrede*, 10). He thereby guards against both denials of divine immanence and false conceptions of divine transcendence.

Herder did call Christianity "der menschenliebendste Deismus," but in so doing he did not mean to signal acceptance of a deistic understanding of God as externally related to the world as artifact. Rather, this phrase signaled his conviction that Christianity, as the religion of humanity, is neither an original perfectly transparent divine revelation which then was obscured by human accretions, nor an original natural religion of reason which then underwent a fall into particular religious forms. Christianity as the religion of humanity emerged in and through the ongoing development of preceding religious traditions, and this process of development is a process of divine self-revelation.[69] Never does religious truth appear naked, shorn of cultural and historical particularity.[70] Herder's historicism is thoroughgoing.[71] The Bible is divine revelation, as Herder's *Älteste Urkunde* (1774) clearly argues, but one that must be understood in the context of an organic conception of historical development: "Grains it was, which veiled in many ways and sown, held much within them, which only with the passage of time and often a great passage of time would develop: out of the train of developed times the Bible came into being."[72]

Herder interprets the truth of the Bible as a "figurative [*bildlische*] truth," adding that some truths can be communicated only through pictures or symbols. A picture, for Herder, is a way of holistically grasping truth, versus attempting to grasp truth through analysis, through distinction and separation. We remain always bound to the texts and narratives and images that have formed our imaginations; we remain always sensuous beings.[73] We do in some sense grow out of a sensuous childhood into maturity, but only in the sense that we recognize these pictures as pictures; man "remains however his life long the child of a higher power: what he recognizes in, on, and around himself, is always infinitely less than what swims before, around, and behind him in a dark mirror."[74] To be an adult is not to move beyond images to grasp an original, but to recognize that our grasp of truth is mediated by pictures, to recognize that we remain surrounded by mystery.

Herder's Aesthetics

As this suggests, aesthetics is key not just to Herder's religious thought but to his overall conception of the human.[75] For Herder's thought is rooted in the insight that ultimate reality is mediated to us, rather than concealed from us, by sense experience. It is through our experience of finite particulars that we arrive at a grasp of the infinite. Herder's aesthetics is rooted in a broader aesthesiology, an account of the senses and of sense experience, rather than merely a focus on the arts or on the beautiful. It is an expression of his concern to develop a more holistic anthropology, broadening out from the narrow rationalism of the (earlier) Enlightenment. Departing from the traditional subordination of confused sense perception to clear rational cognition, Herder, in the footsteps of Baumgarten, who first christened the discipline of "aesthetics," followed instead the order of experience. Our access to the general and universal is through complex, confused wholes and experienced particulars.[76] The special significance of the arts is to be grasped by appreciating that God is the artist of creation, and that human beings, as God's highest artwork, are themselves naturally also artists. The creative capacity of human beings is not a displacement of or competitor to divine creativity but a finite expression of this capacity. In artistic representations crafted by human beings, we glimpse not only ourselves but also the creative nature of God, from which our creativity springs. Herder thus goes so far as to declare art, *Kunst*, the "epitome [*Inbegriff*] and end of our nature" (SW 17:344).

One main focus of Herder's aesthetic reflection is Greek sculpture, which he regards as an important expression of the three-dimensional, and thus particularly holistic, sense of touch. Greek sculpture, in attempting a representation of the ideally beautiful human body, was at the same time offering a concrete symbol of the ideal human being as such.[77] The other central object of Herder's aesthetics is the poetry of the Hebrew Bible, analyzed most fully in the *Älteste Urkunde des Menschengeschlechts* (1774/76). Of all forms of speech, poetry most fully succeeds in preserving the complex whole of experienced feeling. It does so not by imitating feeling but by mediating it through signs and the imagination. Human beings bring the manifold of given experience into unity and in this sense construct the intelligible world, but are able to do so only in contact with the given manifold and through the historically and culturally mediated signs of language. Herder speaks metaphorically of this symbolic expression of felt experience as the construction of *Bilder*—"we don't see, but rather we create images [*Bilder*]"; what we see is not the image projected on the retina but that which is formed by the soul."[78] His most sustained application of this metaphor is to the creation story, which he analyzes as an epic poem in seven strophes, each of which composes a single sensual picture (*Sinnbild*) or hieroglyph (SW 7:79, 212–13).[79] To draw attention to the sensual character of poetry is not to reject it as divine speech; as Buntfuss argues, "Herder in a way characteristic of his thought overcame the one-sidedness both of the thesis of the sensual as of the divine origin of speech, while preserving the moment of truth inherent in each."[80] The poetry of the Hebrew Bible can be understood simultaneously as a human product of a specific cultural-historical context and as revelatory; God's self-revelation takes place through human efforts to imitate divine creativity and to grasp and relate to self, world, and God. Human beings are to be understood "not only as addressee but also as the select medium of the revelation of creation."[81] And this takes place through the imago Dei; in the order of knowing, the original and the image exchange places, such that we know God through conceiving of God in our own image, and can indeed come to know God in this way because we have been created in God's image. The era of Hebrew poetry is over and gone, replaced by more self-conscious, and self-consciously distinct, "religious" and "aesthetic" forms. Yet Herder believes that it remains the case that we approach God more fully through symbolic thinking and intuitive cognition, in our longing for the infinite and the whole, rather than through the inevitable one-sidedness of clear and distinct ideas.

Bildung is then for Herder both divine and human activity. First and foremost it is a divine activity, in which human beings participate willy-nilly like all of nature. Human beings can, though, through advancing Humanity as their own telos, come to participate actively in Bildung. Tellingly, in Herder's dialogue *Gott: Einige Gespräche*, the character Theano (often seen as Herder's mouthpiece) insists that all things must become like God, whether or not they will to do so. Blessed is the one who follows willingly, obeying with reason and serving with love; "he has the sweet, deceptive impression that he forms himself, although God is ceaselessly forming him."[82] Theano goes so far as to call the conviction that one is forming oneself deceptive—in this respect the opposite of an Enlightenment emphasis on autonomous human agency. Herder's own position is that this conscious and willing cooperation with God's purposes just is the highest realization of human freedom and agency.

The Pitfalls of Providentialism

Herder is a fundamentally optimistic thinker, with a providentialist view of history. This does not mean that he idealizes human beings or sees the process of the formation of humanity as smooth or steady. The process involves conflict; competing urges and tendencies cannot equally come to expression but compete with one another. Conquered and repressed peoples can be expected to act in ways destructive to both others and themselves; self-indulgence and domination corrode the wealthy and powerful. Vices as well as virtues come to expression, errors as well as truths. All of these contribute to the ongoing process of Bildung: "folly had to appear, so that wisdom could overcome it."[83]

Herder shelters, then, no starry-eyed illusions about "bildende Tradition." Errors and vices crop up again and again and are even unavoidable in this process of Bildung. Herder, sounding a theme prominent in the century prior, associates error with the very nature of language. Speech can express only names, not natures in themselves, and we reason with names that we ourselves have created. Thus we are bound to stray from the natures or essences of things. On the other hand, he does not conclude that we are cut off from reality, living in a world of mere appearances. It is through speech, and thus through tradition, through faith in the words of our fathers, that we do come to know the world.[84] Reason is thus no escape from tradition or faith. We arrive at truth only by working through the mixture of error and insight we have inherited, not by somehow removing ourselves from this. Similarly, however capable each unique instantiation of humanity is of its own perfection and happiness, it is also the case that horrible evils have been perpetrated and sometimes also perpetuated as traditions by both individuals and nations.[85]

How, then, do we come to distinguish between error and truth, evil and good, vice and virtue? "Rather than construing change and misconception as spelling outright defeat for the subject's rational intentions, philosophical reflection seeks to harness the contingency, error, and negation so pervasive in economic, cultural, and legal life and practice."[86] On the one hand, truth seems to have a tendency to become obscured over time; on the other hand, Herder thinks, it also has a tendency to reemerge. When does the latter take place and when the former, and how do we know? This is, of course, a pressing issue only because Herder insists that human history, and indeed the history of the world, is teleologically structured; that it is a working out of divine purposes directed toward the telos of humanity, the finite reflection of the imago Dei: "by restricting the concept of entelechy to instances of 'good' striving, Herder implicitly concedes that the teleological underpinnings of Bildung serve not just purposes of descriptive correctness but have inherently normative and disclosive standing as truth."[87] Were history simply a directionless succession of organisms and events, the emergence and reemergence of error and evil would come as no surprise. Herder uses a variety of metaphors—of exhaustion, of practice, of contest—to describe how historical development proceeds. Vices and cruelties will exhaust themselves, but goodness will grow stronger; human beings must make repeated attempts, making new pots with the shards of failed pottery, until they manage to make a sound pot; and vices and virtues contend with one another until virtue prevails. His most fully developed account, though, is twofold—one aspect appealing to what he regarded as general natural laws, the other specific to humanity.[88] So first, natural processes at all levels (the solar system, the history of peoples, the individual psyche) proceed from an initial stage of violent opposing forces through a period of mutual correction to arrive at equilibrium, "a sort of regular and harmonic proportion," which Herder also characterizes as a "maximum of cooperative forces."[89] Each system arrives at its own maximum, but as systems come into contact with one another, a new process of opposing forces is initiated, to be resolved in some new harmonious maximum. The importance of variety thus becomes more apparent; the instantiation of various extremes serves the achievement of equilibrium.

Among human beings, development takes place not simply through this kind of mechanical equilibration but also through learning. While reason brings with it the capacity for error as much as for insight, it most importantly signals the capacity to learn precisely through error. For human error does not remain theoretical; human beings live according to their grasp of truth, beauty, and goodness; they form themselves (*sich bilden*) accordingly. And when they lapse, they suffer the practical consequences of their blunders: "if they err or remain standing halfway within an inherited tradition, they suffer the consequences of their error and pay for their own guilt" (SW 14.15.1, 210). No supernatural or otherworldly punishment for human misdeeds is necessary; human beings learn from the natural consequences of their acts. Herder assumes that the "ought" thus makes itself apparent through the "is" of natural consequences. He treats the human process of self-correction as a special instance of the more general natural law of opposing forces arriving at equilibrium. The former is distinct, of course, in that it is or can be a self-conscious process. Human beings can therefore be said to be agents of their own self-perfection in a way that storms at sea or volcanoes on land cannot.

Herder's optimism concerning the progress of humanity appears naive in the wake of two world wars and recurrent genocides; scientific understanding and technological know-how progress, but does humanity? Worse yet, we might view Herder's providentialism as fueling a number of deeply troubling tendencies: to excuse the perpetration of injustice as necessary to the realization of progress, or—the other side of the same coin—to justify past evils and countenance present passivity and fatalism in the face of the inevitable progress of the engine of history. We might also worry that for all his embrace of diversity and his rejection of race and Eurocentrism, Herder remains caught up in a paradigm that actually feeds racism and imperialism, insofar as he thinks of culture in developmental terms, "placing groups on a temporal trajectory, further or closer to the telos" of humanity.[90] It is in relation to Herder's faith in the inevitable progress of the Bildung of individuals and cultures toward *Humanität* (not Herder's affirmations of divine immanence or his notion of scripture as myth, for instance) that Barth is most sharply critical. And the perceptiveness—but also the limits—of Barth's critique will help us take the measure of contemporary critiques of Herder's conception of Bildung.

Barth on Herder

Barth acknowledges that Herder is in many respects seen, and rightly, as a salutary foil to Kant and Enlightenment rationalism more generally. He insists, though, that in one crucial respect Kant came closer than Herder to casting off the blinders of eighteenth-century thought—in his recognition of radical evil. Herder's corrective to Kant therefore nevertheless remained, in Barth's view, within the orbit of autocratic humanism. Precisely in speaking out in favor of feeling and experience over against reason, Herder "not only saved the discovery of man as the measure of all things which was common to Rousseau, Lessing and Kant, and to the eighteenth century as a whole, and ensured its passage into the new era, but meant that it was in turn immensely enriched and strengthened by the discovery of another potentiality inherent in man himself," that of religion itself.[91] Herder's understanding of the imago Dei comes in for particular chastisement as the self-deification of humanity. For Herder "the soul, 'the queen, whose thoughts and wishes are enthroned within us' 'is the image of the Godhead and seeks to stamp everything about her with this image: she creates unity out of diversity, brings forth truth out of untruth, serene activity and achievement out of restless ease, and all the time it is as if she turned her gaze inward and with all the joyous feeling, "I am the daughter of god, and his image" said to herself: "Let us!," and holding sway, were engaged in asserting her will.'"[92] This strikes Barth as utterly antithetical to the recognition that it is Christ who is properly imago Dei and that the human task, far from asserting self-will in stamping all things with our own image, is rather simply to correspond to what has already been perfectly accomplished in Christ. "The most significant word" in Herder's thought, writes Barth, "can be nothing but *humanity*." [93]

Barth recognizes that this does not amount to simple self-absorption; he notes that Herder thinks that it is in grasping ourselves as the image of the Creator that human beings are able truly to love others as also bearing that image. Barth registers, too, Herder's preoccupation with the spread of the sphere of harmonious humanity, understood as the extension of the kingdom of God.[94] But he reads all of this as a bid for human autocracy. As a result, Barth discounts and dismisses, even while duly noting, Herder's appreciation of the concrete reality of history, the historical particularity of different times and peoples and places, of the importance of tradition over against any dream of autonomous subjectivity. "There can be no disputing the significance of these discoveries, made by Herder as they were in complete defiance of the extreme opposite views prevailing in the time before him."[95] Because Herder "finds God in living experience, and this is based upon self-experience," he "is implicitly and unequivocally optimistic in his general view of history."[96] Herder, we might fill in on Barth's behalf, fails to recognize God's Word as coming from *outside*, as forgiving but thereby also standing in judgment on, human experience and activity. Herder thought he possessed the ideal of humanity according to which he could measure all things—"and then he found Christianity, in inspired fashion, but from the well-known lofty watch-tower, to be in accordance with this ideal."[97] He could never really come to terms with the possibility of "the revelation of a majestic claim to Lordship made upon mankind," that is, with the possibility of a judgment on what he had taken to be good and true and right: ideal humanity.[98] Christ for Herder is savior just in the sense that "the human quality in him speaks to the human quality in all of us."[99] In this respect Herder is wholly an Enlightenment thinker, despite his efforts to recover the fully human particularity of Jesus: "the appeal takes root in the universal and pre-known ideal by which Jesus is measured, and which he was found to fit."[100]

Barth's critique of Herder is perceptive. Despite his recognition that the path of the development of humanity would not be one of uninterrupted progress but would involve tension and conflict, and despite his explicit reminders of human error, limitation, and evil, Herder indeed remained fundamentally optimistic that humankind was embarked on a path of Bildung that would lead to the ever-fuller realization of humanity in history. Herder does at times sound like an enthusiast for autocratic humanism: "I, the focal point of all, / Flow through all things and it's I / Who filleth all things in himself!"[101] His Christology was indeed not that distant from Kant's. But this is not the whole story. Herder did not in fact justify the sufferings and evils of the past as necessary contributions to a more glorious future. As we have seen, he insisted that no individual, no culture, may justifiably be treated as merely instrumental to some future state.[102] Herder was sharply critical of contemporaries who offered such rationalizations.[103]

Barth critiques the idolatry of Herder's anthropocentrism; contemporary critical race and postcolonial theorists are more likely to censure Herder's recourse to humanity as a transcendent ideal as a betrayal of his pluralism. These critiques—and their limits—need to be read hand in hand. Herder's ideal of humanity was not an assertion of autocratic humanism, not an imperialistic imposition of false universality, but rather an embodiment of concerns shared by Barth and by contemporary postcolonial and critical race-based critics of Herder who would recognize no kinship with Barth's assertive theocentrism. For all concerned, it is critical that the concrete particularity of the fellow human be acknowledged, that the other be allowed to disturb us with her otherness, jerking us out of our complacent assumption that we ourselves, and our own, represent the ideal of humanity. Sankar Muthu rightly notes that for Herder, "the qualities that fundamentally characterize humanity and that deserve universal respect . . . are among the key sources of cultural differentiation"; what differentiates human beings from one another is integral to what makes them fully human and thus worthy of equal respect, their cultural agency.[104] But beyond this, Herder's humanist commitment is not to any sort of "pre-known ideal" that preempts genuine listening and encounter, but rather to an ideal that mandates listening and encounter and therefore requires ongoing correction and revision. Hence his commitment to what we might label consociationist republicanism, to social and political arrangements that foster the authentic self-realization-in-community of persons and groups who seek one another's recognition and affirmation in all of their concrete particularity.

Barth's critique of Herder, then, ironically serves to convict Barth himself of something of the same failure to listen of which he accuses Herder, rooted in his own sort of commitment to a "pre-known ideal." The significance of Herder's commitment to humanity precisely as openness to encountering the other in all her historical particularity—and to a politics that lives out this commitment—should not be underestimated. Ironically, to *refuse* to judge individuals or cultures for falling short of "humanity" is to become complicit in evil and injustice. Postcolonial anxieties over engaging in ethical judgment of social practices are morally dangerous when they issue in an utter refusal of judgment.[105] Insofar as we do not simply stand aloof from others, clinging to some "lofty watch-tower," but commit ourselves to encountering them in all of their concrete particularity as historically formed formers, any judgments we make also open *ourselves* up for assessment and judgment, to a *claim* made on us by the other in the name of a truth or beauty or goodness we have not yet conceived.

Yet Herder's providentialism, his optimistic philosophy of history, must give us pause. It fortifies a temptation to countenance and excuse at least past evils as necessary to the emergence of greater goods, even if Herder drew back from this conclusion. It is telling that Herder considers and rejects the term *Menschheit* as telos of *Bildung*; where *Humanität* signifies for him the fulfillment of the dignified character of the species, *Menscheit* refers rather to its frailty and fallibility.[106] He is unable to hold together an unblinking acknowledgment of human sinfulness with acceptance of the task of the formation of humanity. To participate hopefully in the ongoing formation of humanity without falling into these traps requires an eschatological reference, a refusal to regard history as capable of serving as the site for human perfection. And this eschatological reference Herder lacks.

Ethical Formation and the Invention of the Religion of Art   4

Theorists of Bildung were agreed that freedom was essential to the realization of humanity. Authentic human development could not be merely passive, something received from the outside; it had to be a kind of *self*-development, whatever else it was. Yet Bildung was not merely a matter of freedom from external constraints, not simply a liberty for self-indulgence. It involved *formation* of the self. What sort of education, though, could rightly form self-formers? This was an essential question. Family, school, trade, journals, salons, political institutions—theorists of Bildung reflected on all of these, and more, as sites of ethical formation. One of the most distinctive features of this period, though, was the way in which art and literature took center stage and were seen as peculiarly important for the project of Bildung. In their efforts to think through the role of the arts, of *Kunst*, in ethical formation, theorists of Bildung created something new: *Kunstreligion*, the Religion of Art.[1] The churches and their associated religious institutions, those "ultimate soul-forming institutions," were suspect because of their associations with authoritarianism and censorship.[2] Art, in contrast, was being conceived through the infant "science" of aesthetics as integrally bound up with freedom, both moral and political.

The present chapter situates the rise of *Kunstreligion* in the thought of Wilhelm von Humboldt (1767–1835) and Friedrich Schiller (1759–1805), with some attention to theories of aesthetic disinterestedness developed by Karl Philipp Moritz and Kant. Wilhelm von Humboldt is best known today for his work as an educational reformer, but his work in linguistics and language philosophy was also pathbreaking.

His liberal political stance and his efforts to establish civil liberties inspired John Stuart Mill, who chose a quotation from Humboldt as the motto for *On Liberty*. It was above all a concern for Bildung that united all of Humboldt's various areas of research and activity.[3] It was also Humboldt who was responsible for forging a lasting link in the minds of German speakers between the term *Bildung* and pedagogical theory. Not only did he institute a radical reform of the Prussian educational system, introducing publicly funded education for all citizens (1809–10), and establish the University of Berlin (1810), which became the model for the modern research university, but he defined what we know today as the ideal of liberal education. Humboldt mediated philosophical conceptions of Bildung to a broader public. In the process he elevated the role of art to new heights. The towering neoclassical poet-philosopher Schiller, sharing Humboldt's liberal sensibilities, saw in aesthetic education the answer both to the ineffectual austerities of Kant's moral theory and to the excesses of the French Revolution. So did many others. As we have seen, Herder's relationship with Kant, his former teacher, was somewhat combative. And Herder deeply influenced Goethe and other contemporaries. Humboldt was no exception to this influence.

Both Herder and Humboldt could affirm that Bildung involved the holistic development of human capacities in a way that respected variety and individuality. Both understood Bildung as oriented to the telos of the full realization of ideal humanity, even if Herder preferred the term *Humanität* and Humboldt *Menschheit*. Both regarded this ideal as having far-reaching political implications: they agreed that the realization of Bildung was incompatible with political repression and tyranny. Both are best understood not as counter-Enlightenment thinkers but rather as seeking to complete while also transforming and deepening Enlightenment ideals.[4]

But there was no simple, unitary neohumanistic conception of Bildung shared by Herder and Humboldt. Herder understood Bildung as both an individual and a shared social undertaking, indeed ultimately as a matter of participating in the divine project of the finite realization of the imago Dei in a colorful harmony of creative consociational common projects. Humboldt tilted away from republicanism toward liberalism, and toward a humanly constructed Religion of Art aimed at a merely human end. To be sure, he championed not mere negative freedom, not freedom for self-indulgence, but rather freedom for Bildung, for authentic human development. Yet he saw this fundamentally as an individual project, and the task of the state most fundamentally as enabling independent self-creation. Humboldt's conception of Bildung has long been tarred as egocentric individualism, as a turning away from society and world to focus on narcissistic self-cultivation.[5] It is important to correct these distortions. Self-development was possible, Humboldt thought, only by way of social engagement. The telos of Bildung, however, was fully realized *individuals*, and it was individuals, too, who were the agents of Bildung, even if they could realize themselves only insofar as they grasped themselves as devoted to an ideal transcending their private interests and concerns—the ideal of *Menschheit*.

Influential as Herder was, it was Humboldt's understanding of Bildung that had the greater impact on Goethe and Schiller, and indeed on common understandings of the importance of a liberal arts education and of a liberally educated public, a *Bildungsbürgertum*, up to the present. It was only with Hegel, as we shall see in chapter 7, that *Kunstreligion* and the project of Bildung were restored to a participatory framework. When they were, however, history was taken up into the process of divine self-realization in ways that problematically legitimized historical evils.

Humboldt on Bildung

Humboldt conceives of Bildung, most fundamentally, as the development of the capacities of the individual into a harmonious whole. This is "the true goal of humankind," he writes, "the highest and most proportionate development [*Bildung*] of all his powers into a whole."[6] Like Herder, Humboldt emphasizes that variety is a good; uniformity (*Einförmigkeit*) he regards as a dangerous threat to the Bildung of humanity.[7] Given human variety, can we say anything in general about the character of the truly developed (*gebildete*) human being? Surprisingly much: "in the character of the perfected human, vivacious senses, a fiery imagination, warmth of moral feeling, strength of will, would all be led and governed through the power of critical reason."[8] It is evident that Humboldt does think in terms of a given set of capacities common to all persons, each of which must be developed in harmonious relationship with the others in order to achieve wholeness, even if it is also the case that individual characters or personalities vary according to which capacities or aptitudes dominate.

For Humboldt, Bildung is primarily conceived of as a matter of unfolding from within rather than as a process of being formed or shaped from without. Yet Humboldt is insistent that Bildung cannot occur in individual isolation. It requires a coming forth, an engagement with the natural world, with society, with other human subjects. "What man necessarily needs is simply an object that makes possible the interplay of his receptivity with his self-activity."[9] Broadly speaking, this object with which the individual must engage in order to develop harmoniously her receptive as well as active capacities, is the world. Humboldt speaks repeatedly of the *verknüpfung*, the linking or association, literally, the knotting together, of the self, our "I," with the world.[10] The individual finds herself only by leaving herself, only by engagement; our senses require objects to perceive, our activity requires stuff with which to work; if this going out is a kind of *Entfremdung*, alienation, it is one in which the individual does not lose himself.[11]

Is the world here simply an instrument for the individual's self-development?[12] Humboldt indeed treats this as the ordinary initial perspective of the would-be agent: "In the midpoint of all special sorts of activity stands the man who, without an intention directed toward anything specific, only seeks to strengthen and elevate the powers of his nature, to furnish his being with worth and duration."[13] The individual starts off seeking to exercise his own capacities to the full, "to become free and independent in himself."[14] But this instrumentalizing relationship to the world is transformed through the process of Bildung, through the act of engaging with the world. Through Bildung the individual rises above the pursuit of his own perfection as a kind of self-interested project or private possession. Instead he pursues it as "the notion of humanity in our own person."[15] It is this devotion to a self-transcending ideal that saves the individual from narcissism. It is also, in Humboldt's view, what lends unity of purpose and a sense of meaning to life.[16] The individual's task is not to become a useful part of some larger social whole but to become in herself a perfected whole.

Engagement with the world, then, preserves the pursuit of Bildung from becoming a kind of narcissistic self-cultivation. More specifically, it is our encounter with other persons that is key. When the individual catches a glimpse in others of the ideal of perfection toward which he himself strives, "he goes out of himself, flows over into the other, and reaches finally the most elevated and blessed of all feelings, the feeling of giving all of his enjoyment and activity for the well-being of others."[17] In encountering others we recognize that the ideal of *Menschheit* transcends the realization of this ideal in our own person. We also recognize that our own instantiation of the ideal may require self-sacrifice, and that this sacrifice can be the realization rather than frustration of our pursuit. As Humboldt puts it in a letter to Schiller, "It is the nature of mankind to recognize oneself in another; out of this springs his need and his love."[18] This is, then, neither narcissism nor atomism; independence of agency is not a kind of isolation but is realized only in and through relation with others.

Crucial to this sense of meaning, for Humboldt, is the fact that through Bildung the individual participates in something transcendent. She does not simply seek to fulfill her subjective desires, whether a desire to fit in, to be cherished, to be useful, or to be exceptional or independent. Neither does she simply accept constraints placed upon her by the natural world or objective demands made on her by the social world. Rather, the individual discerns an ideal, not yet realized, toward the instantiation of which all of her energies can fittingly be directed—the ideal of *Menschheit*. This ideal does not coerce her either from within, like an overwhelming desire, nor from without, like the laws of the state. But neither is it an ideal that has no point of contact with individual agency. She encounters it as an ideal that *ought to be* realized, as a duty or moral demand, not a duty to act in a particular way but to become a particular kind of person, a self-realized person.[19] "He no longer wants merely to prepare knowledge or tools for human use, no longer merely to help to promote just one single part of his formation [*Bildung*]; he knows the goal that is set for him."[20]

While it is critical for Humboldt that Bildung be oriented toward the realization of a transcendent ideal, he does not conceive of this in terms of the imago Dei. He asserts explicitly that humanity is merely a concept abstracted from individual human beings; it has no reality apart from them.[21] Humboldt's thought, as has been noted, reverses the Platonic priority of Form to individual instantiation. "In Humboldt the idea of *Menschheit*, like all ideas, becomes a fact only when it becomes manifest as individuality."[22] True, the idea of *Menschheit* cannot be fully manifested in any single individual; it requires a manifold of individuals in which to be realized. Humboldt does speak of an infinite power in which the capacity for Bildung is grounded. He resists, however, any objectification of this power; this power "cannot . . . be isolated from what has been created; it cannot be hypostatized."[23]

The agent of the process of Bildung has, then, decisively shifted. For Herder the primary agent of Bildung is God; Bildung is a cosmic process operative at many different levels throughout the universe. Human beings can actively participate in this process insofar as we, unlike other creatures, are capable of understanding it and making it into the telos of our own activity, just as Aquinas regarded human capacity to grasp the natural law as the special sort of participation in the eternal law possible for rational moral agents. For Humboldt, in contrast, Bildung is not a cosmic process nor a divine activity; the agents of the process are simply individual human beings. *Menschheit* in our own person cannot be realized through any sort of imitative process. For *Menschheit* in our own person just is our own individuality, and for its expression there is no model: "the former [*Bildner*] does not actually intend to depict the image of a God, but rather to express and fix the fullness of his plastic imagination. Each activity possesses its own particular mood, and only within it lies the true spirit of its perfection."[24]

Bildung and Religion

Humboldt is willing to grant that religion has a positive role in the process of Bildung—for some. His approach is thoroughly functionalist. He announces at the outset of his reflections in *On Religion* (1789) that he will consider religion purely from the perspective of the subjective needs that it satisfies, abstracting from the question of objective truth, since the influence of religion is quite independent of whether it is accompanied by a rational grasp of truth on the part of the believer.[25] Kant's Copernican Revolution is palpable here; we can no longer speak with confidence of things in themselves, only of how they appear to the subject, or at most of how a subject with our particular cognitive faculties *must* conceive of things. And indeed Humboldt began a serious study of Kant's thought in 1788, two years prior to the publication of the *Critique of Judgment*.

Most centrally, individuals turn to religion, he speculates, when they confront the dispiriting thought that the ideal of perfection toward which we strive will never be reached, that "the perfection, for which our heart blazes, was only a delusion, only an exhilarating dream, existing nowhere but in our idea."[26] We long to see this perfection, and so we conceive of it as existing in some being and then seek to unite ourselves with this being through love and imitation. We encounter this tendency, Humboldt thinks, even in peoples at the most primitive stages of development, and the conception of deity varies only according to the idea of perfection held by each people in each age, whether one centered on sensual beauty or on intellectual or moral perfection. Such conceptions can, Humboldt grants, have a positive impact on the process of Bildung: "all things appear to us in an altered form, when they are the creations of methodical intention, rather than the result of irrational chance. . . . Our search after truth, our striving after perfection gain more solidity and security when there is for us a being that is the source of all truth, the quintessence of all perfection."[27] We are better able to cope with setbacks, trusting that they are not ultimate; the belief that we receive all things "out of the hands of Love" makes us happier and releases our own goodness; we are filled with thankfulness and trust and are better able to open ourselves to others.

Having said all this about the positive role of religion in Bildung, Humboldt quickly adds that there is no *necessary* dependence of Bildung or the realization of *Menschheit* on religious faith: "the mere idea of spiritual perfection is great and fulfilling and uplifting enough, in order no longer to need another hull or form."[28] One who strives purely after the idea of perfection knows that the worth of his own achievement remains even when he himself is gone; he is not threatened by the possibility of his own extinction, for his deceptive imagination no longer feels "the nonbeing [*Nichtsein*] in nonbeing."[29] He knows that no fate can touch or damage his soul. Such a one is strong and independent. Humboldt's admiration for such characters is palpable:

> His spirit feels itself independent through self-sufficiency, through the fullness of his ideas, and the consciousness of being elevated above the changefulness of things through his inner strength. When he goes back into his past, searches step by step, to see how

he used each incident in this or some other way, how he gradually became what he now is, when he now sees cause and outworking, end and means, united in himself, full of the most noble pride, of which finite beings are capable, he calls out:

Did you not perfect everything yourself
Passionate heart?

We must then banish all ideas of loneliness, of helplessness, of lack of protection, and comfort, and assistance, that one often believes to be present, where a personal, rational, ordering cause of the chain of finitude is lacking.[30]

Humboldt's quotation here, appropriately enough, is from Goethe's poem *Prometheus* (1778). While Humboldt here admires a promethean stance, however, we shall see in chapter 6 that Prometheus is not a conduit for the expression of Goethe's own understanding of Bildung. For Goethe conceived of Bildung less as a matter of independent self-creation and more as an enterprise of discerning Nature's immanent norms through the messy and confusing medium of life experience.

For Humboldt, the conviction of being self-formed, of having brought about one's own perfection, more than makes up for the lost comfort of the religious perspective. For the religious believer is "deprived" of the "uplifting feeling" of being able to thank himself alone for what he is, and exchanges this for the "delightful" (*entzükkende*) feeling of living in the love of another being.[31] The religious outlook is comforting but betrays a certain weakness. Is there a danger, though, that one who relies solely on the idea of perfection and on his own agency will be narcissistic, will fail to care about others? No, argues Humboldt. This will not "render him hard and insensitive to other beings, not lock his heart against sympathetic love and every benevolent tendency."[32] Why not? Because the idea of perfection is not merely a cold idea of reason but can also be a warm feeling of the heart, which expands his consciousness to include that of others; it "carries his being over into the being of others." In fact, we can say that no one is fully possessed by the highest ideal of perfection as long as he conceives of perfection only in relation to himself or some other individual, "as long as the individual perfections strewn among all spiritual beings do not flow together in his vision of them."[33] In fact, argues Humboldt, perhaps one's identification and unification with other human beings is all the more profound the more the fate of humanity is seen as resting solely on human shoulders.

Humboldt holds back, though, from concluding that the religious perspective has thus been decisively superseded. Instead he settles for the conclusion that moral perfection has no necessary dependence on religion, that it can without religion be just as pure, just as strong, and just as fruitful. The idea of self-perfection as a duty incumbent on us arises out of "the inner nature of the human soul": virtue is in accord with the original tendencies of human nature.[34] Despite the variability of human character, this human nature is universal. The need for religion, on the other hand, is not. It rests on individual characteristics and "is in the strongest sense subjective."[35] Religion will take root in those who are strongly impressionable, in whom thought and feeling are closely entwined. There is no rationale for attempting to foist it on to others.

Bildung and *Kunst*

Religion is for Humboldt a dispensable form of the more fundamental category of art. In an argument akin to that developed more fully by Schiller in his letters collected as *Aesthetic Education of Humankind*, Humboldt noted that human beings are neither purely rational nor purely sensual creatures. There is a third element in human nature that relates these other two capacities of the soul to one another and unites them into a single whole. This is a capacity "to knit sensuous conceptions together with extrasensory ideas, to draw general ideas, which are no longer sensuous, out of sensuous impressions, to regard the world of the senses as a sign of the nonsensuous, and to lend extrasensory objects the shell of sensuous images [*Bilder*]."[36] Humboldt struggles to find an adequate linguistic expression for this capacity. Aesthetic feeling, he notes, captures it in part; but this refers more narrowly to the capacity to perceive harmony and symmetry, so it is not wholly satisfactory. He settles finally on imagination, *Einbildungskraft*, as the capacity that forges this crucial link between our rational and sensual natures. Through the power of imagination, "all nonsensuous conceptions become more lively, the inclinations that they elicit, become stronger, and the desire to realize them becomes stronger through the sensuous image [*Bild*] in which one wraps them."[37] The imagination thus conceived plays a pivotal double role in Bildung. For it is only because we have this capacity that we are able, first, to arrive at the concept of humanity, abstracting it from all of the individual (partial) instantiations we encounter. And it is also only through the imagination that this abstract idea of perfection is then clothed in a sensuous picture capable of engaging human desire and agency.

It thus becomes clear how important a role art (*Kunst*) must play in Bildung. "Nothing," writes Humboldt, "has such an extensive effect on the whole character as the expression of the nonsensuous in the sensuous, the sublime, the simple, the beautiful in all products of art that surround us."[38] In fact Humboldt credits artistic taste with lending harmony and unity to all of our inclinations and sensations, directing them toward a single point—much as he speaks of the idea of humanity as unifying human agency in the pursuit of perfect humanity. The goal of all art, he says, is in the highest sense ethical. This does not mean that art is narrowly edifying or moralistic; it is not the case that each product of art must support some moral teaching or directly foster ethical conduct. The mistake that is often made in this respect, he argues, is to attempt through art to bring about good attitudes and actions directly, rather than seeking to equip the agent to do so herself. Art accomplishes the latter by bringing transcendent values into the realm of sensuous appearance. Religion is thus for Humboldt one particular expression of the power of the imagination. Imagination and art are indispensable to Bildung. Religion is not. Or better, religion is itself a form of *Kunst*, an expression of the imagination—one among many, each of which can play a parallel role. For while it is certainly true, as we have seen, that religion clothes the idea of perfection in the picture of a perfect being, whose love for us and support of our efforts spurs our own pursuit of Bildung, other products of the imagination can provide equally powerful—or more powerful—"pictures" of abstract ideas.

Humboldt thus stands as one of the founding figures of the *Kunstreligion*, or Religion of Art, that was to come to center stage in Romanticism, and which, as Charles Taylor has argued, has remained a live option from that time forward.[39] "Art is supposed to provide the occasion for an enduring, strengthening, and uplifting experience comparable to the kind of experience that used to be found in the religious domain."[40] The artwork is now, at the birth of aesthetic modernity, conceived of as an inexhaustible totality, which issues forth from, and encounters, the equally boundless subjectivities of the artist and the audience. The artwork unites this sense of infinite meaning, of mystery, of hiddenness, of transcendence, with determinate form, order, and structure. *Kunstreligion*'s advocates argued, in fact, that the presence of the latter is indispensable for the ability to grasp the former.[41] It is often observed that with the founding of aesthetics religious markers are transferred from the maker to the thing made; both the artist and the art object itself are in some sense divinized, infused with sacred power, elevated above ordinary existence.[42] In some instances of *Kunstreligion*, "the work of art itself or the artist rises to the rank of a new Holy."[43] There are certainly hints of this divinizing tendency in Humboldt's attraction to Goethe's *Prometheus* and his accompanying celebration of a human agency that claims to have fully formed (*gebildet*) itself. Insofar as art, and the artists who create it, are seen as playing the primary role in elevating the ideal of *Menschheit* to its transcendent status, they too are sacralized. So Goethe, for instance, in a pamphlet celebrating the splendor of the Strasbourg cathedral, is in awe of not so much the glory of the building itself but the genius of its architect; in recognizing this embodied genius and doing it homage, the "beholder is affirmed as another potential artist and creator capable of transcendence."[44] Aesthetic contemplation thus strengthens the beholder's own sense of creative agency, his own sense of inhabiting the human in a way that realizes some new greatness.

More often than not, though, modern art has, as Taylor has argued, thrived on the ambiguity of its ontological commitments. This ambiguity is clearly evident in Humboldt's thought. For instance, although he rejects the objective idealism of Herder's conception of *Humanität*, insisting that the ideal of humanity does not exist outside of its concrete instantiations in particular individuals, he is capable of writing passages such as the following, from the *Ideen zu einem Versuch, die Gränzen der Wirksamkeit des Staats zu bestimmen* (1792): "When the final striving of all our human effort is solely directed at the discovery, nourishing, and creation in ourselves and others of the only thing truly Existent, if eternally invisible in its archetype, when it is this alone that makes the premonition of each symbol so dear and holy; so we tread one step closer to it, regarding the image [*Bild*] of its eternally stirring energy."[45] Humboldt reaches at times, then, for the language of Platonism—not to make ontological claims but to inspire a certain sort of activity. This could almost be Herder speaking; the ideal toward which we strive is spoken of as alone truly existing, our efforts at self-formation, at Bildung, are empowered by our grasp of the *Bild*, the image, of this *Ur-Kraft*. And Herder would agree with Humboldt that the ideal of humanity toward which we strive, as the finite image of the infinite divine reality, does not yet fully exist in time and space but must instead be realized historically, in individual instantiations of more or less imperfect humanity. But for Humboldt such statements are made out of the conviction that this is how we can successfully engage our imaginations in the task of self-formation. We embrace *Kunstreligion* out of the recognition that we are self-formed formers who can look finally only to ourselves in order to become fully human.

We cannot understand the phenomenon of *Kunstreligion* without attending to the political concerns and aspirations of those who promoted it. I have alluded to Humboldt's political liberalism. Seeking to define the appropriate limits of state activity, Humboldt made clear that the primary task of the state is to enable human flourishing.[46] It is a serious mistake, however, for the state to conceive of this in terms of the physical welfare of its citizens. The telos of the state is Bildung, holistic human development, not economic well-being. In this sense Humboldt understands himself to be siding with the ancients over the moderns, and in particular with the project of virtue over against that of happiness. But Bildung is not a project that can be pursued paternalistically by the state on behalf of its citizens. Persons must realize their own humanity, each developing his or her own talents and abilities into a harmonious unity. The responsibility of the state, then, is simply to ensure that its citizens have the freedom to develop themselves in this way. Hence perfectionistic aspirations require political liberalism, a state that protects the freedom of its citizens, not direct soul-shaping on the part of the state. Humboldt, though a liberal, was not a democrat; he did not regard participation in governing as an essential right. Whereas an enlightened monarch could ensure a stable transition to a state confining itself to the protection of its citizens, democracy was likely to crumble into chaos.[47] The French Revolution served as inspiration, to be sure, but also as warning; the people were no reliable protectors of liberty and equality before the law.

Humboldt's laissez-faire liberalism was uncompromising. Not only should the state not be involved in promoting or regulating industry, trade, or religion, but it should also not be in the business of providing social services. "Humboldt distrusted all these aspects of state activity because he feared they would undermine the autonomy and self-reliance of the individual. Rather than exercising their own powers in the struggle to survive, individuals would become passive and dependent on the state."[48] Humboldt published the main lines of his theory of the limits of state action in open letters published in the *Berlinische Monatschrift*. His major work developing these ideas in full, the *Ideen zu einem Versuch, die Gränzen der Wirksamkeit des Staats zu bestimmen*, was completed in draft by 1792. When Humboldt ran into trouble with the Prussian censor, Schiller worked to help him find a publisher elsewhere. But Humboldt never published the work. Despite his conviction that individuals must be responsible for their own self-development, "he confessed that he had doubts about his central thesis because his minimal state cannot provide its citizens with the necessary means for their *Bildung*."[49] Perhaps freedom alone was not sufficient.

Politics, Aesthetic Disinterestedness, and the Tasks of Aesthetic Education: Schiller

If Humboldt argued that political freedom was the essential precondition for Bildung, Schiller inverted the claim, showing that the critical place of art and imagination in ethical formation was itself integrally bound up with the project of forging lasting and stable freedom. Aesthetic education, grasping the freedom involved in giving form to matter, is a precondition of lasting political freedom. Schiller bemoans the fact that in contemporary society, "out of the piecing together of innumerable but lifeless parts, a mechanical kind of collective life ensued."[50] The individual has become a mere cog in the social machine, of worth only insofar as she is useful for the functioning of the whole. In such a situation, individuals develop only those isolated capacities that prove useful; the division of labor means that one worker needs nimble fingers, another a quick eye, and neither brings a work to completion. Kant, too, had invoked the image of a machine to critique bureaucratic society: as an employee of the state, he noted, one "acts as part of the machine," behaving "purely passively," obeying orders, and not exercising one's own discretion. While this is appropriate when one is acting as an employee, it is critical that such persons retain the freedom to engage in the public use of reason, "the use which anyone may make of it *as a man of learning* addressing the entire *reading public*."[51] While Kant, as we have seen, insisted on the freedom to argue, Schiller sought to correct this modern situation of self-alienation by an emphasis on balanced, harmonious development.

Understanding the role of freedom in Schiller's aesthetics requires some appreciation for the rise of the notion of aesthetic disinterestedness. The pivotal figures here are Karl Philipp Moritz (1756–93) and Kant. Kant's *Critique of Judgment* is generally recognized as a key work in the development of autonomy aesthetics. But the *Critique of Judgment* was preceded five years earlier, in 1785, by an essay by Karl Phillip Moritz that espouses a significantly stronger claim to aesthetic autonomy. Best known today as the author of the autobiographical Bildungsroman *Anton Reiser* (1785), Moritz also wrote "Attempt at a Unification of all Beautiful Arts and Sciences under the Concept of *That Which Is Perfected in Itself*," which appeared that same year in the *Berlinische Monatschrift*.[52] Moritz argued that artworks are self-sufficient totalities whose perfection is purely intrinsic, not arising through relationship to anything external. They are to be contemplated disinterestedly, for their own sake. In asserting the autonomy of the artwork, Moritz was rejecting a long-standing aesthetic theory initiated by Christian Wolff and extended by Alexander Gottlieb Baumgarten, which understood the beauty of art as derived from its imitation of the objective perfections of natural beauty.[53] Moritz argued that the perfection of an artwork does not depend on its capacity to perfect the observer or even on its capacity to elicit pleasure in the observer. The artist, Moritz argued, should not seek to please the public but only seek the intrinsic perfection of the artwork. There is, he acknowledged, a pleasure that attends reception of the perfect artwork, but this is a purely disinterested pleasure. "Only insofar as you [the artist] know that I have become accustomed to take pleasure in that which is truly perfect in itself, is my pleasure dear to you" (6).

While Moritz's view anticipates later Romantic and Idealist conceptions of the autonomy of art, it was not a position widely accepted at the time. This was no doubt in part because Moritz does not so much offer a substantial account of the intrinsic value of the artwork as a simple inversion of the concept of the useful (*Zweckmässig*).[54] If an object is useful only when it serves the purposes of a user, he argued, it is beautiful only if it serves a purpose lying wholly within itself — but he had nothing to say about what this purpose might be or about the nature of the intrinsic perfection of the artwork, beyond that "the lack of outer usefulness/purposiveness [*Zweckmässigkeit*] must be replaced through its inner purposiveness [*Zweckmässigkeit*]; the object must be something perfected in itself" (6).

Neither Kant nor Schiller follows Moritz's claims of aesthetic autonomy, even if both accept that aesthetic judgments are in some sense disinterested.[55] Kant's view is not that works of art or judgments of beauty have nothing to do with other kinds of value or value judgments. Quite the contrary: he argues that both the existence of beauty and judgments of taste serve morality. When he says that judgments of taste are disinterested, Kant's point is that such judgments must be free of determination by any and all rules, including rules of morality. Beautiful objects please in an immediate way, prior to any conceptualization of them and therefore antecedent to any conception of them as useful for some purpose or function. Precisely because of their freedom from determination by concepts, such judgments can offer a symbol of the freedom of moral self-determination. It is because "paradigmatic judgments of taste are disinterested in their origin," then, that they can "serve the supreme interest of morality."[56] Judgments of taste are analogous to reason's capacity to determine our desires by its own principles instead of heteronomous principles.[57] This analogy arises out of the fact that judgments of beauty are not determined by a concept. Both moral self-determination and aesthetic judgment exemplify freedom from heteronomous determination, though of distinct kinds.[58]

For Schiller, as for Kant, a certain kind of freedom of the aesthetic realm from practical and moral constraints is important precisely because of the way such freedom supports more encompassing ethical and political ends. Deeply influenced as he was by both Kant's moral philosophy and Kant's aesthetics — Kant's insistence that obedience to the moral law not be tainted by self-interest, Kant's account of aesthetic disinterestedness, and the notion that the delight of aesthetic experience is a delight in the free play of the faculties — Schiller was also dissatisfied; Kant's philosophy seemed to him bloodless, sterile.[59] He worried that its "technical form, whereby truth is made manifest to the intellect," "veils it again from our feeling."[60] Pure reason can become genuinely practical, transforming social and political reality, only by way of an aesthetic education that leads persons to act in accordance with the moral law out of, rather than against, inclination. We find the moral law within us in the form of the ideal of humanity. Each individual carries within him, "potentially and prescriptively, an ideal man, the archetype of a human being, and it is his life's task to be, through all his changing manifestations, in harmony with the unchanging unity of this ideal."[61] It is not sufficient, though, that this ideal be realized in any way whatsoever; a political constitution should not sacrifice the variety and individuality of its subjects for the sake of bringing about conformity with that ideal.[62]

Both individual moral perfection and political progress, Schiller argued, require not the mere subordination of emotions and appetites to the rule of reason but rather a harmony between what he regarded (echoing Humboldt) as the two fundamental human drives, the "sense (sensuous) drive" and the "form (formal) drive," the former directed toward ever-changing particularities grasped by the senses, the latter toward universal principles grasped by reason.[63] If we are caught up in the experiences of the moment, we lack any stability, any overarching principles. But an exclusive focus on reason is equally problematic; abstract principles must be applied to specific contexts. Here is where beauty comes into play; beauty is for Schiller an image of "living form," which harmonizes the particular and the universal, sensuous matter and form.[64]

Aesthetic education (Schiller speaks both of *Bildung* and *Erziehung*) requires the development (*Ausbildung*) both of our receptivity to the complex particularities of the world and of our active capacity for imposing form via rational comprehension, and allows us to grasp the possibility of harmonizing these.[65] The kind of independence from moral constraints required by art is specifically a "liberal" relation of human persons to the universe.[66] Our image of the world, its *Schein* or appearance, is not merely given but rather actively constructed by the observer. In contemplating the world, we are no longer passively enslaved to it; it becomes an object for us as we give matter form.[67] The autonomy involved in the free giving of form to matter, the construction of the world as it appears to us, is not for Schiller merely a matter of epistemology; it is a precondition of effective moral autonomy. For it is by way of aesthetic development that human beings learn how to rise above passive slavery to natural inclinations: "the human person in his physical condition simply suffers under the power of nature; in the aesthetic state he frees himself from this power, and in the moral he rules it."[68] Humboldt had focused on imagination as the capacity to abstract general ideas from sensuous experience. While he regarded imagination as relating and uniting the rational with the sensuous capacities of human nature, he conceived of imagination, and its artistic productions, in wholly active terms. Hence his association of imagination with strength and independence, in contrast with religious weakness. Schiller, in contrast, conceives of aesthetic education as achieving a harmony between our active and passive powers. Yet Schiller, too, conceives of aesthetic education as empowering, as enabling ordinary persons to become rulers of nature.

Aesthetic education yields not just autonomy but grace: a joy in acting well. The moral law is no longer experienced as an external constraint but is embraced as that to which the aesthetically formed are inclined.[69] Aesthetic experience must, then, be free from moral constraints in order to serve ethical development in a broader sense.[70] Schiller signals the decisive importance of this theme in the opening paragraphs of the *Letters*. Addressing his Danish patron, the Duke of Augustenberg (to whom an original letter containing the core political ideas of the later letters had been written), Schiller expresses gratitude at having been asked to "submit the results of my inquiry concerning Art and Beauty in the form of a series of letters."[71] "What I would have asked of you as a favor, you in your largesse impose upon me as a duty, thus leaving me the appearance of merit where I am in fact only yielding to inclination. The free mode of procedure you prescribe implies for me no constraint; on the contrary, it answers to a need of my own."[72] Schiller at one and the same time fulfills his duty and revels in his freedom.

Schiller, then, can be seen as reaching back to recover from the Aristotelian virtue tradition the insistence that continence not be equated with virtue. Indeed, Schiller's worry is that the austerity of Kant's moral law, left to itself, cannot succeed even in generating continence, the active principle forcibly containing the passive, but would leave persons and societies mired in weakness of will, unable to realize their own freedom and autonomy, chained to inclination.

"If we learn how to discipline, cultivate, and refine our desires and feelings, we will have created a potent instrument for the execution of our moral ideals. These desires and inclinations will then make us do our duty from inclination rather than against it."[73] Virtue must become second nature. "If . . . we are to be able to count on man's moral behavior with as much certainty as we do on natural effects, it will itself have to be nature, and he will have to be led by his very impulses to the kind of conduct which is bound to proceed from a moral character."[74] This was, for Schiller, not a corruption of moral inclination but a perfecting of it.

What did aesthetic education, the harmonizing of active and passive drives, of duty and inclination, have to do with politics? Everything, Schiller insisted, calling the letters his "profession of political faith."[75] Like Kant and Humboldt, Schiller was more inclined to trust reform from above than revolution from below, even as he passionately advocated for a liberal state that confines itself to the protection of individual liberties. "The state itself is never the end," he wrote. "It is important only as a condition under which the end of humanity [Menschheit] can be attained, and this end of humanity is nothing other than the development [Ausbildung] of all of the powers of man, his advancement."[76] The early days of the French Revolution were exhilarating for anyone to whom the cause of political liberty was dear, and Schiller went so far as to suggest that only the experience of freedom can render a people ripe for it.[77] However, it is the aftermath of the French Revolution that looms in the background of Schiller's *Letters on Aesthetic Education*; his is an urgent search for a kind of liberty that will not degenerate into a Reign of Terror. The freedom Schiller advocated was, as we have seen, emphatically not a freedom from ethical considerations but rather a freedom for something more than mere external conformity to moral constraints. Unlike Humboldt, then, Schiller emerges as a civic republican thinker, concerned that political freedom cannot survive without civic virtue. The French had indeed shown themselves to be lacking in the virtue necessary for a republic to survive and thrive.[78] Not only individuals but also the state must learn to harmonize the form drive and the sense drive, abstract principle and particular desire: "the state should not just honor the objective and generic character of individuals but also their subjective and specific character, and should not depopulate the kingdom of appearances in order to extend the invisible kingdom of morality."[79] Schiller is sometimes charged with having contributed to a form of political disengagement among the educated public that created a vacuum in which National Socialism was ultimately able to take root. Georg Bollenbeck, for instance, while noting that the *Letters on Aesthetic Education* are politically motivated, argues that they essentially worked to indefinitely postpone direct political activity and focus attention instead on self-cultivation.[80] As the passage just quoted makes clear, however, Schiller was aware that the progress he hoped for would likely be possible only if the state itself fostered and honored moral agency. Direct political change is therefore a necessary complement to aesthetic education.

In Conclusion: A Conjured Encounter with Barth

Barth did not devote chapters in his *Protestant Theology in the Nineteenth Century* to either Humboldt or Schiller. Schiller is mentioned only twice in passing, Humboldt not at all. It does not take too much imagination, however, to extrapolate on the basis of his treatment of Herder to what he might have said. Here too we can hear Barth pronouncing: We have to do with autocratic humanism, with thinkers for whom the most significant word is *humanity*, who treat humankind as the measure of all things. Here too we encounter the self-deification of the soul, engaged in stamping everything about itself with its own image, asserting its will. Here too, then, claims made on behalf of humanity are fundamentally in danger of feeding self-deception, a failure to recognize their limits, their parochial character, even their sinful distortion by pride or fear. The soul engaged in imposing its image on reality is not open to encounter, not ready to listen, not prepared either for forgiveness or for judgment. Here too, as with Herder, the critique must be qualified, insofar as all of these thinkers share the recognition that we become fully human only as we commit ourselves to acknowledging the concrete particularity of our fellow human beings. Yet the Barthian critique meets its mark here, I want to suggest, more squarely than in the case of Herder, its intended target. And it is these issues, rather than the ontological ambiguities of *Kunstreligion* in themselves, that should claim our attention.

Humboldt, to be sure, insists that the individual can realize himself only by encountering others who themselves embody some dimension of the ideal of *Menschheit*. Yet this encounter is framed as a means to the end of self-realization, not as an end in itself. This is not incidentally related to Humboldt's infatuation with strength and independence. Living in the love of others is delightful but weak, effeminate. One who does so, rather than independently perfecting himself, trades uplifting sublimity for the comforts of the beautiful. We may suspect that in one inflated by the glorious sense of having formed himself, the warm feeling of the heart that expands his consciousness to absorb others precludes, rather than enabling, a genuine encounter with their concrete otherness.

Schiller does not valorize activity over receptivity to the extent that Humboldt does. Indeed he conceives of aesthetic education precisely as bringing about a harmony between active and passive capacities. Yet neither he nor Humboldt acknowledges, as Herder does, the ways in which human beings are socially formed formers; neither grapples with cultural particularity, and neither sees fellowship-in-difference as itself the realization of humanity. For all their insistence that the state ought to respect the individuality of its subjects, that true humanity will be realized only when that individuality is given freedom to develop, not when it is quashed, neither develops anything like Herder's consociationist political vision of smaller wholes joining together in a shared pursuit of common goods.

For Humboldt, only political freedom could provide the conditions under which Bildung could unfold; for Schiller, only Bildung could bring about a citizenry equipped to sustain freedom. There was, then, plenty to do, Schiller thought, to ensure that when political reforms came, as they surely would, they would find fertile soul. In Goethe, Schiller found a crucial ally, a literary giant prepared to take hold of the novel—that suspect new genre that was taking the world by storm—and direct it to the ends of Bildung and *Kunstreligion*. To the story of the rise of the Bildungsroman, and to Goethe's *Wilhelm Meister's Apprenticeship* as its exemplar par excellence, I turn in the following two chapters.

Could the novel play the part envisioned for it? Two particular challenges loomed. It might claim a false, idolatrous authority to limn the fully human. Or it might simply cave in to the pressures of the market and fail to create genuine dialogical encounter with the "infinite incommensurabilities" of being human. Insofar as the novel was designed for private reading and *Kunstreligion* eschewed the thick communal "cultus" of lived religious practice, these challenges were difficult to overcome. Novels that succumbed to commodification were consumed privately in ways more likely to abet than to transform individual and collective fantasies. Novels that resisted commodification could challenge fantasy, but at the risk of cultural marginalization—even if marginalization by way of elevation to elite high-culture status.

The Rise of the Bildungsroman and the Commodification of Literature 5

As we saw in chapter 2, the Pietist movement played an important role in preparing the ground for the novel conceived as an instrument for Bildung. Mainstream Pietists guarded against charges of works-righteousness by insisting that any good that Pietist Christians did was in truth worked by God, growing out of the seed of God's Word. Pietist hostility to worldly literature reflected the conviction that it represented an assertion of human autonomy; by rejecting such expressions of *menschen-kunst*, human creative agency, they preserved their passivity to divine agency and their commitment to being formed by the Word of God alone. Yet the Pietist movement was an important source for eighteenth-century literary innovations. While Pietism conceived of itself as focused around the small-group study of scripture, devotional works such as Arndt's *Wahres Christentum* were equally important. Moreover, given the emphasis on individual conversion, the reading and writing of personal spiritual narratives became a central feature of devotional life. In the process, habits of examining subjective experience were cultivated, together with a rich vocabulary to be employed in this self-examination. Once in place, these were ripe for appropriation by secular literature, and in particular by the novel. Where spiritual life-writing sought to trace the transformative agency of God, the novel provided a context for tracing—and fostering—human self-forming agency. The novel, then, became closely associated with the project of Bildung. Nowhere was this more evident than in the subgenre of the Bildungsroman.

The emergence of the Bildungsroman, and indeed of the novel in Germany as such, took place within a broader cultural context in which, as we have seen, art was being hailed as bearer of salvation for modern humanity, capable of reconciling all that Enlightenment reason had torn apart, cultivating integrated, autonomous human beings and ushering in the liberal state. The year 1795 witnessed both the publication of Goethe's *Wilhelm Meister's Apprenticeship* and the first appearance of Schiller's landmark literary journal, *Die Horen*, a project in which Goethe was also a key collaborator. The former was to become *the* exemplary Bildungsroman, the latter the cornerstone of German classicism and a key avenue for realizing the project of transforming society via neohumanistic *Bildung*. The first nine of Schiller's *Letters on Aesthetic Education* appeared in the very first issue of *Die Horen*, setting the tone. Aesthetic education would allow Germany to avoid repeating the horrors of the French Revolution, and the fact that Germany had cultivated an aesthetic and philosophical elite rather than a politically engaged elite would in the end prove a strength rather than a weakness.[1] Long before the restoration of the old regime at the Congress of Vienna in 1815, however, Schiller had already begun to worry that the emancipatory potential of literature was in fact rather limited. Only a small elite would recognize great art; the reading public at large would glut themselves with escapist fantasy. Market forces would cater to the preferences of the uneducated many, and the taste of the truly cultivated would survive with difficulty.[2] Two years later, Schiller abandoned the project of *Die Horen*. Friedrich Schlegel, initially enthusiastic about the project of aesthetic education, grew pessimistic about the capacity of the novel to "bind poetry in such an unmediated way to reality, and to wish to depict in poetry something not fully soluble into that medium."[3] Goethe, meanwhile, wrote works that proved increasingly inaccessible to the public; he remarked in a letter written toward the end of his life that "my works cannot be popular. . . . They are written, not for the multitude, but only for individuals who desire something congenial, whose aims are like my own."[4] Goethe and Schiller did not relinquish their conviction that Bildung was central to the development of individual, nation, and indeed humankind as such, but their hopes of catalyzing a rapid social or political transformation were chastened.

Within this general project of aesthetic education, of reconciling through art universality and particularity, reason and feeling, agency and belonging, the novel came to hold a special place. While both the genre of the Bildungsroman and its definition are hotly contested, the earliest accounts, which reach back to the eighteenth century, defined the Bildungsroman as a novel that depicts the unfolding development of the protagonist, focusing on the interaction between inner character and social forces. Precisely in so doing, the Bildungsroman was seen by its first theorists as furthering "the development [*Bildung*] of the reader to a greater extent than any other form of novel."[5] So Bildung was understood as taking place both within the fictional narrative—in the protagonist—and in reality, in the reader. What was at stake here was the possibility of a nondidactic art that nevertheless served individual projects of ethical formation precisely by way of the creative imagination. More generally at issue was the very identity of art, of ethics, and the relation between them, and implicit in this nexus was also the question whether and in what sense the Bildungsroman could take on something like the formative role played by scripture itself within Pietist communities.

In order to see how these issues played out we must attend to some of the key social changes associated with the emergence of the novel in the eighteenth century and with the impact of these changes both on the cultural place of scripture and other religious texts and on ethical formation. After examining the conditions for the rise of the novel generally speaking, and the special characteristics that set novels apart from previous literary forms, I will turn to the Bildungsroman in particular. The claim that novels have an important part to play in ethical formation is familiar to us today from contemporary philosophical and theological retrievals of virtue ethics. Fine-grained perception of particulars is essential, and narrative fiction excels in the depiction of such particulars; moral principles do not apply themselves. Moreover, narrative fiction cultivates our capacity for empathy with others, expanding our capacity to care.[6] It was in the mid-eighteenth century that a keen sense of the chasm between universal moral principle and the particularities of lived experience developed, along with the sense that art, and the novel in particular, could assist in navigating this divide. This was also an era preoccupied with the power and limits of sympathy, with the ways in which it could powerfully connect observers with the ups and downs of others' experiences—or fail to be extended to those perceived as too distant, too alien. All of these features of literature were in the mid-eighteenth-century German context regarded as resources for the enterprise of authentic self-realization, within the broader cultural enterprise of the formation of humanity. Novels provided mirrors in which to scrutinize one's own experience and discern one's own emerging self.

For the purposes of the present project, the critical questions have to do with authority. For *Kunstreligion* is always in danger of falling into idolatry, in which either the artist or the artwork is regarded as a final authority on the good or beautiful. Neither human agency nor the search for immanent form (the authentic self) is suspect in itself. They are problematic only when they are taken to be capable of certifying themselves. For then they become closed to critical interrogation, refusing, as Barth would have it, to listen to the Word of Judgment—to the disturbing otherness of God, confronting us in our fellows. Novels that catered to promethean fantasies, whether by feeding desires stoked by the market or by being drafted into the service of nationalist ambitions, could not succeed in becoming "secular scripture" or assist in forming a humanity sustained by ongoing dialogical engagement.

The Novelty of the Novel

Over the course of the eighteenth century, a wide-ranging shift in reading habits took place as "intensive" reading gave way to "extensive" reading.[7] Instead of reading a few texts over and over again, committing long passages to memory and internalizing them, the growing middle class began to read a much broader variety of texts. They did not stop reading scripture and devotional literature, but they began, alongside these, to read more and more newspapers, practical manuals, historical works, travel narratives, literary journals, and novels. This represented a profound reorientation to the world: no longer toward the past, toward a received wisdom that needed only be appropriated in order to live well, but toward the present and the future, toward a rapidly expanding base of knowledge and range of experience available to the enterprising. This was, of course, a departure from Pietism's focus on devotional literature, but it was also a departure from all previous reading practices, which centered on a canon that was quite narrow, even if (as opposed to Pietist practice) it included both pagan and Christian works.

While perhaps not quite as ephemeral in content as newspapers, the novel was exactly that, an upstart on the literary stage, lacking the cultural authority of poetry or even of theater, whose status and moral legitimacy was itself still contested. So named because they did not employ the inherited plots accepted without question by the likes of Shakespeare and Milton, novels reflected a departure from the premise that only the lasting and universal is worthy of literary attention, that, as Ian Watt has put it, "since Nature is essentially complete and unchanging, its records, whether scriptural, legendary, or historical, constitute a definitive repertoire of human experience."[8] Both newspapers and novels, then, are oriented toward what is "new," what is "novel," rather than toward received wisdom. Social history has shed light on some of the reasons behind this dramatic seventeenth- and eighteenth-century literary shift: increased knowledge about the natural and social worlds, the introduction of new technologies, differentiation of labor, and a more linear sense of history. What emerged was a sense of the present and future as quite other than the past, as introducing new things into the world. Hence the passion for accounts of events happening around the world, for travel narratives, historical treatises, and practical manuals to direct household and business affairs. But why a new form of fiction?

Novels are characterized not only by an invented rather than an inherited plot but also, even more centrally, by their focus on the day-to-day life experiences of ordinary people. Gone is the conviction, common to epic and chivalric romance, that serious literature must deal with that which is most significant, that it is the exceptional hero who is most representatively human. The inventory of a mediocre mind or of a threadbare wardrobe is perfectly worthy of novelistic attention—think of *Moby Dick*'s exhaustive account of the production of whale oil, or the orphan protagonist of Dickens' *Oliver Twist*. The focus of attention shifts from the universal to the particular, from the ideal to the real, from timeless, unchanging Forms to empirical happenings.[9]

The Novel and the Dignity of the Individual

Two basic conditions have been identified for the emergence of the novel, with its "formal realism": the individual must be considered a worthy subject for serious literary treatment, and ordinary lives must be varied enough to be interesting.[10] Both can be construed as expressions of a new individualism which can itself be seen as seen as indebted to the influence of Reformed Protestantism and the emergence of capitalism. Ultimately, however, it was a new preoccupation with subjective experience—a development heavily indebted to Pietism—that was decisive.

This first condition, the conviction of the value of every individual, is inconceivable without Christianity and may seem sufficient in itself: the closest literary antecedent of the novel's formal realism is found in the Bible.[11] For in the Bible too any differentiation between high and low styles, between tragic and comic, was set aside; ordinary people, in fact, the poor, the disfigured, the powerless, become the "heroes" and take center stage. As Erich Auerbach has influentially argued, "the true heart of the Christian doctrine—Incarnation and Passion—was . . . totally incompatible with the principle of the separation of styles. . . . [Christianity] engenders a new elevated style, which does not scorn everyday life and which is ready to absorb the sensorily realistic, even the ugly, the undignified, the physically base."[12]

The conviction that each and every individual is significant enough to be the subject of serious literature seems, then, to be present at the birth of Christianity. And certainly if it is present there, it is rooted in the Hebrew Bible, where little David fells Goliath, Jacob receives his elder brother's inheritance, and Sarah conceives in her old age. Within the New Testament the emphasis on the individual, however humble, is undeniable; Jesus summons not just the poor but the outcast—prostitutes, tax collectors—stressing that his Father's loving care is directed toward each one. "However much the New Testament directs attention to the social, and emphasizes and furthers the charitable, nevertheless it thinks of the person as irreplaceable."[13] The church is certainly corporate, but it is a *gathered* people who respond to the call. Christians are baptized, not born into the faith. It is not social elites who display the essentially human but ordinary, flawed persons.[14]

While the notion of the dignity of the individual is thus rooted deeply in the biblical faiths, it does not follow that its full social and political expression is found there or that the Bible is simply an expression of the same literary realism that animates the novel. Auerbach argues that in the Bible the individual is significant not in his or her own right but in relation to God; it is vertical, not horizontal, relationships that have ultimate meaning.[15] It is because the peasant bears the image of God that the scandal that Christ died for her is in some way fathomable, and it is only insofar as the peasant images Christ, that is to say becomes a saint, that she merits literary attention. We might note as well that David, Jacob, and Sarah are properly tropes for the beleaguered Chosen People, important for how they shed light on Yahweh's relationship with his beloved Israel. In the New Testament, meanwhile, humble individuals play key roles in the narrative, to be sure, but prostitutes and tax collectors are as much tropes as were little David and aged Sarah, if now standing in for Samaritans and members of other despised groups. The disciples, too, stand in for later doubters or faithful followers. The individual has irreducible worth in the Bible, we might then say, but not precisely in her concrete individuality.

Social, economic, and religious changes come together in modernity to render the significance of the individual socially salient in a new way: increasing economic mobility, increasing division of labor, expanding scope for individual decisions. T. H. Green saw economic specialization as particularly important in making the novel's attention to ordinary life a potential subject of serious literature: "In the progressive division of labour, while we become more useful as citizens, we seem to lose our completeness as men. . . . The perfect organization of modern society removes the excitement of adventure and the occasion for independent effort. There is less of human interest to touch us within our calling."[16] The reverse side of this coin is that the lives of other ordinary people are unknown enough to us to render their description interesting. At the same time the drama shifts inward; it plays out in the subjective consciousness of the protagonist. Puritan and Pietist autobiographies had paved the way, for here too it is not the external action of the narrative but the inner emotional life of the character that is held up as significant. Pietist life-writing sought to discern the hand of God in the changing inflections of subjective experience, where these were taken to be infinitely varied rather than following some uniform pattern or course. But one might scrutinize this same experience for direction signs from one's authentic self, the core of one's being. Novels could and did incorporate documentary elements and thereby record the diverse occupations that keep a modern economy afloat. What the novel attended to peculiarly well, however, was not this but subjectivity, the experiential life of the individual as it unfolds in time. What is crucial to the novel is neither, then, simply the notion of the intrinsic worth of the human person nor the distinctiveness of various occupations. Rather, it is the notion of the individuality of subjective experience and of its significance. Pietism had ably prepared the way.

Popular Fiction and the Creation of a "Secular Scripture"

The theater was criticized for its masks and disguises, for the way it meddled with identity, and actors were seen as a disreputable social element.[17] But theater—or at least tragedy—had in any case a high and ancient pedigree to which its defenders could appeal. The same could not be said for the novel. The novel was for multiple reasons not a respectable literary genre. It was, after all, new, and novelty is rarely respectable. It broke with the conventions that governed established literary genres. Beyond this, it was able to come into being because of changing conditions for literary production. Literary patronage by courts and nobility was on the decline, while publishers and booksellers were on the rise. This made it easier for works to be published which did not conform to established critical standards—but only if a market existed for them. Thus a new freedom from traditional literary conventions coincided with dependence on the expanding reading public, which in concrete terms meant dependence on the dictates of the market.[18]

What did the eighteenth-century reading public want? Easy reading that was entertaining and informative—and novels fit the bill.[19] Novels were easy to read because of their minute transcription of experience in its temporal and spatial details; readers did not need to master complex literary conventions, possess specialized knowledge, or have good memories.[20] Somewhat counterintuitively, the materiality of the novel, its many words on paper, the pages to be turned, the volume to be held, could rather easily become transparent to the reader. Readers could vividly imagine and strongly identify with the characters of a novel. "The mechanically produced and therefore identical letters set with absolute uniformity on the page are, of course, much more impersonal than any manuscript, but at the same time they can be read much more automatically: ceasing to be conscious of the printed page before our eyes we surrender ourselves entirely to the world of illusion which the printed novel describes."[21]

Novels' capacity to entertain also derived from the powerful illusion of reality they created. In particular, novels allowed unparalleled access to the inner lives of their characters and thus a more intense identification with them.[22] Novels were informative, finally, because, as already noted, they gave insight into the lives of other ordinary people, lives that differed enough from one's own to be stimulating.

If novels were popular because they were easy to read and created powerful illusions and strong identification, these characteristics were also reason for concern. Many bemoaned what they took to be a general decline in literary standards. Oliver Goldsmith, in "The Distresses of a Hired Writer" (1761), spoke with regret of "that fatal revolution whereby writing is converted to a mechanic trade; and booksellers, instead of the great, become the patrons and paymasters of men of genius."[23] This meant that "men of genius" were being assessed by those lacking any qualification to do so. It also followed that writers themselves could be successful without possessing any degree of genius; they need only ape some already popular piece of literature. "The sagacious Bookseller," wrote James Ralph in *The Case of Authors* (1758), "feels the Pulse of the Times, and according to the stroke, prescribes not to cure, but flatter the disease."[24] In particular, novels fed escapism—the monotonous drudgery of daily life could be traded for gratifying fantasy. Samuel Richardson criticized the popular romances of his day on these grounds, failing to see that the same objection could be raised against his own *Pamela*; "his narrative skill was actually being used to re-create the pseudo-realism of the daydream, to give an air of authenticity to a triumph against all obstacles and contrary to every expectation."[25] The novelist was free from inherited critical principles and therefore free to innovate aesthetically—but this freedom brought with it the danger of becoming enslaved to the market of popular taste.

The situation in Germany was somewhat different from that in England. The novel had come to Germany from the British Isles, with *Robinson Crusoe* (1719) often regarded as its earliest exemplar. Germany at the time was oriented toward England, and to a lesser extent France, for both philosophical and literary models. This was important in defining the German novel for two reasons. First, it meant that the earliest novels in Germany were in part an expression of a general intellectual inferiority complex, an attempt to catch up with the leading nations of the world.[26] It was almost inevitable that artistic creation would be caught up in nationalistic impulses, by the desire to create not just literature in the German language but a distinctively German literature that could display German greatness. Second, though, it meant that German novelists could observe the pitfalls that had attended the rise of the popular book market in England and attempt to avoid these.

Karl Phillip Moritz, articulating in 1785 his influential statement of aesthetic autonomy, argued that the masses are incapable of disinterested pleasure in the autonomous artwork; they consume literature, art, and music as diversions, for the sake of the sensations these arouse. Therefore lack of public appreciation is no sign of artistic failure. The misunderstood, alienated artist becomes for Moritz the rule rather than the exception. It is perhaps not surprising that Moritz himself felt misunderstood and alienated. He managed to survive in the literary marketplace, but he did so by churning out pages, recycling material, and more generally compromising his own aesthetic sensibilities. When he attempted, as with his essay on aesthetics, to focus on quality rather than on what would sell, his works were not well received by the public, even if they were granted recognition by cultural elites. While it would be a mistake to conclude that his aesthetic theory is discredited because of the circumstances of its origin, the irony of the fact that Moritz's theory of aesthetic disinterestedness is not itself disinterested has not gone unnoticed.[27] The notion of aesthetic autonomy was conceived in resistance to the pressures of the literary marketplace. The category of art (*Kunst*), which united sculpture, painting, music, and literature, had up to that point included the works of the *Dichter*, or poet, but not those of the *Schriftsteller*, or writer. The *Schriftsteller* was understood as a craftsman who pumped out fiction to feed the insatiable appetite of the public. The *Dichter*, on Moritz's account, served not the public but art itself.[28]

As one scholar notes, "Moritz, Kant, Goethe, and Schiller favored self-contained works that rewarded repeated study, neither intoxicating the readers with sensory stimuli, nor browbeating them with moral lessons."[29] Goethe and Schiller aspired not simply to write popular fiction but literary works of lasting significance, works that would merit the kind of intensive attention—in the form of reading, rereading, and internalization—that scripture and devotional literature had received from the Pietists. They sought to create a kind of "secular scripture," texts that would serve the high purposes of the formation of humanity.[30] The only way to genuinely serve the public, thought Goethe and Schiller, was *by way of* serving art.

Goethe coined the term *Weltliteratur* (world literature) in 1827. He did so in service of a cosmopolitan vision of Bildung: "Everywhere one hears and reads of the progress of the human race, arising out of a broadening view of the world and human relationships. . . . I am persuaded that a common world literature is forming [*es bilde sich*], in which an honorable role is reserved for us Germans" (WA 41.2, 265). The end of this *Weltliteratur* is not German power or glory; it is the progress of humankind. And yet one can contribute to this goal by way of collective creations, by way of a national literature. Cultural rootedness, pride in particularity, are here seen not as competing with, but as contributing to, the task of the formation of humanity. Goethe's theory of translation embodied recognition of the demands of cultural difference, mandating a deep encounter with the language and culture one is translating, and the recognition that translation alters and extends the language into which a text is translated; translation is itself a form of cultural encounter and thereby an extension of humanity.[31]

If Goethe early on worried that the lack of German political unity might pose a barrier to literary excellence, he came in the course of the 1790s to think that political division specially situated German writers to contribute to the formation of humanity.[32] His later concern was over the threat posed by the very success of print capitalism; popularity spelled homogenization and undermined formative potential. For if embodied in the very genre of the novel is the notion that a novel could potentially be written about anyone, it did not of course follow that every novel was worth reading, let alone that every novel was worth rereading. Goethe and Schiller certainly wanted to write fiction capable of engaging the expanding reading public. Only if they succeeded could their works have the kind of broad and lasting political impact to which they aspired. The task as they saw it was to engage the expanding bourgeoisie in reading practices that would transform them from passive audience into active social and political agents, capable of taking charge of their own lives.[33] And the danger was that the masses were so enslaved to their proclivities that they were effectively insulated from the transformative possibilities of art.

In the context of earlier humanist education, theater had been used as a key tool for moral education. The assumption there had been that the enactment of exemplary characters could serve in the cultivation of the virtues. Theater could form students to be effective public leaders by effectively presenting themselves *as* leaders. The emphasis then, was on public self-presentation.[34] The novel, and the spiritual autobiographies that paved the way, shifted the focus to authentic self-understanding and self-development. But could the novel form the backbone of a new literature of formation, taking the place not just of scripture as it had come to be imbibed by Pietists but also of the humanist canon of the Latin schools that remained unchanged until the middle of the eighteenth century? Part of the challenge here lay in the fact that, as already noted, the reading public had not just expanded but also undergone a significant transformation. As Engelsing writes, the ordinary reader now sought "what fit him, that in which he could recognize himself (in however arbitrary a fashion), with which he could establish himself in his environment or have some influence on that environment."[35] As Habermas comments, "the relations between author, work, and public changed. They became intimate mutual relationships between privatized individuals who were psychologically interested in what was 'human,' in self-knowledge, and in empathy."[36] This went hand in hand with a new understanding of society as composed of essentially equal individuals capable of engaging with one another in a symmetrical fashion.[37]

In some respects the transformation was a gradual one—devotional classics like Arndt's *Wahres Christentum* were edged out by devotional poetry and fiction (Klopstock, Gellert), not by more daringly worldly works of fiction.[38] But the attitude even to these new devotional works, however conventionally pious, changed, in that those who read Klopstock, for instance, did so not because he was a received authority but because they felt that his works spoke to them personally. And pious novels like Gellert's *Schwedische Gräfin* prepared the ground for the reception of more worldly novels.

The Pietists, as we saw in chapter 2, found it necessary to read a vast array of spiritual autobiographies in order to find resonances with the particular features of their own experience. Readers of fiction, similarly, now took up a book in the hope of finding something that could speak personally to them, to their idiosyncratic predilections and sympathies. No longer did they seek the reinforcement of a familiar model or ideal. If they sought a canon, it was a canon as idiosyncratically defined by George Steiner, rather than what is normally called a literary canon (and dubbed by Steiner a "syllabus"). While a syllabus, on Steiner's account, embodies a cultural consensus concerning not only aesthetic but also political and economic values, a "canon" is "a profoundly personal construct" that is "the guarded catalogue of that in speech, music, and art which houses inside us, which is irrevocably familiar to our homecomings."[39] Steiner argues, moreover, that while arguments over respective excellence are at home in the realm of the syllabus, they are out of place when it comes to one's canon: "No man or woman need justify his personal anthology, his canonic welcomes. Love does not argue its necessities." Steiner does not locate his distinction between syllabus and canon historically, but it is one that begs for historicization. While it is in all likelihood always the case that some works, some passages, some notes resonate more fully with some readers than others, and thus that even in the presence of a tight "syllabus" that is intensively read, a kind of personal canon is created, this is something that comes to consciousness, and is validated, only in the mid-eighteenth century.

Of course no authors are more canonical (in the traditional sense) to the German literary tradition today than Goethe and Schiller, and Schiller in particular achieved renown through more traditional genres, poetry and drama. While Schiller experimented with the novel, Goethe embraced it wholeheartedly. The canonization of these two literary figures occurred in tandem with a concerted effort in the late nineteenth century to carve out a distinctively German identity for a nation united by language but not by a history of political unity, colonial exploits, or military greatness. Transfigured in support of German nationalism, their works lost their potential to assist dialogically in catalyzing the formation of humanity. Long before the texts of Schiller and Goethe came to serve as cultural syllabus, however, they resonated with the yearning for a personal canon, with its powerful and deeply personal identification.

Given its precarious standing as a new and somewhat disreputable genre, the novel was a particularly unlikely candidate for the status of "secular scripture." But as we have seen, what was sought was also something distinctively new, to go hand in hand with new understandings of individuality.[40] Each individual was seen as "an independent figure equipped with original spontaneity," with his or her own capacities and predilections, which had to be honored if development was to be authentic. Authentic moral development could not involve the stamping out of personal identity by social expectations and the universal moral law, and yet just this was the nagging worry.[41] How, in the face of conflicting drives and inclinations within, could the essential—the authentic—be distinguished from the dross, and a coherent whole be created? And how, in the face of the demand to subordinate inclination and serve the common good, could selfhood be honored? This was in some sense the age-old task of cultivating a virtuous character, but now transformed by a new sense that no ideal of virtue, no moral law, could simply be received from without; it could be embraced only if it spoke to, or emerged from, something deeply personal within. Pietist autobiography had created a form of literature scrutinizing subjective experience and centering on the spiritual development of an ordinary individual.[42] Following this model, the novel was seen as an ideal fictional arena for delving into subjectivity, he inner life of individual feeling, emotion, and reflection, and for tracing the gradual development of a character worthy of being claimed as one's own. Like Pietist autobiographies, early German novels focused on the interplay between the inner development and the social context of a single individual. But where Pietist autobiographies sought to trace the hand of God in the inner history of the individual, displaying how idiosyncratic individuality at the same time displayed the grace-filled hand of God, the script of the novel was not conversion but Bildung.

The autobiography of Johann Heinrich Jung-Stilling (1740–1817) is a particularly fascinating example of mutual influence. Jung-Stilling was a Pietist who rose from the lower middle class to become a physician and university professor. In the course of his studies he became personally acquainted with both Herder and Goethe, and it was Goethe who urged him to write his spiritual autobiography, publishing the first part without the author's knowledge in 1777. Further parts were published in 1778, 1789, 1804, and 1816/17, and the whole has a claim to being the most well-known Pietist autobiography, probably because of its association with Goethe. Jung-Stilling named the fifth part *Heinrich Stilling's Lehrjahre* (apprenticeship) in a deliberate reference to Goethe's *Wilhelm Meisters Lehrjahre*.[43]

Jung-Stilling sets out to show that his entire life has been guided by the hand of Providence.[44] His constant striving is to give himself utterly over to divine direction; he consistently stresses that one's own will has no rights before God's plan.[45] In the face of critiques from other Pietists suspicious of his successful career and his embrace of worldly learning, Jung-Stilling seeks to justify his rise in the world, together with all the myriad intimate details of his life, as providentially determined.[46] Hence utter resignation to God's will and agency issues in energetic activity in the world, constantly accompanied by spiritual exegesis of his inner life for evidence of God's leading: "the mortification of the self reveals itself as a hidden self-elevation, when Stilling interprets himself as the chosen instrument of God."[47] His apprenticeship is not the simple unfolding of an inner nature; God must remake human nature. Jung-Stilling must be molded, formed, made pliable to God the potter, in order to be a site for the realization of God's will.[48]

The fact that Jung-Stilling could see himself (aided and abetted by Goethe) as successfully reappropriating Goethe's Bildungsroman in service of an increasingly worldly Pietism shows just how much the secular literary innovations of the novel owed to the tradition of spiritual autobiography in general, and to Pietist scrutiny of spiritual psychology in particular.[49] For Goethe and his protagonists, however, the certainty of God's guiding hand has melted away, as we shall see, leaving in its place a bootstrapping tongue-in-cheek mythology indifferently evoking entelechy, Fate, and Providence.

Theorizing the Bildungsroman

Even the earliest critical reflection on the novel in Germany, which in turn shaped the authorship of subsequent novels, unequivocally supported this new literary form as tool for Bildung. Friedrich von Blanckenburg's *Versuch über den Roman* (1774; Essay on the novel) broke critical ground in defending the novel, despite the continuing sway of theater, as the exemplary narrative form for the modern era.[50] And the clear task of the novel, on his account, is to portray the development and formation (*die Ausbildung, die Formung*) of the hero's character; its preoccupation is with the hero's inner history, not outer plot development.[51] As Rolf Selbmann notes, "Blanckenburg was basically describing a form of the novel that did not yet exist."[52] He was able to appeal, alongside Henry Fielding's *Tom Jones* and the novels of Samuel Richardson, only to a single German example, Wieland's *Story of Agathon*, which was published in 1766/67; Goethe's *Wilhelm Meister's Ap-*

prenticeship, the novel most often cited as exemplifying the Bildungsroman par excellence, appeared only in 1795/96.

Although he did not employ the term *Bildungsroman*, Blanckenburg's conception of the novel as such is largely continuous with later definitions of the subgenre. The term itself was coined in 1803 by Karl Morgenstern, a professor of rhetoric and aesthetics, and further developed by him in a series of lectures and articles over the next several decades.[53] (Goethe himself never used the term, whether to describe his own fiction or that of others.) Consciously building on Blanckenburg's theory of the novel, Morgenstern defined the Bildungsroman as a novel that "depicts the development [*Bildung*] of the hero as this begins, continues, and reaches a certain level of perfection."[54]

For a long time Morgenstern's contribution was forgotten, and the invention of the term was attributed to Wilhelm Dilthey, who in his 1870 biography of Schleiermacher proposes it as a category for German novels in the "school of Wilhelm Meister."[55] Thematically, Dilthey understood the Bildungsroman as depicting the process by which an individual achieves both inner integration and harmony with society; it shows how a young man "enters onto life's stage, searches for soulmates, encounters friendship and love, how he enters into conflict with the hard realities of the world and so matures in the course of varied life experiences, finds himself and becomes certain of his task in the world."[56] This followed a line of interpretation established as early as 1796, when Christian Gottfried Körner wrote in a letter to Schiller that what we encounter in *Wilhelm Meister* is the "depiction of a beautiful human nature that gradually forms itself through the interaction of its inner capacities and outer relationships. The goal of this process of formation [*Ausbildung*] is a perfected equilibrium."[57] Dilthey's definition set the tone during the crucial period of the canonization of German literature in imperial Germany (1871–1918): Goethe and Schiller lay at the heart of the literary canon that defined Germanness and thus demanded the creation of a German nation, and the Bildungsroman was regarded as the characteristically German genre of the novel, expressing quintessentially German depth and inwardness.[58] So understood, the genre of the Bildungsroman was easily exploited by the politically conservative cultural elites that dominated following the failure of the democratic movements of 1848; personal cultivation rather than political action should preoccupy the greatest talents of the age. Not surprisingly, then, German authors with progressive aspirations arrayed themselves against the Bildungsroman, giving rise to a phenomenon that has been dubbed the Anti-Bildungsroman.[59] This tradition continued well into the twentieth century. Thomas Mann's *Doktor Faustus*, for instance, was written both as an Anti-Bildungsroman and as a critique of National Socialism; Mann saw the genre, and the ideal of Bildung it enshrined, as a compensation for the public's lack of access to political power and argued that it assisted the rise of Fascism.[60]

In recent decades, however, scholars have begun to question the fit between even the most canonical examples of Bildungsroman and the theoretical construct. In one would-be Bildungsroman after another, it has been shown, the protagonist in fact fails to arrive at integrated maturity and fails to reconcile individual gifts and proclivities with surrounding social circumstances.[61] Rather than achieving self-confidence, much less harmonious autonomy, the main characters end up alienated, despairing, or at best merely resigned. Even Wilhelm Meister himself, as we shall see in the next chapter, hardly seems to display anything like exemplary self-formation; he is quite passive in the face of the Masonic-like Tower Society that has orchestrated his life from backstage, and contemporary interpreters detect a tone of irony in Goethe's novel that was overlooked in the Imperial period.[62] Schiller argued that it was a mistake to focus too exclusively on the character of Wilhelm Meister; more important was his function within the whole constellation of energies in the novel: "everything takes place on and around him, but not actually because of him, because the things around him depict and express these energies, while he expresses malleability [*Bildsamkeit*]."[63]

Some, then, have dismissed the genre altogether. The term can continue to be useful, however, even if the inadequacy of the traditional definition is conceded.[64] The Bildungsroman is not best understood as a genre defined solely by its formal features which then turns out to have been instantiated only or best by German novels. Rather, it is a tradition or lineage of novels, the later exemplars of which establish their membership by referring intertextually to earlier novels, most particularly to *Wilhelm Meister* but also to Wieland's *Agathon* as the earliest claimant to the title. Moreover, like *Wilhelm Meister* and *Agathon*, these novels establish their identity in that they "have something to do with *Bildung*, that is, with the early bourgeois, humanistic concept of the shaping of the individual self from its innate potentialities through acculturation and social experience to the threshold of maturity."[65]

What are we then to make of the fact that even the most exemplary Bildungsroman hardly seems to depict the successful achievement of Bildung? One might go so far as to regard the Bildungsroman as depicting the *difficulties* standing in the way, the *obstacles* to achieving a harmony between individual potentialities and social realities.[66] The Bildungsroman, so understood, problematizes any easy solution to these challenges. This, of course, renders the category of Anti-Bildungsroman superfluous, since every Bildungsroman is then in some sense also an anti-Bildungsroman. On such an account, any novel that depicts a successful course of Bildung would seem to be liable to being dismissed as mere popular literature; "the great texts sustain the dialectic of practical social reality on the one hand and the complex inwardness of the individual on the other, whereas the minor writers tend (to borrow D. H. Lawrence's term) to put their thumb in the scales, to load the issue either in favor of the hero's cherished inwardness or in favor of the practical accommodation to society."[67] It is only the lesser texts that conform to the late eighteenth- and early nineteenth-century characterizations of the genre by portraying the successful Bildung of the protagonist. In the great texts, either no clear resolution is forthcoming, or it is undermined by irony. In Wieland's *Geschichte des Agathon*, for instance, the fictional editor of Agathon's manuscript notes that he is providing the original manuscript's happy ending, but at the same time the editor ironizes this ending by questioning how plausible it is.[68]

An approach that champions negativity and absence of closure embodies modernist assumptions foreign to the time of the early Bildungsroman. We can, though, go so far as to say that "it does not much matter whether the process of *Bildung* succeeds or fails, whether the protagonist achieves an accommodation with life and society or not."[69] For depictions of both successful and failed projects of self-definition can offer points of orientation for readers. And from the outset the depiction of Bildung within the novel was secondary to the aim of actually fostering the Bildung of the reader. Blanckenburg saw the two as straightforwardly linked: the novel, in depicting the Bildung of the protagonist, would also serve the Bildung of the reader: "The poet should form [*bilden*] the feelings of humanity" (435). Morgenstern, similarly, argued that precisely in depicting the formative development of the hero, the Bildungsroman "furthers the development [*Bildung*] of the reader to a greater extent than any other form of novel."⁷⁰ But the artists of the period saw the matter as more complex. Friedrich Schlegel, for instance, argued that Goethe's *Wilhelm Meister* novel was indeed aimed at forming (*bilden*) readers into able artists and competent human beings, but not that it did so by presenting Wilhelm's own development as exemplary.⁷¹ And recent scholarship, attentive to the ironic and fragmentary quality of texts such as *Wilhelm Meister*, *Geschichte des Agathon*, and Karl Philipp Moritz's *Anton Reiser*, have further emphasized the crucial role of reader reception. "Goethe and his Romantic contemporaries attempted to create a new type of reader by means of innovative and daring narrative strategies that challenge the reader to unlock the meaning of their poetic texts; this goal, not the simple telling of a story, constitutes the educative value of these novels."⁷² This makes perfect sense, given that Bildung was understood as not merely coming from the outside but as a process of self-development requiring the active engagement of the agent. The Bildung tradition sought to disrupt the notion that ethical formation could take place by way of either mere obedience to authoritative commands or imitation of authoritative models. The task of Bildung was the task of becoming human by becoming an authentic individual.

Once we grasp that membership in the Bildungsroman category is established less through any formal features than simply by the act of engaging, within the context of narrative fiction, with the task of Bildung, particularly by commenting intertextually on earlier examples of Bildungsroman, it becomes natural to treat the genre as a kind of metafiction—that is, as "fictional writing which self-consciously and systematically draws attention to its status as an artifact in order to pose questions about the relationship between fiction and reality."⁷³ The self-reflexive features of these novels, the fact that they often centrally deal with reading, writing, or competing literary genres such as theater, allow them to comment both on the "successive stages in the transformation of the German literary institution" and on the transformative power of literary art more generally.⁷⁴ Karl Philipp Moritz's title character Anton Reiser, for instance, alienated from his Pietist upbringing, becomes an avid consumer of contemporary fiction, through which he temporarily escapes the misery of his impoverished existence. Wilhelm Meister's youth, meanwhile, is governed by a passion for theater, through which he experiments with possible identities, commenting on the results by way of the reflective space afforded by the novel. The Bildungsroman thus provided a literary forum for reflecting on the significance for ethical formation of the shift from intensive reading of the Bible and devotional literature to extensive reading of popular novels, from public theatrical spectacles to private reading in the parlor, from literary patronage by the nobility to competition in the literary market, and from authoritative exemplars to personal authenticity.

What theorists of the Bildungsroman grasped is that a reader's imaginative encounter with the obstacles and inconclusiveness experienced by a fictional character could stimulate their own active engagement in the process of self-formation as much as if not more than the display of Bildung accomplished. What they failed to see is that formation of character through moral exemplars can never be, and has never been, a matter of mere imitation or conformity. It is not enough that an individual, whether fictional or actual, be held up as exemplary, officially endorsed by recognized authorities. A would-be exemplar has formative power only insofar as he or she evokes the emotional response of admiration.[75] If we admire someone or their actions, we regard them as exemplifying something good or beautiful. Admiration moves us, naturally evoking emulation, the desire to become like someone in relevant respects. Admiration powerfully focuses our attention on an exemplar as we seek to identify more precisely what it is about him or her that is admirable (and what is not). When we are moved to become like an exemplar, our attention is focused on acquired traits and dispositions rather than natural talents. We imagine ourselves in the image of the one we admire.[76] But this is a complex imaginative process, for each of us inhabits our own embodied particularity. If I am to emulate the courage and integrity of Stephen, the first Christian martyr, I cannot simply steel my resolve to receive the stones being hurled at me, for there are none. I must identify what it would mean to be relevantly like Stephen in my own context—how Stephen might respond to a domineering colleague, perhaps, or a friend whose off-color jokes one has finally recognized constitute harassment. In doing so, we construct narratives that weave together our own contexts with our projection of how our exemplar—and therefore our own ideal self—would respond, feel, and act in particular situations. Fictional narratives can play an important role in fostering the various steps of this process—by sketching potential exemplars in rich detail, displaying ways in which a would-be exemplar is or is not admirable, and exposing potential exemplars' patterns of perceiving, feeling, responding, and acting.

The Bildungsroman, then, was indeed suited to foster ethical formation. The task of forming authentic individuals was not, though, the dramatic departure from the past that theorists of the Bildungsroman tended to conceive it to be. Yes, society was more complex, with more highly differentiated social roles and more movement among them. But ethical formation had never been simply a matter of copying an authoritative model. Nor was it inherently paradoxical to provide a *model* for becoming *oneself*. Yet as the Bildungsroman was conceived as a dramatically new departure, tasked with modeling independence from models and an impossibly independent mode of self-realization, its theorists became preoccupied with its problematic status.

The fact that the Bildungsroman, as metafiction, repeatedly draws attention to its artefactual character undermines its realism. But formal realism is one of the generic strengths of the novel. Like perspectival painting, which depicts the world as it appears from one particular point, the novel, with its detailed account of the minutiae of experience, was capable of giving the reader the illusion not just of watching the unfolding events but of participating intimately in the inner lives of the characters. A typical feature of the Bildungsroman, though, was repeated disruption of this illusion. In some instances, as in Wieland's *Geschichte des Agathon*, this was the result of repeated authorial intrusions, particularly of an ironic sort. These jolted the reader out of the illusion of the novel. It also resulted from the fact that "the Bildungsroman too rarely operates with a precise sense of the moral integrity and otherness of the people with whom the protagonist comes into contact."[77] Characters other than the protagonist are not rendered fully; they are sketched only insofar as they come into contact with the protagonist. Friedrich Schlegel, in the first significant published review of *Wilhelm Meister*, hailed it as showing "how the Bildung of a striving spirit unfolds in silence, and how the development of the world rises quietly out from within."[78] It is not that these novels do not employ the same techniques used by other novelists to achieve the illusion of reality, but that these techniques are employed quite selectively. It is not surprising, then, that the Bildungsroman did not achieve the level of popularity achieved by the great nineteenth-century English novels, even though it was hailed as an expression of literary genius—and by the early twentieth century as capturing a particularly German spiritual and intellectual genius.[79] In fact, even today scholars continue to criticize the Bildungsroman as too difficult or too theoretical. Even though Bildungsroman authors sought to exploit the popularity of the novel, they were at the same time so suspicious of this popularity that they deliberately interfered with some of the features that fed it. These interferences make the Bildungsroman more challenging not because they require knowledge of elite literary conventions but because they stimulate reflection in the reader. Instead of offering readers an emotionally gripping, easy escape from the responsibilities of ordinary life, they make the reader aware of the act of reading, stimulate the reader to think about the relationship between fiction and reality, and lead the reader to reflect on her own response to the fiction.

The Bildungsroman, then, was an attempt to subvert the tendency of the popular literary market to feed rather than transform desire. It was an effort to create, within the genre of the novel, a form of literature that would demand intensive reading and rereading rather than extensive consumption, that would be canonical rather than disposable. The challenge was to do this in a way that could avoid becoming elitist. For the rise of the novel coincides with the emergence of a reading public broad enough to create a literary market. Thus with the novel literature becomes commodified; it falls under the sway of market forces. And as soon as the Bildungsroman became something appreciated and read only by cultural elites, its capacity to transform the broader reading public was undermined. It became a badge of cultural achievement, of the *Bildungsbürgertum*, not a force for broad social—and political—transformation.[80] This pitfall was keenly appreciated by authors of the Bildungsroman, yet it proved nearly impossible to avoid. Schiller's final letter on Aesthetic Education conceded that his ideal aesthetic state was for the time being confined to "some few chosen circles, where conduct is governed, not by some soulless imitation of the manners and morals of others, but by the aesthetic nature we have made our own."[81]

What these thinkers did not see was something that Hegel, as we shall see in chapter 7, seeks to articulate in his thesis that art loses formative power insofar as it attains cultural autonomy. Religious formation takes place through a complex web of mutually reinforcing social practices: prayer and worship, individual devotional reading, catechetical instruction, public proclamation of scripture in the gathered assembly of worshipers, liturgical enactments and sacramental actions, self-conscious and collectively reinforced efforts at "application," and so forth, all of these historically extended over millennia and thus accompanied by layers upon layers of interpretation and reinterpretation. Novels, in contrast, are generally read in private and only rarely become objects of collective reflection—as today in university classrooms or neighborhood book discussion groups. They powerfully draw readers into the imaginative worlds they create, but they lack well-developed structures for sustaining those worlds beyond the actual experience of reading, however intense it may be. This makes them easy prey for the forces of commodification. Perhaps because Pietism so emphasized personal religious experience, it was easy to overlook the fact that the formative power of scripture, devotional literature, and spiritual autobiography was in Pietism nevertheless still mediated by communal practices of Bible study, worship, and living out the love of Christ for neighbor. While Hegel grasped this and therefore underscored the ongoing importance of the "cultus" of Christianity, champions of *Kunstreligion* and the Bildungsroman adopted a Pietist psychology and vocabulary of experience without this web of social practices. They rightly worried that admiration is not always directed toward the truly admirable and that they were entering a form of society in which market forces would increasingly dictate what was seen as admirable and worthy of emulation. They fretted over the emerging cult of personality. But they were equally suspicious of authoritarian religious traditions that had sought tight control over models and demonized the creative imagination. They never quite found a way out. The greatness of Goethe's *Wilhelm Meister* lay in the ways in which he drew attention to both his character's and his theory's incompleteness and inadequacy, thereby gesturing beyond the limits of the imaginative worlds he created. It was in recognizing that he could *show* more than he could *tell* that Goethe best succeeded in writing a model Bildungsroman—as we shall see in the coming chapter.

Authorship and Its Resignation in Goethe's *Wilhelm Meister's Apprenticeship*   6

The transition from Pietist autobiography to the Bildungsroman might seem to be a natural and easy one. To be sure, these novels are written in the third rather than the first person, but they reveal the inner experience of a single protagonist and thus retain much of the feel of a first-person narrative. Moreover, Pietist confessions and conversion narratives might be written in either first or third person, with the latter following the established genre of saints' lives. Both Pietist life-writing and Bildungsroman dealt with the lives and experiences of ordinary people; both explored the nuances of subjective feeling—indeed in a letter to Herder Goethe referred to *Wilhelm Meister* as a "Pseudo-Konfession," a pseudo-confession.[1] But the discontinuities are nonetheless dramatic. For however attentive Pietist life-writing was to the subjective life of the individual, this attention was directed toward discerning in the midst of irreducible particularity and meaningless contingency a familiar pattern, of encountering in the depths of personal feeling and apparent coincidence the hand of God. Insofar as early German models took their point of departure from Pietist life-writing, they were governed by a distinctive problematic: How could one narrate the individual's course of Bildung in the absence of authoritative exemplars, a preestablished path of Bildung, a recognized endpoint for ethical formation? If we are not to be remade after the image of God in Christ, after whose image, then, and how can any form or norm that is *imposed* on the self become what the self truly *is*? If we are to form *ourselves*, in what relation does this self-forming stand to the circumstances in which we find ourselves, the relationships in which we stand, the experiences we undergo—

that is, to the ways in which we are formed prior to any forming we may be said ourselves to undertake?

For Goethe, the central challenge was finding a form or order for one's life that brings it into harmony with the natural and social worlds and that is not merely contingent, alien, or heteronomous but native to the self and so embraced freely.[2] He took some hints toward a solution from Pietism. By delving within, into the inner experience and feeling of the subject, one could hope to distinguish between what was native and what was adventitious to the self. The task, as Goethe conceived it, was not to discover the workings of a transcendent deity, but neither was it simply to discover one's unique authentic self. Rather, with an understanding of Bildung clearly indebted to Paracelsus's understanding of entelechy and filtered through "a Spinoza transposed into life-categories," Goethe hoped to discern an immanent teleology in nature.[3] There was, he believed, no deity external to the universe, guiding its workings or providentially watching over individual creatures. Rather, each organism had an immanent form and a drive to realize that form by way of successive phases of metamorphosis.[4] In so doing, that organism also contributed to the self-realization of the larger wholes of which it was a part, from the species up through the universe itself, also conceived of as a kind of organic entity. While there was in this sense a harmony between self-realization and the realization of the whole, this did not mean that the realization of immanent form was a process free of conflict and uncertainty; it required struggle against disorder, against inertia, and in particular instances there was no guarantee of success, no pre-established harmony.[5] Moreover, the development of human character could not simply be assimilated to the metamorphosis of plants, influential as his study of the latter was for Goethe's understanding of organic transformation.[6] For consciousness and agency transform this process: On the one hand, human moral agents form intentions and act for the sake of ends, they are not simply vessels for the unfolding of inbuilt tendencies.[7] On the other hand, neither can they transparently grasp and so actively realize their immanent form. Rather, they struggle through experience, through acting on the world and experiencing the consequences of their actions, through trying on various identities, through admiring and emulating others, grasping how they are perceived by others, and engaging and relating with others. Only in the course of this messy concrete experience, full of conflict and failure and confusion, do they move toward understanding of self, others, and the world.

Goethe clearly did not understand Bildung as something achieved through a straightforward self-assertion of the will. Nor did he regard the endpoint as self-sufficient autonomy. Nevertheless, the earliest reception of the novel helped to cement a distorted view of *Wilhelm Meister* and, subsequently, of popular conceptions of the Bildungsroman and of Bildung itself: Wilhelm was alternately praised for having successfully formed himself and arrived at a point of independent activity, on the one hand, or criticized for his passivity and therefore viewed as having failed at the task of Bildung. In one of the most influential statements about the novel, Schiller wrote that Wilhelm was stepping "from an empty and undefined ideal into a defined active life, but without losing his idealizing power in the process."[8] There is truth in this depiction of Wilhelm's movement from indeterminacy to determinacy, but it is important to add that Wilhelm himself is depicted throughout the novel less as active and self-assertive than as sensitive and responsive; in the rare moments in which he seeks to impose his life-plan on the world, his efforts consistently backfire. He sets out to become all things and learns that he must become something specific and therefore limited; he sets out to realize himself and learns that he must serve others; he sets out in adolescent rebellion against the life of commerce to which his father summons him, and learns that technical rationality is not simply to be dismissed in favor of dreamy ideals but to be placed in service of the common good. He learns, further, that the process of becoming himself is inherently social and relational, that he cannot narrate his own identity without the help of other narrators and narrations, and cannot meaningfully act without interacting with, and finally acting together with, other agents.

Goethe shared Humboldt and Schiller's sense that art had a critical role to play in reversing the emerging dominance of instrumental reason and restoring the possibility of integral personal and social fulfillment in harmony with nature. Among the various artistic genres, narrative fiction could best both display and foster the messy process of discerning—primarily through the experience of failure and conflict—one's given talents and capacities and how these could be realized in service to the common good, the realization of humanity.

To grasp the character of this process was also to see, however, that the artist's contribution could not be simply a matter of finding the right sensuous clothing for pregiven abstract ideas. Resisting Schiller's advice to make his philosophy of Bildung more explicit within the novel, Goethe sought instead to take a backseat to the immanent unfolding of the characters and circumstances he had set in motion. This suggests that Goethe grasped that his understanding of Bildung rendered his own role as author problematic. On the one hand, he clearly brought his understanding of immanent teleology and of organic Bildung to the task of writing. On the other hand, he shied away from taking on the role of an external Providence, determining the characters from without. Even if this is in some sense necessarily the place of the author of a novel, Goethe set a question mark over the author's authority to assume such a role. As we shall see, he thereby also set a question mark over the adequacy of his own theory of Bildung. The novel itself succeeds where the theory fails, however. It succeeds by way of its very refusal of tidy closure. In repudiating claims to final authority and remaining ever open to dialogical encounter, Goethe grasps that genuine Bildung requires resisting the temptation to self-authorizing human autarchy.

Fate in *Wilhelm Meister*

The plot of *Wilhelm Meister's Apprenticeship* is long and complex but can nevertheless be summed up briefly: Wilhelm, growing up in a bourgeois household where he is expected to follow his father into the life of commerce and thereby become a productive middle-class citizen, instead entertains aspirations of helping to cultivate a cultured public through the establishment of a German National Theater. Sent on a business trip, he falls in with a traveling theatrical troupe and indulges his acting fantasies, only to realize after some time that he has idealized the tawdry reality of theatrical life. Groping around for a sense of direction, Wilhelm discovers that a mysterious Tower Society has intervened at various stages of his journey to influence the course of events and offer him veiled guidance. When Wilhelm seeks direction, they retreat, yet when he attempts to act independently, he discovers that they have anticipated and outmaneuvered him. Via a series of dramatic reversals and unexpected revelations, the tale ends happily: Wilhelm is extricated from a misguided engagement to the capable but unimaginative Therese, becomes involved in the noble Lothario's enterprise of dismantling feudalism on his estates, and wins the heart and hand of the benevolent and aristocratic Natalie. But instead of settling down into some specific form of active life, he sets out on yet another journey, postponing marriage and settled adult life.

It is obvious that *Wilhelm Meister* places the ideal of a useful, productive business life in question. Like Schiller in the *Letters on Aesthetic Education*, Wilhelm Meister rebels against becoming a cog in a wheel or having his varied talents and capacities reduced to a means to profit, an end that itself is an empty means. To his friend Werner, whose end in life is to accumulate cash, he says, "You are treating form as though it were substance, and in all your adding up and balancing of accounts you usually ignore the true sum total of life."[9] Wilhelm resists doing what is socially expected of him, but he is much less clear about what he should do or become. Before leaving home, he experiments with writing fiction, but Werner points out that he never finishes the projects he undertakes. Even midway through the novel, having experienced firsthand the tawdry side of theatrical life and looking on bourgeois business life with new respect, he remains unsure which direction to go. He asks himself whether it was simply rebellion against bourgeois respectability that led him to the theater, or whether it was something higher and more worthy; he works to disentangle a sense of inner vocation from external occasion. He thus grapples with the question of what constitutes genuine self-determination. What distinguishes a whim from an authentic sense of inner vocation? What if a sense of calling turns out to be self-deceptive illusion? Or manipulation from without? Hanging in the balance, he wishes that some outer force would tip the scale, and in the next moment he hints at the thought that it already has. His most central need is to develop and form his inner predispositions to the good and beautiful, and the opportunity to do so, in the form of an offer to go on stage with the troupe he has been accompanying, has fallen into his lap. "Must I not respect the power of Fate for having, without any cooperation on my part, brought me to the goal of all I wish?"[10] What he most hoped for has happened by coincidence, without his having actively brought it about.

There is a certain irony when a character in a novel wonders aloud whether his or her development is being determined by some outer force, since of course the author providentially determines not only the inner capacities of all of the characters but also the outer circumstances in which these come to expression. But Goethe sharpens this point and thus induces the reader to reflect on agency in ethical formation, in a variety of ways.[11] Most dramatically, he embodies this external guiding hand in the form of the Tower Society. But he also uses an extended discussion of Hamlet in the novel's fourth and fifth books as an opportunity for meta-level reflection both on literary genre and on fate.

Different as their external circumstances are, Hamlet is in an important sense Wilhelm's double. He is, at least in Wilhelm's eyes, defined not by his action but by his sentiments; he is passive and is determined by Fate.[12] *Hamlet* is thus peculiar in uniting characteristics that Wilhelm associates respectively with the novel and with drama. The hero of a novel, he argues, is typically passive, he undergoes the action of the novel rather than acting, and in so doing his sentiments are revealed as they develop through the play of contingency. The hero of a drama, in contrast, is typically active, yet his action is governed, often tragically, by Fate.[13] Hamlet is passive and delves into his sentiments rather than acting, yet the course of events, as is typical in dramatic fiction, is determined by Fate. *Wilhelm Meister*, meanwhile, represents the same idiosyncratic combination of characteristics in novel form, for here too what appears to be mere coincidence turns out to be Fate—or at least the guiding hand of the Tower Society.

Wilhelm argues with conviction that *Hamlet* is a work of genius even if it refuses to deliver what the audience expects—a hero with a sharply defined character whose action is energetically directed at a particular goal. Here "the hero has no plan, but the play has" (HA 7:4.15, 254; E 151). Serlo, actor and manager of a quality standing theater that agrees to employ the vagabond actors, is not persuaded that Wilhelm has in fact succeeded in capturing the meaning of the play: "You don't much compliment providence by thus elevating the poet. You seem to be assigning to the glory of the poet what others attribute to providence, namely a purpose and a plan that he never thought of."[14] Heavily ironic as Serlo's comment is, it underscores an important point: that the poet, Goethe as much as Shakespeare, stands in for Providence in the artistic work—or, perhaps, on Goethe's view, offers the model on which the whole notion of Providence has been constructed; a hidden hand operating at a level outside the actual action of the plot, which nevertheless determines its course and outcome. Goethe thus deliberately disrupts the artistic illusion at which the novel can so excel — of suggesting how meaning and form emerge out of mere contingency and accident. Goethe rubs the reader's nose in the fact that an authorial mind stands behind this appearance of contingency, working to introduce characters and plot developments in a natural way and leading them to a satisfying conclusion.

Looking back on the novel thirty years after its publication, Goethe suggested that "the whole seems to want to say nothing other than that the human being, despite all stupidity and error, is led by a higher hand and does arrive finally at a happy end."[15] Yet this judgment is not left unproblematized, either. He clearly does not mean simply to assert that his authorial role as Providence was successfully achieved in the novel and that this summary statement reflects his intention for the work. For he several times calls *Wilhelm Meister* one of the most "incalculable" (*inkalkulabelsten*) productions, declaring himself almost unable to assess it.[16] Goethe seems thereby to identify himself with Wilhelm, who knows full well that he has not earned his good fortune and who can hardly believe that it is real. That is, Goethe himself seems to suggest that the novel was hardly mere putty in the hands of its creator and that it rather became something he had never quite intended. In calling it "incalculable" Goethe seems to confess that he, its author, cannot in any straightforward way be identified with the higher hand that led it to a happy end, even if by rights he ought to have been. In the midst of writing *Wilhelm Meister*, he communicates to Schiller, hardly sounding sovereign over his artistic production: "I have just held tight to my idea and will rejoice, if it leads me out of this labyrinth."[17] Reading the novel again in 1821, he finds it highly symbolic, speaking through the various characters of something more general and higher.[18]

Wilhelm himself is eager throughout the novel to attribute the course his life takes, whether of a happy or tragic cast, to Fate. He takes the fact that his first love, Mariane, is an actress as an indication that he is indeed destined for the theater: "Fate, he decided, was extending its helping hand to him, through Mariane, to draw him out of that stifling, draggle-tailed middle-class existence he had so long desired to escape."[19] When the reader becomes aware of the Tower Society, it seems natural to conclude that it has served as a natural substitute for Providence, working behind the scenes to influence Wilhelm's development, sending emissaries at various points who in "chance" encounters with Wilhelm slip him veiled bits of advice. It is therefore particularly significant that these mysterious strangers repeatedly take it upon themselves to warn Wilhelm against a passive faith in Providence. So, for instance, the stranger who meets him in the first book, and who turns out to know more about his family background than he himself, declares himself troubled to hear the word *fate* in the mouth of a young man who instead of using his reason and understanding to negotiate his own path in life, ascribes to pure accident a kind of reason "and accepts this religiously."[20] But when Wilhelm presses the stranger, asking whether he really denies that there is any power that reigns over us and directs everything to our benefit, the man refuses to be pinned down. What matters at the moment is not what he himself thinks but what is productive for Wilhelm's development: "Here it's just a question of which way of picturing it [*Vorstellungsart*] is for our best [*zu unserm Besten gereicht*]."[21] The phrase Goethe uses here, "zu unserem Besten gereicht," is commonly used in Pietist circles to speak specifically of the character of God's providential care of the individual. While the Tower Society is acting as Providence in Wilhelm's life, it can do so successfully only insofar as Wilhelm remains unaware of the society's machinations and takes responsibility for his own life.

The stranger Wilhelm meets in book 1 does not merely warn against a passive acceptance of Fate. In its stead he offers an understanding of how it is that human beings can "deserve to be called an earthly divinity": "The fabric of this world is formed out of necessity and chance. Human reason situates itself between the two and knows how to master them: it treats what is necessary as the ground of its existence; it knows how to direct, lead, and use what is contingent."[22]

In order to master necessity and chance in this way, one must of course properly distinguish them; but this is just the problem: how to do so? The necessary lies both within and without, in both subjective and objective forms—in the natural laws of matter and motion, of course, but more importantly for the purposes of this novel, in the subjective necessity of one's inner being. The individual's central talents and capacities are regarded as given, constituting a kind of law for that person, constraining his or her possibilities. To attempt to become someone else, to realize a form of life alien to oneself, is an enterprise bound to be frustrated. But it is also a mistake to confuse contingency with necessity—that is, to take some passing impulse as an expression of one's deepest being, or some external constraint as unalterable. Wilhelm is repeatedly depicted as confusing these; he rightly senses that he has an inner need to help others but thinks that he must accomplish this through the theater. Or again, at some level he senses his need for Natalie, but he wrongly assumes that their union is an impossibility.

How successful is the society in its efforts to assist Wilhelm? The whole idea of the Tower Society is bound to be resented by most contemporary readers as an alien, even far-fetched element. Within its own historical context, however, it was no more an artificial intrusion than the voice given to Pietism in the person of the Beautiful Soul. The Freemasons and other secret societies enjoyed a considerable vogue in the closing decades of the eighteenth century, as one expression of the effort to construct a kind of transnational brotherhood and a naturalistic substitute for inherited religious traditions. Indeed Goethe plays throughout the novel with some of the conceits of Masonry, centrally with the very idea of Wilhelm Meister's "apprenticeship," following the Masonic degrees of initiation from apprentice to journeyman to master. Within *Wilhelm Meister*, however, the society is more than this; it is a way of grappling with the role that external guiding forces or authorities can take when the very notions of external providence and external authority are problematized in favor of organic, internal teleology. On the one hand, Goethe uses the society as a mouthpiece for his own philosophy of ethical formation. On the other hand, he treats the aociety and its efforts with a light irony that invites the reader to further test and probe that philosophy rather than simply taking it as authoritative.

The Tower Society and Its Limits

It seems excessive to term the society's interventions "bumbling," as one critic would have it, but it is certainly the case that the society, however it seeks to employ the props of transcendence, remains thoroughly human and fallible.[23] It becomes clear, for instance, that the Abbé, the doctor, and Jarno, the three leading lights of the Tower Society, are not of one mind when it comes to the best means by which to further Wilhelm's development.[24] Nor is Natalie, though perhaps the most unqualifiedly successful "product" of the society's efforts, uncritical of the approach they have taken; certainly she does not herself emulate it, and she hints that the Abbé's own ideas may have undergone some transformation over time.[25]

The Abbé is obviously the leader of the *Turmgesellschaft*, and it is thus his educational philosophy, Rousseauian in inspiration, that holds the greatest sway. The key to education, in his mind, is identifying an individual's central inborn talents and creating an environment in which these can flourish. While he concedes that following one's instincts and drives can lead into error, he insists that learning through one's own blunders is often the best path toward grasping the way of life that is truly appropriate to one's own nature.[26] The task of the educator is thus to work behind the scenes to manipulate external circumstances in a productive way so that nature can take its course; not attempting directly to change or even mold the individual's actions or character. Whereas the Pietist must discern God's hand in her life, Rousseau's educator can remain backstage. In this way individuals will quickly grasp the natural consequences of their actions and learn from their successes as well as failures how best to realize their inner drives within the world. "In order to promote a child's education [*Erziehung des Menschen*], one must first find out where its desires and inclinations lie, and then enable it to satisfy those desires and further those inclinations as quickly as possible. If someone has chosen a wrong path, he can correct this before it is too late, and once he has found what suits him, stick to this firmly and develop [*fortbilde*] more vigorously."[27]

Natalie admits that she personally has no complaint to lodge against the Abbé's philosophy of education, since she considers herself to have been well guided by it. But she recognizes that the results are rather questionable in the case of her sister, the somewhat frivolous Countess, and her younger brother Friedrich, who seems incapable of taking anything in earnest (HA 7:8.3, 521). Within her own sphere of influence, among the peasants she takes under her wing, Natalie proceeds very differently from the Abbé. As her basic impulse is to respond immediately to every need she sees, she is not capable of watching from behind the scenes as someone goes astray. She insists on articulating clear rules and impressing (*einschärfen*) them upon the children in her care, to give their lives a certain support or security (*Halt*). She claims no infallible authority to discern these rules or laws; her point is the rather more skeptical one that "it is better to err because of principles than to do so from arbitrariness of nature, and my observation of human beings tells me that there is always some gap in their natures which can only be filled by a principle expressly communicated to them."[28] She sees in the idiosyncratic individual not a native law that must be discovered by delving within, but a gap that must be filled in order to give life a steady direction. Jarno, meanwhile, confesses that he can't stand to watch people err, and so he has often argued with the Abbé over how best to foster Wilhelm's development, with the Abbé insisting that Wilhelm has to learn from his own errors and Jarno wanting to confront him with the blunt truth in order to save him from wasting his energies on aspirations doomed to fail.[29] And in fact Jarno acts accordingly on occasion, telling Wilhelm bluntly that he is not cut out to be an actor and will never transform society through the theater. It is also Jarno who reveals the conflicts within the society and who describes how they have evolved over the years. So the Abbé's philosophy does not go unquestioned. The Abbé's approach clearly is nevertheless ascendant. Both Jarno and Natalie describe their own differences from that approach as stemming from their own peculiar personalities, and in various ways acknowledge the authority of the Abbé, Jarno by calling himself a very bad teacher (*Lehrmeister*) who has contributed the least to the society and to humankind, and Natalie by praising the Abbé's tolerance of her own approach. But the novel does not offer any reconciliation of these tensions—by, for instance, suggesting that Natalie's approach is appropriate for young children or that Jarno's brisk honesty simply serves to underscore lessons already learned from experience.

Not only are there conflicts within the Tower Society that impede it from acting in a fully coordinated way; it is also clearly hampered by its lack of omniscience. When Jarno arrives to announce the good news that the seemingly unsurmountable obstacles to a match between Therese and Lothario have been cleared away, as Therese is not in fact the daughter of a woman with whom Lothario had a passing affair, he is shocked to discover that Wilhelm has in the meantime become engaged to the wonderfully able but prosaic Therese. The society apparently neither anticipated nor knew of this turn of events.[30] Even Jarno, despite the warnings he has delivered against relying on Fate, can now do little more than offer high-sounding words that ring empty in Wilhelm's ears and hope for the best: "It is not our fault that we got ourselves into this muddle.... Let us hope that good fortune will get us out of it."[31]

The Tower Society is humanized in a third way in that it is portrayed as itself a work in progress, continually reinventing itself, in process of development even as it seeks to influence the development of individuals under its survey. It employs some of the ritual trappings of speculative Freemasonry; at the key moment when the Tower Society decides to reveal itself to Wilhelm, it does so by summoning him to a ritual up in the tower of Lothario's castle, a space rendered mysterious and unfamiliar through the presence of darkness, tapestries, a cloth-covered table "instead of an altar," and figures who appear suddenly from behind curtains, speak, and again disappear. Clearly there is a deliberate attempt here to draw on the power of religious ritual to construct a sense of an alternate, deeper reality alongside ordinary mundane experience. It is in this context that Wilhelm is informed, "You are saved, and on the way to your goal," and presented with his certificate of completed apprenticeship.[32] Yet a few pages later Jarno pokes fun at the ritual: "Everything you saw in the tower was the relics of a youthful enterprise that most initiates first took very seriously but will probably now just smile at."[33]

Wilhelm is aghast: "So they are just playing games with those portentous words and signs? . . . We are ceremoniously conducted to a place that inspires awe, we witness miraculous apparitions, are given scrolls containing mysterious, grandiose aphorisms which we barely understand, are told we have been apprentices and are now free—and are none the wiser."[34]

Jarno makes an effort to defend the practices, at least as props for the young, who "have an unusually strong hankering after mysteries, ceremonies and grandiloquence"; a young person wants "to feel, albeit dimly and indefinitely, that his whole being is affected and involved."[35] Jarno's own unusual passion for knowledge and clarity almost derailed the entire enterprise; aware now of the excesses of his own prosaic bent, he still regards disenchantment as salutary, even if he recognizes that it is destructive for most if it comes too soon. Wilhelm, meanwhile, is offended at having been subjected to yet another level of patronizing manipulation, although he certainly does want to feel that his whole being is affected and involved in discerning his path forward in life.

Much as Wilhelm has wished at various points in his journey that Fate would make his path clear, when it is revealed to him that the Tower Society has been working behind the scenes on the project of his formation, he suffers under the knowledge. He feels himself to have been robbed of his independent agency, and his engagement to Therese issues out of his determination to initiate an act that is genuinely his own.[36] When the result of this act is a mess from which he sees no way of extricating himself, Wilhelm is close to despair; he resents the thought that he has been manipulated by the society but can only hope in desperation that they have some way of helping him out of the fix in which he finds himself. He is particularly aggrieved that they have already declared his apprenticeship over; he is now officially a "Meister" but has no clue what to do with himself.[37] By refraining from idealizing the Tower Society, Goethe refuses to offer a kind of closure that would falsify the genuine problematic of Bildung—the ordinary human being is not a fictional character created by an author and does not have a Tower Society looking over her shoulder. How is she to distinguish between the necessary and the contingent and so discover the inner laws according to which she can authentically live? It is not enough to be able to articulate this as a general principle. Hence Wilhelm's anger when, in the midst of his anguish over his engagement to Therese and his painfully suppressed love for Natalie, Jarno reads to him from his *Lehrbrief*, instructing him that "a person who has great potentiality for development will in due course acquire knowledge of himself and the world."[38] This pronouncement further confuses Wilhelm; despairing equally over himself and over the prospect of help from the society, he is on the brink of trying to lose himself in aimless travel when he discovers that Natalie loves him and that Therese has secretly made his engagement with Natalie the condition of her own engagement with Lothario. The novel thus offers a happy ending, but without implying either that the society is sovereign or that Wilhelm has arrived at mature self-confidence; Wilhelm is just as dumbfounded as before. He never seems to realize the ideal laid down by the mysterious stranger in book 1, for he is never shown as sovereign in his employment of reason, situating himself confidently between chance and necessity. His general attitude throughout and his final words in the novel seem rather to instantiate the attitude roundly chastised by the stranger: "We imagine [*bilden uns ein*] we are God-fearing people [*fromm*, pious] if we saunter through life without much thought, we let ourselves be carried along by happy chance, and then finally declare that our wavering existence was a life governed by divine guidance."[39]

Wilhelm's Theatrical Apprenticeship

This is not to say that Wilhelm has learned nothing about himself or has made no progress in his task of self-formation. By the end of the novel he has given up his dream of elevating humankind through the theater. He has discovered that he has a son, Felix, and has accepted responsibility for raising him. He has declared himself willing to collaborate with Lothario by managing an estate in a way that will promote freedom and equality. And he has discovered the importance of finding a mother for Felix who can at the same time be his genuine soulmate. Thus there is much to be said for interpretations that read Wilhelm's Bildung as having been successfully accomplished by the end of the novel:

> Wilhelm's superficially wayward and inconsequential history of errors and perplexities figures as the inevitably complex and apparently untidy process of clarification and expression of the immanent form of his unique personality, and of the concrete possibilities of bringing that personality into fruitful engagement with the outer world available to him. What we follow in all its sometimes tortuous detail is the working-out through experience of just what is necessary and just what is contingent in Wilhelm's initially given selfhood and in the given world in which he finds himself.[40]

The genius of the novel is that it displays this process of gradual self-realization and reconciliation with reality, but without offering the kind of closure that would falsify the ongoing existential challenge facing both Wilhelm and the reader.

What does Wilhelm learn by way of his lengthy detour through the world of theater? To some extent, the dominance of this theme reflects the earliest form of the novel, in which Goethe envisioned that Wilhelm's theatrical ambitions would be realized. Goethe worked on the novel from 1777 to 1785, and it reflected his own involvement in the Weimar court theater and the hopes of many of the time to transform society by establishing National Theaters throughout Germany. The notion of a "National Theater," while reflecting the ideal of a national literature rooted in the special character of the German language, was not quite what the name indicates. These were theaters, the first of which was established in Hamburg in 1767, that performed plays in German, but many of the plays were translated from French and Italian, as there was not an adequate supply of original German material. The idea was that court-subsidized theaters would raise theater to cultural respectability, improve the lives of actors by giving them a steady income and taking them off the road, and by relieving these economic pressures also release the inherent power of theater to form sounder, more elevated public taste.[41] In a 1784 lecture to the German Society at Mannheim, Schiller expressed the aspirations of the day: "The stage is the channel, open to all, into which the light of wisdom pours down from the superior, thinking part of the people, to spread from there in milder beams through the whole state. More correct ideas, sounder principles, purer feelings flow from here through all the veins of the people. The mists of barbarism, of dark superstition vanish, night gives way to victorious light."[42] When Goethe picked up work on *Wilhelm Meister* nearly a decade later, he retained but extensively reworked the material from the original sketch in *Wilhelm Meister's Theatrical Mission*, which now helps to make up the first five books of *Wilhelm Meister's Apprenticeship*. Thus Wilhelm's involvement with theater remains a strong element in the novel, even if its significance for the whole is transformed; it becomes, as for Anton Reiser, an avenue more for self-realization than for public transformation.

In childhood, Wilhelm is entranced by the puppet theater. He first encounters it as something transcendent and mysteriously powerful, and uncovering its secrets and learning himself how to bring the puppets to life gives him a sense of divine power: echoing Genesis 1, he relates how, "[his] imagination brooding over that little world," he played with the puppets.[43] Together with this sense of creative power comes an experience of self-discovery as he imagines himself in a colorful panoply of roles; he memorizes all of the parts in the puppet comedy of David and Goliath, though most often he casts himself as the young hero.[44]

Later, leaving behind the puppets, Wilhelm indulges the wish to inhabit these roles bodily and animates his friends to put on amateur theatricals, in which they acquire a certain facility of expression; self-discovery is paired with self-cultivation.[45] Already at this point of his youthful development, he identifies a deep tension between the world of commerce and the world of theater, which he personifies in a poem written at the age of fourteen; commerce is an old housewife, always busy and scolding, while the muse of tragic poetry is a beautiful goddess, daughter of freedom—"her sense of herself gave her dignity without pride."[46] His infatuation with Mariane is deeply intertwined with his theatrical aspirations; in her presence all of his childhood dreams are revived and strengthened, and in the unbounded confidence of first love he imagines himself as already the creator of a future National Theater (HA 7:1.10, 35; E 17). All of this is treated with droll irony: Wilhelm's imagination is stronger than his persistence, and most of his theatrical projects remain mere fragments: he creates a set and costumes for *Das befreite Jerusalem* but forgets to teach his cast their lines; he begins to write dramas, but only isolated scenes. All of this gives the reader not just a sense of the typical characteristics of childhood but a glimpse into Wilhelm's character: imaginative, eager, enthusiastic, but with an energy that is not channeled in a clear, focused direction.

As we have already seen, through his involvement first with Melina's traveling troupe and then with Serlo's standing theater, Wilhelm is by book 5 well on the way to becoming an accomplished and well-received actor. In the meantime his aspirations seem to have shifted slightly or become clarified. As he writes to Werner, rejecting his friend's offer to improve and manage a newly acquired estate, "Even as a youth I had the vague desire and intention to develop [*auszubilden*] myself fully, myself as I am."[47] Now the means have become more evident. A focus on personal formation and cultivation ("eine ... allgemeine ... personelle Ausbildung") is possible only for the nobility; the middle classes are expected to be useful.[48] No one asks who he is but only what he has; his capacities, insights, and knowledge are means to external ends, not organic components of a personal whole. Irresistibly drawn to the kind of harmonious development (*Ausbildung*) of his nature denied to him by class, Wilhelm finds it possible only in the world of theater.

This ideal of harmonious personal development has often been lifted out of its book 5 context as a clear statement of Goethe's own conception of Bildung. Certainly it echoes Schiller's complaints about the mechanical, instrumentalized character of bourgeois existence and his vision of aesthetic education as therapy. But it has also rightly been noted that this ideal, as grasped and expressed by Wilhelm at this point, still betrays his own naiveté and a certain superficiality. For

Wilhelm dwells on particulars such as the nobleman's "formal grace" and "relaxed elegance," his sonorous voice and measured manner.[49] He himself has made progress in self-cultivation by devoting himself to physical exercise and overcoming his physical awkwardness, to training his voice and speech, so as to become presentable as a public person.[50] Such preoccupations with external appearances are placed incongruously side by side with Wilhelm's expectation that life in the theater will enable him finally to take as good only what truly is good and find beautiful only what truly is beautiful.[51] "We can only understand the emphasis [Goethe] makes Wilhelm lay on these externals and Wilhelm's extraordinary expectation that as an actor he will, though a mere '*Bürger*,' find in displaying himself on the stage a similar satisfaction in his own all-round development, if we take Goethe's attitude toward his hero as ironical, here as in so many other places."[52] Wilhelm has long since come face to face with the faults and foibles of actors, and in book 3 his first encounter with actual nobility (in the form of a count who invites the troupe to stay in his mansion and prepare a performance for his guests) has also made painfully clear that hereditary aristocracy does not necessarily bring with it either good taste or genuine cultivation. Nevertheless, at this particular crossroads, the point at which his father's death has freed him from parental expectations, and at which both the commercial possibilities represented by Werner and the theatrical life offered to him by Serlo lie equally open, Wilhelm opts for the theater.

It is only in book 7 that these dreams finally appear to him as illusions. Jarno, as usual, makes fun of Wilhelm's enterprise: "How is it now with that old fancy of yours of achieving something good and beautiful in the company of gypsies."[53] This time Wilhelm responds savagely. Actors are full of themselves. Each wants to be the one and only, and doesn't see that even as a band they can achieve very little. They expect to receive the utmost respect from others and cannot bear with the slightest fault in their fellows. They are self-deceived and utterly lack self-understanding. Jarno, overcome with laughter, for once takes the part of the actors. Wilhelm has offered a wonderful account of human nature itself, and these qualities are amply displayed by every social class. "I would gladly excuse an actor for any fault that arose from self-deception and a desire to please, for if he does not appear as something to himself and others, he is nothing at all. His job is to provide appearances [*Schein*], and he must needs set high store on instantaneous approval, for he gets none other. He must try to delude and dazzle, for that's what he's there for."[54] But the same is not to be said of human beings as such: "I can readily forgive an actor all the human failings, but not humans for an actor's failings." Hard-nosed realism must not become an excuse for moral failing; off stage, Jarno's words imply, *Sein*, being, precedes *Schein*, shining appearances. Self-deception and egoism must be replaced by a genuine self-knowledge that allows also for genuine respect and concern for others.

The play here on *Sein* and *Schein* has been introduced earlier, back in Wilhelm's book 5 letter to Werner, defending his decision to opt for the theatrical life. Here *Schein* is seen as a special attribute of the nobility that the middle classes can cultivate only on stage. "A nobleman can and must be someone who represents by his appearance [*scheinen*], whereas the burgher simply is [*sein*], and when he tries to put on an appearance [literally 'to appear'], the effect is ludicrous or in bad taste. The nobleman should act and achieve, the burgher must labor and create, developing some of his capabilities in order to be useful."[55] Wilhelm here connects the right to shine, to cultivate an impressive appearance, with the opportunity to achieve a fully developed personality.

By book 7 he has learned to be more suspicious of outer appearances. They still appear to be revealing, as when Werner appears and marvels over the change in Wilhelm's appearance: he now looks positively noble. The changes seem to extend even to physical characteristics: "Your eyes are more deep set, your forehead is broader, your nose is more delicate and your mouth is much more pleasant."[56] Werner, in contrast, has become skinny and bald and round-shouldered, his voice shrill, his face pale. We hear echoes here of Lavater's influential theory of physiognomy (1775), according to which physical features expressed specific character traits. But it is telling that it is Werner who draws attention to these features and who sees them as significant. Even here, his focus is on the economic significance of these external characteristics, their instrumental rather than intrinsic meaning. "With your figure you should be able to get me a rich heiress.[57] Wilhelm has acquired the shining appearance he longed for, but he now more clearly sees that it is not this that guarantees the capacity to find beauty and goodness only in the truly beautiful and good, any more than membership in the hereditary nobility guarantees the possession of true virtue.

Narrating Bildung

If acting offers Wilhelm the opportunity to cultivate the external appearance of nobility, life-writing—his own and others'—represents a pathway to a fuller form of self-discovery and development. The actor imaginatively inhabits a variety of roles, at least to the extent of being able to offer an external appearance (*Schein*) commensurate with audience expectations. But the task of narrating one's biography is explored as a personally demanding one, a site of painful honesty and genuine discovery, and encountering the life stories of others is no less significant and revelatory. The multiplicity of narratives testifies to the uniqueness of the individual and to the absence of a single authoritative life narrative, a single exemplar of the fully human.

Wilhelm's impulse to narrate his development appears very early in the novel, as springing from his desire to reveal himself fully to his new love.[58] The flaw in his relationship with Mariane, its asymmetrical character, is revealed in her failure to reciprocate; she knows him—his naive confidence that a childhood obsession with puppetry will lead naturally through an affair with an actress to the founding of a new National Theater—but he does not know her, and most centrally does not know that she is engaged to another. Variations on this theme recur throughout the novel. So, for instance, Serlo's sister Aurelie relates her story to Wilhelm, confiding in him her anguish over losing Lothario's love, but Wilhelm soon discovers that though her story is genuine, it does not give him adequate grounds for assessing Lothario's character.[59] Each life story has its own integrity; knowing one does not give the audience the right to judge another. Therese, too, opens her soul to Wilhelm almost as soon as they meet, and he experiences her as the embodiment of trust and clarity.[60] By this point, though, Wilhelm has lost confidence in the narrative coherence of his own life. When Therese, picking up the thread of her story partway through, suggests that it is hardly fair that he has said next to nothing about himself to someone who has already revealed herself so fully to him, he replies, "Unfortunately . . . I have nothing to relate except one mistake after another, one false step after the other, and I cannot think of anybody I would rather not tell about the constant confusion I was and still am in, than you."[61] He is sure that her life has contained no wrong turns, no uncertainties, no lost time, but she assures him this is not the case.

In fact, it is in good measure through the recognition that others have had dark and winding paths to follow that Wilhelm regains confidence in his ability to persevere in the search for his own narrative coherence. It is not through the provision of an authoritative narrative form or set of stages, nor a flawless exemplar, that Wilhelm is able to proceed. The very thought of such an exemplary biography had destroyed his confidence; now he takes comfort in the thought that others have been able to forge intelligible form out of experiences of failure and suffering.

Biographical narratives that are read rather than personally related also play an important role in *Wilhelm Meister*, most notably the *Confessions of a Beautiful Soul* (*Bekenntnisse einer Schönen Seele*), which makes up the whole of book 6. Like the narrations offered by Wilhelm, Aurelie, and Therese, this one plays an instrumental role within the novel, revealing background information crucial to making sense of the unfolding plot. The "Beautiful Soul" is an aunt of Lothario, Natalie, the Countess, and Friedrich, and her story gives the reader a crucial glimpse into their upbringing and thereby into the philosophy of the Abbé, who oversaw their ethical formation. But the *Bekenntnisse* is much more than this. The inclusion of a fictional Pietist autobiography within his novel gave Goethe a way of drawing attention to the deep connections between these two genres, in their shared attention to shades of inner feeling and focus on personal development. The framing of the *Bekenntnisse* subjects it to critique, but Goethe does not succumb to the temptation to simply parody a stereotypical Pietist conversion narrative. We have to do with a decidedly individualized character, one with an aspiration to transcendence that does not sit comfortably within any received categories. The Beautiful Soul tries to fit her experience within the "system of achieving conversion advocated by the pietist theologians at Halle," but to no avail; where they demand an overwhelming sense of guilt and separation from God, she feels herself constantly in God's comforting presence.[62] She begins to be drawn into the circle led by Zinzendorf in Herrnhut, but here, too, after a brief period of feeling that she has found true spiritual community, she becomes somewhat alienated from the other brethren, noting "how few of them understood the real meaning of delicate words and phrases."[63] In her pursuit of undisturbed communion with God, she withdraws more and more from social contact and breaks off her engagement. From her cultivated, skeptical uncle (who is friends with the Abbé and thus closely linked to the Tower Society) she comes to appreciate the beauty of art to both express and speak to what is highest and best in the human soul. Through his emphasis on the importance of cultivating mind (*Geist*) and taste (*Sinnlichkeit*) in tandem with one another, she comes to feel that some of the little images (*Bildchen*) she has employed have been inadequate to express divine beauty and transcendence.[64] She never gives up her basic conviction that our attention should be directed not to creatures but to their Creator, and feels herself, in her separation from the world and focus on her inner life, to be following an inner drive given her by God and leading her to God.

The immediate significance of the *Confessions* is that reading it, rather inexplicably, allows Aurelie to die peacefully and forgive Lothario for having abandoned her. What makes this particularly intriguing is that Aurelie has not been depicted as a religiously inclined person at all, and moreover that the manuscript has been sent her by the doctor of the Tower Society. Within the *Confessions* this doctor is depicted as striving to correct the Beautiful Soul's tendency to retreat within herself and cultivate the life of the soul to the neglect of that of the body.[65] His refrain is one that we also hear from the Abbé— that the purpose of human life is to be active, and to become familiar with all the outer things of the world that might prove to helpful for carrying out this activity. *Tätigkeit*, activity, is a key word in Wilhelm Meister; it can mean simply job, occupation, or work, but as used here it carries some of the connotations of vocation. It is a form of activity that is genuinely fitting for and expressive of the individual, not an inherited trade or social role, nor a mere means of subsistence or route to profit. For the task of Bildung is to achieve the harmonious integration of all of one's faculties even while devoting oneself to some specific field of activity.[66] The Beautiful Soul does not contradict the doctor and indeed offers a partial echo of his teaching: "Only through our practical activity [*Praktische*] do we become fully aware of our own individual existence," she notes; "and why shouldn't we by this means demonstrate also to ourselves that there is a Being who gives us this power to do good."[67] Her own distinctively nonpractical activity, though, is directed at inward purification, and through this toward God. The doctor's recognition of the at least partial legitimacy of her distinctive *Tätigkeit* comes in the form not of words but of deeds, and shows that she can indeed do good in the world even if her intention is to transcend it: he sends the manuscript to Aurelie, signifying that the life narrative of the Beautiful Soul can assist others to die well, if not to live.

Among the significant life narratives of Wilhelm Meister we must finally of course also include the scrolls Wilhelm is shown in the Tower, containing the *Lehrjahre*, literally the years of apprenticeship (but also termed at one point the confessions, *Konfessionen*, of Lothario, Jarno, himself, and many others unknown to him). While the reader is never allowed to read any of these, Wilhelm is authorized to do so once his apprenticeship is declared complete.[68] He does not actually read his own scroll until after he resolves to ask Therese to marry him. He must now, he knows, finally reciprocate her self-revelation to him. In setting out to tell his story, however, he is quickly at a loss, for "it seemed so totally lacking in events of any significance, and anything he would have to report was so little to his advantage that more than once he was tempted to give up the whole idea."[69] It is at this point that he reads the Tower scroll account of his apprenticeship years, drawing on it in order to present himself to Therese, reciprocating her honesty if not, he reflects, her great virtue and purposeful activity (*zweckmässige Tätigkeit*).

Why does Wilhelm need to read his scroll in order to narrate his life story? What does he learn from the scroll? It offers him a kind of a mirror, a reflection of himself that pulls various events and experiences into a meaningful shape, tracing errors and failures as sources of insight and development, and discerning a direction in what Wilhelm has often experienced merely as confusing change. The suggestion that Wilhelm's relationship with himself is mediated through his relationships with others and through both their life narratives and his own surfaces repeatedly throughout the novel. "How unwilling we are, after we have been sick, to look at ourselves in a mirror!" (HA 7:8.1, 505; E 309). But in this case Wilhelm has been adequately prepared for the shock and is no longer suffering from delusions of grandeur. He is able to read his scroll with gratitude that others have lavished sustained attention on him, on discerning his individual character and path of development: "he saw for the first time his image [*Bild*] outside of himself, to be sure not, as in a mirror, a second self, but rather as in a portrait, an other self: one recognizes oneself to be sure not in every detail, but one rejoices, that a thinking soul has grasped us this way, a great talent has wanted to portray us this way, that an image of that which we were still exists, and that it can endure longer than we ourselves."[70] He does not give the narrative absolute authority to define him, but he regards it as an aid to self-definition. Even if the narrative does not offer him a second self, it does help him clarify his identity just by virtue of what in it he recognizes and what he does not.

The Social Character of Bildung

It is not only his own scroll that offers Wilhelm a *Bild* against which to define himself. In some sense, all of his relationships, not only with his father and his son but also with his friends and mentors and lovers, offer him "other selves," images next to which his own can come into better focus, against which he can take his own measure. The painting of the sick prince is a reflection of Wilhelm that links him to his grandfather and the latter's sense of the significance of artistic creativity. Or again, trying to convince himself that Felix is indeed his son, he lifts him in front of a mirror and searches for external resemblances. Mariane's old maid advises him: "Observe his talents, personality and abilities, and if you don't gradually come to see yourself in him, then you must have bad eyesight."[71] These other selves are significant despite the fact, or perhaps better in part *because* of the fact, that each person and each life narrative is unique and irreducibly personal. So the task of Bildung cannot be carried out in isolation from others. As Wilhelm's *Lehrbrief* informs him, "words [including therefore the speech of which this *Lehrbrief* consists, and the conversation that he is having with the Abbé, and of course finally also the words of which *Wilhelm Meister* itself is constituted!] are good, but they are not the best. The best is not made clear by words."[72] In our search for and our desire to realize in ourselves the best, we must attend to others. This is not an easy task, for "imitation is natural to us all, but what to imitate is not easily ascertained."[73] In part this is because there is much that we encounter that is not worth imitating; in part also because we cannot imitate all of the goodness that we recognize but only that to which our own individual capacities are suited. We also have trouble properly perceiving others well. At first Natalie is for Wilhelm simply "the Amazon." He knows only that she has acted the part of the good Samaritan, has stopped to care for him and his friends when she discovers that he and the troupe of actors have been set upon by highwaymen. When in book 8 Wilhelm finally meets her again as the sister of Therese and Lothario, he struggles to assimilate the image (*Bild*) of the Amazon with that of his new friend Natalie; "the former had been fashioned, as it were, by him, the latter seemed almost to be refashioning him."[74] The images we construct of others serve our fantasies; when we instead attend to them as they truly are, their form has the power to re-form us. They chasten any temptation to autarchy and remind us of the intrinsically dialogical character of our own humanity. Goethe applies this idea to himself as well. Writing in gratitude to Schiller for his enthusiastic reception of the first books of *Wilhelm Meister*, which have given him renewed determination to finish the novel with dispatch, he exclaims, "How much more advantageous it is to contemplate [*bespiegeln*, i.e., mirror] oneself in others as in oneself!"[75]

Not only the process but also the telos of Bildung turns out to be intrinsically social in character. As the conclusion of the novel makes clear, Wilhelm can be said to have finished his apprenticeship only because he has overcome the egocentric tendencies that seem to be built into the aspiration to self-formation. As he formulates this drive in book 5, it seems to concern merely himself. Yet what ends up being worth cultivating in himself is his concern for others—for Mignon and the Harper, for Felix, for Lothario's plans for dismantling feudalism, for Natalie and her charitable enterprises.[76] Jarno suggests that this is a natural transition: "When a man makes his first entry into the world, it is good that he have a high opinion of himself, believes he can acquire many excellent qualities, and therefore endeavors to do everything; but when his development [*Bildung*] has reached a certain stage, it is advantageous for him to lose himself in a larger whole, learn to live for others, and forget himself in dutiful activity for others. Only then will he come to know himself."[77] Jarno becomes a mouthpiece for the words of the Gospels: Wilhelm must lose his life in order to find it again.

Wilhelm learns this most evidently in his care for Felix. His desire to guide and form Felix awakens in him a new interest in the world around him. Immediately after he is assured in the Tower that Felix is indeed his son, the two go out into the garden. It is in some sense clearly a new Eden, but Wilhelm cannot, like Adam, simply name the plants whatever he likes; in order to satisfy his son's curiosity he must turn to the gardener. Wilhelm shoulders the task of passing on to Felix a socially mediated reality he must first receive from others. Human creativity is not ex nihilo. A recurrent theme in the novel has been Wilhelm's failure to attend to the external world, and this seems finally to be overcome. Even if the Tower Society has long since declared his apprenticeship over, this day seems to Wilhelm the first of his true Bildung; "he felt the need to inform himself, being required to inform another."[78] He now desires his own Bildung not for its own sake but in order to pass it along; he becomes capable of his own self-determination only insofar as he recognizes himself as a member of a chain of inheritance, expressed most fully in the bonds of family.

Friedrich's closing words are later echoed by Goethe as the interpretive key to the novel: "You seem to me like Saul, the son of Kish, who went in search of his father's asses, and found a kingdom."[79] Saul, son of Kish, went forth to search for his father's missing donkeys and instead was anointed by the prophet of Yahweh to be king of Israel. Wilhelm goes forth ostensibly on a commission from his father but in fact in flight from the bourgeois commercial life represented by his father and in some sense in search of his grandfather's lost art collection. He is reunited with that collection and thereby with the notion of art as revealing the creative capacities of human nature, but at the same time finds a way to place the commercial management of estates in service of higher humanistic ideals, thereby redeeming his paternal inheritance.[80] Even as on a personal level Wilhelm finds a way of marrying romantic passion with commitment and parental responsibility, he also takes on a broader social role of contributing to a transformation of society that will enable each member to be a meaningful participant.[81] As critics have noted, the political aspects of Wilhelm's vocation are underdeveloped and utopian in character, unsurprisingly so given the quagmire of German society at the time Goethe was writing.[82] The impulse to social and political reform is distinctly present, though, even if the form it takes is more utopian than realistic.

Bildung in *Wilhelm Meister* turns out to be social in one additional respect. For the individual, the telos of the process is the development of his or her particular capacities in a way that allows the individual to take a meaningful place in the world and be productive for others. But no individual constitutes a totality, is in him or herself the perfect human being.[83] Reading from Wilhelm's apprenticeship certificate, Jarno states that "all men make up mankind and all forces together make up the world."[84] All the various aptitudes and tendencies, "from the faintest active urge of the animal to the most highly developed activity of the mind, from the stammering delight of the child to the superlative expression of bards and orators, from the first scuffle of boys to those vast undertakings by which whole countries are defended or conquered," must be developed, but they can be developed only in the totality of humankind, not in a single individual.[85] There is a place for Therese's practicality as for Natalie's idealism, for Jarno's caustic honesty and the contrastive relief of Friedrich's lighthearted wit. The ideal of humanity can only be collectively, and indeed as we have just seen, only communally, realized. Wilhelm does not fall short of the ideal of Bildung inasmuch as he fails to become a Universal Man, but rather the inverse; he realizes that ideal, and with it the nobility that he initially sought through the theater, only insofar as he becomes a *particular* instantiation of the ideal of humanity.

Saul, Son of Kish

The understanding of Bildung captured in the *Lehrbrief* is essentially Goethe's own. Something from Goethe's understanding of plant metamorphosis is carried over here. This can be understood as an unfolding of inner principles, influenced and constrained by environmental conditions. Goethe had argued that this displayed a universal law of nature.[86] However, he recognized as well that no appeal to natural entelechy could give an adequate account of Bildung as the process by which a self-conscious moral agent is formed. Bildung is not a blind process of growth. As one of Goethe's most well-known maxims puts it, "aptitudes, to be sure, develop naturally, but they must be practiced intentionally and gradually improved."[87] Moral agency brings with it both creative power and responsibility. As the Uncle says, "within us there lies the formative power which creates what is to be, and never lets us rest until we have accomplished this in one way or another in or outside ourselves."[88] Bildung is not simply the realization of what in some sense already is but the bringing about of what ought to be; it requires the discernment of which tendencies and drives are to be nourished and which to be neglected.

The words of wisdom read to Wilhelm by Jarno from his *Lehrbrief*, however closely they echo Goethe's own philosophy, simply drive him to distraction. He has puzzled over them before, but they have not helped him with the concrete task of discernment that faces him: "Since that moment of liberation I know less than ever what I can do, or what I desire, or should do."[89] Yet all turns out well for Wilhelm. As we have seen, Fate smiles on him, as on Saul, son of Kish. Not because of own exertions, which are until very late in the game egocentric and in other key ways misdirected, not because of the skill of the Tower Society, but somehow nevertheless Wilhelm has won a prize far greater than the one he sought—not just love but a form of purposeful engagement with the world, a way not just of recognizing but also of realizing goodness and beauty through service to others, even if the concrete form this will take remains sketchy. The references to Fate are not intended to fit within a coherent metaphysics so much as simply to draw attention to the fact that things often turn out well quite apart from any conscious exertion of agency, understanding of the process one is undergoing, or the vision of the goal to which the process is directed. Goethe described his own experience in just such terms, as having been shaped "through many levels of trial, of acting and suffering" (HA 10:307). It is thus not surprising that *Wilhelm Meister* has been described as "fairy-tale like" and "a bit garden-like."[90] As one critic has pointed out, the narrator's optimism is possible only "because the decidedly evil is missing from the world of the *Lehrjahre*."[91]

Yet even if this somewhat naive optimism is present both in the novel and in Goethe itself, what saves *Wilhelm Meister* from mere shallowness and preserves its compelling nature is the fact that the novel at the same time itself signals the unsatisfactory character of this stance. It does so in several ways. One is by refusing to paper over the fact that Fate does not smile on all as it does on Wilhelm. It is not the case that all predispositions, when developed, can harmonize with one another, and *Wilhelm Meister* points to this when it shows how the Harper's incestuous passion, however "natural," bears fruit in Mignon, a child naturally, and tragically, destined to die. Nor has either the frivolous Countess or Friedhelm, though like Lothario and Natalie raised under the Abbé's supervision, found anything like a socially meaningful form of activity, *Tätigkeit*. Goethe recognized as much when he looked about himself; reading Moritz's *Anton Reiser*, for instance, he wrote to Frau von Stein, "He is like my younger brother, of the same nature, only that he was neglected and damaged by fate, where I was favored and preferred."[92] Perhaps even more telling than these various admissions is the irony that characterizes the book. It is the members of the Tower Society, divided among themselves and hardly infallible, and helped out of a tight spot at the end only by the flighty Friedrich, who are made the mouthpiece of Goethe's own philosophy. And the Bildung that is supposed to be Wilhelm's own accomplishment is handed to him on a silver platter, more despite than because of his efforts. As I have already noted, this irony undermines the authority of the Tower Society's wise-sounding pronouncements.

We may in fact have Schiller to thank for the passages in which Jarno reads to Wihlem from the *Lehrbrief*; at any rate, upon reading the draft of book 8, Schiller urged Goethe to make his philosophy more explicit, asking if Wilhelm does not perhaps himself need a bit of philosophical education: "If I could only clothe in your way of expression what I in my own way have said in the 'Kingdom of Shadows' and in the 'Aesthetic Letters,' then we would quickly be united."[93] The hints dropped here and there in the book are not sufficient, Schiller complains.[94] Goethe does not disagree with any of what Schiller has to say about Bildung, but he does resist making things too explicit: "The failing, which you rightly note, comes from my most inner nature, from a certain realistic tick."[95] He allows Jarno to read from the *Lehrbrief*, but he also gives Wilhelm a chance to express his resentment, his sense that these mysterious generalities don't really solve the riddle of his life.

The irony is no mistake; it is Goethe's way of insisting that the narrative form of the novel can do greater justice to the concrete particularities of the experience of ethical formation than can any theoretical statement, even one clothed in the sensuous flow of narrative. Beyond this, though, the irony is also Goethe's acknowledgment of the inadequacy of his own theoretical account of Bildung, of its lack of final authority, and of its inability to guarantee that individual self-realization will at the same time constitute the realization of social harmony and ethical ideal. Goethe's use of irony constitutes an aesthetic, but not a philosophical, solution to this problem.[96]

Goethe hints to Schiller that a more adequate response will require the continuation of the novel. But *Wilhelm Meisters Wanderjahre* is hardly a continuation, to say nothing of a fuller resolution of the aporias of the *Lehrjahre*. While the title character appears in both, the *Wanderjahre* is no longer focused on Bildung but is rather what has been termed an "archival novel," reflecting a commitment to representing in a single artwork disparate elements of contemporary life (including, in the *Wanderjahre*, a technical account of the cotton industry) accompanied by a lack of commitment to narrative unity.[97] Its subtitle, *Die Entsagenden* (The renunciants), refers to the forms of renunciation demanded by modern life. These extend into the realm of aesthetic possibility; the narrator is simply a fictional editor and the task of integration and assessment falls to the reader. If in *Wilhelm Meisters Lehrjahre* Goethe ironically shifted authorial responsibility to Fate, here he goes further, adopting a "poetics of renunciation."[98] Goethe resigns, then, the claim to authority, to being able to author a resolution to the problem of Bildung.

Wilhelm Meister as Secular Scripture

In offering a solution, but one framed ironically, meanwhile, *Wilhelm Meister's Lehrjahre* pointed both beyond itself and beyond its author. In so doing, we might say, it indeed succeeded in becoming secular scripture, not just in the sense of constituting a book worthy of something like the intensive reading practices of the Pietists but also in a sense articulated by Nicholas Boyle as revealing truths "about our shared condition" that transcend the author's own insights.[99] Boyle defines literature as "language free of instrumental purpose, . . . [which] seeks to tell the truth."[100] Literature thus contrasts with other forms of discourse that are straightforwardly utilitarian, aimed at describing things in ways that allow us to manipulate them and thereby fulfill our needs and desires. Secular literature, for Boyle, is distinguished from sacred literature in that its truth-telling feature is subordinated to another aim, that of giving pleasure or entertaining through the use of the written medium (as opposed to simply employing writing as a tool to instruct us how to satisfy our desires).[101] Nevertheless, secular literary works tell us truths about things, about life, about natural, personal, cultural entities, and this renders them potentially revelatory.

The distinction between secular and sacred literature thus has nothing to do with the distinction between fiction and nonfiction. Indeed the fictional character of some literature supports rather than undermines its capacity to be truthful. Where fiction dominates a work, "it hypothetically but systematically postulates the nonexistence of its author."[102] This is not, as it might appear, a falsification, which presents a fictionally constructed world as if it were real; rather, it makes fiction more able to tell the truth:

> In this set of truths, in this represented segment of the world we share, in these people and these their destinies, or, in the case of lyric poetry, in these now known and worded moments and moods and layerings of memory, there is revealed a truth, the truth, which only a text which is all but free of contamination by authorship can reveal: the truth that regardless of who, for example, Shakespeare or Dickens may have been or what they may have meant by, let us say, *Hamlet* or *Great Expectations*, there is life, and there is the wasting of it, and there is the fulfillment of it too—fulfillment gained or lost but always at least present in the redemptive assumption that it is all, however hurtful, or absurd, or even banal, worth putting into words for all of us to share.[103]

By virtue of the way they faithfully attend to the particulars of reality, works of secular literature can reveal truths that transcend the insights of their authors. We might think in this connection also of Martha Nussbaum's defense of the ethical significance of literature; she too regards literature's key contribution as coming by way of resisting reduction into a utilitarian mode of relating to the world, and she emphasizes the truthfulness of literature, which comes by its loving attention to the particular. Resisting any attempt to transcend the risks and constraints of finitude and mortality that, she argues, make us human, she nevertheless leaves room for "a certain sort of aspiration to transcend our ordinary humanity," rooted in the capacity to "soar above" the "dullness and obtuseness of the everyday," by "delving more deeply into oneself and one's humanity."[104] For Boyle this is a possibility that is grounded theologically in the Incarnation:

the Word has become Flesh; God's truth is to be looked for everywhere.[105] Secular literature, even when it is hostile to Christianity or religion as such, can not only convey universal truths but actually participate in the divine act of redeeming a fallen creation. For there is, he argues, a kind of redemption involved even in the mere act of faithful representation, for this requires attending to things as mattering. "An event of representation" is thus "an event of forgiveness, a participation" in God's re-creation of the world. Even when it is actively hostile to God or Christianity, this very "point of trespass" can be read as at the same time the point of forgiveness: God crucified by the world, and in this redeeming the world.[106]

Two points are worth noting here. First, literature's capacity to give pleasure is closely related to this act of redemption, since "you cannot enjoy everybody unless they matter to you as they matter to themselves and to each other."[107] The kind of truthfulness present in realistic fiction is a form of attention or, perhaps better, of love, of caring about others, and this loving vision is attended, insists Boyle, by a kind of enjoyment or appreciation. Second, there is an interesting, perhaps counterintuitive, relationship between particularity and universality expressed here; literature's capacity to convey universal truths does not stand in tension with its focus on particularity. Rather, it is its faithful representation of particularities of experience that enables the reader's identification, an identification that evokes awareness of a shared condition.

Bernd Auerochs has argued that *Kunstreligion* set out to take over the traditional responsibility of religion to articulate with authority final truth. "But works of art," he continues, "do not bring final truth to expression, but rather many different, individual obscure truths."[108] It was, though, precisely insofar as Goethe set aside *Kunstreligion*'s totalizing ambitions that he succeeded in writing what with Boyle we might term secular scripture.[109] It is in its unfailing insistence on the task of Bildung as it confronts the individual, together with its resignation of final authority to determine the path this will take, that the novel *Wilhelm Meister* most succeeds. It is not through successful self-realization or harmonious development as such that Wilhelm Meister finally completes his apprenticeship, but in his yearning, as he puts it in a letter to Werner, "to see good only in what is good, and beauty only in the truly beautiful," a yearning to be *for* the good with all that he has and all that he is.

An additional chapter would be required in order to spell out how this differs from the ideal of striving as depicted in Goethe's later dramatic masterpiece, *Faust*. Put briefly, the latter is no longer a striving to be for the *good*, to discern and embody the admirable, but a striving to find and follow one's deepest *impulse* and, having found no end to the depths, no *there* there, to dissolve into willing itself.[110] Whether this can still be intelligible *as* striving at all is the question posed poignantly by that work. In contrast, whatever Wilhelm's current grasp of the good, true, and beautiful, and of how he with his particular set of capacities and social circumstances can be for that good, he remains open to grasping it anew. He succeeds in becoming human insofar as he remains open to what lies beyond his selfhood as currently constituted, recognizing that whatever obscure truths he grasps, final truth lies beyond them.[111] Not only does the novel thereby rebuke the myth of domesticated Providence to which mainstream Pietism succumbed, but it finally refuses to substitute in its place Goethe's own theories of entelechy, metamorphosis, and art. It invokes, but places scare quotes around, Fate as well as Providence as well as ritual. It thereby embraces the kind of ontological indeterminacy that Charles Taylor regards as potentially open to reappropriation by those who inhabit the "immanent frame" of modern existence in an "open" rather than "closed" fashion.[112] More specifically, it opens the way to recovery of a noncontrastive understanding of divine transcendence, a transcendence that is beyond construal in terms either of identity or of simple contrast with anything within the created order, and with the created order as such.[113] (It is because she assumes that divine transcendence must be contrastive that Nussbaum rejects it; in so doing, however, she robs herself of resources for articulating the question of the authority with which literature can articulate truth.) In *Wilhelm Meister*, Goethe renounces the authority of Providential (self-)authorship while continuing to embrace the project of Bildung, grasping its telos as dialogical humanity. In so doing he repudiates autocratic humanism. In its place emerges a space for listening, for being called into question by the otherness of one's fellows, a space for what we might, with Barth, name listening for the Word of God.

"The *Bildung* of Self-Consciousness Itself towards Science": Hegel   7

As we have seen, Bildung, which for Herder was a matter of participating in a providentially ordered process of the differentiation and harmonious integration of natural and cultural worlds, became in the hands of Humboldt, Goethe, and Schiller a site of independent human self-forming activity. While these thinkers continued to regard Bildung as oriented to the realization of an ideal humanity, they no longer understood this in terms of the divine imago but rather as the overcoming of internal divisions and the reconciliation of opposing psychic forces. And while they considered social relations and political reform essential to this project, the Humboldtian tradition regarded these relational and political goods as instrumental to individual self-realization rather than as constitutive of the ends of Bildung. Humboldt held that political freedom must precede and create the conditions for the realization of Bildung; Schiller was convinced that the project of aesthetic education alone could secure lasting political freedom. Neither, though, followed Herder in grasping human beings as essentially social and political creatures (Goethe came closest to recapturing this vision, not in his theoretical writings but in *Wilhelm Meister*, where he enacted an attentiveness to particularity that enabled his work to transcend the limits of his theoretical statements).

If in this respect later theorists of Bildung parted ways with Herder, all were united in considering art to be critically important to the formation of humanity. For Herder, this had to do fundamentally with the way in which artistic representation gives us an opportunity to glimpse — or even participate in — God's creativity in and through the creativity of human artists. In Humboldt, Goethe, and Schiller, in contrast, art was prized as forming self-formers; *Kunstreligion*, they held, could displace inherited authoritarian forms of religion and foster the development of harmoniously integrated individuals, mature persons suited to a life of political freedom. Yet Goethe and Schiller worried that the very cultural changes that had led to an expanded reading public and allowed authors of secular literature to aspire to take over the formative role of scripture within Pietist circles would undermine the transformative potential of art; the commodification of literature would result in the use of art as means of escape and distraction from the burdens of self-realization. Instead of the Bildung of mature, self-forming and self-governing individuals, literature would create consumers.

Hegel steps decisively into this stream of reflection on Bildung. The novel cannot, he insists, resolve the divisions that beset the individual within modern bourgeois society, and art however broadly construed cannot bear the weight of the task of reconciliation. This does not mean that Hegel repudiates the Bildung tradition. Quite to the contrary: like Herder, but in an even more radical fashion, he understands the Bildung of individuals as intelligible only in light of the Bildung of humanity as such, and indeed of the cosmos itself. While eschewing Herder's optimistic Enlightenment providentialism, Hegel recovers even more fully the *exitus-reditus* scheme in which human beings, created in the image of God as principles of their own actions, play a role in the return of creation to God by accepting the divine invitation to friendship and thus by knowing and loving all creatures in relation to God. The end of this *reditus* is not absorption into the Neoplatonic One but reconciliation, freedom-in-community, harmony-in-diversity.

Kunstreligion, for Hegel, forfeits by virtue of its bid for cultural autonomy the formative capacity once held by art. Hegel returns instead to Christianity. Christianity, on his view, both pictures and enacts the truth of the Concept's self-expression of its own communal character into finite reality. The Concept's creative self-expression, generating ever-expanding networks of harmony-in-diversity, is fulfilled in the mutual recognition of self-realizing persons-in-community, who enact a reconciliatory *reditus* by grasping themselves and others as finite expressions of the Concept. Bildung, for Hegel, is not then a site of autonomous human agency, independent of divine forming and re-forming agency. Rather, in an echo of Boehme, God for Hegel becomes the primary *subject* of Bildung. Bildung is then the story of *divine* becoming, of the coming forth of finite spirit and its recognition of and reconciliation with divine self-giving goodness. For Hegel, unlike Boehme, evil is endured and overcome in the divine reconciling process; it is not divinely posited. It is the possibility and not the actuality of evil that is necessary. Yet in regarding the historical process as necessary to divine self-realization, Hegel does offer a sort of narrative legitimation of conflict and evil. To be sure, according to the *felix culpa* narrative woven through the Christian tradition, God allows evil, bringing out of it a greater good. More than this, God is not aloof but takes evil into the divine life in solidarity with finite spirit. Yet God for Hegel does not simply endure evil; rather, God is fully realized as God only through the historical process. It is *this* move, not Hegel's creative elaboration of the *exitus-reditus* trope, that must be refused by those who would carry on the task of forming humanity, extending ever-renewed gestures of reconciliation.

There is no uncontested interpretation of Hegel. As I understand him, Hegel learned from Kant's critical philosophy, but he was nevertheless engaged in metaphysics; we are not confined to articulating how things must necessarily appear to us but may talk about reality as such. Indeed Hegel reveals metaphysics to be unavoidable; attempts to avoid it fall into pragmatic self-contradiction. This does not, however, mean that metaphysical claims can claim infallibility; they are subject to the same criteria of assessment as any other form of inquiry. My interpretation thus aligns more closely with "revised metaphysical" than with "post-Kantian" interpretations of Hegel.

I will not begin, however, by rehearsing this debate. Given that Hegel is a highly systematic but also dialectical thinker, it is easy to misinterpret individual claims that he makes by failing to see how they fit into his larger argument—something Hegel affirms at one level may be critiqued as inadequate at a further stage of dialectical development, and vice versa. Yet if we begin by sketching Hegel's thought at the most abstract, general level, its relevance to the present project may remain quite opaque. I will therefore proceed by beginning at a very concrete point, which picks up naturally from the previous chapter—Hegel's critique of the modern novel as the apprenticeship of the individual on the resistant prose of the social order. From this point, I take a step back to consider the place of the novel within Hegel's understanding of the development of art and his critique of *Kunstreligion*. This will enable us to see why Hegel could not accept aesthetic education as adequate to the task of Bildung; religion and philosophy are crucial.

Having arrived at this point, we will be able to see why Hegel conceived of his *Phenomenology*, the orienting introduction to his philosophical system, in terms of Bildung. Indeed the *Phenomenology* has been aptly considered a Bildungsroman of the human spirit. Making sense of the *Phenomenology* as the introduction to Hegel's mature philosophical system then requires attention to Hegel's metaphysical project of reconciliation: Hegel sought to illuminate the Conceptual structure of reality, making it possible for consciousness to be at home in the world by finding it intelligible, an expression of reason. The *Phenomenology* itself traces not this path of reconciliation but rather that of failure; it prepares the way for Hegel's system by showing that alternatives to his dialectical metaphysics end in despair. Hegel's philosophical system proper then sets out to show the inadequacy of dualistic or oppositional thinking; universal and particular, subject and object, master and slave, must be understood as reciprocally related to one another. What consciousness makes possible is the articulation of these dialectical relationships, making explicit the "Concept" that animates them. Humankind thus finds itself entrusted with this task of reconciliation, while also discovering itself convicted of having abdicated responsibility for this task. Hegel finds that only theological "picture-thinking" is adequate to enabling us to come to terms both with this responsibility and with this failure. For we are freed to take up this task insofar as we discover ourselves forgiven and invited to participate in the infinitely reconciling life of God. Apart from this, the burden of forming humanity is too great. Hegel emerges not as conservative defender of the established social and political order but as summoning an active commitment to making the rational concretely actual. Where social and political institutions fall short, failing to enable reciprocal recognition and community-in-difference, reconciliation confronts us as task. And yet Hegel is also guilty of embracing a philosophy of history that excused evil—notably the evils of slavery and colonialism—as historically necessary moments in the realization of the Concept. That he did so has everything to do with the way history becomes for Hegel the site of divine self-realization.

Hegel and the Bildungsroman

Perceiving the socioeconomic conditions for the origin of the genre, Hegel dubbed the novel a "modern bourgeois epic." On his account, the novel assumes the task both of depicting and of resolving the "conflict between the poetry of the heart and the opposing prose of circumstances."[1] In contrast to chivalric romances with their emphasis on the accidents of fortune, the protagonist of the novel is confronted by a stable social order and established social institutions—police, courts of law, government, etc. "The heroes with their subjective ends of love, honor, ambition or with their idealistic hopes of bettering the world stand over against this standing order and prose of reality, which places obstacles in their way from all sides."[2] Rather than tilting at windmills, these newfangled knights fight against the substantial social realities of bourgeois society, which oppose themselves to "the ideal and the infinite rights of the heart." Although Hegel does not differentiate the Bildungsroman from the novel as such, Dilthey's later influential definition of the Bildungsroman is a remarkably close echo of Hegel—with one significant difference. Whereas Dilthey, as we saw in chapter 5, insisted that the Bildungsroman provided a *positive* model for a reconciliation of individual aptitudes and desires with practical social realities, Hegel's account is tinged with irony:

> These battles are in the modern world nothing but the apprenticeship [*Lehrjahre*], the training [*Erziehung*] of the individual on the reality at hand. . . . However much one has squabbled with the world or been shoved around by it, in the end he nevertheless usually gets his girl and some kind of job, gets married and becomes a Philistine just like the others; the wife takes care of the house, children are also not left out of the picture, the idolized woman, who at first was the one and only, an angel, acts like all the others, the office is a source of work and irritation, marriage becomes a cross, and the whole *Katzenjammer* of the rest is there.[3]

Given Hegel's use of the term *Lehrjahre*, his comments have understandably been seen as a jibe at Goethe's *Wilhelm Meister*. Some have tried to exonerate *Wilhelm Meister* of Hegel's criticism, or clear Hegel of the charge of having criticized Goethe, by arguing that Hegel's characterization applies much more fully not to the rather challenging novels usually considered to belong to the genre of Bildungsroman but to the popular romantic novels of his own day.[4] This is doubtless true. In fact, *Wilhelm Meister*, as we saw in chapter 6, itself pokes fun at this philistine form of reconciliation. Beyond this, though, we must grapple with the fact that Hegel seems here to parody a notion of reconciliation with prosaic reality that his own understanding of ethical formation and *Sittlichkeit*, concrete ethical life, has seemed to some to embody. What, then, are for Hegel the conditions for the genuine reconciliation of subject and world, poetry and prose? As we shall see, this turns out to be a driving question behind Hegel's philosophy as a whole.

The essential limitation of modern novels, in Hegel's view, is that they falsify the process of Bildung by offering a premature reconciliation, one that never fully comes to terms with the failures of subjective consciousness to arrive at harmony between its self-conception and the truth about itself. The novel sets up the conflict between the ideals of the modern individual, in all of her inwardness and desire for self-realization, and the existing institutions of bourgeois society, but in the end, suggests Hegel, the protagonist simply becomes resigned to society and its existing institutions—marriage, family, work—rather than achieving a genuine reconciliation with and through these institutions.

To this it is only fair to respond that that *Wilhelm Meister* itself, and the novels that followed in its wake, did not in fact depict an easy accommodation of the protagonist with his circumstances; the protagonist remains passive, or immature, or despairing. As we have seen, this phenomenon has been so striking that it has led critics to allege that there were no novels of aesthetic significance that met the expectations set out for the Bildungsroman.[5] However, this suggests that Goethe and the literary artists who followed in the tradition of the Bildungsroman themselves grasped that their novels could accomplish their task only by pointing to genuine Bildung, genuine reconciliation, as lying beyond themselves. As we saw in the last chapter, Goethe places his own philosophy of ethical formation in the mouth of the Abbé, leader of the Tower Society, and in the *Lehrbrief* delivered to Wilhelm. But he also ironizes the society and its efforts to coach Wilhelm toward autonomy. Faced with the task of becoming an active agent of his own formation, of discerning which of his desires and aptitudes ought to be nourished and which left by the wayside, Wilhelm despairs. Yet all turns out well for him, not because he manages to execute this task, nor finally because of the behind-the-scenes activities of the Tower Society, but mysteriously, as it were, by way of Fate. As Goethe's letters to Schiller obliquely hint, this was a way of gesturing aesthetically toward the limitations of Goethe's own abstract philosophy of Bildung and of pointing instead to the novel's fidelity to the particularities of lived existence as displaying truths that outran the reflective consciousness of its author. Bildung is a concrete task entrusted to the agent, Goethe recognized, so delivering an abstract general philosophy is of limited usefulness. The concrete narrative reality of the novel, Goethe thought, could do better by guarding the "incalculable" character of particulars. The fact that *Wilhelm Meister* failed to depict Wilhelm's Bildung and pointed beyond itself to truths Goethe could not express or make explicit, is thus part of its greatness. An ironic *Kunstreligion* that signaled its own insufficiency was a step in the right direction. Hegel, however, wanted to do more than point.

Hegel's Aesthetics

In order to grasp the force of Hegel's comments about the novel, we must place them within the context of his broader theory of art. While focused primarily on the analysis of artworks rather than on reception aesthetics, Hegel's understanding of art built on Schiller's notion of aesthetic experience as vital to Bildung via the harmonious integration of the sensuous and the rational.[6] Art is critically important for embodied rational creatures such as we are, because it allows truth to appear to our senses; art is "the sensuous appearance [*Scheinen*] of the Idea."[7] As sensuous appearance in art, truth is something concrete and particular. Insofar as this particularity is lacking and truth has not become embodied in some particular object, experience, or individual character, the idea is less real or actual. And the particularity cannot be wholly accidental to the truth it makes sensuous; an organic harmony of the two is required. In art, however varied its expressions, Hegel held that human beings give creative expression not just to any truths or ideas but rather to aspects of their self-understanding. The art of a particular historical period expresses the ideals and aspirations, the underlying self-understanding, of *these* people at *this* time. At the same time, art is for Hegel always a kind of revelation or anticipation of the freedom-in-harmonious-relation toward which we are all striving individually and communally, as the inadequacy of one-sided or partial conceptions of self and world are shown to be unstable and to undermine themselves. Objects are beautiful, for Hegel, because they offer created, sensuous expressions of freedom-in-harmony and "afford us a breathing space in which to feel at one with ourselves and with the world."[8]

Hegel depicts art as developing through three primary stages: symbolic, classical, and romantic. He maps these onto particular cultural-historical moments—ancient Egyptian and Persian, Greco-Roman, and Christian—while noting that features characteristic of what he construes as earlier stages can reappear at later historical moments. There are puzzles here, as everywhere in Hegel scholarship. One has to do with Hegel's apparent elevation of Classical over Romantic art, odd since Romantic art is the third, and thus synthetic, moment.[9] Another has to do with the notion—originating in a misreading of Hegel introduced by the student who transcribed and published his lectures on aesthetics—that Romantic art culminates in the "death" of art.

Symbolic art seeks to give sensuous expression to spirit conceived of in an utterly indeterminate way, for which no form can be adequate.[10] Symbolic art thus seeks sensuous expression by distorting natural forms or constructing mysterious riddles. Egyptian art, for instance, distorts natural forms, uniting human with animal bodies. Jewish art, guarding the transcendence of God, refuses to depict the divine and presents human beings as lowly and powerless.

Symbolic art is displaced by Classical art when "instead of indefinite, general, abstract ideas, it is free individuality which constitutes the content and form of the representation."[11] In Classical Greco-Roman art, Hegel argues, we encounter a perfect correspondence between meaning and form. His favorite example is Greek sculpture, in which the human body appears as the perfect sensuous representation of the human spirit, spirit resting in body and not seeking to point to anything beyond itself.[12] While sculpture offers this ideal in its purest form, Greek drama is singled out for presenting this harmony of meaning and form in its most concrete form, in that it displays human beings in the process of development or self-actualization, moving through conflict to arrive at a deeper harmony or reconciliation with Fate. This is not to say that tragedy is a lesser form of drama—indeed

Hegel famously considered Sophocles's *Antigone* perhaps the best exemplar of Greek drama in that the tragic outcome flows organically from the characters and their clearly defined projects and purposes.[13]

Romantic art, meanwhile, has moved beyond the synthesis of Classical art, having grasped that spirit transcends any particular natural body. This deeper inwardness and self-consciousness renders the sensuous realm no longer adequate to the full expression of spirit.[14] Thus Hegel speaks of Romantic art as the dissolution (not the death) of art, in that subjectivity and objectivity no longer hold together and perfectly reflect one another.[15] This does not mean that Hegel considers the movement from Classical to Romantic art as a retrogression. Rather, it is a movement in which art begins to achieve autonomy from religion and philosophy.

Greek art is properly *Kunstreligion*, Art-as-Religion. Art, thought Hegel, was for the Greeks the locus of religious experience and the highest form of consciousness of the truth. This was not art seeking to fulfill some social function belonging to religion (as in the *Kunstreligion* of Hegel's contemporaries) but rather an immediate unity of artistic expression and religious worship. With Christianity's conception of God as utterly transcending the world, accented decisively by the Reformation, the realm of sensuous appearance was no longer seen as adequate to the divine, and spirituality became more inward and subjective. Art and religion were distinguished, and the long process of the secularization and emancipation of art began.

Where religiosity becomes decisively inward, as in Protestantism, art is granted full independence. Ironically, this achievement of autonomy represents for Hegel at the same time a demotion of art's significance. Artists in modernity are free to explore the myriad expressions of human experience: "the artist acquires his subject-matter in himself and is the human spirit actually determining itself and considering, meditating on, and expressing the infinity of its feelings and situations."[16] Aesthetic independence reveals itself to be a freedom for insignificance and triviality. At its best, Romantic art expresses truth by acknowledging finitude and frailty, in and through aesthetic attention to human vulnerability and suffering.[17] If secular forms of Romantic art simply explore the full spectrum of the human heart, explicitly Christian art, for Hegel, shows this in depicting the suffering of the martyrs or of Christ on the cross, and the depths of love in Madonna and Child. Whether in religious or secular forms, Romantic art expresses spirit shining in and through the sensuous sphere. In art, therefore, the truth that genuine freedom is reconciliation finds *direct* aesthetic expression. The reconciliation of spirit and sensuousness "finds its *truest* expression," however, "beyond the aesthetic sphere" in religion and philosophy.[18] In seeking to recover the unity of spirit and body that characterized classical art, but in a way that honors human freedom and subjectivity, Romantic art points beyond itself. The freedom of spirit at home with itself in the other can be expressed more fully, Hegel holds, in religion and philosophy. For Hegel, then, "art, considered in its highest vocation, is and remains for us a thing of the past."[19] Of course art continues, but its autonomy from religion and philosophy means that its "highest vocation" has been relinquished.

Hegel maps his account of the symbolic, Classical, and Romantic stages of art onto a similarly dialectical account of artistic genres, again without claiming any direct historical correspondence. Here architecture, with its highly abstract expression of ideas, corresponds to symbolic art, and sculpture, as we have already seen, to Classical art. Romantic art is constituted by its own inner dialectic of painting, music, and poetry.[20] Painting, music, and poetry are all here considered as arts that accentuate subjective and ideal elements. Painting is capable of capturing the myriad details of the world as perceived, shaped, and constructed by human activity.[21] However, painting depicts human subjects and their environments as external to or merely alongside one another. Music, meanwhile, is the art that most fully expresses feeling.[22] Poetry constitutes a synthetic moment in that it overcomes the highly abstract, indeterminate character of music while displaying subjective inwardness and feeling not merely alongside or as externally related to the objectivity of the natural world and of social institutions, but precisely as these are understood and regarded by human subjects in all their inwardness.[23] It is in this respect that Hegel considers poetry the "most perfect art," the art that most fully reconciles subjectivity and objectivity by expressing spiritual freedom, but in a concrete, determinate way.[24]

Poetry has itself, of course, various forms; for Hegel the most basic are epic, lyric, and drama. These can be seen as repeating within themselves the shape of the movement from painting through music to poetry, from a form that depicts the human subject standing merely alongside an objective, static natural and social world, through a form that emphasizes human feeling and subjectivity but in a way that sacrifices or abstracts from concreteness and determinacy, to a synthetic form. Epic—think, for instance, of Homer—depicts the hero against the backdrop of a world determined by Fate and necessity, triumphing or foundering as the case may be.[25] In drama, by contrast, the hero is active in a new way; action issues from his or her individual will, from subjective desire and intention. "Drama, for Hegel, does not depict the richness of the epic world or explore the inner world of lyric feeling. It shows characters acting in pursuit of their *own* will and interest and thereby coming into conflict with other individuals."[26] Drama represents the synthesis of epic and lyric poetry in that here character is displayed in action in the world, developing through the course of conflict, and arriving at some sort of satisfying resolution.

This brief survey of Hegel's aesthetics equips us to arrive at a fuller understanding of his critical remarks on the novel of Bildung. For while the novel is surely an exemplar of Romantic art, and of poetry within Hegel's further threefold division of poetry, the novel, however "novel" a genre, represents a modern expression of epic. In medieval chivalric epics, the plot, like that of the modern novel, focuses on the deeds of an individual protagonist, but the institutional order of the world is unstable and the protagonist's adventures therefore, argues Hegel, take on a kind of fantastic, mythical character. The modern novel, in contrast, has its setting within a solidly established bourgeois institutional order. The protagonist, experiencing this given order as unreceptive to his subjective aims, battles against it. Like Don Quijote, the protagonist of the novel "finds before him an enchanted and quite alien world which he must fight because it obstructs him and in its inflexible firmness does not give way to his passions but interposes as a hindrance the will of a father or an aunt and civil relationships, etc."[27] These youth are unable to grasp the institutions of family, civil society, and state (i.e., the realm of "objective spirit") as genuine expressions of what is most essentially human and are thus unable to be at home in them. They set off in hopes of "knocking a hole in the order of things," changing the world, or at least creating a little heaven on earth by delivering the princess of their heart from her dragonlike relatives.[28] If the modern novel is indeed the apprenticeship of the individual subject on the institutions of objective spirit, the protagonist ought to come through to a recognition of these institutions not as pure contingencies but precisely as expressions of spirit, as mediums for the collective self-realization of humankind and thus properly also of his own genuine self-realization. And Hegel gestures in this direction, suggesting that "the end of such apprenticeship consists in this, that the subject sows his wild oats, builds himself with his wishes and opinions into harmony with subsisting relationships and their rationality, enters the concatenation of the world, and acquires for himself an appropriate attitude to it."[29] But in the next sentence, with its heavily ironic treatment of the whole *Katzenjammer* to which the idealistic protagonist has in the end become resigned, it becomes clear that the novel does not for Hegel succeed in accomplishing the genuine apprenticeship of the subject. Even at its conclusion it remains in the position characteristic of epic, in which the outer social world and the inner world of the subject are both merely given and thus situated side by side, with no genuine reconciliation between the two: "what is sought and is to count is only its own inner subjective formation, the spirit's expression and mode of receptivity, and not an objective and absolutely valid subject-matter."[30] This is precisely what is missing, however the novel may end with a contingent acceptance of objective reality on the part of the protagonist: genuine *reasons* for this acceptance, as opposed to a mere shift of inclination or mood. The novel does not display socially embodied reason, the objective spirit of ethical life, but simply a fortuitous harmony of subjective inclination and social convention, secured perhaps, by the deus ex machina of Fate but not by rational thought and cognition.[31]

Of course it is hardly clear that drama itself (the synthetic genre) succeeds in displaying a genuine reconciliation of subject and object, freedom and determinacy. In tragic drama, the hero's decisive self-expression in action culminates in disaster and destruction. In comedy, meanwhile, destruction is averted not because a thoroughgoing reconciliation is achieved but because the characters are able to accept their failures and frustrations and not take them—or themselves—too seriously; affirmation is present despite the lack of reconciliation, and in this sense the hero triumphs over circumstances.[32] It is puzzling that the series of nested triads that constitutes Hegel's aesthetics culminates in a dyad: tragedy and comedy. Where, then, is the synthetic form of the drama, which itself is positioned to crown the synthesis both of symbolic-Classical-Romantic art and of the genres of painting-music-poetry? It has been suggested that this points to a third, synthetic dramatic form, the drama of reconciliation.[33] Hegel gestures briefly in this direction, speaking of a third principal form of drama, rather undeveloped, in which genuine harmony is achieved through human action despite profound differences and conflicts among the interests and passions of the various characters.[34]

The underdeveloped character of Hegel's drama of reconciliation serves to underscore his conviction that Romantic act culminates in a dissolution of subjectivity and objectivity that reflects the autonomy of art and thus points beyond art to religion and philosophy for reconciliation. As Stephen Houlgate writes, "according to Hegel, the idea that true freedom is to be found in inner spirituality that is prepared to let go of, or to 'die to,' its own selfish purposes lies at the heart of *religion*, specifically of Christianity. True comedy, therefore, implicitly points *beyond* art to religion."[35] Indeed the genuine drama of reconciliation would for Hegel have to be religious drama—that is, sacramental ritual.

Hegel's aesthetics thus displays *Kunstreligion*'s inadequacy to the task of Bildung. Epic, lyric, and dramatic poetry overcome the one-sidedness of painting and music. They can convey the complex depths of human subjectivity and the conflicts that arise as persons come to terms with social circumstances and institutions. But this cannot be equated with the realization of Bildung. For this, as we shall see, requires the harmony-in-diversity of subjects who, grasping themselves and one another as finite expressions of the Concept, form relationships and institutions that embody mutual recognition and affirmation.

Hegel's *Phenomenology* as the Bildung of Consciousness

While Hegel regarded the novel as incapable of accomplishing the Bildung of the individual toward ideal humanity, and art more generally as sacrificing its formative and reconciling power in proportion to its increase in relative cultural autonomy, this certainly does not mean, as already noted, that Hegel repudiated the Bildung tradition. For his entire philosophical project is nothing less than a project of Bildung, intended to show that the formation of ideal, harmoniously integrated humanity requires not a more concentrated focus on human self-forming subjectivity but rather the proper situating of this creative subjectivity in the most comprehensive possible context. The harmony that Bildung seeks is for Hegel a harmony of subjects and objects, individual and community, particular and universal, persons and world—indeed his aim is nothing short of the reconciliation of all oppositions that divide and alienate, making it possible for individuals to be in harmony not simply with themselves and their communities but also in the natural world and the cosmos as such. He puts this in terms of being "at home" in the world. "The aim of knowledge is to divest the objective world that stands opposed to us of its strangeness, and, as the phrase is, to find ourselves at home in it."[36]

As we seek to get a handle on Hegel's appropriation and transformation of the Bildung tradition, his *Phenomenology of Spirit* is the appropriate next place to turn for several reasons. First, Hegel considered it the introduction to his systematic philosophy. Second, a section of the *Phenomenology* is devoted specifically to Bildung. Third, Hegel describes the project of the *Phenomenology* as such in terms of Bildung. Indeed this has led many scholars to seize upon the characterization of the *Phenomenology* as a Bildungsroman of the human spirit, coming to adulthood in modernity.[37] Like the novels in the tradition of *Wilhelm Meister*, then, Hegel's *Phenomenology* has been read as setting out to resolve the "conflict between the poetry of the heart and the opposing prose of circumstances," where the poetry of the heart is for Hegel alienated subjectivity, while the prose of circumstances is the external social and legal order perceived as constraining rather than expressing the subject's freedom. As in a novel, the development and resolution of tension is in the *Phenomenology* also (at least from chapter 4 onwards) developed narratively. The process of the formation of consciousness, suggests Allen Wood, "occurs not primarily through the imparting of information by a teacher, but instead through what Hegel calls 'experience': a conflict-ridden process in the course of which a spiritual being discovers its own identity or selfhood while striving to actualize the selfhood it is in the process of discovering."[38] So understood, Bildung involves "the frustration of immediate desires and the growth of a capacity, consequent only on this experience of conflict and frustration, to direct one's own agency through a self-conception and rational principles."[39] But there is something peculiar about characterizing the *Phenomenology* as a Bildungsroman, since the *Phenomenology* is "a record of a long series of failures."[40] Hegel is explicit about this: the *Phenomenology* traces "the path of the natural consciousness which presses forward to true knowledge," but the road is "the pathway of doubt, or more precisely . . . the way of despair."[41]

At the same time Hegel also claims that the *Phenomenology*, in tracing "the series of configurations which consciousness goes through along this road is, in reality, the detailed history of the education [*Bildung*] of consciousness itself to the standpoint of Science." Like *Wilhelm Meister*, then, and unlike the popular novels of the day, the *Phenomenology* serves the project of Bildung precisely by depicting the *failure* of Bildung rather than its success.

The *Phenomenology* (1807) was Hegel's first mature work, written with his entire philosophical system in view. It was intended as an introduction to that system, but an introduction of a specific sort, one intended to provide a "ladder" to the special standpoint of Science, describing the "coming-to-be of Science as such or of knowledge."[42] Yet it is if anything more cryptic than Hegel's other works, seems to confuse logic with philosophy of history, and does not fit clearly into the architectonic of Hegel's system. Nevertheless, the fact that Hegel continued to refer to it and was planning a new edition at the time of his death indicates that he continued to regard it as the entry point into his philosophy.[43] What is critical to take into account is the fact that the *Phenomenology* was intended as a negative introduction, a ground-clearing exercise: Hegel seeks to defend his philosophical method by showing that alternatives to it end in irresolvable difficulties: "the title of the work refers to the fact that it is supposed to be a complete record of all the false or merely apparent (hence phenomenal) forms that spirit's knowledge can take."[44] Taking our conceptual categories for granted, and thinking of them in dualistic or oppositional ways, such that the finite excludes and opposes the infinite, the subjective excludes and stands over against the objective, and so forth, we end up in trouble; the only solution is to examine these categories more fully so as to see how our categories are dialectically interrelated.

Like the highly self-reflexive novels in the tradition of *Wilhelm Meister*, the *Phenomenology* alternates between two perspectives: that of ordinary consciousness (at the level of both the individual and society), with its taken-for-granted categories, and the observer's point of view, looking on the trials and travails of consciousness from the standpoint of Science or speculative thought.[45] We as readers are not simply swept up into the maelstrom of ordinary consciousness but are patiently tutored, offered an interpretive key to the action. Many of the categories discussed in the *Phenomenology* appear again from 1812 onward in Hegel's *Encyclopedia of the Philosophical Sciences*, comprising his Science of Logic, Philosophy of Nature, and Philosophy of Spirit, but in the latter texts these are laid out dialectically rather than from the standpoint of the frustrations of ordinary unreflective consciousness. From multiple angles, therefore, Hegel unpacks what has been dubbed the "Chalcedonian logic" of "distinction in inseparable relation," tracing the contours of Bildung.[46]

Hegel as Metaphysician

According to influential contemporary post-Kantian readings of Hegel, Hegel's philosophy is best seen as a continuation of Kant's critical project. Hegel shared with Kant the conviction that we can be intellectually responsible only insofar as we investigate the validity of our conceptual categories. Moreover, on this view he accepted with Kant that we can therefore do no more than articulate how things necessarily must appear to us, given these categories; we cannot engage in metaphysical talk about reality or being in itself. "For Hegel, the issue of the 'determinations of any possible object' . . . has been critically transformed into the issue of the 'determinations of any object of a possibly self-conscious judgment.'"[47] In saying that finite subjectivity becomes intelligible to itself as a "manifestation of the Absolute," according to this reading Hegel "means simply to say that the developmental process of the self-realization of human freedom can be understood, and that every other aspect of any intelligibility depends on, presupposes, the proper understanding of this process," which is thus "absolute."[48] On these readings, the *Phenomenology* is intended to foster human autonomy in the sense of consciousness of ourselves as inhabiting a space of reasons that we collectively have generated, and for which we now take full responsibility."[49] The book "intended to show its readership why 'leading one's own life,' self-determination, had become necessary for 'us moderns' and what such 'self-legislation' actually meant."[50]

This reading runs into problems, however, given the fact that Hegel often speaks favorably of the metaphysical project of speaking of the "really true" and critically of Kant's subjective idealism: "In this self-renunciation on the part of reason, the Notion of truth is lost; it is limited to knowing only subjective truth, only phenomena, appearances, only something to which the nature of the object itself does not correspond."[51] Hegel announces his aspiration to provide an "exposition" of "what . . . the thing in itself is in truth," or again, of "what is truly in itself."[52] It is thus not surprising that a range of metaphysical readings of Hegel have reemerged in recent decades. These do not necessarily embrace Spirit Monism—that is, the view that Hegel sees all of reality as flowing necessarily from an absolute substance that develops to self-consciousness in human beings.[53] Rather, attending in particular to Hegel's philosophy of nature, they regard Hegel as embracing a realism about universals that is critical to arriving at a satisfactory account of laws of nature and of natural kinds.[54] Hegel's stance is not a monistic one on which finite things are merely modifications or appearances of some underlying absolute substance, nor a holistic view on which finite things gain their identity by way of their interrelationships with one another, but rather the view that finite things are expressions of an *infinite* that is not to be thought of as a substance—that is, as another individual entity alongside others. To be an individual entity is to be a "particularized universal"; such things are "embodiments of the infinite, but not in a way that robs them of their individuality."[55] Hegel's thought is thus regarded as centrally concerned with resolving the problem of the relationship between universality and individuality, and in so doing, with moving "beyond a whole series of divisions in our view of the world, between abstract and concrete, ideal and real, one and many, necessity and freedom, state and citizen, moral law and self-interest, general will and particular will, reason and tradition, God and man."[56]

On this revised metaphysical reading of Hegel, he does not blithely ignore the problems Kant's critical philosophy raised for traditional metaphysics. Rather, Hegel can be understood to be arguing that there is no alternative to metaphysics, in the sense that metaphysical assumptions, assumptions about reality, about what is the case, will always be at work in what we think and say and do. Even Kant makes metaphysical claims, such as the claim that space and time are *not* real but simply conditions for the possibility of *our* experience. Like Kant, Hegel thinks that we should examine our assumptions, the categories through which we think. Unlike Kant, however, he does not think that in examining our categories, all we can do is clarify how things must appear to us, without ever being able to say how things actually are. Rather, we are engaged in inquiry into being as such, ontology. The criteria of assessment here are just the same as in any other form of inquiry—the metaphysician appeals "to just the same criteria in settling his disputes as are available to any investigator engaged in a theoretical form of inquiry, such as inference to the best explanation, simplicity, coherence and so on."[57] Metaphysics is just as fallible as any other form of inquiry.

On readings of Hegel currently claiming the "post-Kantian" title, the Bildung of consciousness culminates in a critical acceptance of reality, which is self-conscious of its constructed character and so is capable of being selective, able and willing to critique and correct inherited social norms and practices even while having been formed by them. On this reading, the culmination of philosophy and the arrival at Absolute Spirit is best understood as an open-ended consummation that directs us back to an ongoing self-critical cultivation of human social practices.[58]

On a revised metaphysical reading (which has no lesser claim to the post-Kantian mantle), such an ongoing critical revision of social practices is also endorsed, but Hegel is understood as having claimed in a much more encompassing sense to have made it possible for consciousness to be at home in and to be reconciled with the world. For we have become able to see the world as intelligible, as an expression of reason: to find ourselves at home in the world by ridding it of its strangeness, "which means no more than to trace the objective world back to the notion—to our most innermost self."[59] This is a form of grasping the conceptual structure of reality and thereby of articulating the rational in the real that does not shut down but rather sustains, the ongoing project of forming social practices that are indeed reconciliatory.

The Movements of the *Phenomenology*

On a bird's-eye survey of the *Phenomenology*, we find two triads structuring the whole, the first composed of consciousness, self-consciousness, and reason, and the second of spirit, religion, and absolute knowing. Many of these are composed of their own inner triads—for example, consciousness is made up of "sense-certainty," "perception," and "force and the understanding." The movement is a kind of spiral, with forms of consciousness that have already proved one-sided and unstable reemerging at later, more complex stages — for example, "unhappy consciousness" reemerging as "self-alienated spirit," or "reason as testing laws" returning as "morality" (Kantian *Moralität*). Tracing the dead-ends experienced by ordinary consciousness on its way of despair enables us to see why Hegel considered himself to be tracing "the detailed history of the education [*Bildung*] of consciousness itself to the standpoint of Science." The work of the *Phenomenology* is to show the unsatisfactory character of all efforts to think of ourselves or the world apart from the "infinite interrelatedness" in which these stand, and thus to point us toward the standpoint of Science, from which we grasp individual existents as embodiments of the infinite, and assume the task not just of thinking but of living out the ecstatic reconciliation that lies at the ground of being.[60] Bildung thus releases us for ideal humanity.

The starting point, that of sense-certainty, represents what Hegel takes to be the ordinary commonsense standpoint according to which we can have knowledge unmediated by concepts and this constitutes the most direct knowledge possible of individual things.[61] From this standpoint, knowledge through concepts would disrupt this direct knowledge and separate us from the thing known. However, this standpoint runs into difficulties, since what sense-certainty actually experiences in the object are properties that can be instantiated in many individuals — that is, universals. Trying to exclude these properties from view and gain contact with the individual object by pointing simply to what is "this-here-now" does not help. For in the next instant something else is "this-here-now." "'Here is, e.g., the tree. If I turn round, this truth has vanished and is converted into its opposite: 'No tree is here, but a house instead.'"[62]

In the face of these difficulties, consciousness moves from "sense-certainty" to "perception." From the standpoint of perception, an object is grasped no longer as directly known but as "the thing with many properties."[63] The object is an instantiation of many universals, bundled together in "a *simple togetherness* of a plurality." Hegel's example is "this" salt that is "here," "white," "tart," "cubical," etc.[64] This perspective is no more satisfactory than that of "sense-certainty," however, since it is unclear how such a bundle holds together. The bundle view oscillates, then, with the view that the object is a "one" in which its various properties inhere, as in a substratum.[65] "Consciousness alternately makes itself, as well as the Thing, into both a pure, many-less *One*, and into an *Also* that resolves itself into independent 'matters.'"[66]

Finding this oscillation unacceptable, consciousness then moves to a third way of thinking, one that regards natural forces as the reality underlying what is now taken to be an illusion of stable, individuated objects. These forces cannot be directly perceived by the senses. On this perspective, then, "consciousness has a mediated relation to the inner being and . . . looks through this mediating play of Forces into the true background of Things."[67] This "true background" is conceptualized in terms of laws of nature. Consciousness remains dissatisfied, however, for these laws appear tautological, mere descriptions of the regularities of nature that offer no real explanation of their existence.[68] This dissatisfaction thus precipitates the shift from the first triad, "consciousness," to the second, "self-consciousness," where attention is directed to understanding how consciousness conceives of itself, rather than of the object.

If consciousness one-sidedly elided itself in attempting to grasp the object as such, self-consciousness shows itself to be equally one-sided. In its first form, desire, pure will, destroys the object in order to negate its otherness; in the second, the subject destroys other subjects in a life-death struggle. In its third, Hegel's oft-cited master-slave dialectic, self-consciousness seeks to dominate other subjects through enslavement rather than destroying them. The master seeks affirmation of his self-worth through the conquest of another. In demanding nonreciprocal recognition by the slave, however, the master seeks confirmation of his independent value by way of something that is bound to frustrate that aim; the master becomes in fact *dependent* on the slave's recognition, while the slave possesses a consciousness not dependent on the master's recognition and thus independent.

The failure of alignment between the master's self-conception and the truth of how his self-conception is constituted renders the master-slave relationship inherently unstable and thus drives the movement of consciousness forward into the next set of moments, roughly mapped onto particular historical forms of thought: Stoicism, Skepticism, and the Unhappy Consciousness.[69] Stoicism, with its conception of an immanent Reason governing all of nature, offers self-consciousness a way of recognizing itself, as rational, in the world as rational. However, Stoicism's rationalism remains too abstract: it "turns its back on individuality altogether," fails to satisfy, and hence gives way first to a Scepticism that despairs of knowledge, and then to the Unhappy Consciousness, for which Stoic immanent Reason has retreated into a transcendent and unknowable realm, cut off from consciousness.[70]

In a quest for self-renunciation, the sacrifice of the individual to the universal, self-consciousness gives up its concern "to save and maintain itself for itself at the expense of the world."[71] This marks the transition to the third main movement of the *Phenomenology*, that of individual reason. Here consciousness moves from subjective idealism to the stance of a scientific observer. Subjective idealism takes itself to be all of reality, such that consciousness experiences only itself and thus fails to truly grasp the rational structure of the world. Scientific observation, in contrast, seeks to grasp the rational structure of the world by subsuming observed particulars under universal laws. Frustrated in its efforts to attribute teleology to natural organisms that cannot be said to be capable of purposive activity, however, consciousness seeks instead to identify laws governing consciousness itself, the human mind. This effort founders on the recognition of human freedom, and consciousness therefore shifts from the mode of observer to that of agent.[72] Now consciousness hopes to be at home in the world not by knowing it but by realizing its own purposes within it: "consciousness no longer aims to *find* itself *immediately*, but to produce itself by its own activity."[73] An initial effort to indulge individual whim fully in pleasure-seeking founders in hedonism's failure to bring true satisfaction; the subsequent effort to promote universal happiness meets with resistance from others who "do not find in this content the fulfillment of the law of *their* hearts."[74] Recoiling, consciousness then seeks through virtue to achieve its own happiness apart from others. Such an effort, though, leads to "virtue in imagination and name only, which lacks . . . substantial content."[75]

In the final section of "Reason," Hegel explores three moments of "Individuality which takes itself to be real in and for itself." The first, self-expression, founders in unstable relativism. Consciousness thus seeks to commit itself to universal moral laws but discovers that these must be interpreted and are not in themselves action-guiding. Kant's categorical imperative, argues Hegel, fares no better, since "the criterion of law which Reason possesses within itself fits every case equally well, and is thus no criterion at all"; to the extent to which it is not purely formal, substantial moral content has been smuggled in.[76]

Acknowledging the failures of individual reason, consciousness moves into the final main part of the *Phenomenology*, that of Spirit. Spirit is consciousness that has taken objective shape in cultural institutions. This final section of the *Phenomenology* thus displays the most determinate historical trajectory, beginning with the ethical life (*Sittlichkeit*) of the Greeks, which Hegel on the one hand idealizes as particularly beautiful and harmonious, and on the other hand regards as something necessarily left behind by consciousness: "Spirit . . . must advance to the consciousness of what it is immediately, must leave behind it the beauty of ethical life, and by passing through a series of shapes attain to a knowledge of itself."[77] Greek life, as we have seen in discussing Hegel's aesthetics, was characterized by stable complementarities between man, polis, and human law on the one hand, and woman, family, and divine law on the other; individuals thus found themselves in an immediate and unreflective harmony with their social institutions, experiencing the community and its laws as a perfect reflection of themselves.[78] But immediate forms of harmony are fragile; Antigone displays the way in which these collapse in the face of conflicts between human and divine law.[79]

Consciousness thus reaches the stage of "culture" (*Bildung*). For in addition to characterizing the whole project of the *Phenomenology* as the Bildung of consciousness, Hegel uses the term *Bildung* within the *Phenomenology* to refer to a stage or sphere that he also terms "self-alienated spirit," situated between the immediacy of ethical life (*Sittlichkeit*), in which individuals are fully embedded in the unreflective common life of the community, and a fully self-conscious "moral worldview" (*Moralität*). Here consciousness no longer regards itself as resting in immediate harmony with the social and political order; rather, the social world is seen as something that requires setting aside the natural self.[80] The tension between nature and culture is reflected in tensions between self-interest and the general interest upheld by the state. Alienated consciousness, here associated with medieval Europe, takes refuge from this external reality of force in an ideal world of pure faith. It thus represents the splitting of the original unity of individual and community that was present in Greek ethical life, a splitting that culminates in the Enlightenment and ultimately in the Reign of Terror. Both political and religious authorities having been subjected to Enlightenment critique, the spiritual refuge of reconciliation in the world beyond is destroyed, the world is seen as a neutral material subject to human purposes, and revolutionary consciousness seeks to establish heaven on earth. The French Revolution failed because its conception of freedom and equality was essentially negative: "in this absolute freedom, therefore, all social groups or classes which are the spiritual spheres into which the whole is articulated are abolished; the individual consciousness that belonged to any such sphere, and willed and fulfilled itself in it, has put aside its limitation."[81]

The final moment of the dialectic of Spirit begins with a return to Kantian morality, now focused on Kant's understanding of freedom as autonomy. Hegel argues that Kantian morality erects and polices dualisms between duty and inclination, morality and happiness, practical freedom and natural necessity, only to be then forced to postulate their artificial harmony. Here the problem is that the realization of this harmony "has to be projected into a future infinitely remote; for if it actually came about, this would do away with the moral consciousness. For morality is only moral consciousness as negative essence, for whose pure duty sensuousness has only a negative significance."[82] The echoes of Schiller are palpable.

Within the movement of the *Phenomenology*, the dualisms of Kantian morality give way to the stance of conscience, which "does not give itself an empty criterion to be used against actual consciousness" but rather relies on its own immediate grasp of what is to be done.[83] This proves unsatisfactory, given that the certainties of subjective conscience often clash with those of others or with the established moral order. Consciousness thus seeks to guard purity of intention even more radically, by retreating from action. Here Hegel offers his own rendition of the critique of the "Beautiful Soul" we have already seen in Goethe's *Wilhelm Meister*: "In order to preserve the purity of its heart, it flees from contact with the actual world, and persists in its self-willed impotence."[84]

Having displayed the bankruptcy of the Enlightenment critique of religion and the unsatisfactory character of the way in which Kant seeks to bring God in to overcome the dualisms he inscribes in morality, Hegel turns from the dialectic of Spirit to that of Religion, constituted by the moments of Natural Religion, Religion in the Form of Art (*Kunstreligion*), and Revealed Religion. These constitute the penultimate movement of consciousness in the *Phenomenology*, which concludes with Absolute Knowing. Here we encounter many of the same ideas that Hegel will later develop in his Lectures on Aesthetics and on the Philosophy of Religion. Here they are intertwined, and presented negatively rather than positively—as one-sided moments pointing toward Science. The first two forms of religion correspond with the first two stages of art, which we have already seen: symbolic and Classical; recall that it is only with Romantic art that Hegel regards art as claiming autonomy from religion. Religion thus has to do with human conceptions not just of the divine but of human creative activity: the movement from natural religion to *Kunstreligion* traces efforts to represent the divine. Natural religion begins by divinizing natural powers and representing God in plant and animal forms but moves on in Religion in the Form of Art to conceiving of the divine as artist, like itself. *Kunstreligion*, however appealing, proves as unstable as the immediate *Sittlichkeit* to which it corresponds: the Greek gods, exposed in their arbitrary contingency, fade into abstract Platonic universals, and laws and maxims are left without any validating anchor. "The pure thoughts of the Beautiful and the Good thus display a comic spectacle. . . . They become empty, and just for that reason the sport of mere opinion and the caprice of any chance individuality."[85]

With that, *Kunstreligion* gives way to the "revealed religion," Christianity. Here consciousness encounters God fully revealed or manifest, "as an actual individual man."[86] This divine nature, revealed in its unity with human nature, appears at first to be *confined* to a particular individual. Only with the resurrection and the gift of the Holy Spirit can God's ongoing presence in the life of the community be grasped. In revealed religion, however, consciousness remains caught up in picture-thinking in a way that prevents recognition of the truth at which it has arrived: "the community . . . does not possess the consciousness of what it is."[87] Hence consciousness must move on to Absolute Knowing, a knowing that will overcome the one-sidedness of the various conceptions through which consciousness has moved through the *Phenomenology* and reconcile these with one another in a complex unity.

Beyond the *Phenomenology*: The Movement of the Concept

Consciousness at the end of the *Phenomenology* is thus like Wilhelm Meister, who in looking back on what he took to be a series of failures discovers to his astonishment that they have indeed constituted his successful apprenticeship. Hegel's positive philosophical system consists in some sense of multiple renarrations of the *Phenomenology*, now cast positively rather than negatively. Thinking here is still ceaselessly in dialectical motion, but the motion is no longer along a path of failure and despair but of unfolding and ceaseless return. Hegel is thus essentially a philosopher of reconciliation. The tensions between subject and object, universal and particular, master and slave, God and world, are to be overcome. The way forward lies in grasping the ways in which our concepts and categories are defined by their interrelationships with one another and by their relationship with the whole.

We can begin to see this this if we return to the master-slave dialectic, as Hegel himself does in the third part of his *Encyclopedia of the Philosophical Sciences, The Philosophy of Spirit*. Here the movement no longer ends in failure, with the master's frustrated demand for non-reciprocal recognition, but rather issues in the master's realization that he too is in bondage. Only when the master renounces domination and recognizes the slave as a human being like himself does genuine—because reciprocal—recognition become possible, and with it, reconciliation of master and slave. Here

> the mutually related self-conscious subjects, by setting aside their unequal particular individuality, have risen to the consciousness of their real universality, of the freedom belonging to all, and hence to the intuition of their specific identity with each other. The master confronted by his slave was not yet truly free, for he did not yet see himself in the slave. Consequently, it is only with the release and liberation of the slave that the master also becomes fully free. In this condition of universal freedom in being

reflected into myself, I am immediately reflected in the other person, and conversely, in relating myself to the other I am immediately related to myself.[88]

The "identity" between master and slave is their identity as equally human, and therefore as properly free. In grasping this, they set aside their "unequal particular individuality." Importantly, this does not mean that they set aside their particularity as such. Mutual recognition as equally human is not a matter of relinquishing individuality. Master and slave do not become indistinguishable. What is given up are their identities as "master" and "slave," forms of particularity in which inequality and failure of mutual recognition are embedded.

Hegel's larger claim is that that coming to be at home in the world requires an analogous letting go, repeated in myriad variations and registers. Individual and cultural differences do not always pose a barrier to recognition. Letting go is nevertheless involved in coming to see the inadequacy of construing any of our categories in dualistic or oppositional ways.[89] Whenever we grasp one thing as other to or over against something else, we must come to see their identities as interdefined. Neither is thus independent of the other; they are reciprocally related. To be able to see whatever otherness seems to threaten ourselves and our freedom in this way is to overcome the threat and alienation of this otherness without destroying or being destroyed by it. "Really to think what is other is to discover its otherness as implicated in the act of thinking and the thinking implicated in the otherness: more briefly . . . to think otherness is to be 'reconciled,' to stop seeing what is other as a rival, a competitor with the thinker's reality and so a menace."[90]

When we respond in this way, preserving distinctions by grasping them in their interrelatedness as moments within the process of unfolding reason, we are acting in harmony with the rational character of reality itself. We recognize this underlying rational character, which Hegel terms the Concept, the *Begriff*, as the inner truth of our own being and of the being of the world. This is what it is truly to be free; this is not mere freedom from constraint which reveals itself, like the master's freedom, to be a form of bondage. It is freedom to realize what we most fundamentally are, in the only way that can finally preserve our finite individuality: situating it in relation to the universal infinite. Hence freedom is reconciliation with the true character of reality, grasping the world as the complex movement of the Concept's self-expression.

While the Absolute Concept is the rational ground of *all* that exists, human beings stand in a special relationship to that Concept insofar as they are "Spirit," self-conscious creatures who can therefore be for themselves both subject and object, thinker and that which is thought about. What the arrival of Spirit or consciousness makes possible is the making *explicit* of the way in which all things, nested within the dialectical series of interrelated determinations, are grounded in the Concept. Here finite reason recognizes infinite reason. "Insofar as [human beings] are spirit, they must be in actuality, i.e., *explicitly*, what they are in truth. Physical nature remains in the condition of implicitness [*Ansich*]; it is 'implicitly' the Concept."[91] Spirit makes the Concept explicit not solely through reflection but also through social institutions, "Objective Spirit." Hence Hegel's logic of dialectical interrelatedness, as we shall see, presses beyond contemplation to action. Or rather, contemplation and action are themselves dialectically interrelated, insofar as human beings recognize their relationships and social institutions as permeated by distinctions in opposition, hence as not-yet-adequate to the Concept and therefore as in need of reformation.

Hegel's Theology of Reconciliation

Hegel is irresistibly drawn to theology. Among his earliest writings were essays on the relationship between folk religion and Christianity, the positivity of the Christian religion, on religion and love, and reflections on the spirit and fate of Christianity.[92] Meanwhile, at the other end of his career, from 1821 to 1831, the year of his death, he lectured four times on the philosophy of religion. Although he held that speculative philosophy expresses the truth concerning the dialectical self-expression of the Concept most clearly and precisely, whereas religion makes use of "picture-thinking," he did not think that religion was a ladder to be pushed away once the heights of philosophy had been scaled. Since the task of forging social institutions that make explicit the harmony-in-relation of the Absolute Concept has not been accomplished but lies before us, we stand in need not only of philosophy's contemplative wisdom but of religion's holistic address to heart as well as head, and of religion's cultic and communal expressions. Even Hegel's earliest writings are pervaded with a concern for overcoming social divisions, and indeed divisions of all sorts, and Christianity, as a religion of love and reconciliation, is seen as having a critically important role to play.[93] Hegel's 1797 "Entwürfe über Religion und Liebe" can be read as containing the kernel of his mature philosophy:

> Here life has run through the circle of development [*Bildung*] from an immature to a completely mature unity: when the unity was immature, there still stood over against it the world and the possibility of a cleavage between itself and the world; as development proceeded, reflection produced more and more oppositions (unified by satisfied impulses) until it set the whole of man's life in opposition [to objectivity]; finally, love completely destroys objectivity and thereby annuls and transcends [*aufhebt*] reflection, deprives man's opposite of all foreign character, and discovers life itself without any further defect [*Mangel*; lack]. In love the separate [*das Getrennte*; the twain] does still remain, but as something united and no longer as something separate; life [in the subject] senses life [in the object].[94]

The unfolded ideality of the Absolute Concept, as it is in itself, comes to expression in the myriad particularities of finite existents. The immanent Trinity is the Absolute Concept, the Conceptual ground of reality, "that from which everything proceeds and into which everything returns, that upon which everything is dependent and apart from which nothing other than it has absolute, true independence."[95] With the emergence of finite existent beings comes the possibility of opposition and conflict, as each concept and thing appears to be what it is only insofar as it negates that which it is not. Spirit comes to regard itself as other than and alienated from the world. Yet insofar as Spirit (finite existents evolved to the point of self-consciousness) is capable of grasping this dialectical process of unfolding relationships, and so also of grasping the unity of the Concept within the plenitude of particularity, reconciliation is possible. It is love that best characterizes this reconciliation, insofar as love involves a self-gift to the other in which one finds oneself again without seeking oneself; it is being-for-oneself-in-another, in a shared life or friendship.[96]

Hegel's mature philosophy involved an even fuller reappropriation of Christian theological doctrine. While many Enlightenment thinkers had praised Jesus as moral teacher and Christianity as a religion of love, for Hegel the doctrines of the Trinity, fall, and incarnation were all essential. The truth of the Absolute Concept is expressed, he held, in the trinitarian doctrine of God. God is "the absolutely universal in-and-for-itself," of which we become aware insofar as we grasp concepts.[97] But this Absolute Concept is not adequately conceived of as an undifferentiated unity out of which everything proceeds or in which everything is grounded. So Christianity rightly speaks of the immanent *Trinity*; God is not solely in relation to the world (economically) but in God's own self (immanently) to be grasped as three persons. "God in his eternal universality is the one who distinguishes himself, determines himself, posits an other to himself, and likewise sublates the distinction, thereby remaining present to himself, and is spirit only through this process of being brought forth."[98] And through the doctrine of the incarnation, Christians affirm that God is not aloof from the world but has entered into the world in finite spirit. Christianity is for Hegel the religion of revelation because in it the Absolute Concept is revealed as the truth and ground of finite reality. The Concept is shown to be absolute inasmuch as it is not merely a conditioned other over against finite existents.

God has become human in the finite historical individual Jesus Christ; Jesus reveals that it is in Subjective Spirit that the Absolute Concept comes to self-consciousness: "this is the one and only sensible shape of spirit—it is the appearance of God in the flesh."[99] The scandal of particularity, of God revealed in a specific historical individual, reflects the fact that the Concept's self-differentiation is indeed into the very concreteness of time. In Jesus "this content—the unity of divine and human nature—achieves certainty, obtaining the form of immediate sensible intuition and external existence for humankind, so that it appears as something that has been seen in the world, something that has been experienced in the world."[100] In Jesus humanity is reconciled with God. With the coming of the Holy Spirit, poured out on the community of believers at Pentecost, God is known as present in and with the loving life of the community such that all are caught up in this reconciling movement. "This is the explication of reconciliation: that God is reconciled with the world, or rather that God has shown himself to be reconciled with the world, that even the human is not something alien to him, but rather that this otherness, this self-distinguishing, finitude as it is expressed, is a moment in God himself, although, to be sure, it is a disappearing moment."[101]

Why stress that *even* the human is not alien to God, if finite spirit is the Absolute Concept arrived at self-consciousness and thus self-recognition? Because Hegel also thinks that the doctrine of reconciliation can be appreciated only if the fall too is acknowledged, something he regarded his contemporaries as largely failing to grasp.[102] Human beings are fallen insofar as they refuse to live up to what they are as moral agents and not simply natural creatures; human beings "are implicitly spirit and rationality, created in and after the image of God," but humanity "steps forth" into a "cleavage" from its implicit being, rather than into harmony with that implicit being.[103] To be spirit is to be self-conscious and hence to stand over against oneself, to be divided. Evil is the *refusal* of recognition and reconciliation; it is willing to exist for oneself, as cut off from both the reconciling movement of the Concept and from other finite existents.[104] Jesus brings reconciliation by revealing that "what seems incompatible—the infinite and the inner ego, and [on the other hand] pure essence or God, and fulfillment, is not so, that this antithesis is null and void, and that the truth, or what is affirmative and absolute, is the unity of the finite and infinite, the unity of subjectivity, in its various determinations, and objectivity."[105]

Multiple echoes of Boehme have been heard here.[106] Like Boehme, it is said, Hegel seeks to hold onto a traditional affirmation of divine perfection apart from and prior to creation yet proves unable to do so: divinity *must* come to expression in creation in order to realize itself; the eternal divine is characterized by lack rather than abundance. The drama of unfolding creation *is itself* the drama of unfolding divinity. Hegel, like Boehme, thereby ends up legitimizing suffering, conflict, and evil as necessary elements in divine self-realization, even as his goal is reconciliation rather than conflict.

It is not an easy matter to adjudicate. While it is certainly the case that God for Hegel does not remain aloof from entanglement with history and therefore with evil, Hegel rightly sees that evil proper is the refusal of recognition and reconciliation. And he affirms the life of the immanent Trinity, God's eternal life, as infinite interrelatedness and the fullness of self-gift to the other *free* of this refusal. Harmony-in-realized-differentiation does not stand only at the end of the process of becoming but is present as its eternal, radically transcendent ground.

The most problematic passages in Hegel are those places at which he seems to suggest that evil is somehow necessary to the unfolding of the Concept and to the emergence of Spirit. "Evil as well as good has its origin in the will, and the will in its concept is both good and evil."[107] It is critical to see precisely what Hegel is saying here: not that evil exists necessarily, that is, within the Absolute Concept, but rather just that to have a finite will, that is, to be a finite moral agent, is to be capable of *either* good or evil.[108] What is necessary to the unfolding life of God, then, is the *possibility* of evil, not its actuality.[109] Evil is a falling away from the reconciling life of God. And evil has indeed come to be, or rather, this falling away from being has taken place, insofar as finite spirit has asserted itself in opposition to the good and to responsible agency. Aquinas, echoing Ambrose, Augustine, and a long succession of liturgies, could affirm that "God allows evils to happen in order to bring a greater good therefrom."[110] And Hegel stands in this tradition of the *felix culpa*. The harmonious relating that is the immanent divine life has come forth into actuality; this movement into actuality is a path of diremption and division, but also of reconciliation: "Spirit is the power of rebirth, the inexhaustible movement by which opposing forces are reconciled and new connections established."[111] Yet Hegel's God is not fully or perfectly God apart from the historical process; the immanent Trinity is incomplete. God does not merely permit evils to happen, and stand in solidarity with sinful, suffering spirit, but is realized in and through this process of happening. The price Hegel pays for making the historical process thus essential to divine self-realization is not immediately obvious. It becomes evident, as we shall see below, in Hegel's philosophy of history, and with it, his complicity in racism and colonial imperialism.

The reconciliation embodied in Christ comes to be concretely realized within the community, the church: "the community itself is the existing Spirit, Spirit in its existence, God existing as community.... The Spirit as existing and realizing itself is the community."[112] To recognize what Hegel calls the unity of the divine and human natures is not to *become* the Absolute Concept; human beings and human communities remain finite, embodied, temporal creatures, "disappearing moments" in the flow of the Absolute. But in grasping itself as God existing as community, the community is grasping socially embodied human spirit as the fullest realization yet of the Absolute Idea's self-expression into finite creation—thus grasping itself as Absolute Spirit, and in so doing initiating the *reditus* of all of creation back to the Absolute Idea, the return that is a reflection of and conscious relation of creation to that which grounds it.[113]

Existing in history, the church forms its members through devotional practices, sacraments, and teaching, such that they realize ever more fully this task of being the finite expression of, and reconciliation with, the truth of the Absolute Idea. "Therefore it is the concern of the truth that this habituating and educating of spirit should become ever more identical with the self, with the human will, and that this truth should become one's volition, one's object, one's spirit."[114] Just as it is essential to the Absolute Concept to express itself in that which is other than itself, it is essential that the communal consciousness of divine-human reconciliation be concretely realized "in the worldly realm."[115] This concrete realization will take the form of social practices and institutions that bring the natural and social worlds into conformity with "the Concept, reason, and eternal truth."[116] In other words, the divine-human reconciliation enacted by the church must be expressed in concrete ethical life, in a *Sittlichkeit* that is no longer immediate and thus fragile. This new form of *Sittlichkeit* is not simply a passive formation through experience of nature and participation in social institutions, with their intrinsic goods and immanent norms, but rather an active formation of ourselves and our societies. We are, in other words, to take up the reins of Bildung.

Politics and the Tasks of Bildung

From one perspective, Hegel's philosophical system culminates in philosophical contemplation, in speculative philosophy's clear and precise articulation of the truth of the Concept and its dialectical movement. From the first generation of Left Hegelians onward, Hegel has been accused of quietism and conservatism, summed up for some in an oft-discussed statement in the preface to the *Philosophy of Right*: "What is rational is actual; and what is actual is rational."[117] Yet the philosophical consummation of Hegel's system does not legitimate passivity by reconciling citizens to the status quo. Quite the contrary, it can be seen as mandating a newly self-aware social and political engagement. For it is not the institutions of family, civil society, and state (what Hegel terms "Objective Spirit") as they are or as they have developed up to Hegel's day that are justified; these continue to be riddled by unmediated oppositions. Rather, any social practices and institutions are justified only insofar as they genuinely embody the Concept and thus are "actual" in Hegel's technical sense. And to the extent that they embed failures of recognition, forms of identity that subordinate or demonize others, they are not actual, and critique and change are required. This task of social criticism is not carried out in some thin ether of abstraction. Rather, it is a matter of engaging in thick immanent critique of substantive practices and of the norms embedded in them.[118]

We have seen that the opposition between master and slave is overcome only through mutual recognition, in which each recognizes the other as equally human and therefore equally worthy of affirmation in his or her concrete individuality. Indeed we fully grasp Hegel's understanding of love and reconciliation only if we understand these in terms of recognition.[119] For reconciliation, as we have seen, is for Hegel not a matter of absorption or self-loss any more than it is mastery of the other: "The recognition that is needed cannot be coerced or controlled. Mutual-reciprocal recognition is possible only if coercion is renounced. The authentic 'cancellation' of other-being means that the other is not eliminated but is allowed to go free and affirmed. . . . The release and affirmation of the other is constitutive of the determinately universal identity of the 'We.' The 'We' . . . is a determinate universal that reflects both the common identity and individual differences."[120] Mutual recognition is the prerequisite for genuine community, in which the reconciled enjoy a shared life. The task confronting social and political life (and Hegel's primary focus in the *Philosophy of Right*) is to embed this mutual recognition in all of our institutions, such that individual and collective self-expression in all its plenitude and richness does not result in anyone's domination or marginalization. The immediacy of Greek *Sittlichkeit*, however alluring, reduces persons to pregiven social roles and so is prone to collapse into injustice and strife. The sphere of civil society, in contrast, is composed of distinct individuals, private persons who pursue their own interests and regard the collectivity as purely instrumental to the satisfaction of their own needs and desires. While participants in civil society think of themselves as autonomous agents, in fact their desires and character are being shaped through their participation in its institutions and practices. Notably, even as they conceive of themselves as independent, the division of labor renders them interdependent. At the same time, in order to realize their desires more effectively within civil society, they become more self-disciplined and active. Within civil society, agents are thus transformed neither through their own decision nor through the imposition of some external will, but through social practices and institutions that work through their own self-interested desires to transform them. Hegel is fascinated by the regularities that govern the "system of needs," noting that "this proliferation of arbitrariness generates universal determinations from within itself, and this apparently scattered and thoughtless activity is subject to a necessity which arises of its own accord."[121]

Bringing these empirical regularities to conceptual expression does not justify them, however, but is what makes it possible to discern and express their *inadequacy* as norms for social life. The invisible hand does not prevent economic misery or generate equity. It is therefore necessary for persons to make shared social ends, rather than their private interests, the ends of their action, in a free self-identification with the common good. They are then prepared to generate laws and institutions that secure justice and the common good. Hegel understands this as an embodiment of the universal in the particular, in the concrete social practices and institutions of a particular people, and points to its realization in the state, the distinctive feature of which for Hegel is that in it particularity, "released and set at liberty" in civil society, has been "brought back to universality, i.e., to the universal end of the whole."[122]

Hegel's point in describing the state as particularity brought back to universality is not to say that individuals are to be sacrificed to the collectivity, nor that the power of the state is to be glorified, but rather that a state that protects the rights of its citizens and offers space for the public exchange of reasons provides the social conditions under which genuine freedom, a freedom that seeks the common good in concrete social practices and the institutions of civil society, can be realized. A social contract among self-interested individuals cannot bring about the state; the state is not simply a whole made up of independent parts that remain external to one another despite their relationship.[123] "Mechanism is the individualistic conception of the social, which, lacking any immanent bonds or relations, must be held together by external forces, for example, force itself, by self-interest, illusion, or by a deliberately constructed contract."[124] The state is for Hegel properly rather conceived of as a social organism, persisting only insofar as it continually reproduces itself through the proper functioning of its constitutive powers. Here, part and whole are co-constitutive of one another.[125] The members of the state, instead of uniting simply in order to further their private interests, come together in reciprocal recognition and constitute a larger we; the shared life of the community is an end in itself and not merely a means to the flourishing of its various members. This shared life becomes part of the identity of its members, such that they can continue to be what they are only in and through the community. The state for Hegel is understood not simply as a matter of governmental institutions, the constitution, laws, etc., but includes the "spirit of the nation" or the nation as a sort of spiritual individual.[126] This is not a generic abstraction but includes (as Herder had also insisted) the cultural individuality of the nation. A constitution cannot be imposed on a nation from without but must be an organic expression of the self-understanding of the community:

> Since spirit is actual only as that which it knows itself to be, and since the state, as the spirit of a nation [*Volk*], is both the law which *permeates all relations within it* and also the customs and consciousness of the individuals who belong to it, the constitution of a specific nation will in general depend on the nature and development [*Bildung*] of its self-consciousness; it is in this self-consciousness that its subjective freedom and hence also the actuality of the constitution lie. The wish to give a nation a constitution *a priori*, even if its content were more or less rational, is an idea [*Einfall*] which overlooks the very moment by virtue of which a constitution is more than a product of thought. Each nation accordingly has the constitution appropriate and proper to it. . . . The constitution of a nation must embody the nation's feeling for its rights and [present] condition; otherwise it will have no meaning or value, even if it is present in an external sense.[127]

Existing social and political institutions are rightly subject to critique insofar as they enshrine failures of recognition, that is, various forms of domination and marginalization. However, social criticism will fail unless it is immanent. The legal order must be able to be grasped as an organic outgrowth of the "spiritual individuality" of the nation and its members. This leads Hegel to set aside the question of the ideal form of government; the question is malformed, since what matters is not some particular structure but whether the form is an expression of the spiritual individuality of the nation in a way that honors both universality and particularity: "The principle of the modern world at large is freedom of subjectivity, according to which all essential aspects present in the spiritual totality develop and enter into their right. If we begin with this point of view, we can scarcely raise the idle question of which form, monarchy or democracy, is superior. We can only say that the forms of all political constitutions are one-sided if they cannot sustain within themselves the principle of free subjectivity and are unable to conform to fully developed reason."[128]

In understanding the state as a social organism, then, Hegel envisions it as involving a kind of unity that leaves room for the development of free subjectivities held together by mutual recognition rather than by force or self-interest. There are thus consociationist elements in Hegel's political thought, as in Herder's; "the state is essentially an organization whose members constitute *circles within their own right [für sich]*," Hegel stresses, held together not by coercion but by the rule of law, embodying mutual recognition.[129]

Race, Philosophy of History, and the Underside of Bildung

Hegel's account of the state should be seen more as a summons than a blessing. Hegel is not best understood as complacently regarding either nineteenth-century Lutheran Christianity or the Prussian state as the realization of the kingdom of God. At the same time, we undeniably encounter in Hegel the recurrent tendency to cast the suffering of the innocent, the collapse and destruction of individuals, social practices, institutions, and civilizations, as means to the realization of Spirit in history, and to imply that evils and injustices perpetrated in the course of Spirit's unfolding are palliated, if not justified, by their world-historical role.[130] Hegel shared, moreover, in the general predilection of his era for arraying cultural differences along a single developmental trajectory, even if his dialectical arrays rarely trace a simple linear historical progression. This is amply evident not only in his aesthetics and in his philosophy of religion but also in his philosophy of history, where Hegel's dialectical account treats not just ancient civilizations but also contemporary cultures as having been fundamentally superseded.

These tendencies are starkly clear in Hegel's theorization of race and of Africa. Hegel accepts the existence of physiologically distinct human races, identifying the differences among the races as "still a natural difference, that is, a difference which, in the first instance, concerns the natural soul."[131] He attributes these differences to the influence of geography and climate. In contrast to Herder, who recognized all peoples as essentially and so distinctively cultural, Hegel regards "blacks" (*die Neger*) as prehistorical and preethical, caught in a childlike or natural state; as Robert Bernasconi notes, "Hegel's account of Africa served as a null-point or base-point to anchor what followed."[132] In Africans, Hegel thought, we observe human beings sunk in nature, not yet cognizant of their own spiritual character.

> Negroes are to be regarded as a race of children who remain immersed in their state of uninterested *naïveté*. They are sold, and let themselves be sold, without any reflection on the rights or wrongs of the matter. The Higher which they feel they do not hold fast to, it is only a fugitive thought. This Higher they transfer to the first stone they come across, thus making it their fetish and they throw this fetish away if it fails to help them. Good-natured and harmless when at peace, they can become suddenly enraged and then commit the most frightful cruelties. They cannot be denied a capacity for education; not only have they, here and there, adopted Christianity with the greatest gratitude and spoken movingly of the freedom they have acquired through Christianity after a long spiritual servitude, but in Haiti they have even formed a State on Christian principles. But they do not show an inherent striving for culture. In their native country the most shocking despotism prevails. There they do not attain to the feeling of human personality, their mentality is quite dormant, remaining sunk within itself and making no progress, and thus corresponding to the compact, differenceless mass of the African continent.[133]

On the other hand, Hegel also asserts that "man is per se [*an sich*] rational; herein lies the possibility of equal justice for all men and the futility of a rigid distinction between races which have rights and those which have none."[134] He insists that racial differences do not justify lack of equality before the law; equal human rights belong to all. The point of insisting that racial differences are *natural*, having to do with the *natural* soul, is to underscore that they are not spiritual (*geistige*) differences and do not justify differential ethical or political treatment. Hegel therefore declares the enslavement of Africans to be "wholly unjust."[135] Hegel's understanding of the natural or prehistorical character of the African race, unpacked in greater detail in his *Lectures on the Philosophy of History*, is that extremes of climate arrest human development and are to blame for the childlike character of the Negro race.[136] He insists on the one hand, and in harmony with his affirmation of basic human "spiritual" equality, that Negroes are *capable* of Bildung, but he claims that they display no inner *drive* to culture (*Kultur*). This is evidenced by the fact that despotism rules in their lands, that they allow themselves to be sold without thinking about whether or not this is right, and that they are content with a fetishism that projects "the Higher" onto random objects, which are then discarded at will. The fact that Negroes are nevertheless capable of spiritual development is evidenced for Hegel by the fact that they have here and there accepted Christianity "with great thankfulness."

On Hegel's account, then, European imperialism and colonialism are justified, because the introduction of European culture and religion are necessary for waking African spirit from dormancy; in the absence of this stimulus, it seems that Africans would never have become conscious of themselves as responsible moral agents, properly participants in relationships of mutual recognition. "It is the absolute right of the Idea to make its appearance in legal determinations and objective institutions. . . . [This] entitles civilized nations [*Nationen*] to regard and treat as barbarians other nations which are less advanced than they are in the substantial moments of the state."[137] Bernasconi drives this point home: "Hegel may not have drawn the consequence explicitly himself, but the conclusion to which his theorizing led was that the colonization of Africa would complete the process of introducing Africans to history."[138]

It can hardly be denied that Hegel's account of Africa and of the

Negro race gave comfort to European colonialism. In stating that "the alleged justification of slavery (with all its more specific explanations in terms of physical force, capture in time of war, the saving and preservation of life, sustenance, education [*Erziehung*], acts of benevolence, the slave's own acquiescence, etc.) . . . depend[s] on regarding the human being simply as a natural being [*Naturwesen*]," Hegel convicts himself. He fails to recognize African peoples as having cultures of their own. In treating them as a "null-point," he is able to fit them conveniently into his single developmental trajectory. But this is premised on a failure of encounter, a failure of genuine recognition of the other.

A similar failure of recognition pervades Hegel's understanding of the place of the Jews within Europe. Indeed the figure of the Jewish other, in Hegel as in Kant, served as a kind of template for European-Christian conceptions of race.[139] How, Hegel asks, are those individuals or groups to be treated whose self-understanding does not permit them to consider themselves full members of the whole, because they cannot share in the self-understanding of the nation?[140] He argues that it is right to grant civil rights to the Jews even if they do not regard themselves as members of the nation:

> Although it may well have been contrary to formal right to grant even civil rights to the Jews, on the grounds that the latter should be regarded not just as a particular religious group but also as members of a foreign nation [*Volk*], the outcry which this viewpoint and others produced overlooked the fact that Jews are primarily *human beings*; this is not just a neutral and abstract quality . . . , for its consequence is that the granting of civil rights gives those who receive them a *self-awareness* as recognized legal [*rechtliche*] persons in civil society, and it is from this root, infinite and free from all other influences, that the desired assimilation in terms of attitude and disposition arises.

Jews are to be granted not simply the freedom to practice their religion but specifically the freedom to refuse to recognize the state as their nation, that is, to refuse to regard themselves as members of this social organism, with its shared life. They are properly to be recognized as human beings, and this is not merely "superficial" or "abstract" but rather gives them a new form of self-consciousness precisely *as* recognized. Recognized as *counting* in this way, Hegel hopes, Jews will freely assimilate with Christian Europe. But recognition, he contends, is rightly extended to the Jews regardless of whether it is reciprocated.

One commentator has argued that "Hegel's defense of toleration and inclusion is not a suppression of difference; rather it is a special, exceptional preservation of difference within the totality of recognition constitutive of spiritual-ethical organism."[141] Yet it is hardly clear that what Hegel advocates is a recognition of the equal dignity of the Jews *in all their particularity*. Rather, to recognize the Jews as "primarily *human beings*" is precisely to recognize them as potentially assimilable, able to be remade into ordinary (Christian) Europeans. And this is a form of *mis*recognition. How could Jews come to understand their own particularity as being at home in this social organism, this nation, when it is so patently clear that it is only as *mis*recognized in this way that "belonging" is possible? We might well think here of Jean-Paul Sartre's condemnation of the liberals whose "defense of the Jew save the latter as man and annihilates him as Jew."[142] Jews, unlike Africans, are not for Hegel a cultural "null-point." But resolving the Jewish Question involves treating them as such—that is, treating them as "primarily *human beings*" in a way that disregards their particularity rather than recognizing it. Hegel was unable to see the very distinctive particularities of the Jews as part and parcel of the "spiritual individuality" of European nations.

To indict Hegel's failure to recognize Africans as cultural beings and his misrecognition of Jews as "primarily *human beings*" (and so as essentially a neutral substrate within which proper Christian Europeanness can take root) is to apply to Hegel's own thought his insistence that critique be brought to bear on social and political institutions premised on failures of recognition. As a form of immanent critique, it can champion Hegel even while censuring him. But there is a yet more troubling aspect to Hegel's philosophy of history—the way that it countenances even what it rightly names as evil. To be sure, when it comes to the philosophy of history Hegel distinguishes between a "historically grounded right" and philosophical right.[143] Hence, for instance, he writes that "slavery occurs in the transitional phase between natural human existence and the truly ethical condition; it occurs in a world where a wrong is still right."[144] His point is that human social and political institutions must become adequate to the Concept, to human beings as spiritual equals owing recognition to one another. Until this concept becomes actual, a contradiction exists between the existent and the actual. Hegel did not baldly endorse power positivism or legitimate whatever powers-that-be had the upper hand; social institutions, cultural practices, and states are properly justified only insofar as their practices can withstand critical scrutiny according to the Concept. To reject something as unjustified and unjust is not in itself to bring about what is just; the lasting, stable transformation of institutions is no easy matter, and philosophical proclamations do not in themselves bring these about. In this sense Hegel is correct that we have to recognize and grapple with "historically grounded right." We must indeed assess practices and institutions, and we will find some wanting. We should identify contradictions between the existent and the "actual," even if we sometimes err in our judgments. And practices and norms that are justified in a given context may later be shown to have been wrong; justification is context-relative, even if truth is not. What is most troubling here is not the fact that Hegel issues such judgments but rather that he suggests the movement through the wrong, through injustice, through evil, is somehow made right by the fact that it furthers the process of becoming adequate to the Concept. "Reason cannot stop to consider the injuries sustained by single individuals, for particular ends are submerged in the universal end."[145] It is in this larger sense that such wrongs are, for him, *indeed* right, justified, legitimate. This is no eschatological wiping away of tears but a triumphal march that insists that tears need not be wiped away since the negative is taken up as negated, as overcome, in the progress of Reason. In his interpretation of the fall, as we have seen, Hegel says only that the *possibility* of such evils is a condition of the possibility of the unfolding of the Concept into actuality, not that such evils had necessarily to be actualized.[146] Yet in his *Philosophy of History* Hegel is intent on showing that actual evils are legitimated by their inclusion in the process of divine self-realization. This process is driven by lack, by need at the heart of the divine, not by self-gift out of overflowing abundance.

Hegel and the Bildung Tradition

What, then, shall we say, when all is said and done, about Hegel's inheritance and transformation of the Bildung tradition as reflected in Herder and Humboldt, Goethe and Schiller? What in Herder was a multilayered process of individual and communal self-formation whose primary agent was God became in the hands of Humboldt, Goethe, and Schiller a purely human affair; "Humanity" is progressively realized insofar as individuals are enabled to develop their capacities in a harmonious way, overcoming divisions between reason and sense/feeling, activity and passivity. Bildung is fundamentally a process of free self-realization on the part of individuals. To be sure, these thinkers recognized that individuals could realize themselves in this way only by way of social engagement. Moreover, Bildung involves the realization of an ideal and is thus a matter of self-transcendence, not self-indulgence. But the state and indeed social relationships as such are essentially instrumental to self-realization. Schiller inverted the relationship Humboldt had sketched between political freedom and Bildung, regarding the latter as essential prerequisite for the former, and thus embracing the civic republicans' insistence that virtue is necessary for freedom. He nevertheless remained essentially a liberal individualist, agreeing with Humboldt that the end of the state is the promotion of individual self-realization. Humboldt and Schiller regarded established Christianity as obsolete and authoritarian and looked instead to a Religion of Art, *Kunstreligion*, as the key site for ethical formation. Much the same can be said of Goethe, although Goethe privileged the particularity of literature over what he grasped as the inadequacy of his own theorizing of Bildung; his literary greatness has essentially to do with the ways in which he ironizes, even while participating in, the project of aesthetic education, thereby pointing beyond it.

Goethe and Schiller had nourished high hopes for the project of aesthetic education, but these were soon chastened by their recognition that the burgeoning reading public sought escape, not edification. Similarly, political hopes fueled by the French Revolution were dampened by the denouement of the Reign of Terror. But Hegel's relativizing of the aspirations of *Kunstreligion* was more thoroughgoing. On his diagnosis, the autonomy of modern art undermined the project of Bildung-via-Kunstreligion. Art, to be sure, plays a vital role in allowing truth to appear in sensuous form, anticipating the harmonious freedom-in-relation that is the Concept expressed into actuality. But the novel offers only a contingent reconciliation of individual and society, subjectivity and objectivity. And while drama is more successful than epic literary forms such as the novel in reconciling subjectivity with objectivity, Romantic art as such, including Romantic drama, reflects the split between subjectivity and objectivity that accompanies the increased autonomy of art. Art is now fundamentally a space for the exploration of particularity; it points beyond itself to religion and philosophy as the space of reconciliation. Art in Hegel's day appeared to many to be capable of mediating the work of Bildung, fostering harmonious self-development, only because of its origins within the simpler harmony of a past *Kunstreligion*, for which art and religion were one. Autonomous art could not, argued Hegel, substitute for religion. The greatest creations of Romantic art, in pointing beyond themselves, point to the falsity of autocratic humanism. In lieu of *Kunstreligion*, therefore, Hegel returns to Christianity itself, albeit not to the authoritarian structures that had elicited ire from the Enlightenment onward. In this, as in many other respects, Hegel stands closest to Herder in the Bildung tradition. For Hegel, Christianity is vital because it is true, and because it pictures and enacts the truth in ways vital to the kind of embodied, feeling, social, imagining, thinking creatures that we are. The truth of which Christian theology speaks, and which the Christian *cultus* enacts, is the truth of the Concept's self-expression as community into the realm of finite existence, and of the reconciliation that is the "return" or fulfillment of this expressive self-differentiation. Philosophy's clear expression of Absolute Spirit cannot itself dispose persons and communities to reconciliation in this holistic way.

That Hegel's philosophical system culminates in Absolute Spirit's expressions in religion and philosophy does not mean that the human social and political institutions that constitute Objective Spirit are left behind or are not essential to the work of reconciliation. Insofar as these institutions are not yet actual, not yet in harmony with the Concept, they are subject to critique and reform so that they can become ever more hospitable to freedom-in-community.[147] Like Herder, Hegel embraces both individual and cultural particularity and diversity. Like Herder, too, Hegel insists at the same time on the necessity of judgment; not all forms of particularity are to be affirmed and embraced. Where Herder treats humanity conformed to the image of God as the criterion of assessment, Hegel interprets this in terms of actuality, the conformity of existing reality with the Concept. What Herder and Hegel share is not just a common indebtedness to Christian Neoplatonism's conception of the *exitus* and *reditus* of creation but a concern for reciprocal recognition on the part of creative self-realizing persons-in-community, which generates ever-expanding networks of shared life characterized not by uniformity but by harmony-in-diversity. Yet as we saw, Herder falls into an optimistic providentialism concerning the progressive Bildung of humanity. Hegel wrestles more profoundly, if finally problematically, with the presence of evil in history. Evil arises out of a refusal of responsible agency, on the one hand, and the refusal of reconciliation with the universal, on the other. It is all too real. But it does not have the last word. How, though, to affirm this without looking to the ongoing march of the historical process as making right the sin and suffering of the past?

Listening to Barth

Barth selects Hegel as the culminating figure in his account of the "background" to nineteenth-century theology. Hegel holds a special place in displaying the underlying continuity between the eighteenth and nineteenth centuries, despite all of their differences: "if the eighteenth and nineteenth centuries formed a unity in such a way that the nineteenth century was the fulfillment of the eighteenth, then it was Hegel who represented this unity in his philosophy as no other man did."[148] Barth convicted Schleiermacher, and the liberal theological tradition he inaugurated, of having failed to grasp Hegel's seriousness about theological truth. Instead what they carried forward, Barth charged, was his greatest flaw, an "unqualified and direct affirmation of modern cultural consciousness."[149] For "the kingdom of God, according to Schleiermacher, is utterly and unequivocally identical with the advance of civilization."[150]

For in Hegel as in his eighteenth-century predecessors, Barth insists, we witness a grasping after human autocracy; Hegel "exploited and made fruitful to the last detail Kant's great discovery of the transcendent nature of the human capacity for reason."[151] What was critically missing was any acknowledgment of guilt attendant on self-assertion, "the guilt incurred by the neglect, the overlooking, the covering up and denying of other concerns by the existence of which it was bound to feel itself hindered, limited and channeled in asserting its own concerns."[152] That Hegel was at first glorified and then vilified is the first hint of the recognition of this guilt, "the first harbinger, we might perhaps say, of the catastrophe of 1914."[153] World War I for Barth signifies the shattering of the dream of human autocracy. Hegel is still caught up in that long-lived yet ultimately fragile dream. His is a "philosophy of self-confidence," "confidence in mind which for its own part is one with God and the same with God," even as "there is likewise and in the same sense a final identity between Self and mind, as there is in general between thinking and the thing thought."[154] Hegel carried forward Herder's turn to history, made possible by the affirmation that the rational is the historical and the historical rational. Hegel was right, says Barth, to issue a reminder that truth is "history, event; that it might always be recognized and discovered in actuality and not otherwise."[155] He was right, too, to be concerned first and foremost with knowledge of God, and hence to demand that philosophy be founded on theology.[156] Like Herder, though, Barth charges that Hegel was fundamentally blind to sin. He therefore "understood reconciliation not as an incomprehensibly new beginning, but simply as a continuation of the one eventual course of truth, which is identical with the existence of God himself."[157] "Hegel, in making the dialectical method of logic the essential nature of God, made impossible the knowledge of the actual dialectic of grace, which has its foundation in the freedom of God."[158]

Rooted in his self-confidence that mind is one with God, Hegel can embrace "a fierceness of controversy" which at the same time "is accompanied by a fundamentally conciliatory spirit, and an open-mindedness towards all things."[159] This open-mindedness, though, is not a true encounter but rather a sovereign placing of particulars into a preexisting scheme. "Hegel's method makes it possible for him to have to overlook, suppress or forget nothing, seemingly nothing at all. It enabled him to be open, free and just in all directions. By virtue of it he could meet every request and complaint, no matter how alien it was to him, with the answer that it had already been taken into consideration in its place."[160]

Small wonder, then, that Hegel confidently places reason's childhood in "the oriental world, its time of adolescence and adulthood in the world of Greece and Rome, and its mature old age now in the Germanic world."[161] He misses "the revelation of God to man who is lost in sin, and the revelation of God's incomprehensible reconciling," the revelation that makes possible a wholly different form of open-mindedness, one that allows itself to be called into question and thus truly encounters the other.[162]

Note that Barth does not get distracted by Hegel's idiosyncratic talk of "the Concept" or worry that it leaves no room for an adequate articulation of divine agency. Barth knows as well as Hegel that God is not a member of the class of beings: he could agree that "if we are steered away from a metaphysics of anthropomorphic divine subjectivity and recalled to the recognition that the God of Christian theology is not an agent among others, well and good."[163] Nevertheless, Barth's critique stings. In effect, he convicts Hegel himself of a premature and thus a false reconciliation, one that fails by virtue of its very commitment to reconciling particularity in all its diversity with the Concept. He fails by virtue of his confidence that he has already taken into consideration "every request and complaint" and thus need not listen. Hegel refuses to entertain the possibility of any word from outside, and therefore the critical word that is forgiveness-and-judgment.

But is this fair? While Hegel certainly thinks that human beings are rational, capable of knowing themselves as expressions of the Concept in the form of Subjective Spirit, and of creating the social institutions of Objective Spirit in accordance with the Concept, is this really to be equated with the conviction "that the perfect life consisted in the complete autarchy of rational man in a rational world on the basis of the existence and dominion of a Deity guaranteeing this association and thus too man's complete autarchy"?[164] The Concept in some sense guarantees that the world is rational, since the world just is the self-expression into finitude of the Concept. But this does not, as I have argued, legitimate human complacency. Rather it funds a human task, a human vocation, actually to recognize the Concept and to critique and transform what exists so as to make it actual, i.e. — that is, to bring it into harmony with the Concept.

Human beings thus discover themselves to be responsible to God, rather than finding themselves to be supported or guaranteed in their autocracy by God. Moreover, Hegel recognizes that human beings can and do fail in this responsibility. Hegel takes it to be the "predominant notion of our time" that humanity is by nature good.[165] Were this the case, he insists, were humanity "not cloven, then it has no need of reconciliation; and if reconciliation is unnecessary, then the entire process we are here considering is superfluous."[166] On Hegel's account, humankind is indeed fallen and sinful, having refused to become explicitly what it is implicitly, a spiritual form of life, persons capable of recognizing themselves as the Concept's self-expression into finitude. Human persons are therefore called to repent and accept responsibility for themselves as free creatures, that is, responsibility for working towards reconciliation. Does Hegel thereby fall into a Pelagian trap of thinking that human beings autonomously arrive at this recognition of their responsibility, of their refusal and failure, thereby moving themselves to reconciliation? In repentance, Hegel says, there is an "undoing of what has been done." This wiping out of transgressions is not a literal undoing, of course; it is rather that it becomes possible for one's transgressions not to be counted against one, and so to make a new start.[167] What Hegel affirms is that we grasp the reality of forgiveness when we become aware that nothing we can do can actually cut us off from the love that is God. It is Christ, by way of his reconciling of divine and human natures, who reveals this to us, so we can say that we have been forgiven through Christ.[168] "Acting in the belief that reconciliation has been implicitly achieved, is, on the one hand, the act of the subject, but on the other hand it is the act of the divine Spirit. Faith itself is the divine Spirit that works in the subject."[169] While evil does emerge among human beings, "at the same time it is present as something implicitly null, over which spirit has power: spirit has the power to undo evil."[170] For Barth likewise sin is an "ontological impossibility," utterly at odds with who human beings are as elected in Christ for covenant partnership with God.[171] Yet we do of course sin, insofar as we fail to correspond to this gracious determination of who we are.

This is not to exonerate Hegel, however. His failure is not that of denying human sinfulness. Nor is he wrong to affirm that the infinitely reconciling life of God is capable of overcoming evil because it does not hold itself aloof from the historical process in which evils arise. Rather, the heart of the problem lies in his identification of history as the site of divine self-realization. When it is argued that God's own perfection is attained in and through the historical process, evil is rationalized even if it is contingent and even if it is negated. A different philosophy of history, and a doctrine of creation as divine self-gift beyond all need for self-realization in history, would not, to be sure, have insulated Hegel from possible failures of recognition, of African peoples, for instance, and of the Jewish people. None of us is beyond the need for actual confrontation with the disturbing otherness of the fellows whose voices we have not yet heard. But Hegel placed an unbearable weight on the historical process, the burden of securing perfect reconciliation simply in and through history's dialectical unfolding. The eschatological reference point of history is erased, a reference point that would have made it possible to repent and lament sin and evil—including the sins and evils of colonial empire—without legitimating them.

CONCLUSION

On a bustling city street, with dozens of people watching, police gun down a teenage gang member as he kneels in surrender. The city is Nairobi, but there is an eerie familiarity about the scene. The video goes viral, this being the twenty-first century. A friend of the teen, interviewed by a radio journalist researching the shooting, blurts out, "There's this thing called humanity—you can't just shoot someone like that. That's not humanity. That's insane, I'm telling you."[1] On the other side of the globe, "alt-right" icon Richard Spencer suggests that racial identity can provide whites with the robust sense of belonging once supplied by Christianity. Whites are, he argues, specially called: to strive, to struggle, and to conquer. The alternative is "civilizational suicide."[2]

Both the impulse to protest police brutality in the name of humanity and dreams of a distinctively elevated *Volksgeist* have roots in the Bildung tradition. Herder repudiated race and Eurocentrism in no uncertain terms, to be sure, but he did foster the notion that each people, each *Volk*, has a special contribution to make to the realization of humanity. W. E. B. DuBois was to valorize just this idea as the spiritual significance of race, which remains, he stated, even when not aligned with distinctions of "common blood, descent, and physical peculiarities."[3] Each "race group," DuBois argued, is "striving, each in its own way, to develop for civilization its particular message, its particular ideal, which shall help to guide the world nearer and nearer that perfection of human life for which we all long, that 'one far off Divine event.'"[4] Here is Herder's aspiration to the formation of humanity, poured into a millennialist mold and married to a cultural understanding of race.⁵ Subtract the "Divine event," exchange the striving to contribute to humanity for a striving to dominate, and you have Richard Spencer's brand of white supremacy.

Cosmopolitanism, suggests Anthony Appiah, is "universalism plus difference."⁶ It does not envision "all humanity in its own image" but is rooted rather in a principle of dialogue.⁷ This is a more faithful rendition of the dialogical humanism we have found in Herder and Hegel. Luke Bretherton, similarly, contrasts the false univeralism of "rationalist cosmopolitanism" with a Christian cosmopolitanism that honors particularity while refusing to allow particular communities to become ends in themselves, instead summoning them to listen "to both God and the strangers among whom it lives."⁸ Evidently, though, we have not yet learned to listen rather than to shoot. Sometimes we envision others in our own image, refusing to acknowledge difference. Sometimes we refuse to recognize others as human. Both are failures of recognition, failures to regard ourselves as answerable to our fellows.

Once upon a time we took upon ourselves the task of forming humanity. Discontent with the enterprise of trampling *Menschen-Kunst*, of evacuating agency, we claimed it instead. Internally divided, we sought unity; unsure of our identity but unwilling merely to mimic another's, we worked to locate and realize our inner form. Aware of our creative powers, we drew on imagination to unite reason and feeling, to clothe ideals in enchanting, animating guises. Resentful of censorship and authoritarian rule, we sought to demonstrate our capacity to be seen and heard in public, our capacity for independent judgment and for self-government. Conscious of history and culture, of being formed formers, we strove to assess and transform the social wholes in which we were embedded and to take the measure of their world-historical significance.

Such is the story of Bildung. It can be narrated as a standard secularization saga: formative powers once reserved to God, divine *formatio*, *reformatio*, and *conformatio* to the divine image, Jesus Christ, were taken over by humankind, which declared independence, rebelled against an externally imposed model, and looked instead for a telos within, for a seed of authenticity to claim and cultivate. I have tried to relate a more complicated tale, of a loss but also a partial recovery of the narrative logic of Christian humanism, with its vision of the *exitus* and *reditus* of creation, married to a new sense of historical particularity and creative novelty. Here creation is God's excessive self-gift into finitude, the overflowing of the friendship of the divine life into the constitution of what is other than God, and the invitation of this finite other into the abundant plenitude of shared life with God. Humankind awakes to a task, a task of playing a special role in the *reditus* of creation, as those creatures made to the divine image, capable of responsibility, of responding to God on behalf of creation, of accepting God's offer of friendship and extending it to others, to strangers and enemies. Human beings do not execute this task in a space evacuated of divine agency but as empowered by grace. A radically transcendent God does not compete with the dignity of the human; divine activity does not decrease in proportion to human activity. A radically transcendent God is not cut off from creation but can be most intimate with it.

It was just here that efforts to assimilate awareness of the humanly formed character of culture and of political and economic relations, and of the limitless growth of human knowledge, went awry. Divine and human agency came to be conceived of in contrastive terms, as limiting and excluding one another. Pietist anxiety over human assertiveness was expressed in a suspicion of human artifice, *Menschenkunst*; the imagination was conceived as a subversive power, a power to displace divine formation by humanly conceived images. Fidelity was thus to be expressed through passivity, through a foundational performance of evacuation, such that the Christian could become a mere container, a vessel for divine activity. This elicited, in thinkers such as Humboldt, Schiller, and Goethe, a counterreaction that valorized human imagination rather than seeking to subdue it. This sometimes involved a dismissal of divine formative agency. When it did, it was accompanied by efforts to manufacture some sort of replacement consistent with human autonomy. One form this took was *Kunstreligion*, the Religion of Art. If religion functions to harmonize reason and feeling, to clothe abstract ideas in pictures capable of inspiring and moving us, we can take charge of this process; we need not remain passive recipients of authorized religious traditions but can create our own. Here they grasped, albeit imperfectly, something vitally important about the role of the imagination, and of narrative fiction, in ethical formation: that it takes place by way of a never-ending process of glimpsing in exemplary actions, persons, and lives something admirable and worthy of emulation but as yet only dimly understood, of imagining ourselves in their image and narratively projecting how they would respond and act in our own very different shoes. These thinkers grasped, too, the ways in which commodification could powerfully amplify the attraction of persons and lives that are not truly admirable. What they failed to see, though, was that it had always been thus—ethical formation had never taken place by way of "soulless imitation" but had always been a matter of creative, imaginative engagement of unique persons in all their embodied particularity and difference.[9] There was nothing here to exclude or compete with divine formative agency. There was, though, the ongoing task of seeking to grasp, depict, and embody the truly admirable.

The reaction against the attempted Pietist evacuation of human agency could take another form, equally problematic, as it did in Boehme. Here divine formative agency was not rejected but rather absorbed into the world, into history. Divine and human agency do not compete, not because God is transcendent beyond all possible competition with the human, but because the human, rightly understood, *is* the divine, or a moment in the unfolding process of the divine life. This was a partial recovery of Christian humanism, of the drama of the *exitus* and *reditus* of creation. But the narrative logic was warped: Creation issues not out of abundance but out of lack, a lack at the heart of God. God comes to completion only through the world, only through history. And in this process movement takes place only through conflict, through opposition and the overcoming of oppositions, which give rise to new oppositions to be overcome. Lack, opposition, conflict, evil become necessary to divine self-realization, rather than reflective of the limits of finitude and the fruits of resistance to divine self-gift.[10]

The strands of the Bildung tradition that most fully recovered the logic of Christian humanism were those represented by Herder and Hegel. Herder unwaveringly sustained a commitment to acknowledging the concrete particularity of the fellow human, for seeing in each person and each social formation some realization of the good and beautiful. He pointed to "a universality open to difference and characterized by dynamism: a universality that is constantly tested by the particular, a universality that must give an account of itself, must narrate itself in the face of particularity."[11] If Herder did not name this as a *reditus*, as a grateful response to a divine befriending Creator, he did unwaveringly insist that we resist identifying our own image with the image of God, that neighborly love not be confused with either assimilation or condemnation of difference. Yet at the same time, Herder's vision was clouded by his optimistic providentialism: with history as the arena for the irresistibly progressive realization of humanity, it was tempting to wink at human fallibility and corruption or see it as part of a benign equilibration process.

Hegel's venture, I have argued, was to avoid Herder's naive providentialism while seeking to resist Boehme's dramatic legitimation of evil. Conflict is not necessary to divine self-realization but arises out of the limitations and failures of finite creation, out of an incapacity to fully receive divine self-gift and a refusal to do so. Evil is a holding on to difference in opposition, an exclusion of otherness, a refusal of the other's self-gift. The infinitely reconciling life of God continues to unfold; the light shines in the darkness, and the darkness does not overcome it. Yet Hegel finally regarded the historical process itself as necessary to divine self-realization. He could not but thereby legitimize historical evils. Hence the sordid talk of "historically grounded right" that gave aid and comfort to racism and imperialism.

No wonder, then, that the Bildung tradition had a dark side. It licensed philosophies of history that legitimated injustice, private projects of self-cultivation and the political withdrawal of a cultural elite content to polish itself, and it was easily co-opted by groups seeking to legitimate cultural and racial privilege.

> The concrete sociopolitical embodiment of the idea of a self-regulating aesthetic society was the so-called *Bildungsbürgertum*, the "educated middle classes," who, although excluded from the exercise of serious forms of independent political power virtually everywhere, used their purported possession of a cultivated faculty of aesthetic judgment, their taste, to legitimize the retention of a certain socially privileged position. Membership in this group, the *Bildungsbürgertum*, was not supposed to be guaranteed by noble birth, inherited wealth, or economic success, but was to be granted by the free recognition of one's (good) taste on the part of others who were themselves in a position to judge. The *Bildungsbürgertum* was a self-coopting group whose collective good taste was a tacit warrant (almost) of moral superiority.[12]

The project of Bildung fed lip-service universalisms that proclaimed human fraternity while relegating some to the status of never-to-be-fully-human. It legitimated slavery and colonialism as wrongs that are nonetheless rights. It rebelled against the reduction of human beings to the status of mechanical parts in the gears of commercial society, and announced the right of each to speak and be heard in the public forum, but appropriated to some — to the cultured classes and the civilized nations — the authority to anticipate what all would say and seek.

"What alternative is there, in the final analysis," asks Thomas McCarthy, "to the historically informed diagnoses of the present with an eye to practically possible futures that have been so much a part of modern consciousness?"[13] Humankind finds itself responsible, still confronted with the task of forming humanity. This is not a matter of cultural polish, not a matter of the sovereign placing of particulars into a preexisting scheme, not an expression of human autocracy. Rather, it requires awareness of the fact that growth in knowledge and technological development does not necessarily mean human progress or improvement: "after the horrors of the twentieth century, the most keenly felt deficiency of modern progress may well be . . . the evident gap between massive advances in the available means of power — technological, economic, political, military — and the failure to develop effective normative structures — moral, legal, political — to contain and direct those powers onto paths of peace and justice."[14] It requires, moreover, constant openness to the possibility that one has failed to express, in the spheres of individual and social existence, the infinite harmonious relatedness that Christians name as trinitarian life. It is a matter of recognizing that no one has become fully human as long as anyone is not able to speak and be heard, and that being made to the divine image is not a matter of "colonial mimesis" — "they" do not become more human by becoming more like "us."[15] Only thus can we truly humanize the products of our own individual and collective imaginations.

Taking up the task of forming humanity requires hope, to be sure, but also repentance, acceptance of forgiveness, renewed effort, and an ongoing commitment to listen for the each new "voice and complaint" that questions the actuality of the harmony thus far apparently achieved. Only in this chastened way are we freed to live toward the dignity of the image of God. While the ongoing critique of unjust power and the effort to create and sustain more just and loving social practices and institutions are indispensable, they do not legitimize or compensate for the suffering and loss of the past or bring about the final and total reconciliation for which the Bildung tradition longed. The *Gemeinde*, the community of the Spirit, thus must commemorate and mourn the injustices and sufferings of the past, even while engaging in the anticipatory celebration of a reconciliation that has not yet fully arrived.

Listening to Barth's Praise for Kant

I launched this project with the unlikely suggestion that we might find in Barth, theological critic both of humanism and of modernity, not just reasons to dismiss or discredit the tradition of Bildung but also resources for discerning what in that tradition might remain worthy of appropriation. As we saw, critical as Barth is of autocratic humanism, he himself stands within the tradition of Bildung, recognizing humankind as confronted with the task of becoming human in and through their cultural activity—even as he insisted that every culture be met with sharp skepticism. Along the way, we have listened to his own sharp rebuke of Pietism, Herder, and Hegel. It is time for one last listening session.

Thoroughgoing as Barth's critique of Kant is, he also reserves for Kant greater praise than for any other eighteenth- or nineteenth-century theologian. The critique has to do, once again, with modern humanism's grasping after independence, with the aspiration to "the complete autarchy of rational man in a rational world."[16] So, notes Barth, Kant speaks of the "'God within ourselves,' who must be the authentic interpreter of all revelation, 'because we do not understand anyone but the one who speaks with us through . . . our own reason.'"[17] Kant insists that *we* must measure the God who is proclaimed to us. For there is "something in us that we cannot cease to wonder at," something that "raises *humanity* in its Idea to a dignity we should never have suspected in *man* as an object of experience."[18] This is our ability "to sacrifice our sensuous nature to morality." Because it is supersensible, it is often regarded as supernatural, which, although a pardonable error, is "greatly mistaken."[19] So "the real solution to the problem (of the new man) consists in putting to use the Idea of this power, which dwells in us in a way we cannot understand, and impressing it on men, beginning in their earliest youth and continuing on by public instruction."[20] We find here, then, what for Kant is the key to succeeding in humankind's vocation to Bildung, to the formation of mature humanity.[21]

Yet as insistent as Kant is on human autarchy, on relying solely on autonomous human reason ("the God within"), he bursts the bounds of this aspiration to autarchy by acknowledging the problem of radical evil. It is this that leads Barth to praise him. But Kant's acknowledgment—which in its starkest form regards the subjective basis for the formation of all maxims as corrupt, and which thus acknowledges this corruption to be incapable of being rooted out by human endeavor, since this would ceaselessly simply reproduce corrupt maxims—introduces an instability into Kant's system.[22] Face to face with radical evil, Kant points to the need for, but then withdraws from, the notion of "a righteousness which is not our own."[23] Similarly, he points to a gospel from which one might in fact need instruction, and to the need for divine forgiveness.[24] He notes quite explicitly the problem posed by the notion that education toward humanity rests in the hands of corrupt teachers: "Since, however, good human beings, who must themselves have been educated for this purpose, are necessary for moral education, and since there is probably not one among them who has no (innate or acquired) corruption in himself, the problem of moral education for our species remains unsolved even in the quality of the principle, not merely in degree."[25] Kant "resolutely turns back" from all of this, notes Barth, since it would undermine the human autonomy to which he and his age are committed. The absence of any good teachers throws us back on our own resources, on "the God within." But in at least naming the problem of evil, and so in acknowledging, however imperfectly, the bankruptcy of the aspiration to autarchy, Kant went beyond other thinkers in both the eighteenth and nineteenth centuries.[26]

Kant's failure in Barth's eyes, then, is a failure to follow through on his recognition of radical evil, to admit that the reality of radical evil means that we are not after all suited to be the measure of all things. We need to hear, and be corrected by, something beyond ourselves. Kant refuses to admit that the claim that I possess, through reason alone, all that I need in order to be the judge of all things is itself a sign of that radical evil, which denies human fallibility and incompleteness. This for Barth is a failure to recognize divine sovereignty. But it is not just this. As we saw in the introduction, for Barth the failure of modern human autarchy, one already visible in Pietism, comes in refusing to recognize any "object which is not in the first place really within him" and thus in denying anything that he cannot make his own—incarnation, divine command, sacrament, and, notably, the "fellow man."[27]

One need not claim the name Christian to take up Barth's point about the refusal of the "fellow man" and employ it as a lens through which to consider all that Barth has to say about incarnation, revelation, divine command, and the rest. Kant's treatment of Jesus Christ is symptomatic of this refusal of recognition—"to the religion of reason the Son of God is not a man, but 'the abstraction of humanity.'"[28] This abstraction "resides already in our reason" and hence does not require any historical realization, no encounter with any concrete fellow human, in order for it to serve as the ideal which we strive to actualize through Bildung. Despite Kant's emphasis in "What Is Enlightenment?" on advancing arguments in the public forum, and hence on dialogical encounter, reason in Kant—and the ideal of humanity toward which Bildung strives—remains fundamentally *monological*. "What Kant has in mind by the universal perspective is not an encounter with an other that calls me into question, or an address of an I to a Thou, but rather a reflective act, a judgment in which there is an attempt to take a larger perspective than the merely self-interested and egoistic."[29] As a contemporary scholar notes, "the tendencies toward monoculturalism that surface in Kant's account of progress, the insignificant role he envisions for reciprocal intercultural learning, is prefigured in his fundamentally monological conceptions of reason and rationality."[30] No wonder, then, with this supreme self-confidence in reason, a self-confidence troubled but finally not punctured by the naming of radical evil, that Kant is able to dream that only among whites, and really only among the Germans, had the various drives and dispositions of human nature achieved their ideal harmony, that only here need one look for ongoing advancement toward perfected humanity.

Of course Kant did not speak for the Bildung tradition as such. Indeed the thinkers to whom we have attended in these pages, from Herder and Humboldt to Goethe, Schiller, and Hegel, saw themselves in this respect as critics of Kant, or at least as offering vital supplements to Kant. Goethe, writing to Herder after the publication of Kant's *Religion within the Limits of Reason Alone*, was contemptuous: Kant, he wrote, "had criminally smeared his philosopher's cloak with the shameful stain of radical evil, after it had taken him a long human life to cleanse it from many a dirty prejudice."[31] Repudiating the doctrine of the fall was bound up with gathering the confidence to embark on the task of forming humanity, independent of divine formative agency. Humankind was not tainted, as Kant implied, but innocent. Hegel rightly rejected the superficiality of this proclamation, retrieving the doctrine of the fall together with a notion of the infinitely reconciling life of God and a conception of reason that was anything but monological. Yet Hegel too fell into various failures of recognition, various forms of refusal of the "fellow man." To grasp that humankind is ever prone to premature reconciliation is not sufficient to prevent oneself from failing to see just where one is guilty oneself. The task of forming humanity continues.

Listening for the Word of God on the Margins

Barth's insistence on dialogical encounter with our fellow human beings is apparent where we might perhaps least expect to find it — in his accounts of revelation and of confession.[32] Listening to Barth's 1925 discussion of the possibility of a universal Reformed confession, we might well hear Kant's "What Is Enlightenment?" ringing in our ears. Kant cautions that an ecclesiastical synod should not "be entitled to commit itself by oath to a certain unalterable set of doctrines, in order to secure for all time a constant guardianship over each of its members, and through them over the people." For "one age cannot enter into an alliance on oath to put the next age in a position where it would be impossible for it to extend and correct its knowledge, particularly on such important matters, or to make any progress whatsoever in enlightenment."[33] Barth, strikingly, *agrees*. But he adds to Kant's emphasis on argument in public a commitment to listening and an emphasis on particularity rooted in an orientation to God's truth on the one hand and awareness of shared human sinfulness on the other. It is this that keeps the dialogical articulation of truth from slipping into reason's monological dream of self-sufficiency.

A Reformed creed, for Barth, does not aspire to be universal and for all times and places. A creed is particular to a specific time and place and "open to discussion and improvement, as liable to be superseded."[34] A creed rightly emerges from the assembled community: "behind the Reformed Creed there stands ultimately, if all is rightly done, neither a consistorial nor a royal court, but (at least in theory) the market place or the Town Hall where the citizens of state or country, who are Christian communicants sharing the Lord's Supper, meet together."[35] This statement reflects, to be sure, Barth's assumption of a context in which there is an established state church. But the point is not that this guarantees any kind of uniformity. Quite the contrary, what is key here is the presence of an inclusive public space of dialogical encounter, as is underscored when he adds that "the oldest Reformed Creeds are entirely the result of discussion and subsequent voting, carried on with side-open doors."[36]

A creed seeks to articulate dogma; it is not simply an expression of the views of a particular body of persons. Precisely because of this, because it seeks to hear the truth of *God's* revelation, it is incumbent on those who draft a creed or confession to listen to *all* who would speak.[37] For listening for God's truth is a matter of listening for a truth that comes from outside, that disrupts our assumptions and expectations. And it is further incumbent on them to concede the provisional character of whatever dogma they articulate: "it concerns not conceptions of faith, but dogma; yet fundamentally variable, fluid dogma. Universal Christian truth; yet truth understood now and here in a specific way and expressed by one Christian community," and hence not claiming a false universality or inclusivity.[38] Confession should be rooted in the "concrete visibility" of a particular community in a particular time and place; otherwise it will fall into false claims of universality and inclusivity.[39] This also means that a confession should not seek to articulate all truth but rather to articulate a particular truth; it should say something to a specific situation of the moment "as its own provisional understanding of the Gospel and law of God."[40]

The community in which confession arises is not first and foremost a community of virtue, of shared goodness or wisdom. Rather, it is a community of those able to be vulnerable in listening to one another precisely because they acknowledge their sinfulness, and with it their lack of self-sufficiency. "I can confess my faith . . . ," Barth insists, "only with my neighbours, that is with those known to me as fellow believers — and that means known above all as fellow sinners and fellow prisoners."[41] "We must have found one another mutually, not just in a sentimental brotherly love but in the criminality common to them and to us, and in the pardon for criminals common to them and to us." Hence, he insists, confession takes place "in the muck and misery of this definite earthly place."[42]

The fact that confessions are able to speak God's truth only insofar as they speak from some "definite earthly place" does not mean, though, that we can remain content with whatever confession emerges from our own particular community, however committed to dialogical encounter. We must be ever attentive to those whose confessions emerge from elsewhere, and most particularly to those on the margins: "Also today if the Confession be genuine, it must come from the boundaries. It must be the Creed of those who are forsaken by God and who, as the forsaken, are visited by God; of those who are lost and who, as the lost, are rescued."[43] We should expect confession to come from the margins of society, and from the margins of the globe, because those on the margins in terms of power and privilege are most capable of seeing what those in the center are NOT able to see of the truth. It is thus from margin to center that the most significant dialogical address comes — and yet also the one most likely to be ignored.[44] In another context Barth emphasizes that God's command addresses us as individuals, "responsible partners" in the divine covenant, but also simultaneously as called into solidarity with our fellows: "the one absolute thing which is the object of God's command, and to which we are summoned when it is declared to us, is not something that I am and have alone, but only in the community and solidarity of many, perhaps of all men."[45] As Gerald McKenny notes, "solidarity, he is convinced, is possible only as we know ourselves to be placed under a command that is given to all of us yet is transparent to none of us, for the knowledge of which we must continuously ask God, and in our ultimate ignorance of which we must continuously reaffirm our accountability to one another."[46]

Barth did not regard the stance involved in listening for the Word of God to be confined to the special situations of those engaged in dogmatic theology or those crafting confessions and creeds. It is, rather, the appropriate stance of all seekers of truth. Barth takes up this stance quite explicitly in undertaking the project of writing *Protestant Theology in the Nineteenth Century: Its Background and History*. He notes that the project is a theological task, which is to say that he strives to listen for God's Word in listening to these voices from the past: "history is meant to bear witness to the truth of God, not to our achievements, so that we must avoid any thought that we already know what they have to say and be prepared to hear something new."[47] We are called to be responsible to those "whose work is handed over defenceless to our understanding and appreciation upon their death"; they have "a claim on our courtesy, a claim that their own concerns should be heard and that they should not be used simply as a means to our ends."[48] We are called to suspend our own concerns in order to listen truly to theirs.[49] What did this emphasis on listening for God's Word through attending to the margins mean for Barth's particular context of the World Council of the Alliance of Reformed Churches in 1925, to which Barth's reflections on the desirability and possibility of a Reformed Creed were addressed? "The Church must have the courage to speak today," he insists, ". . . upon the fascist, racialist *nationalism* which since the war is appearing in similar forms in all countries."[50]

Barth's insistence, then, is that God's Word, this word from *outside* ourselves that forgives our evil even as it judges it, is to be heard in and through dialogical encounter with our fellow corrupt, limited human beings. Sankar Muthu has argued that what enabled Enlightenment-era anti-imperialism to take root in thinkers like Herder, however briefly, was the coming together of commitments to "moral universalism, cultural diversity, partial incommensurability, and the delegitimization of empire."[51] It is indeed the case that this made possible a "more inclusive and meaningful" form of cosmopolitanism, a genuine advance over a cosmopolitanism of naked basic human rights.[52] But it is not enough that the self-formation of humanity rely on reason rather than impulse, not enough that it be holistic, embracing feeling as well as reason, nor sufficient that it valorize individuality and historical particularity, or that it recognize the importance of culture and tradition and the ways in which we are formed formers of ourselves and our social institutions, together with their embedded norms. Nor is it adequate to reject expressions of cultural agency that undermine the very capacity for cultural agency.[53] What is essential to acknowledge is that any particular formation of humanity is not simply a particular, contingent, historical expression but also that it is ever prone to denying its own limited character and declaring its own finality and totality. Barth believed that we could sustain this truth and this never-ending task only if we saw humanity is already perfected fully on our behalf by Christ; the *reditus* is already accomplished, and we are invited to become woven into the dance; the task is always already a gift we have been given. But even those unable or unwilling to share Barth's christocentric faith may find his call for humble, listening encounter compelling. Any adequate cosmopolitanism must be essentially dialogical in character.

I suggested at the outset that we might find in contemporary critical theory a kind of echo of Barth's critical appropriation of the Bildung tradition, albeit in a form liable to an idolatry of critical deconstruction. One key to why this is so lies in the ways in which critical theorists contrast "judgment" with "critique." Judgment is here regarded as a way "to subsume a particular under an already constituted category, whereas critique asks after the occlusive constitution of the field of categories themselves."[54] The attitude of critique is then identified with "virtue," where virtue is understood to involve a fundamentally critical relation to norms and to the ways in which any moral code forms particular sorts of subjects.[55] Critique proceeds not by pointing to some more adequate moral or political order but solely by way of desubjugation and suspension of judgment.[56] We might think here also of Walter Benjamin, for whom divine power manifests itself in this world only destructively; it reveals the injustices of the secular world without positively establishing divine justice, which dwells only in the longed-for but ever-receding messianic age.[57] But what if the judgment at issue is not, as Adorno charges, a withdrawal from praxis that wrongfully claims sovereignty, nor, as Benjamin fears, a would-be justice that appeals to ends in order to legitimate unjust means, but rather a never-ending listening for the judgment of God in encounter with our fellow creatures?[58] Or, as Gillian Rose would have it, retrieving for our time something of Hegel's *Phenomenology*, "a ceaseless comedy, according to which our aims and outcomes constantly mismatch each other, and provoke yet another revised aim, action and discordant outcome," so that we find ourselves in an "absolute comedy" in which "comprehension is always provisional and preliminary"—but also always to be ventured anew.[59] Then judgment, too, becomes a moment in attending to tears in the fabric of the epistemological field, and attending to these tears become a moment in the formation of humanity.

Listening to those on the margins was a matter of urgency, of life and death, in Barth's day as now. Today we must listen to those living under regimes propped up by police brutality, and to those whose fear and insecurity feed the cycles of violence in which that brutality gestates. We must listen too to those who find in visions of cultural purity and dreams of racial hegemony a source of purpose and identity. The task of forming a harmoniously diverse humanity is our own, however distant the Bildung tradition: ours the task of self-government, of speaking in public; ours the task of culture, of compelling narration, of the creative work of imagination as of the critical work of reason; ours the task of finding shining exemplars to admire, and of seeking to discern how to emulate what is admirable in them in the context of our own embodied particularity. Ours too is the task of uncovering the mutual dependencies of unexamined oppositions. And ours as well is the work of scrutinizing our social practices, awake to where they prove inadequate to "the Concept."

What is critical to sustaining these tasks is an ever-renewed commitment to listening to precisely those voices we are most tempted to dismiss and rule out of court, or think we have already fully heard. It is not a matter of refraining from assessment, of sliding into relativism, but of commitment to thoroughly dialogical practices of assessment of both self and other. Given the epistemic injustices built into our practices and identities, and shaping our habits of trust, speech, and listening, this is no easy matter.[60] It is incumbent on us too to develop more expansive conceptions of speech and listening, capable of encompassing the full spectrum of our reciprocal relations with the nonhuman as well as the human world. Participating in the *reditus* of creation involves being "attuned to, resonating with, and fulfilling the relations within which we are enmeshed and through which we live and breathe and have our being."[61] These are tasks we can sustain only insofar as we grasp, amidst all this effort, that we are not so much achieving ourselves as receiving ourselves from one another, and insofar as we grant that consummation can only be eschatological and hence beyond our ability to secure. It is in mutual recognition of one another in all of our socially embedded particularity, and in the shared life, the friendship, that this recognition makes possible, that we become more fully human. We are in one another's hands.

ACKNOWLEDGMENTS

I have been at work on this project for a long time and have accumulated many debts along the way. I am glad to have the opportunity to acknowledge them here. Forming Humanity is the fruit of a research fellowship from the Alexander von Humboldt Foundation that enabled me to conduct research at the University of Bielefeld in 2008–9 and again in fall 2011. I am grateful to the Foundation and its very able staff, and also to the warm hospitality of the staff of the Zentrum für interdisziplinäre Forschung at the University of Bielefeld, where my family and I stayed. I could not have asked for a wiser or more generous host than Wolfgang Braungart, professor of German Literature at the University of Bielefeld. Vittorio Hösle and Mark Roche, both of the University of Notre Dame, offered critical support and encouragement in the very early stages of the project. John Cavadini, then chair of the Department of Theology at the University of Notre Dame, granted me leave time from my usual academic duties in 2008–9, as did Harry Attridge, then dean of the Yale University Divinity School, in fall 2011. Greg Sterling, current dean of the Yale University Divinity School, was kind enough to enable me to take a leave from my responsibilities as senior associate dean of Academic Affairs in spring 2017; without that leave the manuscript would have continued to languish.

I have been fortunate in having opportunities to deliver lectures and informal talks on related material to various audiences, including at the University of Bielefeld in spring 2009; the Colloquium in Religion and Critical Thought at Brown University; the Orr Lectures at Wilson College in April 2012; "Forming Humanity: Practices of

Education Christianly Considered," presented at "Everyday Ethics: A Future for Moral Theology?," a conference of the McDonald Centre held in May 2016 at Christ Church, University of Oxford; and "The Problem of Human Making from Pietism to Hegel," Oberlin College, November 10, 2016. I am grateful to my hosts and interlocutors on each of these occasions. Chuck Mathewes and UVA's Religious Studies Department generously hosted a manuscript workshop in September 2017, and I am indebted to all of the participants, most particularly respondents Eric Hilker and Kyle Nicholas, and Chuck Mathewes, who offered judicious written feedback on the entire manuscript. The project also benefited from vigorous discussion by faculty and students in the Religious Ethics Colloquium at Yale University in fall 2017. Various individuals read parts of the manuscript and offered very helpful feedback; I am grateful in particular to James Dunn, Jan Hagens, Ryan McAnnally-Linz, and Timothy Jackson, and hope that I have not failed to acknowledge others. Tal Lewis and Jeffrey Stout have been critical for my engagement with Hegel, even if they would not agree with the reading I offer here; Adam Eitel planted the idea of engaging with Barth. Two reviewers for the University of Chicago Press offered their keen insight, pressing me in the most productive way possible in slightly different directions; they were then kind enough to make themselves known to me, thus enabling me to benefit from their feedback as I made revisions to the manuscript; I am most fortunate in being able therefore to thank Kevin Hector and Gerald McKenny by name. Alan Thomas at the University of Chicago Press cheered the project on and passed me along into the very capable hands of my editor Kyle Wagner; I am grateful to both, as well as to Ruth Goring, with whom I had the pleasure of working for a second time, and to the entire production team. I gratefully acknowledge financial support provided by a grant from the Frederick W. Hilles Fund of Yale University. There are many others with whom I have engaged in imagined conversation throughout the process of writing this book; while they remain unnamed, I am indebted to them as well, and to the ways in which their arguments and questions have shaped my own. Amidst all of this bounty of support and assistance, I am acutely conscious of the limitations of the book, and of my own finitude. I am solely responsible for whatever blind spots and errors remain.

My final debt is to my husband, Jan, and children, Cora and Adam. They have accompanied me on all the ups and downs that the adventure of writing a book entails. Without their steadfast love and support, it would never have seen the light of day.

NOTES

INTRODUCTION

1. Immanuel Kant, "Beantwortung der Frage: Was Ist Aufklärung?" in *Gesammelte Schriften*, Deutsche Akademie der Wissenschaft zu Berlin (Berlin: Walter de Gruyter, 1907-) (hereafter AA), 8:35, translated in "An Answer to the Question: 'What Is Enlightenment?,'" in *Kant's Political Writings*, ed. Hans Reiss, trans. H. B. Nisbet (Cambridge: Cambridge University Press, 1991), 54.

2. Thomas Pfau, "Beyond Liberal Utopia: Freedom as the Problem of Modernity," *European Romantic Review* 19.2 (2008): 83–103; here 97.

3. Alasdair MacIntyre, *Ethics in the Conflicts of Modernity* (Cambridge: Cambridge University Press, 2016), 315.

4. Terry Pinkard, *German Philosophy 1760-1860: The Legacy of Idealism* (Cambridge: Cambridge University Press, 2002), 7.

5. Benedict Anderson, *Imagined Communities: Reflections on the Origin and Spread of Nationalism*, 2nd ed. (1st ed. 1983; London: Verso, 1991), 7, 11, 43.

6. Madame de Staël, *De l'Allmagne*, 2nd ed. (Paris, 1814), 31–32.

7. Bruce Lincoln's account of Herder's key role in the positive retrieval of "myth" as the primordial expression of *Völker* attends to the ways in which Herder's thought was appropriated for nationalist projects, but elides the humanist character of Herder's own project: *Theorizing Myth: Narrative, Ideology, and Scholarship* (Chicago: University of Chicago Press, 1999), 52–56.

8. Martha Nussbaum, "Patriotism and Cosmopolitanism," *Boston Review*, October 1, 1994.

9. E.g., Martha Nussbaum, *Poetic Justice: The Literary Imagination and Public Life* (Boston: Beacon, 1995).

10. Anthony Appiah, "Cosmopolitan Reading," in *Cosmopolitan Geographies: New Locations in Literature and Culture*, ed. Vinay Dharwadker (New York: Routledge, 2001), 223.

11. See Pinkard, *German Philosophy*, 7; Robert B. Pippin, *Modernism as a Philosophical Problem*, 2nd ed. (1st ed. 1991; Oxford: Blackwell, 1999), 13–14; refuting the notion of the "apolitical" German character is a central thesis of Frederick Beiser's *Enlightenment, Revolution, and Romanticism: The Genesis of German Political Thought 1790-1800* (Cambridge, MA: Harvard University Press, 1992), see esp. 7–9.

12. Kant, "What Is Enlightenment?," AA 8:36/55 (henceforth number following solidus is page in English translation).

13. Kant, "What Is Enlightenment?," AA 8:36/55.

14. Kant, "What is Enlightenment?," AA 8:41–42/60.

15. Quoted in Jürgen Habermas, *The Structural Transformation of the Public Sphere*, trans. Thomas Burger (Cambridge, MA: MIT Press, 1989). Translation of *Strukturwandel der Öffentlichkeit* (Darmstadt, Germany: Hermann Luchterhand Verlag, 1962), 25.

16. While the thinkers on whom I focus in this study understood themselves as correcting and supplementing Kant, Kant did consider moral formation imperative; the moral law must provide both the objective and the subjective ground of motivation, but this is possible only through the feeling of respect for the moral law, and this feeling is elicited through cultivation. Moreover, Kant argues in the *Doctrine of Virtue* that there is a duty to cultivate feelings (notably sympathetic joy and sadness) that make it easier to act well: "Nature has already implanted in human beings receptivity to these feelings. But to use this as a means to promoting active and rational benevolence is still a particular, though only a conditional, duty. It is called the duty of humanity (*humanitas*) because a human being is regarded here not merely as a rational being but also as an animal endowed with reason," AA 6:456, trans. in Immanuel Kant, *Practical Philosophy*, ed. Mary Gregor (Cambridge: Cambridge University Press, 1996). As inadequate and limited as he found natural compassion to be, Kant nevertheless regarded it as "one of the impulses that nature has implanted in us to do what the representation of duty alone might not accomplish" (AA 6:457). Important recent work recovering these aspects of Kant's thought include Robert Louden, *Kant's Impure Ethics* (Oxford: Oxford University Press, 2000); John H. Zammito, *Kant, Herder, and the Birth of Anthropology* (Chicago: University of Chicago Press, 2002); Ian Hunter, "The Morals of Metaphysics: Kant's *Groundwork* as Intellectual Paideia," *Critical Inquiry* 28.4 (2002): 908–29; and Chad Wellmon, *Becoming Human: Romantic Anthropology and the Embodiment of Freedom* (University Park: Pennsylvania State University Press, 2010). Kant's contemporaries nevertheless found his efforts to relate human beings as free subjects of the moral law to human beings as creatures of inclination to be profoundly unsatisfying.

17. Habermas, *Structural Transformation*, 25–26.

18. Habermas, *Structural Transformation*, 28.

19. For this understanding of a broad tradition of Christian humanism, discussed in chapter 1, see, e.g., R. W. Southern, *Medieval Humanism and Other Studies* (Oxford: Basil Blackwell, 1970), 31–32; Alasdair MacDonald, Zweder von Martels, and Jan Veenstra, eds., *Christian Humanism: Essays in Honor of Arjo Vanderjagt* (Leiden: Brill, 2009), ix–x; John Bequette, ed., *A Companion to Medieval Christian Humanism* (Leiden: Brill, 2016), 6; Amos Edelheit, *Ficino, Pico, and Savonarola: The Evolution of Humanist Theology 1461/2-1498* (Leiden: Brill, 2008), 9–10.

20. My undertaking here has certain resonances with another recent project that defends the theological significance of modern German theologians from Kant to Tillich in terms of concerns with ethical formation; Kevin Hector's *The Theological Project of Modernism: Faith and the Conditions of Mineness* (Cambridge: Cambridge University Press, 2015), which persuasively argues that these thinkers are all concerned with the conditions of the possibility of experiencing one's life as self-expressive, and with God as overcoming oppositions that make this sort of identification difficult.

21. Other contemporary theological retrievals of humanism include David Klemm and William Schweiker, *Religion and the Human Future: An Essay on Theological Humanism* (Oxford: Wiley-Blackwell, 2008), and William Schweiker, *Dust That Breathes: Christian Faith and the New Humanisms* (Oxford: Wiley-Blackwell, 2011). Schweiker characterizes Christian humanism as "a legacy steeped in a love of learning, the examination of life, a practical take on Christian faith, and open to truth wherever it can be found," x. While the present project shares in the affirmation of these goods, Christian humanism is here understood in the more determinate way sketched above.

22. Habermas, *Structural Transformation*, 46–47.

23. Habermas, *Structural Transformation*, 48.

24. Max Horkheimer, *Autorität und Familie*, 64, quoted in Habermas, *Structural Transformation*, 48.

25. Martha Nussbaum, *Poetic Justice: The Literary Imagination and Public Life* (Boston: Beacon, 1995), 27.

26. Nussbaum, *Poetic Justice*, 31.

27. Nussbaum, *Poetic Justice*, 38.

28. Nussbaum, *Poetic Justice*, 24.

29. Martha Nussbaum, *Love's Knowledge: Essays on Philosophy and Literature* (New York: Oxford University Press, 1990), 375.

30. Martha Nussbaum, *Upheavals of Thought: The Intelligence of Emotions* (Cambridge: Cambridge University Press, 2001), 547.

31. Nussbaum, *Upheavals*, 590; see also 552.

32. Taylor, *Secular Age*, 697, 701.

33. Charles Taylor, *A Secular Age* (Cambridge, MA: Belknap, 2007), 359; on ontic indeterminacy, see also 404, 757–69; open and closed readings of the "immanent frame," 272, 550.

34. Jeffrey Stout, *Blessed Are the Organized: Grassroots Democracy in America* (Princeton, NJ: Princeton University Press, 2010), 219.

35. Charles Mathewes, *A Theology of Public Life* (Cambridge: Cambridge University Press, 2007), 74. Mathewes puts forth a vision of Christian civic participation as liturgical and ascetic—that is, as part of Christians' fundamental vocation, rather than as a foray into alien ("secular") territory.

36. Stout explicitly defends the usefulness of the term "sacred value" (*Blessed Are the Organized*, 219), in contrast to Nussbaum, who argues that the language of *sacred* or *infinite* value has "generated much confusion" and is too vague to be useful (*Poetic Justice*, 69). Stout notes that his thinking on sacred value has been most strongly influenced by Robert Merrihew Adams's *Finite and Infinite Goods* (Oxford: Oxford University Press, 1999), chap. 4, and Marilyn McCord Adams's *Horrendous Evils and the Goodness of God* (Ithaca, NY: Cornell University Press, 1999), though he also acknowledges common ground with the argument Ronald Dworkin makes about sacred value in *Life's Dominion: An Argument about Abortion, Euthanasia, and Individual Freedom* (New York: Alfred A. Knopf, 1993). Iris Murdoch, like Adams heavily influenced by Plato, argues that moral philosophy ought to retain as a central concept "a single perfect transcendent non-representable and necessary real object of attention." *The Sovereignty of Good* (1970; repr. Oxford: Routledge, 2001), 54.

37. Raymond Geuss, *Morality, Culture, and History: Essays on German Philosophy* (Cambridge: Cambridge University Press, 1999), 37–38, 42.

38. Immanuel Kant, "On the Different Human Races" (1777), in *The Idea of Race*, ed. Robert Bernasconi and Tommy Lott (Indianapolis: Hackett, 2000), 8–22; Mark Larrimore, "Sublime Waste: Kant on the Destiny of the 'Races,'" in *Civilization and Oppression*, ed. Cheryl J. Misak (Calgary: University of Calgary Press, 1999), 103; J. Kameron Carter, *Race: A Theological Account* (Oxford: Oxford University Press, 2008), 89–92; Sara Eigen and Mark Larrimore, eds., *The German Invention of Race* (Albany: State University of New York Press, 2006); Chad Wellmon, *Becoming Human*, 141–163. However, Sankar Muthu, while acknowledging that Kant's writings in the 1770s contributed to biological notions of race, has argued that "the hierarchical and biological concept of race disappears" in Kant's later writings (*Enlightenment against Empire* [Princeton, NJ: Princeton University Press, 2003], 183). This is not supported by the analyses of others, e.g., Thomas McCarthy, *Race, Empire, and the Idea of Human Development* (Cambridge: Cambridge University Press, 2009), 48–49.

39. Wellmon, *Becoming Human*, 275.

40. Theodore Vial, *Modern Religion, Modern Race* (Oxford: Oxford University Press, 2016), 254. On the ways in which premodern notions of providence were transformed and taken up into modern notions of progress, see Genevieve Lloyd, *Providence Lost* (Cambridge, MA: Harvard University Press, 2008), 279–301.

41. McCarthy, *Race, Empire*, 18.

42. Karl Barth, *Protestant Theology in the Nineteenth Century: Its Background and History* (London: SCM Press, 1972; orig. German ed. 1952), 76.

43. Barth, "Church and Culture," in *Die Theologie und die Kirche* (Zollikon-Zürich: Evangelischer Verlag, 1928), 337. Timothy Gorringe similarly turns to this lecture in his *Furthering Humanity* (Aldershot, Hampshire, UK: Ashgate, 2004); while Gorringe draws some inspiration from Herder, he does not engage with the broader Bildung tradition, and his project is centrally that of constructing a theology of culture and mission; mine is a moral anthropology.

44. Barth, "Church and Culture," 338.

45. Barth, "Church and Culture," 339.

46. Barth, "Church and Culture," 339.

47. Barth, "Church and Culture," 339.

48. Barth, "Church and Culture," 341.

49. Barth, "Church and Culture," 342, 345.

50. Karl Barth, *Church Dogmatics*, ed. G. W. Bromiley and T. F. Torrance (London: T&T Clark, 1932–67), 3/1:185.

51. Barth, "Church and Culture," 343.

52. Barth, "Church and Culture," 343.

53. Barth, "Church and Culture," 344. Or see *The Christian Life*, where Barth writes, "There are some things possible which, more than others, are able to bear witness, are full of hints, parables of the coming world, the new world, the Kingdom of God. Not as if the Kingdom of God dawned with such deeds, such human activity. We cannot build the Kingdom of God. But we will honestly say: There we are dealing with the Church—or to express it less theologically: the good," Trans. J. Strathearn McNab (London: SCM Press, 1930), 59.

54. Barth, "Church and Culture," 346.

55. Barth, "Church and Culture," 346.

56. Barth, "Church and Culture," 349, 354.

57. Barth, *Protestant Theology*, 407.

58. Barth, *Protestant Theology*, 407.

59. Barth, *Protestant Theology*, 414.

60. Bruce L. McCormack, *Karl Barth's Critically Realistic Dialectical Theology: Its Genesis and Development 1909-1936* (Oxford: Oxford University Press, 1995), 38–67.

61. Anders Odenstedt, "Hegel and Gadamer on Bildung," *Southern Journal of Philosophy* 46 (2008): 559–80.

62. Barth, *Protestant Theology*, 114.

63. Barth, *Protestant Theology*, 114–22.

64. Barth, *Protestant Theology*, 116.

65. Gerald McKenny, *Analogy of Grace* (Oxford: Oxford University Press, 2010), 281; Karl Barth, *Church Dogmatics (CD)*, ed. G. W. Bromiley and T. F. Torrance (London: T&T Clark, 1932–67), II/2, 632–36/702–7.

66. McKenny, *Analogy of Grace*, 285, discussing Barth, *CD* II/2, 637/708.

67. Barth, *CD* I/1, 55. Barth's theology was to become not just christologically grounded but christocentric only after 1936, as Bruce McCormack has shown: *Karl Barth's Critically Realistic Dialectical Theology* (Oxford: Clarendon, 1995), 328, 453–63. After this point (beyond CD I/1 and I/2), Barth is committed to understanding all Christian doctrines "from a centre in God's Self-revelation in Jesus Christ" (454). He remained, however, a dialectical theologian: "the eternal Son is present in history indirectly, never becoming directly identical with the veil of human flesh in which He conceals Himself" (366). Even here the dialectic of "veiling and unveiling" in revelation remains; God unveils Godself by veiling Godself (18). That all Christian doctrines are to be understood only in and through Jesus Christ does not mean that one ought to listen for the Word of God only there. We may take hints here on how a humanism worthy of the name will be something other than anthropocentrism; we can listen for God in those who cannot speak to us, even if it is those who speak who must hold one another accountable for our hearing and failure to hear. Given the scope of the current project, these hints will not be developed further here, but such development is a critically important task of the present moment of climate change crisis, coming to terms with the failure of anthropocentrism in the context of the Anthropocene.

68. This is not, however, to reduce the theological claim to a political claim. What Barth offers toward a critical appropriation of the Bildung tradition will hardly be heard in the same way by Christian and non-Christian readers. The former will take Christ's humanity, together with scripture and preaching, to be decisively revelatory of the Word of God; it is Christ's humanity that establishes true humanity and in which we find our own and others' humanity to be established. The latter will listen rather for "sacred value" or "the good." The agenda here is not to reduce one to the other but to open fruitful lines of communication between them.

69. Dipesh Chakrabarty, *Provincializing Europe: Postcolonial Thought and Historical Difference* (Princeton, NJ: Princeton University Press, 2008), 254, discussed with reference to Herder's thought by John Kenneth Noyes, *Aesthetics against Imperialism* (Toronto: University of Toronto Press, 2015), 302–3.

70. *Christ and the Common Life: A Guide to Political Theology* (Grand Rapids, MI: Eerdmans, forthcoming 2019), chap. 10.

71. This raises not just pressing political questions but also urgent questions concerning disability and nonhuman life, even if these questions remain unarticulated within the Bildung tradition; this is one reason that an eschatological frame of reference presses itself on us, together with the need for an expansive notion of speech capable of making sense of the psalmist's proclamation that "the heavens are telling the glory of God"; "human activity as cultivation of the garden should seek to fructify creation, and so enable the wonder and goodness of what God has created to shine forth as part of fostering reciprocal relations of praise and thanksgiving with creation" (Bretherton, *Christ and the Common Life*).

72. Judith Butler, "What Is Critique?" in *The Judith Butler Reader*, ed. Sarah Salih (Oxford: Basil Blackwell, 2004), 314; discussing Michel Foucault, "What Is Critique?" in *The Politics of Truth*, ed. Sylvère Lotringer and Lysa Hochroth (New York: Semiotext(e), 1997).

73. Theodor Adorno, "Cultural Criticism and Society," in *Prisms* (Cambridge, MA: MIT Press, 1984), 29.

74. The notion of "the tear in the fabric of our epistemological web" as the site for the practice of critique comes from Butler, "What Is Critique?" 308.

75. G. W. F. Hegel, *Vorlesungen über die Geschichte der Philosophie 3, Werke* 20 (Frankfurt: Suhrkamp, 1971), 91–119.

76. "The structural principle of irony manifests itself as a perpetual oscillation of the project of *Bildung* between the chaotic and the systematic, between random projections of desire and the stability of a logos intimated by the protagonists' occasional, brief flashes of self-awareness," "Romantic *Bildung* and the Persistence of Teleology," 20. What Thomas Pfau reads as mere oscillation I read as an implicit acknowledgment that no merely immanent teleology can suffice, and hence as an opening to a transcendent conception of the good.

77. Kathryn Tanner, *God and Creation in Christian Theology* (Minneapolis: Fortress, 1988; 2005).

78. See, e.g., Cyril O'Regan, *The Heterodox Hegel* (Albany: State University of New York Press, 1994), 175–80; William Desmond, *Hegel's God: A Counterfeit Double?* (Aldershot, UK: Ashgate, 2003), 2–5, 74.

79. For an acute analysis of the problematic ways in which recent trinitarian theologies continue to "introduce aspects of sinful and finite human existence into the immanent trinity in order to overcome them there, rather than through the trinity's transformative work in history," see Linn Marie Tonstad, *God and Difference: The Trinity, Sexuality, and the Transformation of Finitude* (New York: Routledge, 2016), 10.

CHAPTER ONE

1. Günther Dohmen, *Bildung und Schule* (Weinheim: J. Beltz, 1964), 1:29.
2. *Luther Bibel* (1545), 1. Mose 1:27.
3. Gerhart B. Ladner, *The Idea of Reform: Its Impact on Christian Thought and Action in the Age of the Fathers* (Cambridge, MA: Harvard University Press, 1959).
4. Ernest L. Stahl, *Die Religiöse und die Humanitätsphilosophische Bildungsidee und die Entstehung des deutschen Bildungsromans im 18. Jahrhundert* (Bern: Paul Haupt, 1934; Liechtenstein: Kraus Reprint, 1970), 6–8.
5. The classic account is that of Stahl, *Bildungsidee*. Stahl's account is followed, e.g., by Todd Kontje, *The German Bildungsroman: History of a National Genre* (Columbia, SC: Camden House, 1993), 1–4, and Wilhlem Voßkamp, *Ein anderes Selbst: Bildung und Bild im deutschen Roman des 18. und 19. Jahrhunderts* (Göttingen: Wallstein Verlag, 2004), 14–15.
6. Werner Jaeger, *Paideia*, trans. Gilbert Highet, 2nd ed. (New York: Oxford University Press, 1945), 1:xxiii.
7. Jaeger, *Paideia*, 1:316–21.
8. Henry Marrou, *A History of Education in Antiquity*, trans. George Lamb (New York: Sheed and Ward, 1956), 223, 322 — classical education was "supposed to result in a kind of indeterminate human product of very high intrinsic quality, ready to respond to any demand made upon it by the intellect or circumstance."
9. Jaeger, *Paideia*, 1:xxiii, 417n6. Of course Jaeger's interpretation of classical paideia was itself formed by his own inheritance of the Bildung tradition. Jaeger emphasized, for instance, that paideia was "not an empty abstract pattern, existing outside time and space," but rather "the living ideal which had grown up in the very soil of Greece" (xxiv). It was therefore not an aspiration to shape character into a "fixed and final" standard. Ironically, while Jaeger recognized that paideia was an aristocratic ideal, he also sees in it the source of the affirmation of universal human dignity, which Christianity merely spread (xix). Where he comes closest to acknowledging a tension between the aristocratic character of classical paideia and the affirmation of basic human equality, he protests that "the fact that culture in the humanistic sense was originally restricted to a special class" has never "prevented later generations from asking that more men might share its benefits" (417).
10. There were, of course, multiple competing visions of classical paideia. Whereas Isocrates, for instance, was relatively optimistic that public deliberation would advance the common good, Plato was less sanguine. Kathryn Morgan, "The Education of Athens," in *Isocrates and Civic Education*, ed. Takis Poulakos and David Depew (Austin: University of Texas Press, 2009), 134.

See also Josiah Ober, *Mass and Elite in Democratic Athens* and *The Athenian Revolution* (Princeton, NJ: Princeton University Press, 1991).

11. Jaeger, *Paideia*, 1:416n5.

12. Jaeger, "Classical Philology at the University of Berlin 1870–1945," in *Five Essays*, trans. Adele M. Fiske (Montreal: M. Casalini, 1966), 70–71.

13. Jaś Elsner, "Paideia: Ancient Concept and Modern Reception," *International Journal of the Classical Tradition* 20 (2013): 136–52.

14. Elsner, "Paideia: Ancient Concept," 144.

15. Marrou, *History of Education*, 101; Elsner, "Paideia: Ancient Concept," 145.

16. *Noctes Atticae* 13.17.1, quoted in Richard A. Bauman, *Human Rights in Ancient Rome* (London: Routledge, 2003), 20.

17. Bauman, *Human Rights*, 20.

18. "They recognized that a complementary expansion of ancient Roman *virtus* was necessary for their hegemony in this part of the world [Greece]: the extension and supplementation of this *virtus* through the *humanitas* displayed by the Greeks." Wolfgang Schadewaldt, "Humanitas Romana," in *Aufstieg und Niedergang der römischen Welt* 1.4 (Berlin: Walter de Gruyter, 1974), 56.

19. Bauman, *Human Rights*, 25.

20. 4.12, 23, discussed in Bauman, *Human Rights*, 26.

21. Bauman, *Human Rights*, 22.

22. *Ad Q. fr.* 1.1.3–8, 10, 17, 20–25; Cicero *De off.* 1.35, 1.88, Leg. agrar. 2.87; see Bauman, *Human Rights*, 24.

23. Schadewaldt, "Humanitas Romana," 60.

24. Cicero, *De re publica* 1.28–29; *De legibus* 1.8.25. Translations in Cicero. *On the Republic, On the Laws*, trans. Clinton W. Keyes, Loeb Classical Library 213 (Cambridge, MA: Harvard University Press, 1928). Cf. *Tusculan Disputations* 5.66.

25. *De legibus* 1.8.24.

26. *De legibus* 1.8.24.

27. *De officiis* 1.50; *On Duties*, translated by Walter Miller, Loeb Classical Library 30 (Cambridge, MA: Harvard University Press, 1913).

28. *Pro scauro* 44, In *Orations*, trans. N. H. Watt, Loeb Classical Library 252 (Cambridge, MA: Harvard University Press, 1931).

29. Ralph Haeussler, *Becoming Roman? Divergent Identities and Experiences in Ancient Northwest Italy* (Oxford: Routledge, 2013), 53.

30. Tacitus, *Agricola*, trans. Maurice Hutton (London: Heinemann, 1914), 21.

31. Christopher B. Krebs, *A Most Dangerous Book: Tacitus's "Germania" from the Roman Empire to the Third Reich* (New York: W. W. Norton, 2011), 45.

32. Geoffrey Chaucer, *The Canterbury Tales*, ed. Norman F. Blake (London: Arnold, 1980), 210–11.

33. Maurice Keen, *Origins of the English Gentleman: Heraldry, Chivalry and Gentility in Medieval England, c. 1300-c. 1500* (Gloucestershire: Tempus, 2002), 16–18.

34. Lawrence Stone, *The Crisis of the Aristocracy, 1558-1641* (Oxford: Oxford University Press, 1962), 23.

35. Nicholas Upton, *De Studio Militari*, ed. Bysshe (London: 1664), quoted in Keen, *Origins of the English Gentleman*, 103–4.

36. On these social transitions, see J. G. A. Pocock, "Virtues, Rights, and Manners: A Model for Historians of Political Thought," in *Virtue, Commerce, and History* (Cambridge: Cambridge University Press, 1985), 37–50; and Markku Peltonen, *The Duel in Early Modern England: Civility, Politeness and Honour* (Cambridge: Cambridge University Press, 2003).

37. Paul Oskar Kristeller, *Renaissance Thought II* (New York: Harper & Row, 1965), 178.

38. Kristeller, *Renaissance Thought II*, 4.

39. R. W. Southern, *Medieval Humanism and Other Studies* (Oxford: Basil Blackwell, 1970), 31–32. Recent scholarship continues to support the usefulness of identifying a twelfth-century humanist movement and of studying it hand in hand with Renaissance humanism—e.g., Alasdair MacDonald, Zweder von Martels, and Jan Veenstra, introduction to *Christian Humanism: Essays in Honor of Arjo Vanderjagt*, ed. (Leiden: Brill, 2009), ix–x. Both movements were committed to the reconciliation of pagan learning and Christian theology. See, e.g., Amos Edelheit's defense of "humanist theology" over against Kristeller's tendency to erect a total separation between theology and humanism: *Ficino, Pico, and Savonarola: The Evolution of Humanist Theology 1461/2-1498* (Leiden: Brill, 2008), 9–10. Edelheit rightly emphasizes that the humanists cannot be understood unless their literary studies are seen as part and parcel of theological and political concerns, following along a path of interpretation laid out by Charles Trinkaus, *In Our Image and Likeness: Humanity and Divinity in Italian Humanist Thought* (London: Constable, 1970), and John O'Malley, *Praise and Blame in Renaissance Rome* (Durham, NC: Duke University Press, 1979).

40. Southern, *Medieval Humanism*, 37.

41. Paul Ramsey influentially argued that there are two basic understandings of the imago Dei within Christian theology: a substantial, or structural, view, and a relational view: *Basic Christian Ethics* (orig. 1950; Louisville, KY: Westminster John Knox, 1993), 250–54. According to the structural view, the image of God is located in certain attributes or capacities of the human person, notably the intellect or the will, while the relational view regards the imago as arising out of a relationship between the human person and God and thus not as a possession or structural element of human nature. Each relies on a primary metaphor: the structural view on clay formed by a pot-

ter (or wax imprinted by a seal), and the relational view on a mirror that can reflect someone's image only when placed before that person. Stanley Grenz supplements Ramsey's distinction with the notion of imago as eschatological destiny, a conception he finds rooted in the patristic theology of Irenaeus and emerging again in the eighteenth century with Herder: Grenz, *The Social God and the Relational Self* (Louisville, KY: Westminster John Knox, 2006), 147–48. Of course a teleological dimension is rarely absent from understandings of the imago, embedded as it is in the doctrine of creation, fall, reconciliation, and eschatological consummation. And even the most emphatically relational understandings of the *imago* assume some structural ground for the possibility of mirroring.

42. *Summa theologica* (ST), translated by Fathers of the English Dominican Province (Westminster, MD: Christian Classics, 1981), prologue to vols. 1–2. References indicate sequentially volume, question, and article.

43. ST 1.93.1.

44. ST 1.93.2.

45. ST 1.93.6.

46. Augustine, *De Trinitate* 374–76, trans. Edmund Hill, Works of Saint Augustine 1/5 (Brooklyn, NY: New City, 1991).

47. Augustine, *De Trinitate* 383–85.

48. On the functional understanding in Genesis, see J. Richard Middleton, *The Liberating Image: The Imago Dei in Genesis 1* (Grand Rapids, MI: Brazos, 2005), 88.

49. Adam Eitel, "*De Beata Vita*: Love and Friendship in Thomas Aquinas," PhD diss., Princeton Theological Seminary, 2015, 156–202.

50. *Summa theologica* 1.93.4.

51. This aspect of Thomas's account is often overlooked, as it comes to fruition only in the neglected third part of the *Summa*. See Joseph Wawrykow, "Jesus in the Moral Theology of Thomas Aquinas," *Journal of Medieval and Early Modern Studies* 42.1 (2012): 13–33; Wawrykow argues that Jesus models not independently acquired virtue but humble reception of divine grace, while other human beings now become virtuous through their reception of Christ's saving grace. Grenz, for instance, misses this and faults Aquinas's understanding of the imago Dei as insufficiently christological: *Social God*, 153.

52. Indeed so much so that while it is still often hailed as providing an indispensable foundation for universal human dignity, it has also been dismissed as ill-suited to doing dignity work, e.g., by David Kelsey, *Eccentric Existence* (Louisville, KY: Westminster John Knox, 2009), 938.

53. Hans-Georg Kemper's *Gottebenbildlichkeit und Naturnachahmung im Säkularisierungsprozess* (Tübingen: Niemeyer, 1981) is quite a wide-ranging and suggestive study of the imago Dei theme in relation to German Enlight-

enment and Romantic thought. Kemper is right to note that the impulse to engage with and transform the world, common to humanism and the Reformation, did not emerge from a promethean declaration of human autonomy but was made possible by understandings of the natural world as revelatory of its Creator and of human nature as made in the image of God. Unfortunately, he works within a procrustean set of assumptions concerning an irresistible "Sakularisierungsprozess," contrastive understandings of divine transcendence, and a tidy division between "Christian" and "non-Christian" thinkers (in which Jewish Aristotelians like Maimonides, Neoplatonists like Agrippa of Nettesheim and Paracelsus, deists like Tindal, rationalists like Kant, and romantics like Herder, Schleiermacher, and Novalis fall together into the "non-Christian" category).

54. Bernard McGinn, *The Mystical Thought of Meister Eckhart* (New York: Crossroad, 2001), 1; Jeremiah Hackett, *A Companion to Meister Eckhart* (Leiden: Brill, 2012), xxvii.

55. *Meister Eckhart: Die deutschen und lateinischen Werke*, ed. Josef Quint (Stuttgart: Kohlhammer, 1936–); translations from *The Complete Mystical Works of Meister Eckhart*, trans. Maurice O'C. Walshe (New York: Crossroad, 2009), 2.39. References are given by the volume, sermon number, and page of the Quint edition (Q), followed by the sermon number and page of the English translation (W), 4.1.102.410; 2.39.

56. Q 1.1.5; W 6.66.

57. Q 4.1.101.335; W 1.29.

58. Q 4.1.101.346; W 1.31.

59. Q 4.1.101.345; W 1.30.

60. Q 4.1.101.343; W 1.29; see also Q 4.1.102.409; W 2.44, and Q 4.1.103.474; W 4.55–56.

61. Q 1.1.12; W 6.68.

62. Q 4.1.101.350; W 1.32.

63. Q 4.1.101.351; W 1.32.

64. Q 4.1.101.352; W 1.32.

65. Q 4.1.101.358; W 1.34, quoting Dionysius the Areopagite, *De divinis nominibus* 9.6.

66. Q 1.16b.266; W 14b.115.

67. Q 1.16b.266–267; W 14b.115.

68. Q 2.25.13; 10.93.

69. Q 4.1.104.581; W 3.48.

70. Q 4.1.104.579; W 3.48.

71. Q 4.1.104.584; W 3.49.

72. Q 4.1.104; 587; W 3.49.

73. Q 1.5a.78; W 13a.106.

74. Q 4, *Book of Divine Comfort*, 30; W 535.
75. Q 2.27.48; W 12.101.
76. Q 2.25.17; W 10.93.
77. Q 3.65.97, W 5.62–63; Q 1.1.4, W 6.67; Q 4.1.102.407, W 2.44; Q 4.1.103.474, W 4.58.
78. Bernard McGinn, *The Harvest of Mysticism in Medieval Germany* (New York: Herder & Herder, 2005), 87–88; McGinn notes that "in pagan Neoplatonism, especially in Plotinus, there are equivalent formulations" (12) and argues that it was this notion of mystical identity and indistinction that was most novel and most prone to elicit censure as heretical (56).
79. Q 1.5b.86, W 13b.108; Q 2.25.18, W 10.94.
80. Q 1.5a.79, W 13a.105.
81. Q 5.28; W 534.
82. *Disputatio de Homine*, sentence 35, "pura materia Dei ad futurae formae suae vitam." D. Martin Luthers Werke (WA) (Weimar: Herman Böhlhaus Nachfolger, 1897), 39:1. Gerhard Ebeling translates this as "blosser Stoff," versus WA as "reine Materie." Gerhard Ebeling, *Disputatio de Homine*, Erster Teil, Text und Traditionshintergrund (Tübingen: Mohr, 1977), 23. English translations are my own if unmarked, or if indicated, from *Luther's Works* (LW) (Philadelphia: Fortress, 1957), 34:137–39; see Kemper, *Gottebenbildlichkeit*, 189.
83. *Lectures on Genesis*, 1535–45, WA 42:46b; LW 1:30–31. Hence claims that Luther turns his back on the tradition of speculation concerning Adamic existence, and that he is willing to say only that Adam lived with God in a relationship of love and trust rather than fear and dread, are overblown; Ivar Asheim, *Glaube und Erziehung bei Luther* (Heidelberg: Quelle & Meyer, 1961), 209–12.
84. WA 42:48b; LW 1:31–32.
85. WA 45:274–275b.
86. WA 10.1:1, 155.
87. "Du solch bilde wol fassest und als ein guter spigel rechten widerblick gebest," WA 37:452.
88. "Wenn wir solch bilde fassen . . . so spiegelt oder malet er sich jnn unser hertz, das wir von tag zu tag, jhe mehr und mehr jnn das selbige bilde verkleret werden, bis es gar volkomen werde," WA 37:453.
89. WA 37: 453b.
90. "Da verleuret er das bilde, das Gott gemalet hat, und bildet sich nach dem bild, das der Teuffel gemalt hat," WA 37:454a.
91. WA 7:75; LW 31:347; WA 40.1:443, 448, 452; LW 26:284, 288, 290; Mark Mattes, "Luther on Justification as Forensic and Effective," in *The Oxford Handbook of Martin Luther's Theology*, ed. Robert Kolb, Irene Dingel,

and Lubomir Batka (Oxford: Oxford University Press, 2014), 264–73. I am indebted to conversations with James J. Dunn on this topic.

92. See Robert Kolb, "Luther on the Two Kinds of Righteousness: Reflections on His Two-Dimensional Definition of Humanity at the Heart of His Theology," *Lutheran Quarterly* 13 (1999): 449–66.

93. This aspect of Luther's theology has been recently recovered and underscored by the so-called Finnish School, although they wrongly conclude that Luther lacked a forensic understanding of justification; see, e.g., Tuomo Mannermaa, *Christ Present in Faith: Luther's View of Justification*, ed. Kirsi Stjerna (Minneapolis: Fortress, 2005), 4, 17–22, 54; Mannermaa, "Justification and Theosis," in *Union with Christ: The New Finnish Interpretation of Luther*, ed. Carl E. Braaten and Robert W. Jenson (Grand Rapids, MI: Eerdmans, 1998), 38; Mannermaa, *Der im Glauben gegenwärtige Christus: Rechtfertigung und Vergottung* (Hannover: Lutherisches Verlagshaus, 1989).

94. *Disputatio*, sentence 38, WA 39:1.

95. Luther always holds together two perspectives simultaneously, what Wilfried Joest terms the *Totalaspekt* and the *Partialaspekt*, according to which the Christian is both wholly justified (through grace) and also partially sinner / partially justified (through the indwelling transformative gift of Christ/faith), *Gesetz und Freiheit* (orig. 1951; Göttingen: Vandenhoeck & Ruprecht, 1968), 24–25; WA 8:106–7; LW 32:227–29; Gilbert Meilaender, *The Freedom of a Christian: Grace, Vocation, and the Meaning of Our Humanity* (Grand Rapids, MI: Brazos, 2006), 15–77. I discuss this more fully in *Putting On Virtue: The Legacy of the Splendid Vices* (Chicago: University of Chicago Press, 2008), 178–89.

96. Stahl, *Bildungsidee*, 76–78.

97. *Theophrast von Hohenheim, gen. Paracelsus Sämtliche Werke*, ed. Karl Sudhoff and Wilhelm Matthiessen (Munich: R. Oldenbourg, 1922–33), 1.xii.59–60; English translation from *Paracelsus*, ed. Nicholas Goodrick-Clarke (Berkeley: North Atlantic Books, 1999), 9.20, 118–19; hereafter references are given to the part, volume, and page number of the Sudhoff-Matthiessen edition, followed by the part, section, and page number of the Goodrick-Clarke translation, marked G-C.

98. Kemper, *Gottebenbildlichkeit*, 66–67.

99. Paracelsus, 1.xii.36–40; G-C 9.15–16, 116–17.

100. Paracelsus, 1.xii.41–42; G-C 9.17, 117.

101. Paracelsus, 1.ix.71; G-C 6.8, 80–81.

102. Paracelsus, 1.ix.72–73; G-C 6.9, 81.

103. Paracelsus, 1.ix.73–74, G-C 6.10, 82.

104. Paracelsus, 1.i.254; G-C 3.2, p. 58–59.

105. Kemper, *Gottebenbildlichkeit*, 65.

106. See Dohmen, *Bildung und Schule*, 1:68–77.
107. Paracelsus, 4:265–73. On imagination in Paracelsus, see Walter Pagel, *Paracelsus: An Introduction to Philosophical Medicine in the Era of the Renaissance* (Basel: Karger, 1958), 121–25.
108. Paracelsus, 1.i.262–3; G-C 3.4, p. 60.
109. Paracelsus, 1.i.181–182; G-C 2.3, 47.
110. Paracelsus, 1.xii.56–57; G-C 9.19, p. 118.
111. Paracelsus, 2.i.107; G-C 11.8, pp. 156–57; see also 1.xii.8–9; G-C 9.2, p. 111.
112. Paracelsus, 2.i.94–5; G-C 11.6, p. 156.

CHAPTER TWO

1. Karl Barth, *Protestant Theology in the Nineteenth Century: Its Background and History* (orig. German ed. 1952; London: SCM Press, 1972), 84–85. In situating Pietism alongside the Enlightenment in this way, Barth explicitly opposes Troeltsch and aligns himself with F. C. Baur and A. Ritschl.
2. Barth, *Protestant Theology*, 94.
3. Barth, *Protestant Theology*, 98.
4. Barth, *Protestant Theology*, 105.
5. Barth, *Protestant Theology*, 98; cf. CD II/2, 540/599 f.
6. Barth, *Protestant Theology*, 114.
7. Barth, *Protestant Theology*, 115.
8. Barth, *Protestant Theology*, 117.
9. Martin Brecht, "Einleitung," in *Der Pietismus vom siebzehnten bis zum frühen achtzehnten Jahrhundert*, ed. Martin Brecht (Göttingen: Vandenhoeck & Ruprecht, 1993), 3–9. Ernest Stoeffler, *The Rise of Evangelical Pietism* (Leiden: Brill, 1965), also argues for a broader definition, encompassing English Puritanism.
10. Johannes Wallmann surveys both broad and narrow definitions in "Was ist Pietismus?," in *Pietismus und Neuzeit: Ein Jahrbuch zur Geschichte des neueren Protestantismus*, ed. Martin Brecht, Friedrich de Boor, et al. (Göttingen: Vandenhoeck & Ruprecht, 1994), 20:11–27.
11. Spener, "Wahrhaftige Erzählung dessen, was wegen des sogenannten Pietismi in Deutschland vor einiger Zeit vorgegangen" (1697), quoted in Brecht, "Einleitung," 5.
12. Quoted in Wallmann, "Pietismus," 13.
13. Lucinda Martin, "Jacob Boehme and the Anthropology of German Pietism," in *An Introduction to Jacob Boehme: Four Centuries of Thought and Reception*, ed. Ariel Hessayon and Sarah Apetrei (New York: Routledge, 2014), 121, 127; Glenn Alexander Magee, "Hegel's Reception of Jacob Boehme," in

Introduction to Boehme, 225–27. Martin argues further that Boehme's influence extended even into the mainstream Pietist movement within the established churches (123).

14. James J. Dunn, "Arndt's Tauler / Arndt's Eckhart: The Indexing of a Self-Effacing Theological Tradition," unpublished manuscript.

15. Daniel Ross van Voorhis, "A Prophet of Interior Lutheranism: The Correspondence of Johann Arndt," sheds light on Arndt's self-understanding through a close examination of his letters (PhD diss., University of Saint Andrews, 2008). Many thanks to James Dunn for this reference.

16. Dorothea von der Mücke, *The Practices of the Enlightenment* (New York: Columbia University Press, 2015), 7.

17. Johann Arndt, *Sechs Bücher vom wahren Christentum nebst dessen Paradies-Gärtlein* (1605–10) (repr. Bielefeld: Missionsverlag der Evangl.-Luth. Gebetsgemeinschaft, 1991), 68.

18. Arndt, *Wahres Christentum*, 68.

19. Arndt, *Wahres Christentum*, 231.

20. Arndt, *Wahres Christentum*, 230.

21. Arndt, *Wahres Christentum*, 70.

22. Arndt, *Wahres Christentum*, 101.

23. Arndt, *Wahres Christentum*, 70.

24. Arndt, *Wahres Christentum*, 134.

25. Arndt, *Wahres Christentum*, 148.

26. Arndt, *Wahres Christentum*, 86.

27. Günther Dohmen claims that Arndt speaks of Bildung only in connection with the inner spiritual renewal of the image of God, not when he deals with practical Christian discipleship and imitation of Christ's example, and appeals to this separation as a basis for arguing that the concept of divine formation stood in fundamental tension with the practical imitation of Christ. *Bildung und Schule* (Weinheim: J. Beltz, 1964), 1:86. But while it is true that Arndt does not think that a mere external copying of Christ's actions effects a renewal of the divine image, his own understanding of the practical imitation of Christ is fundamentally connected with the renewal of the imago Dei.

28. I am indebted to James J. Dunn for conversations on this point.

29. Arndt, *Wahres Christentum*, 214.

30. Kemper, *Gottebenbildlichkeit*, 217–22.

31. Ariel Hessayon, "Boehme's Life and Times," in *Boehme*, ed. Hessayon and Apetrei, 27–29.

32. Andrew Weeks, *Boehme: An Intellectual Biography of the Seventeenth-Century Philosopher and Mystic* (Albany: State University of New York Press, 1991), 147.

33. References to Boehme's works will be to the 1731 edition: *Theosophia*

Revelata. Das ist: Alle Göttliche Schriften des Gottseligen und Hocherleuchteten Deutschen Theosophi Jacob Böhmens, 21 vols., ed. Johann Wilhelm Überfeld (Leiden, 1730), 2:36/4.31–32.
34. Boehme, 1:340/23.16–17.
35. Boehme, 1:24/1.3.
36. Boehme, 2:12/1.11–12.
37. Boehme, 2:13/1.13.
38. Boehme, 2:372–91/25.72–26.40.
39. Weeks, *Boehme*, 109.
40. Boehme, 2:11/1.9.
41. Boehme, 14:97/9.3 Weeks, *Boehme*, 192.
42. Boehme, 5:127/2.3.5; Weeks, *Boehme*, 149.
43. Boehme, 32:3–34/4.23.
44. Weeks, *Boehme*, 151; Pagel, *Paracelsus*, 121–25. While granting the influence of Paracelsus, Cyril O'Regan argues that "nothing in his predecessors justifies granting to them, rather than Boehme, credit for providing imagination with an ontotheological status by emphasizing not only its cosmogonic power but its power to constitute the divine as such." *Gnostic Apocalypse: Jacob Boehme's Haunted Narrative* (Albany: State University of New York Press, 2002), 118.
45. Boehme, 5:88/1.2.8.
46. Boehme, 14:78, B.
47. Boehme, 9:158/5.45.
48. Boehme, 17:103/16.14.
49. Boehme, 9:125/4.1–2; 5:96/1.12.17 M.
50. Boehme, 14:226–227/15.43–46.
51. Weeks, *Boehme*, 96; Weeks's intellectual biography of Boehme has permanently transformed Boehme interpretation by painstakingly reconstructing details of his shifting social and political context.
52. Boehme, 3:228/11.94; 3:245–46/12.28.
53. Boehme, 3:228/11.91.
54. Boehme, 3:241/12.16.
55. Weeks, *Boehme*, 107.
56. Boehme, 6:15/1.68–69. As Linn Tonstad insists, arguing against Boehmian moves in recent trinitarian theology, "death cannot belong to God, and—I would argue—should not be made the translation of *any* aspect of inner-trinitarian relations. Death is, in the theological sense, what stands opposed to God, what has no being. It ought not be made internal to God." *God and Difference: The Trinity, Sexuality, and the Transformation of Finitude* (New York: Routledge, 2016), 134.
57. Boehme, 14:231/16.2–3.
58. O'Regan's *Gnostic Apocalypse* traces in rich detail Boehme's "narrative

swerves" from the pre-Reformation and Reformation traditions, identifying it as a recovery of Valentinian Gnosticism that continues to haunt modernity. While tracing a host of such deviations and arguing that they function to disfigure and refigure the biblical narrative, O'Regan emphasizes these same points: the shift from a drama of God-world interaction to a drama of divine self-constitution, and with this the positing of lack and longing, conflict, fall and suffering, in God. *Gnostic Apocalypse*, 103–27.

59. Lucinda Martin, "Jacob Boehme and the Anthropology of German Pietism," in *An Introduction to Jacob Boehme: Four Centuries of Thought and Reception*, ed. Ariel Hessayon and Sarah Apetrei (New York: Routledge, 2014), 120–41.

60. Glenn Alexander Magee, "Hegel's Reception," in *Introduction to Jacob Boehme*, 225–27.

61. Georg Wilhelm Friedrich Hegel, *Werke in zwanzig Bänden* (Frankfurt: Surhkamp, 1970), 20:92, 94; translation in *Lectures on the History of Philosophy* (LHP), 3 vols., trans. E. S. Haldane and Frances H. Simson (London: Kegan Paul, Trench, Trübner, 1892), 3:189; Magee, "Hegel's Reception," 227, 228, 230.

62. *Werke* 20:96; LHP, 3:191.

63. *Werke* 20:98; LHP, 3:196.

64. Hegel, *Werke*, 20:109; LHP, 3:206.

65. Philipp Jakob Spener, *Pia Desideria, Schriften*, ed. Erich Beyreuther (Hildesheim: Georg Olms Verlag, 1979, facsimile of 1680 ed.), 1:182.

66. Spener, *Pia*, 1:193, 196.

67. Spener, *Pia*, 1:240, 237.

68. Spener, *Pia*, 1:196.

69. Dohmen, *Bildung und Schule*, 1:22.

70. Spener, *Pia*, 196.

71. Dohmen, *Bildung und Schule*, 1:135–37; on the negative conception of *Einbildung*, see also August Langen, *Der Wortschatz des Deutschen Pietismus*, 2nd ed. (Tübingen: Max Niemeyer, 1968), 41.

72. Dohmen, *Bildung und Schule*, 1:142.

73. "Den Leuten fleissig einzubilden das Christenthum bestehe nicht in wissen sondern in der praxi" (248).

74. Spener, *Pia*, 235, 261.

75. Gerhard Teerstegen, *Geistliche und Erbauliche Briefe über das Inwendige Leben und Wahre Wesen des Christenthums. . .*, 4 vols. (Solingen: P. Schmitz, 1773–75), 1:2, 221.

76. Teerstegen, *Geistiges Blumengärtlein inniger Seelen* (1727) (Bern: Gabriel Gaudard, 1766), 188.

77. Teerstegen, *Geistiges Blumengärtlein*, 213.

78.

Solches wird auf das kurtzprüfende Leiden
welches sein Feuer der Schmeltzung nur macht
bringen uns grosse und ewige Freuden
wann nur sein Bild an uns völlig erwacht
weil Er mit deme sich gäntzlich vertraut
als seiner aus Ihm erbaueten Braut.

Jesu! Lass in mir dein Schmeltzen fortgehen
zu meiner völligen Läuterung hier
dass ich dann in nur dein Bildniss auch sehen
möge/ aufgehen/ und brechen herfür
nach und nach in seinem völligen Glantz
und mich darinnen vereinget dir gantz.

"Jesus Ein Schmeltzer Unsrer Seelen" aus dem *Gesangbuch für die Inspirationsgemeinde* [von Eberhard Ludwig Gruber,] *J.J.J. Jesus-Lieder für seine Glieder...*, vol. 3, *Weitere Jesus-Lieder Für seine Glieder*, o.O. 1725, 35; quoted in Hans-Jürgen Schrader, "Vom Heiland im Herzen zum inneren Wort: 'Poetische' Aspekte der pietistische Christologie," in *Pietismus und Neuzeit*, 20:67.

79.

Herr Jesu! Werde Mensch in mir
Dass ich vergöttert werd in dir,
So wirst du Mensch, und ich werd Gott,
Und ist der Feind zu Schand und Spott.
So bin ich in dir wiederbracht
Zu Gottes Ebenbild gemacht.

Johann Friedrich Rock, *Aufrichtige und wahrhafftige EXTRACTA Aus dem allgemeinen Diario Der Wahren Inspirations-Gemeinen*, XII Sammlung, o.O. 1751, 243, quoted in Schrader, "Poetische Aspekte," 69.

80. Langen, *Wortschatz*, 41–42.
81. Spener, *Pia*, 181; see also *Pia*, 282, 296.
82. Spener, *Pia*, 196.
83. Spener, *Pia*, 240.
84. Spener, *Pia*, 247.
85. Spener, *Pia*, 241–245.
86. Wallmann, "Was ist Pietismus?," 22–24.
87. Spener, *Pia*, 292.

88. More generally on Pietism as essentially modern in the ways it sought to make knowledge practical, see Martin Gierl, "Pietism, Enlightenment, and Modernity," in *A Companion to German Pietism, 1600-1800*, ed. Douglas H. Shantz (Leiden: Brill, 2015), 348-92.

89. Rolf Engelsing, *Der Bürger als Leser, Lesergeschichte in Deutschland 1500-1800* (Stuttgart: J. B. Metzlersche Verlagsbuchhandlung, 1974), 37.

90. Albrecht Schöne, *Säkularisation als Sprachbildende Kunst: Studien zur Dichtung deutscher Pfarrersöhne* (Göttingen: Vandenhoeck & Ruprecht, 1968), 11-13; on the general issue of the relationship between world and gospel in Luther's thought, see Ivar Asheim, *Glaube und Erziehung bei Luther* (Heidelberg: Quelle & Meyer, 1961), 81-87.

91. Engelsing, *Bürger als Leser*, 27-30.

92. "Anfang und Fortgang der Bekehrung A. H. Franckes," in *Pietismus und Rationalismus*, ed. Marianne Beyer-Fröhlich (Darmstadt: Wissenschaftliche Buchgesellschaft, 1970), 24; translation from *Pietists: Selected Writings*, ed. Peter Erb (New York: Paulist, 1983), 103.

93. Francke, *Bekehrung*, 26; 105.

94. Francke, *Bekehrung*, 27; 105.

95. Francke, *Bekehrung*, 27; 105.

96. *A Sermon on the Resurrection of Our Lord Preached on Easter Sunday* (London, 1732), excerpted in *Pietists*, ed. Erb, 134.

97. Engelsing, *Bürger als Leser*, 63.

98. Engelsing, *Bürger als Leser*, 64-67.

99. Johann Henrich Reitz, *Historie der Wiedergebohrnen*, vol. 1, pts. 1-3 (1698-1701), ed. Hans-Jürgen Schrader (Tübingen: Max Niemeyer Verlag, 1982).

100. Reitz, *Historie der Wiedergebohrnen*, 35.

101. Spener, *Pia*, 299.

102. Von der Mücke, *Practices of the Enlightenment*, 90.

103. Von der Mücke, *Practices*, 103.

104. Langen, *Wortschatz*, 385.

105. Von der Mücke, *Practices*, 9.

106. See, e.g., Wolfgang Braungart, "Literaturwissenschaft und Theologie: Versuch zu einem schwierigen Verhältnis, ausgehend von Kafkas Erzählung 'Ein Hungerkünstler,'" in *Schreiben ist Totenerweckung: Theologie und Literatur*, ed. Erich Garhammer und Georg Langenhorst (Wurzburg: Echter, 2005), 43-69, here 55; Langen, *Wortschatz*, 433-35; Schrader, "'Poetische' Aspekte," in *Pietismus und Neuzeit: Ein Jahrbuch zur Geschichte des neueren Protestantismus* (Göttingen: Vandenhoeck & Ruprecht, 1994), 20:66; Hans-Georg Kemper, "'Göttergleich': Zur Genese der Genie-Religion aus pietistischem und hermetischem 'Geist,'" in *Goethe und der Pietismus*, ed. Hans-Georg Kemper und Hans Schneider (Tübingen: Max Niemeyer Verlag, 2001), 171-208,; here 173.

107. Johann Wolfgang Goethe, "Zwo wichtige bisher unerörterte Biblische Fragen zum erstenmal gründlich beantwortet von einem Landgeistlichen in Schwaben," in *Goethes Werke* (Weimar: H. Böhlau, 1887–1919) (WA), pt. 1, vol. 37, 186–87. See also Johann Wolfgang Goethe, "Brief des Pastors zu *** an den neuen Pastor zu ***," WA 1:37:155–73.

108. Johann Wolfgang Goethe, *Aus meinem Leben. Dichtung und Wahrheit*, bk. 4, chap. 16, WA 1:29:14.

109. Langen, *Wortschatz*, 435.

110. Schrader, "Poetische Aspekte," 72.

111. As Hans-Georg Kemper perceptively notes, "Gerade dort, wo sich [die Kunst] diese angeblich ihre Autonomie errungen hat wie in der Romantik oder bis in die Abstraktion einer reinen Lautdichtung hinein gesteigert hat wie beispielsweise im Dadaismus, hat sie an dieses im Gegenständlich-Sinnlichen das Urbild anschauende und zeugende, einheitstiftende und mit den "höheren Welten" vermittelnde Verständnis von Nachahmung angeknüpft und damit zugleich auch die Tradition des "ältesten Gottesdienstes" fortgesetzt." *Gottebenbildlichkeit*, 28.

CHAPTER THREE

1. Isaiah Berlin, *Vico and Herder: Two Studies in the History of Ideas* (London: Chatto and Winduss 1976). Berlin returned to Herder in one of his last books, *Three Critics of the Enlightenment: Vico, Hamann, Herder* (Princeton, NJ: Princeton University Press, 2000). Charles Taylor's attention to Herder primarily in terms of expressivism, while important, has not decisively changed that picture; e.g., *Hegel* (Cambridge: Cambridge University Press, 1975), 13–27. In Germany, too, Herder has often been seen, together with Hamann, as a pious irrationalist and philosophical dilettante, significant primarily through his inspiration of the revolutionary Sturm und Drang movement. For a brief sketch of Herder's reception in Germany, see Markus Buntfuss, *Die Erscheinungsform des Christentums: Zur ästhetischen Neugestaltung der Religionstheologie bei Herder, Wackenroder und De Wette* (Berlin: De Gruyter, 2004), 12–14.

2. Sankar Muthu, *Enlightenment against Empire* (Princeton, NJ: Princeton University Press, 2003), 212.

3. Muthu, *Enlightenment against Empire*, 260–61. For a particularly pointed critique of Berlin's treatment of Herder, see Robert Norton, "The Myth of the Counter-Enlightenment," *Journal of the History of Ideas* 168, no. 4 (2007): 635–58. Norton is among those working to place Herder's thought firmly within its Enlightenment context; see especially his *Herder's Aesthetics and the European Enlightenment* (Ithaca, NY: Cornell University Press, 1991).

4. F. M. Barnard, *Herder on Nationality, Humanity, and History* (Montreal: McGill-Queen's University Press, 2003), 64. Barnard's scholarship has done

a great deal to correct misperceptions of Herder on this score, starting with *Herder's Social and Political Thought: From Enlightenment to Nationalism* (Oxford: Clarendon, 1965). It has been joined by a wealth of recent Herder scholarship emphasizing Herder's critique of Eurocentrism and imperialism, notably Muthu, *Enlightenment against Empire*; John K. Noyes, *Herder: Aesthetics against Imperialism* (Toronto: University of Toronto Press, 2015); Sonia Sikka, *Herder on Humanity and Cultural Difference: Enlightened Relativism* (Cambridge: Cambridge University Press, 2011); Vicki Spencer, *Herder's Political Thought: A Study on Language, Culture, and Community* (Toronto: University of Toronto Press, 2012); and Nicholas Robinette, "The World Laid Waste: Herder, Language Labor, Empire," *New Literary History* 42 (2011): 193–203. All of these make valuable contributions. I would, though, argue against Sikka that Herder is not best termed a relativist, and note that Robinette seems to me to read into Herder's later thought an increasing conservatism that is not there. Noyes's study is very rich, and his alignment of Herder with postcolonial theory is perceptive, but while it is certainly true that "pointing to the limits of both universalism and relativism, he demonstrates why attempts to think cultural diversity together with common humanity continue to encounter such intense conceptual difficulty to this very day," I would take issue with Noyes's irrationalist conclusion that "the insights themselves must be viewed as inherently contradictory" (16).

5. Nicholas Boyle, *Sacred and Secular Scriptures* (Notre Dame, IN: University of Notre Dame Press, 2005), 15.

6. The standard edition of Herder's works is still *Herder's Sämtliche Werke*, ed. Bernhard Suphan (Berlin: Weidmannsche Buchhandlung, 1877), and I will for the most part cite from it as SW; the best modern edition is not complete: Johann Gottfried Herder, *Werke in zehn Bänden*, ed. Günther Arnold et al. (Frankfurt am Main: Deutscher Klassiker Verlag, 1985–2000). The only complete translation of *Ideen zur Philosophie der Geschichte der Menschheit*, trans. T. Churchill, was published in 1800 (reprint ed., New York: Bergman, 1966); an abridged edition of this translation was published by the University of Chicago Press in 1968, ed. Frank E. Manuel. Several of Herder's important texts are excerpted and translated in *Herder: Philosophical Writings*, ed. Desmond M. Clarke and Michael N. Forster (Cambridge: Cambridge University Press, 2007). All translations given here are my own.

7. On Leibniz's importance for later conceptions of Bildung, see Georg Bollenbeck, *Bildung und Kultur. Glanz und Elend eines deutschen Deutungsmusters* (Frankfurt: Insel Verlag, 1994), 114. On Herder's modification of Leibniz's monads, which are no longer either windowless nor independent, see Buntfuss, *Erscheinungsform*, 56–57.

8. John H. Zammito works to identify the various strands of influence

in *Kant, Herder, and the Birth of Anthropology* (Chicago: University of Chicago Press, 2002); Chad Wellmon places the discussion in the context of the rise of physical and moral anthropology, and the relation between them: *Becoming Human: Romantic Anthropology and the Embodiment of Freedom* (University Park: Pennsylvania State University Press, 2010).

9. Immanuel Kant, introduction to *Anthropology from a Pragmatic Point of View*, ed. Robert B. Louden (Cambridge: Cambridge University Press, 2006), vii. See also Kant's 1784 "Idee zu einer allgemeinen Geschichte in weltbürgerlicher Absicht," *Gesammelte Schriften*, vol. 8, Deutsche Akademie der Wissenschaft zu Berlin (Berlin: Walter de Gruyter, 1907–) (hereafter AA), 15–31, trans. as "Idea for a Universal History with a Cosmopolitan Purpose" in *Kant's Political Writings*, ed. H. Reiss (Cambridge: Cambridge University Press, 1991), 41–53.

10. Kant, *Anthropology*, 3; AA, 119.

11. Kant, *Anthropology*, 228; AA, 324.

12. Kant, *Anthropology*, 230; AA, 325.

13. Kant, *Anthropology*, 229–30; AA, 324–25.

14. Kant, "Idea for a Universal History with a Cosmopolitan Purpose," 42.

15. Sharon Anderson-Gold, "Kant's Ethical Commonwealth: The Highest Good as Social Goal," *International Philosophical Quarterly* 26, no. 1 (1986): 23–32.

16. John Pizer, "Cosmopolitanism and Weltliteratur," *Goethe Yearbook* 13 (2005): 175.

17. On the problematic character of Kant's notion of human development, see Thomas McCarthy, "Kant on Race and Development," in *Race, Empire, and the Idea of Human Development* (Cambridge: Cambridge University Press, 2009), 42–68, and Genevieve Lloyd, *Providence Lost* (Cambridge, MA: Harvard University Press, 2008), 287–98.

18. Muthu, *Enlightenment against Empire*, 183, 186, 257.

19. See Frederick Beiser, *Enlightenment, Revolution, and Romanticism* (Cambridge, MA: Harvard University Press, 1992), 214, 209.

20. Taylor, *Hegel*, 17.

21. Taylor, *Hegel*, 18. For a fuller development of these themes, see also Taylor's *Ethics of Authenticity* (Cambridge, MA: Harvard University Press, 1992); an earlier classic is Lionel Trilling's *Sincerity and Authenticity* (Cambridge, MA: Harvard University Press, 1973).

22. See, e.g., Beiser, *Enlightenment, Revolution, and Romanticism*, 214. "Only because Herder posits human flourishing as a goal, and thinks that some things genuinely contribute to this goal while others do not, can he pass critical judgment on the societies he considers": Sikka, *Herder on Humanity*, 21.

23. SW 13.4.6, 157.

24. SW 13.4.6, 160.

25. See my fuller discussion in "Calvin's Legacy for Contemporary Reformed Natural Law," *Scottish Journal of Philosophy* 67, no. 4:425.

26. Thomas Aquinas, *Summa Theologiae* 1–2.94.2.

27. Aquinas, *Summa Theologiae*, 1.93.4.

28. Knud Haakonssen, *Natural Law and Moral Philosophy from Grotius to the Scottish Enlightenment* (Cambridge: Cambridge University Press, 1996); Jerome B. Schneewind, *The Invention of Autonomy: A History of Modern Moral Philosophy* (Cambridge: Cambridge University Press, 1998), 58–166.

29. SW 13.4.6, 154.

30. Taylor, *Hegel*, 174.

31. Ernest L. Stahl, *Die Religiöse und die Humanitätsphilosophische Bildungsidee und die Entsehung des deutschen Bildungsromans im 18. Jahrhundert* (Bern: Paul Haupt, 1934; Liechtenstein: Kraus Reprint, 1970), 84. Stahl argues that Herder placed somewhat more emphasis on unfolding from within, while still recognizing the significance of outer context.

32. SW 13.9.1, 348.

33. It was Fredrich Meinecke who in 1959 noted that Herder had coined the term *Einfühlung* to translate the English sentimentalists' term *sympathy*: *Historism: The Rise of a New Historical Outlook*, trans. J. E. Anderson (London: Routledge & Kegan Paul, 1972), 297. See Muthu, *Enlightenment against Empire*, 233; Barnard, *Herder on Nationality*, 5, 12, 101.

34. See Barnard, *Herder on Nationality*, 47–49; *Herder's Social and Political Thought*, 72–87. In this sense Pascale Casanova's influential recent account of the ways in which Herder's invention of the notion of a national literature, related organically to the genius of a particular people, worked to seal literatures off from one another may be accurate as an account of how Herder's ideas were appropriated for both political and literary nationalism, but it does not succeed in capturing the way in which Herder's accent is never just on the ways in which cultures are marked off from one another but also on the ways they encounter one another. See Casanova, *The World Republic of Letters* (Cambridge, MA: Harvard University Press, 2004), 75–78, 105–6.

35. Barnard, *Herder on Nationality*, 48, also 27, 62–63. Barnard does not use the term *consociationism* to describe Herder's thought, but it is clearly appropriate and places Herder in continuity with the important Calvinist federalist Johannes Althusius (1563–1638) before him and Jacques Maritain (1882–1973) after him. See Luke Bretherton, "State, Democracy, and Community Organizing," in *A Companion to Public Theology*, ed. Sebastian King and Katie Day (Leiden: Brill 2017), 101–3.

36. See, e.g., SW 18:137, 271, 300–302, 408, see also 13:346; 14:227; 16:119, 551; 17:116; 24:375; 29:129, 133.

37. On Herder's anarchism, see Beiser, *Enlightenment, Revolution, and Romanticism*, 212.

38. Barnard, *Herder on Nationality*, 45; Beiser, *Enlightenment, Revolution, and Romanticism*, 213; see, e.g., Herder SW 13:384.

39. Barnard, *Herder on Nationality*, 138.

40. SW 5:524.

41. SW 18:222–23, see also SW 29:426; 13:384; 17:108; 18:222; 14:32; 13:263.

42. SW 13:250, SW 29:426; see the discussion in Samson Knoll, "Beyond the Black Legend: The Anticolonialism of Johann Gottfried Herder," *North Dakota Quarterly* 57, no. 3 (1989): 55–64. Even if Bruce Lincoln is right to see Herder as a key turning point in the recuperation of the category of myth, "marking it as primordial and authentic," it was a distortion of Herder to appropriate him in service of the glorification of Germans or Aryans: *Theorizing Myth: Narrative, Ideology, and Scholarship* (Chicago: University of Chicago Press, 1999), 209, 55.

43. Noyes, *Aesthetics against Imperialism*, 16.

44. SW 18:247–49.

45. Muthu, *Enlightenment against Empire*, 226; Barnard, *Herder on Nationality*, 74, 78; Noyes, *Aesthetics against Imperialism*, 96.

46. Herder, *Philosophical Writings*, 328–29.

47. Immanuel Kant, "On the Different Human Races" (1777), in *The Idea of Race*, ed. Robert Bernasconi and Tommy Lott (Indianapolis: Hackett, 2000), 14; McCarthy, "Kant on Race and Development," 42–68. On the broader eighteenth-century German discussion of race, see Sara Eigen and Mark Larrimore, eds., *The German Invention of Race* (Albany: SUNY Press, 2006).

48. Kant, "Human Races," 19.

49. AA 15.878; see J. Kameron Carter, *Race: A Theological Account* (Oxford: Oxford University Press, 2008), 89.

50. See Christopher B. Krebs, *A Most Dangerous Book: Tacitus's "Germania" from the Roman Empire to the Third Reich* (New York: W. W. Norton, 2011), 154–57.

51. Krebs, *Tacitus's Germania*, 161.

52. See, e.g., Noyes, *Aesthetics against Imperialism*, 212–17; Barnard, *Herder on Nationality*, 35, 65.

53. SW 13.7.1, 257.

54. SW 17.3.28, 141.

55. SW 13.7.1, 258.

56. Alfred Rosenberg, *The Myth of the Twentieth Century* (1930) sought to legitimate Nazism by appeal to Herder, but later scholarship has shown how Nazi appropriation was a distortion of Herder's own thought; see, e.g., Richard Shorten, *Modernism and Totalitarianism: Rethinking the Sources of Nazism*

and Stalinism (New York: Palgrave Macmillan, 2012), 137–38, although even Shorten misses Herder's dialogical universalism when he claims that Herder bounded "all authentic experience within the limits of the nation" (137).

57. Barnard, *Herder on Nationality*, 93.

58. See, e.g., Dorothea von der Mücke, *The Practices of the Enlightenment* (New York: Columbia University Press, 2015), 51.

59. Von der Mücke, *Practices of the Enlightenment*, 57.

60. Stahl, *Bildungsidee*, 38–39.

61. Stahl, *Bildungsidee*, 101–9, 112–14. Other interpreters have read Herder as moving in quite another direction, from Enlightenment skepticism toward anti-Enlightenment Lutheran piety: Rudolf Haym, *Herder nach seinem Leben und seinen Werken* (Berlin: Gaertner, 1954), 1:572–73; Robert T. Clark, *Herder: His Life and Thought* (Berkeley: University of California Press, 1955), 179–213. Beiser's interpretation is closer to the mark: Herder moves from an early Enlightenment deism to a position heavily influenced by mystical pantheistic thought: "like the radical Aufklärung, this tradition is vitalist, humanist, and pantheist; yet it also insists on the value of religious experience," understood as "awareness of God in the whole of nature" (*Enlightenment, Revolution, and Romanticism*, 205).

62. These most likely stem from the fact that Stahl read Herder through the lens of a preformed conception of *Humanitätsphilosophie* that owed more to Wilhelm von Humboldt's thought than to Herder.

63. Buntfuss, *Erscheinungsform*, 45.

64. Hans-Georg Kemper, *Gottebenbildlichkeit und Naturnachahmung im Säkularisierungsprozess* (Tübingen: Niemeyer, 1981), 111.

65. The imitation of Christ is not a matter of picking out particularities such as the way Jesus dressed or ate, as Herder explained in a 1772 sermon, "Von den Schranken und Misslichkeiten bei Nachahmung auch guter Beispiele und Vorbilder," SW 31:172–94. Stahl wrongly takes this to be a repudiation of the imitation of Christ: *Bildungsidee*, 109.

66. Frederick Burkhardt, introduction to *God: Some Conversations* (Indianapolis: Bobbs-Merrill, 1940). See also Kemper's treatment of how Herder moves beyond deism and Spinozism by leaving behind a static ontology and thinking historically and developmentally about God's presence in the world: *Gottebenbildlichkeit*, 100.

67. ST 1.93.3; see Brian Gerrish's discussion in "The Secret Religion of Germany: Christian Piety and the Pantheism Controversy," *Journal of Religion* 67, no. 4 (1987): 451.

68. Gerrish, "Secret Religion," 447.

69. Kemper, *Gottebenbildlichkeit*, 101.

70. Kemper, *Gottebenbildlichkeit*, 101; Buntfuss, *Erscheinungsform*, 58.

71. SW 5:519–521.

72. SW 7:242.

73. Kemper, *Gottebenbildlichkeit*, 104.

74. SW 7:242.

75. This is a point argued at length by Noyes, *Aesthetics against Imperialism*, particularly with respect to connections between Herder's anti-imperialism and his aesthetics.

76. Buntfuss, *Erscheinungsform*, 23.

77. Buntfuss, *Erscheinungsform*, 36, 41.

78. SW 15:526; SW 7:214, 215.

79. Herder here makes fun of both metaphysical and theosophical interpretations (naming Boehme directly): both are equally beside the point, failing to grasp the poetical character of the creation narrative (SW 6:208).

80. Buntfuss, *Erscheinungsform*, 51. We might think in this context of Karl Barth's treatment of Genesis 1 as "an intuitive and poetic picture of a prehistorical reality of history which is enacted once and for all within the confines of space and time," rejecting "any ideas of the inferiority . . . of a 'non-historical' depiction and narration of history" as "only a ridiculous and middle-class habit of the modern Western mind which is supremely phantastic in its chronic lack of imaginative phantasy." *Church Dogmatics* 3/1, ed. G. W. Bromiley and T. F. Torrance (London: T&T Clark, 1960), 81.

81. Buntfuss, *Erscheinungsform*, 62.

82. SW 16:563.

83. SW 13.9.1, 352. Similar issues hound Kant's philosophy of history; see Lloyd, *Providence Lost*, 287–98.

84. See Charles Taylor's analysis of Herder's holistic theory of language in *The Language Animal: The Full Shape of the Human Linguistic Capacity* (Cambridge, MA: Belknap, 2016), 12–20.

85. SW 13.9.1, 342.

86. Thomas Pfau, "Romantic *Bildung* and the Persistence of Teleology," in *A Companion to German Romantic Philosophy*, ed. Judith Norman and Elizabeth Milan (Leiden: Brill, 2018), 2.

87. Pfau, "Romantic *Bildung*," 6. Pfau regards Hegel as engaging in a "conscious revival of Aristotelian *entelechia*" that "advances not only a formal but an ontological truth claim" in ways resisted by Herder. On my reading, Herder does not resist such claims as much as he fails fully to grapple with how they might be justified.

88. Barnard explores the complexities of Herder's understanding of historical progress at length: *Herder on Nationality*, e.g., 9, 36, 92, 117, 125, 147.

89. SW 14.15.3, 226.

90. Theodore Vial, *Modern Religion, Modern Race* (Oxford: Oxford University Press, 2016), 250. Vial here is speaking of Schleiermacher, who conceives of the telos in terms of "free sociability," but he offers a parallel analysis of

Herder, arguing that both must be seen as "unfamiliar sources of racism" since they develop philosophies of language and culture that lead us to link particular behavioral and mental characteristics to groups of people and then to array these along a developmental spectrum, such that some are backward and others advanced (155–87).

91. Karl Barth, *Protestant Theology in the Nineteenth Century: Its Background and History* (London: SCM Press, 1972; orig. German ed. 1952), 317.

92. Karl Barth, *Protestant Theology*, 322, citing Herder, *Vom Erkennen und Empfinden der menschlichen Seele* (1778), 68; on "correspondence" in Barth, see CD 3/4, 474/543; 2/2, 578/642–43.

93. Barth, *Protestant Theology*, 324.

94. Barth, *Protestant Theology*, 325.

95. Barth, *Protestant Theology*, 326.

96. Barth, *Protestant Theology*, 326.

97. Barth, *Protestant Theology*, 332.

98. Barth, *Protestant Theology*, 333.

99. Barth, *Protestant Theology*, 336.

100. Barth, *Protestant Theology*, 337.

101. Herder, *Seele*, 72; quoted in Barth, *Protestant Theology*, 323.

102. Herder, SW 5:524–5.

103. See Barnard, *Herder on Nationality*, 107–11.

104. Muthu, *Enlightenment against Empire*, 277, 274.

105. Richard Miller offers a deft refutation of moral relativism and defense of a critical value pluralism akin to that of Herder, arguing that "to have moral authority a critic must show general moral and epistemic probity along with giving reasons in an argument that is disciplined by due diligence, perspective-taking, and context sensitivity," thereby expressing respect for their interlocutors in and through their critical engagement with them. *Friends and Other Strangers: Studies in Religion, Ethics, and Culture* (New York: Columbia University Press, 2016), 92.

106. SW 17:137–38.

CHAPTER FOUR

1. The term itself is was apparently coined by Schleiermacher; see *Über die Religion: Reden an die Gebildeten unter ihren Verächtern* (Berlin, 1799), 169. A recent comprehensive study is Bernd Auerochs, *Die Enstehung der Kunstreligion* (Göttingen: Vandenhoeck & Ruprecht, 2006).

2. Yuval Levin, *The Fractured Republic: Renewing America's Social Contract in the Age of Individualism* (New York: Basic Books, 2016), 204.

3. Dietrich Benner, *Wilhelm von Humboldts Bildungstheorie: Eine problem-

geschichtliche Studie zum Begründungszusammenhang neuzeitlicher Bildungsreform, 3rd ed. (Weinheim: Juventa Verlag, 2003), 14.

4. Erhard Wicke, Wolfgang Neuser, and Wolfdietrich Schmied-Kowarzik, eds., foreword to *Menschheit und Individualität: Zur Bildungstheorie und Philosophie Wilhelm von Humboldts* (Weinheim: Deutscher Studien Verlag, 1997), 7. Building on Horkheimer and Adorno, Wicke argues that "classical German humanism's concept of Bildung is a legitimate child of the Enlightenment, but it is a rebellious child, which contradicts and so relates itself dialectically to the dialectic of Enlightenment," thereby contributing to the Enlightenment's own enlightenment (Wicke, "Beitrag der Bildungstheorie," 12). Contrast this interpretation with that of Georg Bollenbeck, who sees only a detached individualism here: *Bildung und Kultur. Glanz und Elend eines deutschen Deutungsmusters* (Frankfurt: Insel Verlag, 1994), 158.

5. For Georg Bollenbeck, this disengagement from the practical world is ultimately responsible for the disaster of National Socialism (*Bildung und Kultur*, 29, 143–48). There is something to this, in terms of the way these ideas were adapted by pedagogues and transformed into the animating ideals of the *Bildungsbürgertum*, but that in itself does not show that it had to unfold this way or that Herder's or Humboldt's conceptions of Bildung were themselves disengaged from practice. In fact, Bollenbeck recognizes that this was not the case for Herder, whose notion of *Kultur* is not limited to art and philosophy, and whose notion of Bildung is not limited to the individual (124–26).

6. Humboldt, *Ideen zu einem Versuch, die Gränzen der Wirksamkeit des Staats zu bestimmen* (1792), in *Werke in fünf Bänden* (W), ed. Andreas Flitner und Klaus Giel (Darmstadt: Wissenschaftliche Buchgesellschaft, 1960), 1:64.

7. *Theorie der Bildung des Menschen* (1793), in W 1:240.

8. "Über Religion," W 1:15.

9. *Theorie der Bildung*, W 1:237.

10. *Theorie der Bildung*, W 1:235.

11. *Theorie der Bildung*, W 1:237.

12. Bollenbeck goes even further, arguing that Humboldt's view was preformationist. *Bildung und Kultur*, 146.

13. *Theorie der Bildung*, W 1:235.

14. *Theorie der Bildung*, W 1:235.

15. *Theorie der Bildung*, W 1:235.

16. Erhard Wicke, "Der Beitrag der Bildungstheorie Wilhelm von Humboldts zur Selbstaufklärung der Aufklärung," in *Menschheit und Individualität*, 11.

17. "Über Religion," W 1:14.

18. Letter to Schiller, September 1800 (the so-called *Wallenstein* Brief,

written in response to having just read Schiller's dramatic trilogy *Wallenstein*, in *Der Briefwechsel zwischen Friedrich Schiller und Wilhelm von Humboldt*, ed. Siegfried Seidel (Berlin: Aufbau Verlag, 1962), 208.

19. "Über Religion," W 1:13.
20. *Theorie der Bildung*, W 1:238–39.
21. *Theorie der Bildung*, W 1:236.
22. Wicke, "Beitrag der Bildungstheorie," 26.
23. *Über das Studium des Alterthums, und des griechischen insbesondere* [1793], W 2:28.
24. *Theorie der Bildung*, W 1:239.
25. "Über Religion," W 1:19.
26. "Über Religion," W 1:19.
27. "Über Religion," W 1:20–21.
28. "Über Religion," W 1:21.
29. "Über Religion," W 1:22.
30. "Über Religion," W 1:22.
31. "Über Religion," W 1:21.
32. "Über Religion," W 1:22.
33. "Über Religion," W 1:23.
34. "Über Religion," W 1:23, 29.
35. "Über Religion," W 1:23.
36. "Über Religion," W 1:10.
37. "*Über Religion*," W 1:10.
38. "*Über Religion*," W 1:12.
39. See, e.g., Charles Taylor, *A Secular Age* (Cambridge, MA: Belknap, 2007), 757–58.
40. Dorothea von der Mücke, *The Practices of the Enlightenment* (New York: Columbia University Press, 2015), 65.
41. Wolfgang Braungart, *Literatur und Religion in der Moderne* (Paderborn: Wilhelm Fink, 2016), 200.
42. Nicholas Boyle, "'Art,' Literature, Theology: Learning from Germany," in *Higher Learning and Catholic Traditions*, ed. Robert E. Sullivan (Notre Dame, IN: University of Notre Dame Press, 2001), 97; Wolfgang Braungart, "Literaturwissenschaft und Theologie," in *Schreiben ist Totenerweckung: Theologie und Literatur* (Würzburg: Echter, 2005), 61.
43. Wolfgang Braungart, "'Alle Kunst ist symbolisch'—Und alle Religion auch," in *Literatur und Religion in der Moderne*, 220. Braungart identifies Wackenroder and Tieck's *Herzensergiessungen* of 1796—seven years after Humboldt's "On Religion"—as the inaugural text of *Kunstreligion*.
44. Von der Mücke, *Practices*, 69.
45. W 1:136.
46. W 1:57; Frederick C. Beiser, *Enlightenment, Revolution, and Romanticism:*

The Genesis of Modern German Political Thought, 1790-1800 (Cambridge, MA: Harvard University Press, 1992), 130-37.

47. On Humboldt's ambivalent reaction to the French Revolution, see Beiser, *Enlightenment, Revolution, and Romanticism*, 114-21.

48. Beiser, *Enlightenment, Revolution, and Romanticism*, 134; see W 1:72, 74.

49. Beiser, *Enlightenment, Revolution, and Romanticism*, 136-37, referring to a February 8, 1793, letter to Brinkmann, in *Wilhelm von Humboldts Briefe an Karl Gustav von Brinkmann*, ed. Albert Leitzmann, Bibliothek des historischen Vereins in Stuttgart, no. 288 (Leipzig, 1939), 54.

50. Friedrich Schiller, *Über die Ästhetische Erziehung des Menschen in einer Reihe von Briefen*, (AE) in *Sämtliche Werke*, vol. 5 (München: Carl Hanser Verlag, 1975), letter 6, para. 7, 584; translation from *On the Aesthetic Education of Man*, ed. and trans. Elizabeth M. Wilkinson and L. A. Willoughby (Oxford: Clarendon, 1967), 35.

51. Kant, "Was Ist Aufklärung?" in *Gesammelte Schriften*, Deutsche Akademie der Wissenschaft zu Berlin (Berlin: Walter de Gruyter, 1907-) (hereafter AA), 8:37; "What Is Enlightenment?" in *Kant's Political Writings*, ed. Hans Reiss (Cambridge: Cambridge University Press, 1970), 55.

52. Karl Phillip Moritz, "Versuch einer Vereinigung aller schönen Künste und Wissenschaften unter dem Begriff des in sich selbst Vollendeten," *Berlinische Monatschrift* (1785), reprinted in Karl Philipp Moritz, *Schriften zur Ästhetik und Poetik*, ed. Hans Joachim Schrimpf (Tübingen: Max Niemeyer Verlag, 1962), 3-9.

53. Paul Guyer, *Kant and the Experience of Freedom: Essays on Aesthetics and Morality* (Cambridge: Cambridge University Press, 1993), 83-84.

54. Guyer, *Experience of Freedom*, 141-44. Guyer helpfully distinguishes between the "similar-sounding but very different" Kantian notion of the "subjective purposiveness" of beautiful objects and Moritz's notion of the "internal purposiveness" of such objects. For Kant beauty is a firmly relational concept, having to do with the appeal of an object to creatures like us; Moritz's concept is nonrelational.

55. This is the core of Guyer's argument in *Experience of Freedom*, chaps. 2-4.

56. Guyer, *Experience of Freedom*, 96.

57. Guyer, *Experience of Freedom*, 107.

58. Guyer, *Experience of Freedom*, 108. The existence of beautiful objects is also important for morality, in offering evidence of the reality of the highest good (115), evidence through their harmony of form and content that nature is hospitable to morality.

59. Elizabeth M. Wilkinson and L. A. Willoughby, introduction to Friedrich Schiller, *On the Aesthetic Education of Man* (AE) (Oxford: Clarendon, 1967), xxiv-xxv.

60. SW 5, letter 1, para. 4, 571; AE, 5.
61. SW 5, letter 4, para. 1, 576; AE, 17.
62. SW 5, letter 4, para. 3, 577; AE, 19.
63. SW 5, letter 13, para. 2, 607; AE, 86–87.
64. SW 5, letter 15, para. 2, 614; AE, 101.
65. SW 5, letter 13, para. 3, 608; AE, 87–88.
66. SW 5, letter 25, para. 1, 651; AE, 183.
67. SW 5, letter 26, para. 8, 658; AE, 195–196.
68. SW 5, letter 24, para. 6, 646; AE, 177.
69. SW 5, letter 24, 645–651; AE, 171–81.
70. On Herder's relation to aesthetic autonomy, see Buntfuss, *Erscheinungsform des Christentums*, 85.
71. On Schiller's relation to the Duke of Augustenberg, see Wilkinson, introduction, xvi–xviii.
72. SW 5, letter 1, para. 1, 2, 570–73; AE 3.
73. Beiser, *Enlightenment, Revolution, and Romanticism*, 101; SW 5, letter 4, 576–79.
74. SW 5, letter 4, para. 1, 576, AE, 17.
75. Letter to Garve, 24.i.1795, quoted in Wilkinson, introduction, xviii.
76. University Lectures of 1789, *Schiller's Sämtliche Werke*, Säkular-Ausgabe, ed. E.v. d. Hellen (Stuttgart: J. Cottasche), 13:79.
77. See Wilkinson, introduction, xviii.
78. See Beiser, *Enlightenment, Revolution, and Romanticism*, 94.
79. SW 5, letter 4, para. 4, 578; AE, 19.
80. Bollenbeck, *Bildung und Kultur*, 140.

CHAPTER FIVE

1. Todd Kontje, *Private Lives in the Public Sphere: The German Bildungsroman as Metafiction* (University Park: Penn State University Press, 1992), 3; Todd Kontje, *The German Bildungsroman: History of a National Genre* (Columbia, SC: Camden House, 1993), 5.
2. Kontje, *National Genre*, 6. George Steiner argues that well into the nineteenth century, literature and the arts "came to be a partial surrogate for certain modes of political action" and that this in fact remains the case in large modern democracies, where the citizen is rarely an actual political actor. *Real Presences* (London: Faber & Faber, 1989), 29.
3. Friedrich Schlegel, *Geschichte der alten und neuen Literatur*, in *Sämtliche Werke* (Wien: J. Mayer, 1882), 1:198–99.
4. Johann Peter Eckermann, *Gespräche*, October 11, 1828, in *Goethes Werke: Hamburger Ausgabe in 14 Bänden* (HA), ed. Erich Trunz (Hamburg: Christian Wegner Verlag, 1950–68; München: C. H. Beck, 1981), 7:620; translation

from Goethe, *Conversations with Eckermann*, trans. John Oxenford (San Francisco: North Point, 1984), 220.

5. Johann Karl Morgenstern, "Über das Wesen des Bildungsromans," in *Zur Geschichte des deutschen Bildungsromans*, ed. Rolf Selbmann, *Wege der Forschung* 40 (Darmstadt: Wissenschaftliche Buchgesellschaft, 1988), 64.

6. Martha Nussbaum's work has been particularly influential here, e.g., "'Finely Aware and Richly Responsible': Literature and the Moral Imagination," *Journal of Philosophy*, October 1985, republished in *Literature and the Question of Philosophy*, ed. Anthony Cascardi (Baltimore: Johns Hopkins University Press, 1987), 167–91; *Poetic Justice: The Literary Imagination and Public Life* (Boston: Beacon, 1995). Among theologians, the contributions of Stanley Hauerwas are particularly significant, e.g., "Constancy and Forgiveness: The Novel as a School for Virtue," in *Dispatches from the Front: Theological Engagements with the Secular* (Durham, NC: Duke University Press, 1994), 31–57.

7. Rolf Engelsing, *Der Bürger als Leser: Lesergeschichte in Deutschland 1500-1800* (Stuttgart: Metzler, 1974), 182–83.

8. Ian Watt, *The Rise of the Novel: Studies in Defoe, Richardson and Fielding* (orig. 1957; London: Penguin, 1970), 14.

9. Watt, *Rise of the Novel*, 22–23.

10. Watt, *Rise of the Novel*, 62.

11. Watt, *Rise of the Novel*, 81.

12. Erich Auerbach, *Mimesis: The Representation of Reality in Western Literature* (orig. 1946; Princeton, NJ: Princeton University Press, 1953), 72.

13. Wolfgang Braungart, "'Ich suche / Mich selbst, und finde mich nicht mehr': Das Selbst und die Tragödie unter den Bedingungen des Christentums (Sophokles, Kleist, Corneille, Racine, Schiller)," in *Notions of the Self in Antiquity and Beyond*, ed. Alexander Arweiler and Melanie Möller (Berlin: Walter de Gruyter, 2008), 239–70, here 245.

14. Braungart, "Ich suche," 242.

15. Auerbach, *Mimesis*, 74.

16. T. H. Green, "Estimate of the Value and Influence of Works of Fiction in Modern Times," in *Works*, ed. Nettleship, 3:40, quoted in Watt, *Rise of the Novel*, 74.

17. I discuss some of these traditional critical tropes in *Putting On Virtue: The Legacy of the Splendid Vices* (Chicago: University of Chicago Press, 2008), 128–37, 288–91. The classic study is Jonas Barish, *The Antitheatrical Prejudice* (Berkeley: University of California Press, 1981).

18. Selbmann, introduction to *Zur Geschichte*, 2, which associates the rise of the novel as a genre with the emergence of the bourgeoisie as a social-political factor.

19. Watt, *Rise of the Novel*, 54.

20. Watt, *Rise of the Novel*, 33–34.

21. Watt, *Rise of the Novel*, 205.
22. Watt, *Rise of the Novel*, 208.
23. In *New Essays*, ed. Crane (Chicago, 1927), 135, quoted in Watt, *Rise of the Novel*, 55.
24. *The Case of Authors* (1758), 21; quoted in Watt, *Rise of the Novel*, 57.
25. Quoted in Watt, *Rise of the Novel*, 212.
26. On the relation between the notion of national literature and political nationalism, and on the ways in which literatures played into conceptions of national significance or insignificance (including Herder's contribution to these developments), see Pascale Casanova's *The World Republic of Letters* (Cambridge, MA: Harvard University Press, 2004).
27. Martha Woodmansee, "The Interests in Disinterestedness: Karl Philipp Moritz and the Emergence of the Theory of Aesthetic Autonomy in Eighteenth-Century Germany," *Modern Language Quarterly* 45, no. 1 (1984): 22–47; reprinted in *The Author, Art, and the Market* (New York: Columbia University Press, 1994).
28. Nicholas Boyle, "'Art,' Literature, Theology: Learning from Germany," in *Higher Learning and Catholic Traditions*, ed. Robert E. Sullivan (Notre Dame, IN: University of Notre Dame Press, 2001), 100–101.
29. Kontje, *Private Lives*, 4.
30. Kontje, *Private Lives*, 9.
31. Fawzi Boubia, "Goethes Theorie der Alterität und die Idee der Weltliteratur: Ein Beitrag zur neueren Kulturdebatte," in *Gegenwart als kulturelles Erbe*, ed. Bernd Thum (Munich: Iudicum, 1985): 269–301. There is an extended (and distinguished) discussion of Goethe and the idea of *Weltliteratur*, grappling with the threat of cultural homogenization but recognizing that Goethe's own vision was of a harmonious interplay of unity in diversity: Fritz Strich, *Goethe und die Weltliteratur* (Bern: A. Francke, 1946); Erich Auerbach, "Philologie der Weltliteratur," in *Weltliteratur: Festgabe für Fritz Strich, zum 70. Geburtstag*, ed. Walter Muschg and Emil Staiger (Bern: A. Francke, 1952), 39–50; Maire and Edward Said, introduction to Auerbach, "Philologie and Weltliteratur," trans. Maire and Edward Said, *Centennial Review* 13 (1969): 1–17.
32. John Pizer, "Cosmopolitanism and Weltliteratur," *Goethe Yearbook* 13 (2005): 166.
33. Literature "provided the training ground for a critical public reflection still preoccupied with itself—a process of self-clarification of private people focusing on the genuine experiences of their novel privateness": Jürgen Habermas's *The Structural Transformation of the Public Sphere*, trans. Thomas Burger (Cambridge, MA: MIT Press, 1991), 29. Habermas explores the political significance of the emergence of a "bourgeois public sphere" in the context first of coffee houses, taverns, and theaters, then in literature and

journals. See also the recent study by Dorothea von der Mücke, *The Practices of the Enlightenment* (New York: Columbia University Press, 2015), which explores how eighteenth-century authors drew on the classical resonances of the Latin *publicum*, "this phantasm of a glorious open debate among equals in support of the common good," despite their awareness of its anachronism (182).

34. See the discussion in Herdt, *Putting On Virtue*, 128–73.
35. Engelsing, *Bürger als Leser*, 184–85.
36. Habermas, *Structural Transformation*, 50.
37. Ernst Manheim, *Die Träger der Öffentlichen Meinung* (Brünn: Rudolf M. Rohrer, 1933), 82–83; literary, scientific, and secret societies formed in the eighteenth century enabled persons of different social classes to come together on an equal footing, and this was at times articulated quite explicitly as a driving desideratum.
38. Engelsing, *Bürger als Leser*, 192.
39. Steiner, *Real Presences*, 184.
40. Interestingly, David Friedrich Strauss in 1872 looked to the newspaper as offering the possibility for a *Neubildung*, an alternative to the church as locus for ethical formation. He spoke of the news media as a "new organization of the ideal elements in the life of the people." *The Old Faith and the New*, 8, cited in Ward Blanton, *Displacing Christian Origins: Philosophy, Secularity, and the New Testament* (Chicago: University of Chicago Press, 2007), 35.
41. Jürgen Jacobs, *Wilhelm Meister und seine Brüder: Untersuchungen zum deutschen Bildungsroman* (Munich: Wilhelm Fink Verlag, 1972), 17. Jacobs relates this to changing social conditions in which the bourgeoisie were faced with a broad array of occupational options (29).
42. Von der Mücke, *Practices*, 80.
43. Jürgen Jacobs, *Wilhelm Meister und seine Brüder*, 41.
44. *Heinrich Stillings Jugend, Jünglingsjahre, Wanderschaft und haüsliches Leben* (Leipzig: P. Reclam, 1904), 402.
45. *Heinrich Stillings Jugend*, 558.
46. Dieter Cunz, afterword to *Heinrich Stillings Jugend, Jünglingsjahre, Wanderschaft und haüsliches Leben* (Stuttgart: Reclam, 1994), 397–98.
47. Jacobs, *Wilhelm Meister*, 40.
48. *Heinrich Stillings Jugend*, 343, 555.
49. Cunz, afterword to *Heinrich Stillings Jugend*, 404.
50. Fritz Martini, "Bildungsroman—Term and Theory," in *Reflection and Action: Essays on the Bildungsroman*, ed. James Hardin (Columbia: University of South Carolina Press, 1991), 19.
51. Friedrich von Blanckenburg, *Versuch über den Roman*, Faksimiledruck der Originalausgabe von 1774, Nachw. v. Eberhard Lämmert (Stuttgart, 1965). On Blanckenburg's contribution, see Selbmann, *Zur Geschichte*, 3–6.

52. Selbmann, *Zur Geschichte*, 4.

53. Karl Morgenstern, "Über den Geist und Zusammenhang einer Reihe philosophischer Romane (1817), "Über das Wesen des Bildungsromans" (1820), "Zur Geschichte des Bildungsromans" (1824), reprinted in Selbmann, *Zur Geschichte*, 45–99.

54. Morgenstern, "Über das Wesen des Bildungsromans," in Selbmann, *Zur Geschichte*, 64.

55. Wilhelm Dilthey, *Leben Schleiermachers* (Berlin, 1870), 1:282. He further developed the concept in *Das Erlebnis und die Dichtung* (1906). It was Fritz Martini who uncovered Morgenstern's contribution: "Bildungsroman—Term and Theory," 1–3.

56. Wilhelm Dilthey, *Das Erlebnis und die Dichtung*, 14th ed. (Göttingen: Vandenhoeck & Ruprecht, 1965), 272–73 On Dilthey's definition as playing into the idealistic outlook of imperial Germany, see Hartmut Steinecke, "The Novel and the Individual," in *Reflection and Action*, 92–93.

57. November 5, 1706, in *Schillers Werke*, Nationalausgabe, ed. Lieselotte Blumenthal and Benno von Wiese (Weimar, 1943–), 36, 1:370.

58. Jeffrey Sammons, "The Bildungsroman for Nonspecialists," in *Reflection and Action*, 32; and "The Mystery of the Missing Bildungsroman, or What Happened to Wilhelm Meister's Legacy?" *Genre* 14 (1981): 229–46.

59. Gerhart Mayer, "Zum deutschen Antibildungsroman," *Jahrbuch der Raabe-Gesellschaft* 15 (1974): 41–64.

60. Kontje, *Private Lives*, 21, 35.

61. Sammons, "Missing Bildungsroman."

62. Hartmut Steinecke, "The Novel and the Individual," in *Reflection and Action*, 93.

63. Letter from Schiller to Goethe, November 28, 1796, HA 7:651.

64. Dilthey's definition, unlike Morgenstern's, was historicized; he saw the Bildungsroman as the literary expression of an epoch preoccupied with subjective ethical formation that began with Lessing and Kant and ended with the deaths of Goethe, Hegel, and Schleiermacher: Selbmann, *Zur Geschichte*, 21. But Dilthey failed both to see how the genre is intertextually rather than formally defined and how the novels concerned wrestle actively with the task of Bildung. He therefore forecloses the possibility of a tradition that extends past the cultural heyday of Bildung.

65. Sammons, "The Bildungsroman for Nonspecialists: An Attempt at Clarification," in *Reflection and Action*, 41.

66. Notably, Martin Swales, *The German Bildungsroman from Wieland to Hesse* (Princeton, NJ: Princeton University Press, 1978).

67. Swales, *German Bildungsroman*, 6.

68. As Swales notes, *German Bildungsroman*, 53.

69. Sammons, "Bildungsroman for Nonspecialists," 41.

70. "Über das Wesen des Bildungsromans," in Selbmann, *Zur Geschichte*, 64.

71. Friedrich Schlegel, *Geschichte der alten und neuen Literatur* (1798), KA 6:274.

72. Dennis Mahoney, "The Apprenticeship of the Reader," in *Reflection and Action*, 101. This thesis is further developed in Mahoney's *Der Roman der Goethezeit* (1774–1829), Sammlung Metzler: Realien zur Literatur 241 (Stuttgart: Metzler, 1988).

73. Patricia Waugh, *Metafiction: The Theory and Practice of Self-Conscious Fiction* (London: Methuen, 1984), 2. Waugh's understanding of metafiction is applied to the Bildungsroman by Kontje, *Private Lives*, 11. While Michael Beddow does not employ the term metafiction, he, too emphasizes this as the crucial feature of the Bildungsroman in the tradition of Wilhelm Meister in *The Fiction of Humanity* (Cambridge: Cambridge University Press, 1982), 5.

74. This is the fruitful approach employed by Kontje in *Private Lives*, 6; Wilhlem Voßkamp, *Ein anderes Selbst: Bildung und Bild im deutschen Roman des 18. und 19. Jahrhunderts* (Göttingen: Wallstein Verlag, 2004), identifies in reflection on *Bild* also a kind of self-reflexive feature.

75. See Linda Trinkaus Zagzebski, *Exemplarist Moral Theory* (Oxford: Oxford University Press, 2017), 33–34, 60, 136. I discuss the role of admiration and emulation more fully in relation to the virtue of integrity in particular in "Enacting Integrity," in *Integrity, Honesty, and Truth-Seeking*, ed. Christian Miller and Ryan West (Oxford: Oxford University Press, forthcoming).

76. David Velleman, "Motivation by Ideal," *Philosophical Explorations* 5, no. 2): 101.

77. Swales, *German Bildungsroman*, 32.

78. Friedrich Schlegel, "Über Goethe's Meister," in *Athenäum. Eine Zeitschrift*, 1.2 (Berlin, 1798; repr. Frankfurt, 1973), 323.

79. Selbmann, *Zur Geschichte*, 24.

80. The classic text here is Max Horkheimer and Theodor Adorno's *Dialectic of Enlightenment* (1947), trans. Edmund Jephcott (Stanford, CA: Stanford University Press, 2002), with its critical analysis of the "culture industry," 94–96.

81. Friedrich Schiller, *Über die Ästhetische Erziehung des Menschen in einer Reihe von Briefen*, (AE) in *Sämtliche Werke*, vol. 5 (Munich: Carl Hanser Verlag, 1975), letter 27, para. 12, 669; translation from *On the Aesthetic Education of Man*, ed. and trans. Elizabeth M. Wilkinson and L. A. Willoughby (Oxford: Clarendon, 1967), 219.

CHAPTER SIX

1. Undated letter to Herder (first half of 1794), HA 7:617. Where possible, I shall refer to the Hamburger Ausgabe (HA), which is the best modern edition: *Goethes Werke: Hamburger Ausgabe in 14 Bänden*, ed. Erich Trunz (Hamburg: Christian Wegner Verlag, 1950–68; Munich: C. H. Beck, 1981); remaining references to Goethe's works are to the Weimar edition (WA), which is the complete edition: *Goethes Werke* (Weimar: H. Böhlau, 1887–1919).

2. Jürgen Jacobs, *Wilhelm Meister und seine Brüder: Untersuchungen zum deutschen Bildungsroman* (Munich: Wilhelm Fink Verlag, 1972), 17–18.

3. Charles Taylor, *Hegel* (Cambridge: Cambridge University Press, 1975), 27.

4. Thomas Pfau, "Of Ends and Endings: Teleological and Variational Models of Romantic Narrative," *European Romantic Review* 18, no. 2 (2007): 233–34.

5. Michael Beddow, *The Fiction of Humanity: Studies in the Bildungsroman from Wieland to Thomas Mann* (Cambridge: Cambridge University Press, 1982), 136.

6. In fact, Goethe went so far as to insist that metamorphosis is a universal law of life. See, e.g., the *Elegy on the Metamorphosis of Plants*, HA 1:199–201, and the botanical essay *On the Metamorphosis of Plants*, HA 13:64–101, and the letter to Wackenroder of January 21, 1832, WA 4.41:209–11.

7. Jacobs, *Wilhelm Meister*, 79.

8. Schiller's statement comes in the course of an exchange of letters, subsequently published and well-known, between Schiller and Goethe: letter from Schiller to Goethe, July 8, 1796, HA 7:642.

9. HA 7:1.10, 37; E 18.

10. HA 7:4.19, 276; E 165, translation modified.

11. As Beddow argues, Wilhelm Meister testifies to the conviction "that there is something about imaginative fiction, and something about authentic humanity, which makes the former an especially suitable medium of insight into the latter." *Fiction of Humanity*, 6.

12. HA 7:5.7, 308; E 185–86.

13. HA 7:5.7, 308; E 185.

14. HA 7:4.15, 255; E 151.

15. Conversation with Eckermann, January 18, 1825, in HA 7:620.

16. "Tag- und Jahreshefte, geschrieben 1819–1824, aus dem Abschnitt "1796," HA 7:619. Thomas Saine, while rightly emphasizing the significant role of Fate in the novel and grasping the question mark this places over the enterprise of self-formation, seems to me to underestimate the complexity of the novel when he says that "the novel is not by any stretch of the imagination a Bildungsroman in the teleological sense. Wilhelm gets to the happy end because the author intends for him to do so." "Was *Wilhelm Meister's*

Lehrjahre Really Supposed to be a Bildungsroman?" in *Reflection and Action*, ed. Hardin, 131.

17. Letter to Schiller, December 10, 1794, HA 7:622.
18. HA 7:619.
19. HA 7:1.9, 35; E 16.
20. HA 7:1.17, 71; E 38.
21. HA 7:1.17; E 38, translation modified.
22. HA 7:1.17, 71; E 38, my translation.
23. James N. Hardin, introduction to *Reflection and Action*, xxi. On the irony with which the Tower Society is treated, see also Lukacs's perceptive comments, alluded to by W. H. Bruford: *The German Tradition of Self-Cultivation: "Bildung" from Humboldt to Thomas Mann* (Cambridge: Cambridge University Press, 1975), 55.
24. HA 7:550.
25. HA 7:8.3, 520–21, 527.
26. HA 7:8.3, 520.
27. HA 7:6, 419; E 254.
28. HA 7:8.3, 527; E 323.
29. HA 7:8.5, 550.
30. HA 7:8.4, 533.
31. HA 7:8.5, 550; E 337.
32. HA 7:7.9, 495; E 303.
33. HA 7:8.5, 548; E 335.
34. HA 7:8.5, 548, E 335–336.
35. HA 7:8.5, 548–49; E 336.
36. HA 7:8.1, 506.
37. HA 7:8.5, 548.
38. HA 7:8.5, 550; E 337.
39. HA 7:1.17, 71; E 38, translation modified.
40. Beddow, *Fiction of Humanity*, 126.
41. Bruford, *Self-Cultivation*, 31–32.
42. Quoted by Bruford, *Self-Cultivation*, 31.
43. HA 7:1.6, 23; E 9.
44. HA 7:1.5, 21; E 8.
45. HA 7:1.8, 31; E 14.
46. HA 7:1.8, 32; E 15, translation altered.
47. HA 7:5.3, 290; E 174.
48. HA 7:5.3, 291; E 175.
49. HA 7:5.3, 290; E 174; Bruford, *Self-Cultivation*, 37.
50. "Goethe one last time caught the reflection of the representative publicness whose light, of course, was refracted in the French rococo court and refracted yet again in its imitation by the petty German princes." Jürgen

Habermas, *The Structural Transformation of the Public Sphere*, trans. Thomas Burger (Cambridge MA: MIT Press, 1989), 13. Habermas focuses on the contrast between nobility as displaying or embodying authority in one's cultivated personality and the bourgeois need to prove oneself through making, production: "The nobleman was what he represented; the bourgeois, what he produced." However, what Wilhelm yearns for is a "freely self-actualizing personality" that he thinks at this point is to be found among the nobility, as opposed to the bourgeois, but that he must learn is in fact yet to be realized; it is a matter not simply of *appearing* but of *being* a certain way.

51. HA 7:5.4, 292; E 175.
52. Bruford, *Self-Cultivation*, 37.
53. HA 7:7.3, 433; E 265.
54. HA 7:7.3, 435; E 266.
55. HA 7:5.3, 291; E 175.
56. HA 7:8.1, 499; E 306.
57. HA 7:8.1, 499; E 306, translation modified.
58. HA 7:1.3.
59. HA 7:4.16.
60. HA 7:7.6.
61. HA 7:7.6, 446; E 273.
62. HA 7:6, 388; E 236.
63. HA 7:6, 400; E 243.
64. HA 7:6, 409; E 248.
65. HA 7:6, 415; E 253. This is often understood as expressing Goethe's own critique—e.g., Dorothea von der Mücke, *The Practices of the Enlightenment* (New York: Columbia University Press, 2015), 144. However, the positive role played by the *Schöne Seele* in assisting Aurelie's healing suggests that Goethe's judgment is more nuanced.
66. Goethe thought the task was much harder in modernity than in the ancient world, where the division of labor was less pronounced; see von der Mücke, *Practices*, 60.
67. HA 7:6, 420; E 255.
68. HA 7:7.9, 497; E 303.
69. HA 7:8.1, 504; E 309.
70. HA 7:8.1, 505, my translation.
71. HA 7:7.8, 488; E 298.
72. HA 7:7.9, 496; E 303.
73. HA 7:7.9, 496; E 303.
74. HA 7:8.2, 516; E 316.
75. Letter to Schiller, February 18, 1795, HA 7:623.
76. Jacobs, *Wilhelm Meister*, 84.
77. HA 7:7.9, 493; E 301.

78. HA 7:8.1, 498; E 305, translation modified.
79. HA 7:8.10, 610; E 373; conversation with Eckermann, January 18, 1825, HA 7:619–20.
80. HA 7:8.5, 540; E 336; Michael Minden, "The Place of Inheritance in the Bildungsroman," in *Reflection and Action*, 275.
81. HA 7:7.3, 430; E 263.
82. Jacobs, *Wilhelm Meister*, 37–38.
83. Bruford, *Self-Cultivation*, 55.
84. HA 7:8.5, 552; E 338.
85. HA 7:8.5, 552; E 338.
86. WA 2/6, 286; HA 13:109.
87. Goethe, *Maximen und Reflexionen*, ed. Max Hecker (Leipzig: Insel, 2003), no. 423.
88. HA 7:6, 405; E 246.
89. HA 7:8.5, 550; E 337.
90. Jacobs, *Wilhelm Meister*, 82, 85.
91. Jacobs, *Wilhelm Meister*, 85.
92. Letter to Frau von Stein, December 14, 1786, cited by Jacobs, *Wilhelm Meister*, 51.
93. Letter from Schiller to Goethe, July 6, 1796, HA 7:647.
94. Letter from Schiller to Goethe, July 8, 1796, HA 7:642.
95. Letter from Goethe to Schiller, July 9, 1796, HA 7:643.
96. This is Jürgen Jacobs's key insight: *Wilhelm Meister*, 89.
97. Ehrhard Bahr, "*Wilhelm Meisters Wanderjahre, oder die Entsagenden* (1821–1829): From Bildungsroman to Archival Novel," in *Reflection and Action*, 163–94.
98. Bahr, "*Wilhelm Meisters Wanderjahre*," 179, 183.
99. Nicholas Boyle, *Sacred and Secular Scriptures* (Notre Dame, IN: University of Notre Dame Press, 2005), 130. Sacred scripture, argues Boyle, reveals not only the truth of what is but the *ought* within the *is*, the response that this reality demands from us: it is "an ethical kerygma proclaimed in the name of the Unnameable" (81). Secular literature hints at this ought but cannot issue it as command. In order to utter this ought, God's will, a text must be authoritative. So it is finally sacred scripture's authority that distinguishes it from its secular counterpart. This authority cannot be demonstrated but is grounded in the faith of the church, the Spirit-inspired reception and interpretation of the Spirit-inspired text (85). The Bible here offers a semiotic universe or conceptual scheme not to rival others but rather as pointing us *through* the worlds of various literary texts, in all of their particularity and contingency, to a further revelation of how we are called to *respond* to these worlds (70–72). In this literary text we are not simply formed and determined by that particular world; in being so formed we discover the world

we inhabit in common (71, 135). In Shakespeare or Austen we are shown "things that before we heard and saw them we did not know we knew. But now that we know them, we all know them, for secular literature does not merely imitate truly. It publishes truths" (135).

100. Boyle, *Sacred and Secular*, 125.

101. Boyle, *Sacred and Secular*, 126.

102. Boyle, *Sacred and Secular*, 134.

103. Boyle, *Sacred and Secular*, 135.

104. Martha Nussbaum, *Love's Knowledge: Essays on Philosophy and Literature* (New York: Oxford University Press, 1990), 379. Boyle's points of reference, however, are Hegel, Ricoeur, and Levinas; Nussbaum's are Plato, Wittgenstein, and Murdoch.

105. Boyle, *Sacred and Secular*, 120. It would be fruitful to juxtapose this further to Steven Kepnes, who from a Jewish perspective writes of how scripture becomes "a model in the West for the revelatory and redemptive capacity of all writing and literature." *Jewish Liturgical Reasoning* (Oxford: Oxford University Press, 2007), 16; also "A Handbook of Scriptural Reasoning," *Modern Theology* 22, no. 3 (July 2006): 367–83.

106. Boyle, *Sacred and Secular*, 144.

107. Boyle, *Sacred and Secular*, 132.

108. Bernd Auerochs, *Die Entstehung der Kunstreligion* (Göttingen: Vandenhoeck & Ruprecht, 2006), 511.

109. On Goethe's self-distancing from the project of *Kunstreligion*, see Auerochs, *Entstehung*, 358–60.

110. Alfred Hölzel, "The Conclusion of Goethe's *Faust*: Ambivalence and Ambiguity," *German Quarterly* 55, no. 1 (1982): 1–12. Bernard Williams expresses something like this aspiration as responding to a demand for authenticity: "Find your deepest impulse and follow that." Here the idea "that there *is* something that is one's deepest impulse, that there is a discovery to be made here . . . and . . . that one trusts what is so discovered, although unclear where it will lead—these . . . are the point." *Morality: An Introduction to Ethics* (New York: Harper & Row, 1972), 86.

111. "The perfection and completion of a life consists in an agent's having persisted in moving toward and beyond the best goods of which she or he knows." Alasdair MacIntyre, *Ethics in the Conflicts of Modernity* (Cambridge: Cambridge University Press, 2016), 315.

112. Charles Taylor, *A Secular Age* (Cambridge, MA: Belknap, 2007), 359; on ontic indeterminacy, see also 404, 757–69; open and closed readings of the "immanent frame," 272, 550.

113. Kathryn Tanner, *God and Creation in Christian Theology* (Minneapolis: Fortress, 2005).

CHAPTER SEVEN

1. Georg Wilhelm Friedrich Hegel, *Vorlesungen über die Ästhetik*, *Werke in zwanzig Bänden* (Frankfurt: Surhkamp, 1970), 14:219. In 1835 (and then again in 1842) one of Hegel's students, Heinrich Gustav Hotho, published two editions of Hegel's lectures on aesthetics, based on Hegel's manuscripts and his own lecture transcripts. The English translation is G. W. F. Hegel, *Aesthetics: Lectures on Fine Art*, trans. T. M. Knox, 2 vols. (Oxford: Clarendon, 1975); here 1:557.
2. Hegel, *Werke* 14:219; *Aesthetics*, 1:557.
3. Hegel, *Werke* 14:220; *Aesthetics*, 1:557.
4. Rolf Selbmann, ed., *Zur Geschichte des Deutschen Bildungsromans* (Darmstadt: Wissenschaftliche Buchgesellschaft, 1988), 18.
5. Jeffrey Sammons, "The Mystery of the Missing Bildungsroman, or What Happened to Wilhelm Meister's Legacy?" *Genre* 14 (1981): 229–46.
6. *Werke* 13:89–92; *Aesthetics* 1:61–63; Stephen Houlgate, *An Introduction to Hegel: Freedom, Truth, and History*, 2nd ed. (Oxford: Blackwell, 2005), 212.
7. *Werke* 13:151; *Aesthetics* 1:111; see also *Werke* 13:61; *Aesthetics* 1:39; and Vittorio Hösle, *Hegels System: Der Idealismus der Subjektivität und das Problem der Intersubjectivität* (Hamburg: Felix Meiner Verlag, 1998), 602.
8. Houlgate, *Freedom*, 218; *Werke* 13:135; *Aesthetics* 1:97–98; *Werke* 13:233; *Aesthetics* 1:177.
9. See, e.g. Hösle, *Hegels System*, 619.
10. *Werke* 13:393; *Aesthetics* 1:303.
11. *Werke* 13:406; *Aesthetics* 1:313.
12. *Werke* 13:263; *Aesthetics* 1:201. Hegel nevertheless dismissed the "science" of physiognomy; the particularities of bodily form in individuals are accidental and not meaningful; *Encyclopedia Philosophy of Spirit*, §411, *Werke* 10:192.
13. *Werke* 15:550 *Aesthetics* 2:1218.
14. *Werke* 14:144; *Aesthetics* 1:531.
15. *Werke* 15:572–73; *Aesthetics* 2:1236. See Houlgate, *Freedom*, 237.
16. *Werke* 13:237–38; *Aesthetics* 1:607.
17. *Werke* 14:133; *Aesthetics* 1:522.
18. Houlgate, *Freedom*, 234, emphasis added.
19. *Werke* 13:25; *Aesthetics* 1:11.
20. *Werke* 13:120–22; *Aesthetics* 1:87–89.
21. *Werke* 15:17–18; *Aesthetics* 2:797.
22. *Werke* 15:152; *Aesthetics* 2:904.
23. *Werke* 15:145; *Aesthetics* 2:900; on poetry's synthetic character, see Hösle, *Hegels System*, 630.

24. *Werke* 15:224; *Aesthetics* 2:960.
25. *Werke* 15:339; *Aesthetics* 2:1053.
26. Stephen Houlgate, "Hegel's Aesthetics," *Stanford Encyclopedia of Philosophy*, ed. Edward N. Zalta (Spring 2016), 6.3.5.2, plato.stanford.edu/archives/spr2016/entries/hegel-aesthetics/.
27. *Werke* 14:219; *Aesthetics* 1:593.
28. *Werke* 14:219; *Aesthetics* 2:593; my translation.
29. Werke 14:220; *Aesthetics* 1:593.
30. Werke 14:221; *Aesthetics* 1:594.
31. Hegel's critique of the novel thus echoes his critique of Romantic religion as evidenced by Jacobi and Schleiermacher: see VPR 1:50–52; LPR 1:135–37, and Charles Taylor, *Hegel* (Cambridge: Cambridge University Press, 1975), 507–8.
32. *Werke* 15:552–54; *Aesthetics* 2:1220–22.
33. Hösle, *Hegels System*, 631n; Hösle, *Die Vollendung der Tragödie im Spätwerk der Sophokles* (Stuttgart-Bad Cannstatt: Frommann-Holzboog, 1984), 26–30; Allen Speight, *Hegel, Literature and the Problem of Agency* (Cambridge: Cambridge University Press, 2001), 96.
34. *Werke* 15:531–32; *Aesthetics* 2:1202–4.
35. Houlgate, "Hegel's Aesthetics," 6.3.5.2.
36. *Werke* 8:351, para. 194; translation from *Hegel's Logic*, trans. William Wallace, ed. J. N. Findlay (Oxford: Clarendon, 1975), 261.
37. Among these are M. H. Abrams, *Natural Supernaturalism* (New York: W. W. Norton, 1973), 510nn; H. S. Harris, *Hegel's Development: Night Thoughts* (Oxford: Clarendon, 1983), 222–23, 561; Walter Kaufmann, *Hegel, a Reinterpretation* (New York: Doubleday, 1965), 158; John H. Smith, *The Spirit and Its Letter* (Ithaca, NY: Cornell University Press, 1988); Mark Taylor, *Journeys to Selfhood* (Berkeley: University of California Press, 1980), 77. Cyril O'Regan surveys this trope in *The Heterodox Hegel* (Albany: State University of New York Press, 1994), 49–57, rightly noting that "the shift in the subject of inquiry from paradigmatic individual self to community and, more specifically, the shift in discourse from concern with the pedagogy of the individual to concern with the pedagogy of the community within which the individual is constituted is an important one" (51).
38. Allen Wood, "Hegel on Education," in *Philosophers on Education: New Historical Perspectives*, ed. Amélie O. Rorty (London: Routledge, 1998), 301.
39. Wood, "Hegel on Education," 301.
40. Wood, "Hegel on Education," 303.
41. *Werke* 3:72; *Hegel's Phenomenology of Spirit*, trans. A. V. Miller (Oxford: Oxford University Press, 1977), 49, para. 78.
42. *Werke* 3:29; *Phenomenology*, 14–15, para. 26.
43. On the problem of the *Phenomenology*, see Terry Pinkard, *Hegel's Phe-

nomenology: The Sociality of Reason (Cambridge: Cambridge University Press, 1996), 1–3.

44. Wood, "Hegel on Education," 303. On the ground-clearing function of the *Phenomenology*, see Robert Stern, *Hegel and the Phenomenology of Spirit* (London: Routledge, 2002).

45. Stern, *Hegel and the Phenomenology*, 24–25.

46. It is Nicholas Adams who perceptively identifies Hegel's reconciliatory logic as Chalcedonian: *Eclipse of Grace: Divine and Human Action in Hegel* (Oxford: Wiley-Blackwell, 2013), 23.

47. Robert Pippin, *Hegel's Idealism: The Satisfactions of Self-Consciousness* (Cambridge: Cambridge University Press, 1989), 250.

48. Robert Pippin, *Hegel's Practical Philosophy: Rational Agency as Ethical Life* (Cambridge: Cambridge University Press, 2008), 11.

49. Terry Pinkard, *German Philosophy, 1760–1860* (Cambridge: Cambridge University Press, 2002), 242, 278.

50. Pinkard, *German Philosophy*, 222; see also Pinkard, *Hegel's Phenomenology*, 16–17.

51. *Werke* 5:38; *Hegel's Science of Logic*, trans. A. V. Miller (Altantic Highlands, NJ: Humanities Press International, 1969; 1990) (SL), 45–46.

52. *Werke* 5:130; SL 121.

53. For this reading, see, e.g., Taylor, *Hegel*, 92.

54. See, e.g., Frederick Beiser, *Hegel* (London: Routledge, 2005); Rolf-Peter Horstmann, "Hegel's *Phenomenology of Spirit* as an Argument for a Monistic Ontology," *Inquiry* 49 (2006): 103–18; James Kreines, "The Logic of Life: Hegel's Philosophical Defense of Teleological Explanation in Biology," in *The Cambridge Companion to Hegel*, 2nd ed., ed. F. Beiser (Cambridge: Cambridge University Press, 2008), 344–77; Robert Stern, *Hegelian Metaphysics* (Oxford: Oxford University Press, 2009). For an overview of these developments, see James Kreines, "Hegel's Metaphysics: Changing the Debate." *Philosophy Compass* 1, no. 5 (2006): 466–80; and Paul Redding, "Georg Wilhelm Friedrich Hegel," in *Stanford Encyclopedia of Philosophy*, plato.stanford.edu/archives/spr2016/entries/hegel/.

55. Stern, *Hegelian Metaphysics*, 66, 64.

56. Stern, *Hegel and the Phenomenology*, 20.

57. Stern, *Hegelian Metaphysics*, 11. While the post-Kantian interpretation has sometimes been seen as having particular affinities with pragmatism, Stern argues persuasively for a stronger connection between this fallibilist metaphysical reading of Hegel and pragmatism, particularly in its Peircean strand. See "Hegel and Pragmatism," "Peirce on Hegel: Nominalist or Realist?," "Peirce, Hegel, and the Category of Secondness," "Peirce, Hegel, and the Category of Firstness," "James and Bradley on the Limits of Human Understanding," in *Hegelian Metaphysics*, 209–344.

58. Pippin does to his credit tackle head on Hegel's claims about nature as the finite manifestation of the Concept (*Begriff*) and of spirit as the truth of nature. He translates such claims into a point about the impossibility of a naturalistic reduction of spirit (i.e., human "mindedness"). "The suggestion Hegel appears to be making is simply that at a certain level of complexity and organization, natural organisms come to be occupied with themselves and eventually to understand themselves in ways no longer appropriately explicable within the boundaries of nature or in any way the result of empirical observation." Pippin, *Hegel's Practical Philosophy*, 46. The social project of studying nature, too, resists such a reduction. Pippin grants that one of our capacities is "the attempt to understand nature properly, in its truth, to get it right." However, he regards getting it right simply as a matter of arriving at an explanation that *we* find satisfying, that satisfies *our own standards* for explanation. Hegel, however, seeks through his dialectical inquiry to distinguish between better and worse standards for explanation, concept formations that uncover essential structures of reality and those that simply reflect parochial needs and interests. (On this point, see Hilary Putnam's classic essay on natural kinds, which attends to the contribution to cognition of both society and the "real world": "The Meaning of 'Meaning,'" in *Mind, Language and Reality* [Cambridge: Cambridge University Press, 1975], 215–71.) We do this not by checking our concept formation against reality, of course, but from within, by seeking to resolve gaps and tensions within our categorizations of reality. In so doing, though, we are becoming aware of nature as an expression or embodiment of reason or the Concept (*Begriff*). Nature lends itself to conceptual understanding in terms of natural kinds, natural law, mathematical relationships, because it is conceptually structured, and with the evolution of creatures who inhabit the space of reasons, this conceptual structure begins to come into view. John McDowell helps us to see why the alternatives to conceiving of reality itself as conceptually structured are unacceptable and end in pragmatic self-contradiction; this is, as Hegel recognized, the strongest sort of argument that can be offered in its favor: *Mind and World* (Cambridge, MA: Harvard University Press, 1994); "Two Sorts of Naturalism," in *Mind, Value and Reality* (Cambridge, MA: Harvard University Press, 1998), 167–97.

59. *Werke* 8:351, para. 194; *Hegel's Logic*, 261.

60. The phrase "infinite interrelatedness" is that of Rowan Williams, "Logic and Spirit in Hegel," in *Wrestling with Angels: Conversations in Modern Theology* (Grand Rapids, MI: Eerdmans, 2007), 36.

61. My account of the movements of the *Phenomenology* is indebted in particular to Stern, *Hegel and the Phenomenology*, and Houlgate, *Freedom*, 48–66.

62. PS §98, 60–61.

63. PG 94; PS §112, 67.

64. PG 95; PS §113, 68–69.
65. Stern, *Hegel and the Phenomenology*, 54–55.
66. PG 101; PS §122, 74.
67. PG 116; PS §143, 86.
68. PG 126; PS §155, 95.
69. I abstract here from the question whether these failures always amount to the kind of determinate negation that has been thought requisite to drive the dialectic forward in a necessary direction.
70. PG 168; PS §216, 130.
71. PG 178; PS §232, 139.
72. PG 232; PS §307, 184–85.
73. PG 261; PS §344, 209.
74. PG 278; PS §373, 224.
75. PG 290; PS § 391, 234.
76. PG 319; PS §431, 259.
77. PG 326; PS §441, 265.
78. PG 336; PS §457, 275.
79. PG 342–43; PS §464–65, 279–80.
80. PG 364; PS §489, 298.
81. PG 433; PS §586, 357.
82. PG 446; PS §603, 368. I set aside here the question whether Hegel properly understood Kant, and the question of what sort of harmony Kant entertains between duty and inclination.
83. PG 466; PS§§634, 385.
84. PG 484; PS §658, 400.
85. PG 543–44; PS §746, 452.
86. PG 552; PS §758, 459.
87. PG 573; PS §787, 477.
88. *Werke* 10:26; *Encyclopedia Philosophy of Mind* §436, 176.
89. Houlgate, *Freedom*, 41.
90. Williams, "Logic and Spirit," 36.
91. *Vorlesungen über die Philosophie der Religion*, vol. 3, *Die vollendete Religion*, ed. Walter Jaeschke (Hamburg: Felix Meiner, 1984).(VPR), 221; The English critical edition, edited by Peter Hodgson, includes multiple distinct versions based on lecture manuscripts and auditors' transcripts. *Lectures on the Philosophy of Religion*, 3 vols. (Oxford: Clarendon, 2007) (LPR), 3:297.
92. See *Werke* 1, *Frühe Schriften*; *Early Theological Writings* (ETW), trans. T. M. Knox (Philadelphia: University of Pennsylvania Press, 1948).
93. Thomas Lewis helpfully situates Hegel's early theological writings in the context of his perduring concern for social cohesion in *Religion, Modernity, and Politics in Hegel* (Oxford: Oxford University Press, 2011), 16–56.
94. *Werke* 1:246; ETW 305.

95. VPR 1:267, LPR 1:368.

96. Lewis argues that Hegel became disillusioned with the reconciliatory possibilities of love: "Hegel will go on to argue that the unity of love lacks the mediation necessary to preserve genuine difference" (*Religion, Modernity, and Politics*, 48). However, while it is correct that Hegel finds unacceptable any form of unity that involves the cancellation or destruction of difference, in his mature philosophy of religion he continues to insist that something importantly true is affirmed in saying that God is love and that ethical life, *Sittlichkeit*, is properly expressed in love; VPR 3:201; LPR 3:276; VPR 3:211, LPR 3:286; VPR 3:246, LPR 3:322. O'Regan, meanwhile, argues that "Hegel is vehement in combating any vision of the divine which does not include moments of exile and return," arguing that Hegel owes this emphasis on the essential role of conflict to Jacob Boehme's apocalyptic thought (*Heterodox Hegel*, 48, 283). The movement of the *immanent* Trinity, however, is more aptly captured in Hegel as self-gift rather than exile, suffering, or pain.

97. VPR 1:281, LPR 1:385.

98. VPR 3:209, LPR 3:285. As Williams comments, "a God whose identity is mediated *simply* through the world won't do. We have first to think about what it is in talking about God and the world that makes God's self-relation and God's relation to the world inseparable" ("Logic and Spirit in Hegel," 40).

99. VPR 3:146, LPR 3:214.

100. VPR 3:237, LPR 3:312–13.

101. VPR 3:250; LPR 3:327.

102. VPR 3:221; LPR 3:296.

103. VPR 3:221–22; LPR 3:296–98.

104. VPR 3:138, LPR 3:206. This is one of two forms of evil. The other is to refuse to become spirit, and to attempt to remain in a state of natural immediacy. VPR 3:222–23; LPR 3:298.

105. VPR 3:143; LPR 3:211.

106. For an exhaustive critical discussion of Boehme's influence on Hegel, see O'Regan, *Heterodox Hegel*, especially 175–80.

107. *Werke* 7, §139; *Elements of the Philosophy of Right* (PR), trans. H.B. Nisbet, ed. Allen W. Wood (Cambridge: Cambridge University Press, 1991), 169.

108. For a compelling theological account of self-createdness as the finite perfection (approaching the goodness of divine uncreatedness) that can make sense of why possessing a capacity to refuse the good is a good for temporal creatures, see Ross McCullough, "Divine and Human Freedom: Sin and the Doctrine of Creation," PhD diss., Yale University, 2018, 138–43.

109. On this point, see Dieter Wandschneider, "Die Dialektische Notwendigkeit des Negativen und Ihre Ethische Relevanz," in *Hegel-Jahrbuch 1987*,

ed. Heinz Kimmerle, Wolfgang Lefèvre, and Rudolf Meyer (Bochum: Germinal Verlag, 1987), 185–94.

110. *Summa theologica* (ST), trans. Fathers of the English Dominican Province (Westminster, MD: Christian Classics, 1981), 3.1.3 ad 3.

111. Peter C. Hodgson, *Hegel and Christian Theology: A Reading of the Lectures on the Philosophy of Religion* (Oxford: Oxford University Press, 2005), 277–78. I am grateful to a reader for the Press who called me to attend more carefully to the nuance of Hegel's position on these matters. This reader noted that the statement that evil is included in the divine identity may not mean that evil is thereby authorized. By analogy, "my identity may depend upon my relationship with another person, and that relationship may depend upon mutual forgiveness. In that case, the relationship upon which my identity depends may include misdeeds—even evil misdeeds—but it will include these misdeeds only as repudiated and 'negated' through forgiveness."

112. VPR 3:254; LPR 3:331.

113. Hösle, *Hegels System*, 590.

114. VPR 3:260; LPR 3:337.

115. VPR 3:263; LPR 3:340.

116. VPR 3:264; LPR 3:341.

117. *Werke* 7, §24–25; PR 20.

118. See Jeffrey Stout, *Democracy and Tradition* (Princeton, NJ: Princeton University Press, 2004), 193–95, and Molly B. Farneth's elaboration of these themes in *Hegel's Social Ethics: Religion, Conflict, and Rituals of Reconciliation* (Princeton, NJ: Princeton University Press, 2017).

119. For an important argument to this effect, see Robert R. Williams, *Hegel's Ethics of Recognition* (Berkeley: University of California Press, 1997), building on but also departing in some important respects from Axel Honneth, *The Struggle for Recognition*, trans. Joel Anderson (Cambridge, MA: Polity, 1995), 107. Due in large part to the influence of Alexandre Kojève's interpretation of Hegel, according to which the master-slave conflict of the *Phenomenology* is never resolved and the need for recognition always issues in struggle, this has often been overlooked: e.g., *Introduction to the Reading of Hegel*, ed. Allan Bloom, trans. J. H. Nichols Jr. (New York: Basic Books, 1969), 7. Other interpreters of Hegel have argued that intersubjectivity is suppressed in Hegel's mature thought in favor of a monological subjectivity: e.g., Michael Theunissen, "The Repressed Intersubjectivity in Hegel's Philosophy of Right," in *Hegel and Legal Theory* (London: Routledge, 1991). Williams regards Honneth and also Habermas to be unduly influenced by Theunissen's account. On Williams's own reading, which I find persuasive, mutual recognition is possible and brings about reconciliation without erasure of difference.

120. Williams, *Ethics of Recognition*, 56.
121. *Werke* 7, §189; PR 228.
122. *Werke* 7, §260; PR 283.
123. For Hegel's account of the part-whole relationship, see *Werke* 8:267–68; *Encyclopedia Logic* §135, 198.
124. Williams, *Ethics of Recognition*, 308, and Williams's broader account of Hegel's state as a social organism, which I follow here, 293–333.
125. *Werke* 7, §269Z; PR 290.
126. *Werke* 7, §352–53; PR 376–77.
127. *Werke* 7, §274; PR, 312–13. Note that Hegel uses *Bildung* here to talk about the highly individual character of national development.
128. *Werke* 7, §273; PR 312.
129. *Werke* 7, §303; PR 344.
130. See, e.g., *Werke* 7, §350–51; PR 376.
131. *Werke* 10, §393Z, *Encyclopedia Philosophy of Spirit*, 41.
132. Robert Bernasconi, "Hegel at the Court of the Ashanti," in *Hegel after Derrida*, ed. Stuart Barnett (London: Routledge, 1998), 52. A more sympathetic, but not fully successful, account is given by Sandra Bonetto, "Race and Racism in Hegel: An Analysis," *Minerva* 10 (2006), http://www.minerva.mic.ul.ie//v0110/Hegel.html. Susan Buck-Morss shows that Hegel shifted from an earlier, more radical view, shaped by unfolding events in Haiti: "Hegel and Haiti," *Critical Inquiry* 26, no. 4 (2000): 821–65.
133. *Werke* 10, §393Z, *Encyclopedia Philosophy of Spirit*, 42–43.
134. *Werke* 10, §393Z, *Encyclopedia Philosophy of Spirit*, 42–43, translation modified.
135. *Lectures on the Philosophy of Right, 1824-25*, cited by Bernasconi, "Ashanti," 58. *Vorlesungen über Rechstphilosophie*, ed. Karl-Heinz Ilting (Stuttgart-Bad Cannstatt: Frommann-Holzboog, 1974), 4:89, trans. Alan S. Brudner, "Prefatory Lectures on the Philosophy of Law," *Clio* 8, no. 1 (1978): 68.
136. *Vorlesungen über die Philosophie der Weltgeschichte*, ed. J. Hoffmeister (Hamburg: Felix Meiner, 1955), 1:212–71; *Lectures on the Philosophy of History*, trans. H. B. Nisbet (Cambridge: Cambridge University Press, 1975), 173–220.
137. *Werke* 7, §350–51; PR 376.
138. Bernasconi, "Ashanti," 59.
139. J. Kameron Carter, *Race: A Theological Account* (Oxford: Oxford University Press, 2008), 79–121.
140. See Williams's discussion, *Ethics of Recognition*, 327–33.
141. Williams, *Ethics of Recognition*, 333.
142. Jean-Paul Sartre, *Anti-Semite and Jew: An Exploration of the Etiology of Hate*, trans., George Becker (New York: Schocken Books, 1948), 57.
143. *Lectures on the Philosophy of Right, 1824-25*, cited by Bernasconi,

"Ashanti," 58. *Vorlesungen über Rechstphilosophie*, ed. Karl-Heinz Ilting (Stuttgart-Bad Cannstatt: Frommann-Holzboog, 1974), 4:89, trans. Alan S. Brudner, "Prefatory Lectures on the Philosophy of Law," *Clio* 8, no. 1 (1978): 68.

144. *Werke* 7, §57; PR 88.

145. *Lectures on the Philosophy of World History: Introduction*, trans. H. B. Nisbet (Cambridge: Cambridge University Press, 1975), 43; *Vorlesungen über die Geschichte der Philosophie*, ed. Johannes Hoffmeister (Leipzig: Felix Meiner, 1940).

146. See Wandschneider, "Dialektische Notwendigkeit."

147. PR 270 Zusatz, p. 302.

148. Karl Barth, *Protestant Theology in the Nineteenth Century: Its Background and History* (orig. German ed. 1952; London: SCM Press, 1972), 385.

149. Barth, *Protestant Theology*, 437.

150. Barth, *Protestant Theology*, 435.

151. Barth, *Protestant Theology*, 385.

152. Barth, *Protestant Theology*, 389.

153. Barth, *Protestant Theology*, 396.

154. Barth, *Protestant Theology*, 391.

155. Barth, *Protestant Theology*, 415.

156. Barth, *Protestant Theology*, 414.

157. Barth, *Protestant Theology*, 418.

158. Barth, *Protestant Theology*, 420.

159. Barth, *Protestant Theology*, 396.

160. Barth, *Protestant Theology*, 406.

161. Barth, *Protestant Theology*, 404.

162. Barth, *Protestant Theology*, 418.

163. Rowan Williams, "Hegel and the Gods of Postmodernity," in *Wrestling with Angels: Conversations in Modern Theology*, ed. Mike Higton (Grand Rapids, MI: Eerdmans, 2007), 33.

164. Barth, *Protestant Theology*, 76.

165. VPR 3:221; LPR 3:296.

166. VPR 3:221; LPR 3:296.

167. Houlgate, "Religion, Morality and Forgiveness in Hegel's Philosophy," in *Philosophy and Religion in German Idealism*, ed. E.-O. Onnasch and P. Cruysberghs (Dordrecht: Kluwer, 2004), 104-5.

168. Houlgate, "Forgiveness," 106.

169. LPR 3:337n239, from transcripts of the 1831 lectures.

170. VPR III, 3:259; LPR 3:336.

171. Karl Barth, *Church Dogmatics* (CD), ed. G. W. Bromiley and T. F. Torrance (London: T&T Clark, 1932-67), 4/1:419.

CONCLUSION

1. Eyder Peralta, "Video Shows Police Officer in Kenya Shooting Gang Member Repeatedly," *Morning Edition*, NPR, May 2, 2017.

2. Graeme Wood, "His Kampf," *Atlantic*, June 2017, www.theatlantic.com/magazine/archive/2017/06/his-kampf/524505/.

3. W. E. B. DuBois, *The Conservation of Races* (Washington, DC: Baptist Magazine Print, 1897), 7; Wood, "His Kampf," draws the connection between Spencer and DuBois.

4. DuBois, *Conservation of Races*, 9.

5. Jonathon Kahn argues that "DuBois's use of the idea of 'folk' is deracinated from an oppressive Herderian metaphysics that endows *Volk* with characteristic essences that defy historical processes." "There Are No Clean Souls," in *Race and Political Theology*, ed. Vincent W. Lloyd (Stanford: Stanford University Press, 2012), 126. But this is to underestimate Herder's historicism.

6. Anthony Appiah, "Cosmopolitan Reading," in *Cosmopolitan Geographies: New Locations in Literature and Culture*, ed. Vinay Dharwadker (New York: Routledge, 2001), 202; see also Appiah, *Cosmopolitanism: Ethics in a World of Strangers* (New York: W. W. Norton, 2006).

7. Appiah, "Cosmopolitan Reading," 174.

8. Luke Bretherton, *Christianity and Contemporary Politics* (Oxford: Wiley-Blackwell, 2010), 133–34, 213.

9. See my discussion of "mimesis and conversion" in *Putting On Virtue*, 66–71.

10. Ted A. Smith traces the ways in which this same impulse has been at work in narrating the Civil War in a way that makes massive death necessary to sanctify the nation, elevating it into a new sublime. Such narratives, he notes, "supply a sense of direction and purpose to history—and a kind of justification for the violent acts along the way—almost in spite of the author's intentions"; he adds, "When understood as a sacrament, the cleansing violence of the Civil War purified America for the work of empire." *Weird John Brown: Divine Violence and the Limits of Ethics* (Stanford, CA: Stanford University Press, 2015), 169, 170.

11. This is what Chad Wellmon suggests was "intimated" in Kant's proto-anthropology, even as it tended to "subordinate the particular to the historical march of the universal." *Becoming Human: Romantic Anthropology and the Embodiment of Freedom* (University Park: Pennsylvania State University Press, 2010), 189. The task of working out these "intimations" was left to Kant's successors, among them, for Wellmon, Schleiermacher, Novalis, Goethe, and Humboldt. We are still at work on that task.

12. Raymond Geuss, *Morality, Culture, and History: Essays on German Philosophy* (Cambridge: Cambridge University Press, 1999), 42.

13. Thomas McCarthy, *Race, Empire, and the Idea of Human Development* (Cambridge: Cambridge University Press, 2009), 133.

14. McCarthy, *Race, Empire*, 149; "the real problems for progressive thought arise when cognitive advances are connected too quickly with improvements in other aspects of human existence, at the limit with the quality of human life as a whole" (144).

15. Homi Bhabha, "Of Mimicry and Man: The Ambivalence of Colonial Discourse," in *Tensions of Empire*, ed. F. Cooper and A. Stoler (Berkeley: University of California Press, 1997), 152–60.

16. Barth, *Protestant Theology*, 76.

17. Barth, *Protestant Theology*, 282, citing Immanuel Kant, *Streit der Fakultäten, Gesammelte Schriften*, Deutsche Akademie der Wissenschaft zu Berlin (Berlin: Walter de Gruyter, 1907–) (hereafter AA), 7:58.

18. Barth, *Protestant Theology*, 283, citing AA 7:58.

19. Barth, *Protestant Theology*, 283, citing AA 7:59.

20. Barth, *Protestant Theology*, 283, citing AA 7:59.

21. Kant, AA 7:324; translation in *Anthropology from a Pragmatic Point of View*, ed. Robert B. Louden (Cambridge: Cambridge University Press, 2006), 229.

22. Barth, *Protestant Theology*, 296.

23. Barth, *Protestant Theology*, 299, quoting from *Religion within the Limits of Reason Alone*, 1794 ed., 83.

24. Barth, *Protestant Theology*, 300, quoting from a letter from Kant to Jung-Stilling.

25. Kant, AA 7:327; *Anthropology from a Pragmatic Point of View*, 232.

26. Barth, *Protestant Theology*, 266.

27. Barth, *Protestant Theology*, 114.

28. Barth, *Protestant Theology*, 288, quoting *Streit*, 75.

29. Robert R. Williams, *Hegel's Ethics of Recognition* (Berkeley: University of California Press, 1997), 33.

30. McCarthy, *Race, Empire*, 68.

31. Letter from Goethe to Herder, June 7, 1793, quoted in Barth, *Protestant Theology*, 294.

32. Derek Alan Woodard-Lehman, "Reason after Revelation: Karl Barth on Divine Word and Human Words," *Modern Theology* 33, no. 1 (2017): 92–115. I am indebted to Woodard-Lehman's work for drawing my attention to the significance of this strand of Barth's thought.

33. Kant, AA 8:38–39; translation in "An Answer to the Question: 'What Is Enlightenment?,'" in *Kant's Political Writings*, 57.

34. "The Desirability and Possibility of a Universal Reformed Creed," address to the World Council of the Alliance of Reformed Churches, 1925, in *Theology and Church: Shorter Writings 1920-1928*, trans. Louise Pettibone Smith (New York: Harper & Row, 1962), 115.

35. Barth, "Reformed Creed," 116.

36. Barth, "Reformed Creed," 117.

37. While an adjudication of the charge that Barth's conception of the divine command results in a fundamentally voluntarist ethics is beyond the purview of this study, it is worth noting that this picture of the discernment of God's command in and through the exchange of reasons with one's fellows offers an important corrective to any such conclusion. Scholarly discussion of voluntarism in Barth's ethics is extensive; McKenny offers an extraordinarily balanced and exhaustive treatment in *Analogy of Grace*, esp. 183–86. Other important recent correctives to the voluntarist view include Nigel Biggar, *The Hastening That Waits: Karl Barth's Ethics* (Oxford: Oxford University Press, 1993) and William Werpehowski, "Command and History in the Ethics of Karl Barth," *Journal of Religious Ethics* 9 (1981): 298–321.

38. Barth, "Reformed Confession," 119.

39. Barth, "Reformed Confession," 124.

40. Barth, "Reformed Confession," 132.

41. Barth, "Reformed Confession," 125.

42. Barth, "Reformed Confession," 126.

43. Barth, "Reformed Confession," 129.

44. Indeed despite his insistence that genuine confession comes from the boundaries, he did not always succeed in hearing it; as Paul Dafydd Jones notes, "although Barth is nearly peerless in his appreciation for how mainstream Christian thought might assist in formulating dogmatic contentions, he does not reckon sufficiently with marginalized voices." "Liberation Theology and 'Democratic Futures' (by Way of Karl Barth and Friedrich Schleiermacher)," *Political Theology* 10, no. 2 (2009): 277.

45. Barth, *Church Dogmatics*, 2/2:655.

46. McKenny, *Analogy of Grace*, 287.

47. Barth, *Protestant Theology*, 15, 22.

48. Barth, *Protestant Theology*, 22.

49. Barth, *Protestant Theology*, 24.

50. Barth, *Protestant Theology*, 133.

51. Muthu, *Enlightenment against Empire*, 268.

52. Muthu, *Enlightenment against Empire*, 268.

53. Muthu, *Enlightenment against Empire*, 278.

54. Judith Butler, "What Is Critique?" in *The Judith Butler Reader*, ed. Sarah Salih (Oxford: Basil Blackwell, 2004), 305.

55. Michel Foucault, "What Is Critique?"; Butler, "What Is Critique?" 308.

56. Foucault, "What Is Critique?" 47; Butler, "What Is Critique?" 305.

57. Walter Benjamin, "Zur Kritik der Gewalt," in *Gesammelte Schriften*, ed. Theodor. W. Adorno, Gershom Scholem, Rold Tidemann, and Hermann Scweppenhaüser, 7 vols. (Frankfurt: Suhrkamp, 1972), 2.1:199; English translation, "Critique of Violence," in *Selected Writings*, ed. Marcus Bullock and Michael W. Jennings, 4 vols. (Cambridge, MA: 1996–2003), 1:249. Ted A. Smith deploys Benjamin's notion of divine violence to brilliant effect in *Weird John Brown*, 69–83. Something like Benjamin's eschatological reservation ought, however, to be joined with rather than divorced from the ongoing fallibilistic task of casuistical judgment, in an orientation at once more creational and more incarnational.

58. Theodor Adorno, "Cultural Criticism and Society," in *Prisms* (Cambridge, MA: MIT Press, 1984), 30. Barth could agree with Judith Butler that "what conditions our doing is a constitutive limit, for which we cannot give a full account, and this condition is, paradoxically, the basis of our accountability": *Giving an Account of Oneself* (New York: Fordham University Press, 2005), 111. Barth would name this as the grace that precedes and enfolds judgment, and so while concurring "on the necessity of conceiving the human in its fallibility," would refuse Butler's demand to "avow error as constitutive of who we are" (*Giving an Account*, 111). "Original sin" names the way this needle has been threaded in the Christian theological tradition.

59. Gillian Rose, *Mourning Becomes the Law: Philosophy and Representation* (Cambridge: Cambridge University Press, 1996), 72.

60. Nancy Daukas, "Epistemic Trust and Social Location," *Episteme* 3, nos. 1–2 (2006): 109–24; Clifton Granby, "More than Just Testimony" (PhD diss., University of Memphis, 2017).

61. Luke Bretherton, *Christ and the Common Life* (Grand Rapids, MI: Eerdmans, 2019).

INDEX

Adam (biblical), 48–49, 66, 269n83
Adams, Nicholas, 301n46
Adams, Robert Merrihew, 260n36
Adorno, Theodor, 19, 250, 285n4
aesthetics: aesthetic autonomy and, 125–26, 127–28, 142; aesthetic disinterestedness and, 112, 125, 126–27, 142; aesthetic education and, 5, 82, 120, 124–31, 134–35, 154, 160, 171, 188, 191, 194, 229; aesthetic experience and, 194; aesthetic independence and, 196; beauty and purpose of art and, 125–26, 287n54; freedom and, 124–25, 126; Hegel and, 194–200, 211, 299n1; Herder and, 102–4, 283n75; morality and, 126–28, 287n58; truth and, 197. *See also* art; Religion of Art
Agrippa of Nettesheim, 267–68n53
Althusius, Johannes, 280n35
Ambrose, 218
Anderson, Benedict, 2–3
anti-Semitism. *See* Jews and anti-Semitism, Hegel and
Appiah, Anthony, 4, 238
Aquinas: active versus contemplative life and, 45; *exitus* and *reditus* of creation and, 89–90; imago Dei and, 25, 39, 40–41, 257n51; natural law and, 89–90, 117; Neoplatonism and, 39; problem of evil and, 218; transcendence versus immanence of God and, 101
Aristotle, 2, 50, 99, 128, 283n87
Arndt, Johann: Bildung and, 62, 272n27; career of, 60; Christ within the believer and, 63; devotional literature and, 144; divine and human agency and, 31, 63–64; the Fall and, 61–62; imago Dei and, 60–62, 63, 272n27; imitation of Christ and, 60, 62, 63–64, 272n27; influence of, 21; as mediating figure, 54; Pietism and, 60, 71, 78, 133; repentance and, 62–64; *True Christianity* by, 60–61
art: aesthetic education and, 23; autonomy of, 125–26, 196–97, 200, 230; beauty and purpose and, 125–26, 158, 287n54; Bildung and, 120–24; class and, 23–24; Classical, 195–96, 197, 211; cultural autonomy and, 154; death of, 195, 196; divine and human creativity and, 188–89; Enlightenment and, 134; formation of humanity

art (*continued*)
and, 188; freedom and, 124, 195; God's will and, 53; Herder and, 103; humanism and, 82; humanitas and, 35; Humboldt and, 121; Kantian moralism and, 12; Luther and, 74, 76; *Menschheit* and, 122; modern, 122; perfection and, 125–26; Pietism and, 31, 74–75; Pietist suspicion of, 74–75; versus religion, 83; Romantic, 195, 196–97, 200, 211, 230; sacred versus secular, 196–97; salvation and, 134; as surrogate for political action, 288n2; symbolic, 195, 197, 211; truth and, 194, 197; writers as artists and, 142–43, 158–59. *See also* aesthetics; Religion of Art

Atticus, 34
Auerbach, Erich, 138–39
Auerochs, Bernd, 186
Augustenberg, Duke of, 128
Augustine, 11, 40, 50, 61, 218
authoritarianism, 92
Avidius, 34

Barnard, F. M., 277–78n4, 280n35
Barth, Karl: autocratic humanism and, 26, 54, 56, 130; biblical creation story and, 283n80; Bildung and, 14, 16, 243, 250; church and culture and, 14–16; confession and, 246, 247–48; as dialectical theologian, 262n67; divine judgment and, 311n58; fascist nationalism and, 249; Hegel and, 16–17, 69, 231–35, 243; Herder and, 107–11, 130, 232, 243; human autarchy and, 14, 17–18; Humboldt and, 130–31; justification and, 56; Kant and, 243–46; Kingdom of God and, 261n53; listening for God's word and, 26, 187, 248–49, 310n44; non-Christian readers and, 18, 262n68; Pietism and, 17–18, 56–57, 59, 243, 271n1; problem of evil and, 26; *reditus* and, 250; Reformed creed and, 246–47; Schiller and, 130; Schleiermacher and, 16–17, 231; theocentrism of, 109, 262n67; theological lineage and, 17; voluntarist ethics and, 310n37; Word of judgment and, 136; World Council of the Alliance of Reformed Churches and, 249; World War I and, 232

Baumgarten, Alexander Gottlieb, 103, 125
Baur, Ferdinand Christian, 271n1
Beddow, Michael, 293n73, 294n11
Beiser, Frederick, 88, 258n11, 282n61
Benjamin, Walter, 250, 311n57
Berlin, Isaiah, 84, 277n1
Bernasconi, Robert, 224, 225
Biggar, Nigel, 310n37
Bildenden tradition, 94–96, 105
Bildung and the Bildung tradition: aesthetics and, 194; art and, 120–24; authenticity and, 151, 153, 176–77, 181–82, 276n66; autocratic humanism and, 58; Barth and, 243, 250; Bildung generation and, 4; Christianity and, 11, 71, 240–41; classical education and, 23; communitarianism versus individualism and, 24, 27; of consciousness, 200–203, 205, 209; context for development of, 21–22; contradictory points of view and, 19; cosmopolitanism versus particularity and, 3; critical theory and, 19; cultural heyday of, 292n64; dark side of, 223–28, 241–42; dialogic human activity and, 19; *Die Horen* and, 134; divine formation and, 21,

25; divine versus human agency and, 9, 47, 58, 104, 117, 239–40; Eckhart and, 46–47; elitism and, 38, 54; engagement with the world and, 115–16; Enlightenment and, 285n4; eschatological limit to, 16; ethical formation and, 53–54, 112, 156; evil and, 22; family as space for, 9–10; freedom and, 112–14, 123–24, 131, 188, 229; Goethe and, 119, 134, 157–59, 171, 183–84, 188–89, 194, 229; Hegel and, 189–91, 193, 198, 200–203, 219–31, 240–41, 250, 306n127; Herder and, 82–87, 90–92, 97–98, 100, 104–6, 109, 113, 117, 123, 188, 199, 229, 231, 240–41, 285n5; humanitas and, 38; human variety and, 114; Humboldt and, 82–83, 113–19, 123–24, 131, 188, 229, 285n5; imagination and, 74, 121; imago Dei and, 8–9, 20–21, 22, 28, 30–31, 42, 54, 90, 188, 238–39; imitation and practice and, 95; immanent teleology and, 24, 263n76; imperialism and colonialism and, 42, 241–42; inclusion versus exclusion and, 12–13; individualism and, 113–14, 229, 285n4; institutionalization of, 23; integration of natural and cultural worlds and, 188; Jakob Boehme and, 67, 70; Janus-faced nature of, 12–13; Johann Arndt and, 62, 272n27; Kant and, 244, 245; language of, 41; literature and journalism and, 4, 133, 143, 193, 200, 291n40; Luther and, 50; meaning of, 2, 6, 28–30, 33; *Menschheit* and, 113–14, 116–17; as merely human project, 22–23; metaphorical repertoire of, 46–47; before nationalism, 3; National Socialism and, 285n5; nature and, 53, 54, 85–86; Neoplatonism and, 25; the novel and, 146; *paideia* and, 264n8; Paracelsus and, 51, 53; pedagogical theory and, 113; Pietism and, 59; politics and, 2, 23, 219–23; present-day reflections of, 237–38; progress and, 42, 55; of protagonist and reader in Bildungsroman, 149–51; race and racism and, 13, 38, 93, 225, 241–42; realization of humanity and, 188; reconciliation and, 25, 58, 60, 188, 190, 193, 243; religion and, 117–20; Religion of Art and, 24–25, 200, 229–30; Schiller and, 131, 134, 183–84, 188–89, 229; secularization and, 7–8, 238; self-formation and, 188; self-government and, 92; social character of, 178–81; state's role in, 123, 124; telos of, 42, 110–11, 179–81, 187; telos of humanity and, 90, 113; theological task of, unfinished, 17; translation of, 6, 28–29, 32; tributaries of, 20–21; universality and particularity and, 201; vocabulary of, 70–75; voices on the margins and, 250–51. See also Bildungsroman

Bildungsroman: anti-Bildungsroman and, 149, 150; Bildung of protagonist and reader in, 149–53; coining of term, 148; definitions of, 134–35, 148, 149–50, 192, 292n56, 292n64; difficulty of, 154; elitism and, 148–49, 154; emergence of, 133–34; formative role of, 135; Germanness of, 153–54; German politics and, 148–49; Goethe and, 131; Hegel and, 192–94; literary canon and, 154; meaning of, 6; membership in category of, 151; as metafiction, 151, 153–54, 293n73; National Socialism and,

Bildungsroman *(continued)*
149; novel as new genre and, 23–24; *Phenomenology of Spirit* and, 25, 191, 201; Pietism and, 80, 135, 153–56; popularity of, 153–54; readers' emulation of protagonist and, 152–53, 293n75; self-reflexive features of, 151, 293n74; theory of, 147–55; third-person narrative and, 156. *See also* Bildung and the Bildung tradition; *Wilhelm Meister's Apprenticeship* (Goethe)

Blanckenburg, Friedrich von, 147, 148, 150

Boehme, Jakob: apocalyptic thought of, 304n96; Bildung and, 67, 70; biography of, 273n51; censorship of, 69; creation and, 64–66, 68–69; divine and human agency and, 31, 58, 240; Hegel and, 190, 241; Herder and, 104; imagination and, 273n44; imago Dei and, 66–67; influence of, 21–22, 26, 60, 69–70, 271–72n13; influences on, 64, 66, 68, 273n44; as mediating figure, 54; Neoplatonism and, 25, 64; Pietism and, 60, 69; Plotinus and, 26; problem of evil and, 67–69, 70, 217, 240; reconciliation and, 60, 68; Trinity and, 65, 273n56; Valentinian Gnosticism and, 273–74n58; Virgin of Divine Wisdom and, 66, 69

Bollenbeck, Georg, Humboldt and, 130, 285n4, 285n5, 285n12

Boyle, Nicholas, 184–86, 297–98n99, 298n104

Braungart, Wolfgang, 276n106, 286n41, 286n43, 289n13

Bretherton, Luke, 19, 238, 263n71, 280n35, 308n8, 311n61

Bruford, Walter, 295n23, 297n83, 304n83

Buck-Morss, Susan, 306n132

Buntfuss, Markus, 104
Butler, Judith, 19, 263n74, 311n58

Carter, J. Kameron, 260n38, 281n49
Casanova, Pascale, 280n34
Chakrabarty, Dipesh, 18–19
Chaucer, 36
Christianity: ancient pagan thought and, 28; Bildung and, 7, 11, 240–41; birth of Christ within and, 57; Catholicism and, 63; Christian humanism and, 8–9, 259–21; church and culture and, 14–16, 261n43; church community and, 218–19; civic participation and, 260n35; confession and, 247–48; *conformatio* and, 29; conversion and, 76–81; cosmopolitanism and, 238; creation and, 64–66, 68–69; creeds and, 246–47; dialogical Christian humanism and, 17; divine secrecy and, 18; divine versus human agency and, 63–64; doctrine of incarnation and, 21; election and, 78–79; Enlightenment and, 216; *exitus* and *reditus* and, 89–90, 239, 240–41, 250, 251; *felix culpa* tradition and, 190; friendship and, 8, 9, 11, 25; God's relation to the world and, 216–17, 304n98; God's word on the margins and, 246–251, 310n44; Goethe and, 229; grace and, 63; Hegel and, 25–26, 155, 189–90, 211, 214–16, 223, 230, 234–35, 240–41; Herder and, 89, 101–2, 108–9, 282n61; human dignity and, 264n9; humanism and, 238–39, 240; Humboldt and, 229; individualism and, 138–39; interiorization of, 56–57, 59; Kingdom of God and, 261n53; lectionary and, 75; love and, 11; Neoplatonism and, 83; original

sin and, 311n58; otherness and, 59; paganism and, 40, 266n39; *paideia* and, 264n9; political claims and, 18, 262n68; predestination and, 63; race and, 224, 225; reconciliation and, 15, 54, 58–59, 216–19; *reformatio* and, 29; versus Religion of Art, 23, 112; religious formation and, 154–55; religious persecution and, 68; salvation and, 29, 63–64, 71, 72; Schiller and, 229; transcendence and, 11, 25–26, 196; trinitarian life and, 242; understanding of humankind and, 27–28. See also evil, problem of; imago Dei; Pietism; Trinity
Cicero, 34–35, 37–38
Civil War (US), 308n10
colonialism. See imperialism and colonialism
community and communitarianism, 95, 230, 243, 247–48
Congress of Vienna (1815), 134
consociationism, 110, 131, 223
cosmopolitanism, 3–4, 92–93, 238, 250, 279
critical theory, 19–20, 263n74

Dante, 11
Dilthey, Wilhelm, 17, 148, 192, 292n56, 292n64
Dionysius, 44
disability, 263n71
Dohmen, Günther, 272n27
DuBois, W. E. B., 237–38, 308n5
Dworkin, Ronald, 260n36

Eckhart, Meister: Bildung and, 7, 30–31, 46–47; charity and, 45; Christ within the soul and, 43–44, 47, 49, 57, 67; imagination and, 74; imago Dei and, 20–21, 42–47; influence of, 47; introspection and, 50; love and, 45–47;

Luther and, 49; mystical tradition and, 71; Neoplatonism and, 43, 47, 269n78; Pietism and, 60, 73–74; union with God and, 45–47, 269n78
Edelheit, Amos, 266n39
Elsner, Jaś, 33
Engelsing, Rolf, 144
Enlightenment: art and, 134; Bildung and, 6–7, 285n4; Christianity and, 216; deism and, 78; freedom to argue and, 4–5; Hegel and, 210–11; Herder and, 83–85, 107–9, 282n61; human agency and, 104; imago Dei and, 267–68n53; individual and community and, 210; Kant and, 1–2, 4–5, 245, 246; moralism and, 56; Pietism and, 56, 271n1; providentialism and, 9, 189; universalism and, 18–19, 84
Ephrata Cloister, 69
ethics: ethical commonwealth and, 87; imitation and, 240; in Greek life, 209–10; literature and, 82–83, 135; love and, 304n96; sites of ethical formation and, 112; voluntarist, 310n37
Eurocentrism, Herder and, 92–94, 96–97, 107, 237–38, 308n5
Eve (biblical), 61
evil, problem of: Barth and, 26; Bildung, 22; Civil War (US) and, 308n10; divine judgment and, 250, 311nn57–58; *felix culpa* tradition and, 190, 218; forgiveness and, 305n111; forms of evil and, 217, 304n104; Hegel and, 9, 26, 70, 190, 217–18, 223–24, 227–28, 231, 234–35, 241, 305n111; Herder and, 106, 241; human will and, 218, 304n108; imagination and, 70; Jakob Boehme and, 67–69, 70, 217, 240; judgment of others and, 110; Kant and, 244–46; prog-

evil, problem of (*continued*)
ress of humanity and, 109, 110–11; reconciliation and, 26, 59; Trinity and, 263n79; voices on the margins and, 250–51

Fall, the, 61–62, 66–67, 217, 246
Farneth, Molly, 305n118
fascism, 249. *See also* National Socialism
Feller, Joachim, 60
Ficino, Marsilio, 50
Fielding, Henry, 147
Finnish School, 270n93
Foucault, Michel, 19
Francke, August Hermann, 57, 71, 74, 77–78
Frederick the Great (Prussia), 4, 5
freedom: of argument, 4–6, 125; art and aesthetics and, 124–25, 126, 195; autonomy and, 210; Bildung and, 113–14, 123–24, 131, 188, 229; in community, 230; *exitus-reditus* and, 189; formation of the self and, 112; French Revolution and, 210; grace and, 232; Humboldt and, 113–14, 188; reconciliation and, 197, 200, 213–14; Schiller and, 188; virtue and, 129
Freemasonry, 149, 164, 167
French Revolution, 23, 123–24, 129, 134, 210, 229
friendship: being fully human and, 251; Christianity and, 8, 9, 11, 25; in diversity, 12; divine, 15; divine invitation to, 189; Hegel's theology of reconciliation and, 215; imago Dei and, 40; love and equality and, 47; *reditus* of creation and, 239

Gadamer, Hans-Georg, 17
Gellert, Christian Fürchtegott, 144
Gellius, Aulus, 33

Gerrish, Brian, 101
Gnosticism, 273–74n58
Goethe, Johann Wolfgang von: aesthetic education and, 229; authentic humanity and, 296n66; Bildung and, 29, 33, 119, 134, 157–59, 171, 183–84, 188–89, 194, 229; Bildungsroman and, 131, 146–48; Christianity and, 229; dialogical character of humanity and, 179; *Die Horen* and, 134; ethical formation and, 82–83, 292n64; fate and, 182–83; *Faust* by, 187; as fiction writer, 143; Herder and, 156; Humboldt and, 119, 122; immanent teleology and, 24, 263n76; inaccessible works of, 134; individualism and, 81; influences on, 113, 114; Kant and, 246, 308n11; literary canon and, 145, 148; literary preferences of, 142–43; *Menschheit* and, 122; metamorphosis and, 181, 187, 294n6; Neoplatonism and, 83; Pietism and, 80, 157; politics and, 143; *Prometheus* by, 119, 122; purpose of art and, 158; Religion of Art and, 8, 9, 23, 186–87, 189, 229; Schiller and, 131, 179, 183, 194; spiritual autobiographies and, 146–47; teleology in nature and, 157–58; theater and, 169; valorization of imagination and, 239–40; *Weltliteratur* and, 143, 290n31; *Wilhelm Meisters Wanderjahre* by, 184. See also *Wilhelm Meister's Apprenticeship* (Goethe)
Goldsmith, Oliver, 141
Gorringe, Timothy, 261n43
Green, T. H., 139
Grenz, Stanley, 266–67n41, 267n51
Grotius, Hugo, 90
Guyer, Paul, 287n54

Habermas, Jürgen, 5–6, 9–11, 144, 290–91n33, 295–96n50, 305n119
Hamann, Johann Georg, 277n1
Hamlet (Shakespeare), 161
Hector, Kevin, 259n20
Hegel, G. W. F.: Aristotelian thought and, 283n87; art and aesthetics and, 154, 191, 194–200, 211, 299n1; Barth and, 69, 231–35, 243; being at home in the world and, 201n, 213, 213; Bildung and, 7, 189–91, 193, 198, 200–203, 205, 219–31, 240–41, 306n127; Bildungsroman and, 192–94; Charles Sanders Peirce and, 301n57; Christianity and, 17, 25–26, 155, 189–90, 211, 214–16, 223, 230, 234–35, 240, 241; colonialism and, 223–28; the Concept and, 25–26, 189, 191, 200, 212–20, 227–38, 230–31, 233–334, 251, 302n58; consociationism and, 223; contested interpretations of, 190; dialogical humanism and, 17, 238; Enlightenment and, 210–11; ethical formation and, 292n64; *exitus* and *reditus* and, 190, 219, 231; the Fall and, 217; freedom and reconciliation and, 197, 200, 203, 301n46; glorification and vilification of, 232; goodness of humanity and, 234; Hegel and, 191; Herder and, 230–31, 232, 241, 283n87; imperialism and colonialism and, 218, 241; individual and community and, 300n37; individuality and, 213; influences on, 60; Jakob Boehme and, 69–70, 190, 241; Jews and anti-Semitism and, 226–27, 235; Kant and, 190, 203, 204–5, 210–11, 246, 301n57, 303n82; master-slave dialectic and, 207, 212–13, 220, 305n119; metaphysics and, 190, 191, 203–5, 301n57; nature and science and, 202–3, 204, 206, 211, 302n58; Neoplatonism and, 25–26; non-autocratic humanism and, 58; the novel and, 190–93, 198, 200, 300n31; particularity and diversity and, 230–31; Pelagian thinking and, 234; philosophy of history and, 218, 223–28, 232, 241; physiognomy and, 299n12; Plotinus and, 26; poetry and drama and, 197–98, 199–200; politics and, 219–23; post-Kantian interpretations of, 205, 301n57; problem of evil and, 9, 26, 59, 70, 190, 217–18, 223–24, 227–28, 231, 234–35, 241, 305n111; race and racism and, 218, 223–28, 235, 241, 306n132; reconciliation and, 59–60, 189–90, 191, 230, 232–35; Religion of Art and, 8, 24–25, 189, 196, 211, 229; Romantic religion and, 300n31; Schleiermacher and, 16–17; self-awareness and, 25, 26; social cohesion and, 215; social contract and, 221–22; Spirit Monism and, 204; theology of reconciliation and, 212, 213–19, 220, 304n96, 305n119; truth and, 203–4, 230, 283n87, 298n104; universality and particularity and, 204, 208, 221; *Wilhelm Meister's Apprenticeship* and, 24–25, 192–93. See also *Phenomenology of Spirit* (Hegel)
Herder, Johann Gottfried: aesthetics and, 102–4, 283n75; anthropocentrism of, 109; anti-imperialism and, 249; art and, 188–89; authoritarianism and, 92; autocratic humanism and, 109; Barth and, 107–11, 130, 232, 243; biblical poetry and, 103–4, 283n79; *Bildenden* tradition and, 105; Bil-

Herder, Johann Gottfried (*continued*)
dung and, 7, 22–23, 29, 33, 82–83, 85–87, 90–92, 96–98, 100, 104–6, 109, 113, 117, 123, 188–89, 229, 231, 240–41, 285n5; Christianity and, 98, 100–102, 108–9, 282n61, 282n65; communitarianism and, 23, 95; consociationism and, 91–92, 110, 131, 223, 280n35; cosmopolitanism and, 92–93; culture and nations and, 3; deism and, 101; dialogical humanism and, 238; divine and human agency and, 96, 104; Enlightenment and, 9, 83–85, 107–9, 189, 282n61; epigenesis and, 91, 280n31; eschatology and, 111; Eurocentrism and, 83, 92–94, 96–97, 107, 237–38, 277–78n4, 308n5; *exitus* and *reditus* and, 231, 240–41; expressivist anthropology and, 88–89, 90; Goethe and, 156; *Gott: Einige Gespräche* by, 104; Greek philosophy and, 99; Hegel and, 230–31, 232, 341, 283n87; historicism and, 84, 102; human flourishing and, 89, 279n22; humanism and, 58, 107, 110; humanitas and, 94; *Humanität* and, 122; human self-correction and, 106–7; human variety and, 114; Humboldt and, 122–23, 131; imago Dei and, 22, 90–91, 97–102, 104, 106, 108, 113, 241, 266–67n41, 282n62; imitation and, 94–96, 99; imperialism and colonialism and, 88, 92–93, 94, 283n75; influence of, 113, 261n43; innovation and *Erfinder* and, 96–97, 100–101; Kant and, 86, 88, 107–8, 113; myth and, 257n7, 281n42; nationalism and, 91–94, 257n7, 280n34, 281n42; natural law and, 89–91; nature and, 85–86, 100; Nazism and, 281–82n56; Neoplatonism and, 25, 83; as non-Christian thinker, 267–68n53; panentheism versus pantheism and, 101; Paracelsus and, 91; particularity and diversity and, 230–31; pluralism and, 84, 109, 110, 284n105; as poorly understood, 83–84, 277n1, 277–78n4; postcolonial theory and, 92, 109, 110; problem of evil and, 106, 241; progress and, 83; progress of humanity and, 107, 109; providentialism and, 105–11, 241; race and racism and, 13, 83, 85, 93–94, 107, 109, 224, 237–38, 283–84n90, 308n5; realization of humanity and, 88–99; reconciliation and, 232; Religion of Art and, 8; Romanticism and, 84; Schiller and, 131; Spinoza Controversy and, 101, 282n66; spiritual autobiographies and, 146; *Sturm und Drang* and, 97; sympathy and empathy and, 89, 91, 280n33; telos of humanity and, 101, 113; truth and, 105–6, 283n87; universality and particularity and, 240

Hermann, Wilhelm, 17
Hermetic tradition, 50, 59, 60, 64
Homer, 31
Horkheimer, Max, 10, 285n4
Horstmann, Peter, 301n54
Hösle, Vittorio, 299n7, 299n23, 300n33, 305n113
Hotho, Heinrich Gustav, 299n1
Houlgate, Stephen, 200, 300n26, 302n61, 303n89, 307n167
humanism: ancient roots of, 39; art and imagination and, 82; autocratic, 26, 54–58, 109, 130, 243; Barth and, 26, 54; Christian, 238–39, 240; dialogical, 238; divine versus human agency and, 58; education and, 37–38; Herder and,

107, 110; humanist theology and, 266n39; humanitas and, 37–38; imago Dei and, 38–42; medieval versus Renaissance, 38–39, 266n39; neohumanism and, 6–7, 41; Neoplatonism and, 83; Pietism and, 80–81; *reditus* of creation and, 46, 83; Reformation and, 76

humanitas: elitism and, 47; formation of humanity and, 54; gentility and, 36–37; *Germania* myth and, 36; Herder and, 94; as human and divine, 35; humanism and, 37–38; imperial ambition and, 30; imperial rule and, 34–36, 54, 265n18; *paideia* and, 33, 34, 38; Roman origins of, 20, 27, 33–36, 38, 94; virtue and, 29, 33–36, 38, 265n18

humanity: adulthood of humankind and, 1, 27; anthropology and, 278–79n8; art in formation of, 188; authentic, 88, 187, 294n11, 298nn110–11; being fully human and, 27, 82, 242, 251; Christian understanding of, 27–28; dialogical character of, 179; disability and, 263n71; of each and of all, 19; goodness of, 234; individual and collective development and, 86–87; individuality and, 131; judgment of others and, 110; mature, 244; neighbor-love and, 85; nonhuman life and, 263n71; progress and, 88, 107, 109, 242, 309n14; realization of, 44, 47, 50, 83, 86–89, 112–13, 131, 188, 229, 237, 241; self-correction and, 106–7; self-deification of, 108; task of, 1, 2, 27, 41, 53, 86–87, 238, 242; telos of, 87–90, 101, 104, 106–7, 110–11, 113, 117, 283–84n90; universality and, 109–10

human rights, 3, 225

Humboldt, Wilhelm von: aesthetic education and, 5; Barth and, 130–31; Bildung and, 22–23, 29, 33, 82–83, 113–17, 118–19, 123–24, 131, 188, 229, 285n5; censorship and, 124; Christianity and, 83, 229; culture and nations and, 3; education reform and, 112–13; freedom and, 113–14, 188; Goethe and, 119, 122; Herder and, 122–23, 131, 282n62; human drives and, 127; human variety and, 114–15; imagination and, 120–21, 128, 239–40; imago Dei and, 116; individualism and, 23, 24, 113–14; influence of, 112–13; influences on, 113; Kant and, 117, 308n11; laissez-faire liberalism and, 123–24; *Menschheit* and, 113–14, 116–17, 118, 130–31; Neoplatonism and, 83; perfection and, 118–20, 131; Platonism and, 123; politics and, 129, 131; preformationism and, 285n12; Prussian educational system and, 32; purpose of art and, 158; religion and, 117–18, 119–20; Religion of Art and, 8–9, 23, 112–13, 121–23, 189, 229; Schiller and, 114, 116, 124, 127, 131; telos of humanity and, 113

Idealism, 6–7, 125–26

imagination: Bildung and, 74, 121; cosmopolitanism and, 54; creation and, 66; Eckhart and, 54, 74; the Fall and, 66–67; freedom and, 124; humanism and, 82; Humboldt and, 120–21, 128; imago Dei and, 66–67; Jakob Boehme and, 273n44; Luther and, 54; Paracelsus and, 52, 58; Pietism and, 54, 58, 70–75, 239; problem of evil and, 70; self-determination and, 95;

imagination (*continued*)
  union of reason and feeling and, 238; valorization of, 239–40
imago Dei: Adam and, 66; Bildung and, 83, 90, 188, 238–39; in Christian hearts, 48; versus colonial mimesis, 242; degrees of, 40–41; Dionysius and, 44; distinction between human and divine and, 21; doctrine of creation and, 20; Eckhart and, 42–47; Enlightenment and, 267–68n53; the Fall and, 61; fluidity and fecundity of, 30; friendship and, 40; as gift and task, 8–9, 15; God's will and, 50; heart, soul, and body and, 61; Herder and, 29, 90–91, 97–102, 104, 106, 108, 113, 241, 282n62; human agency and, 31; human dignity and, 242, 267n52; humanism and, 38–42; humanitas and, 30; human particularity and, 22; Humboldt and, 29, 116; imagination and, 66–57; implications of, 30; Jakob Boehme and, 66–67; Jesus Christ and, 61–62, 267n51; Johann Arndt and, 60–62, 63, 272n27; love and, 83; Luther and, 28, 47–50, 61, 63; malleability of, 41–42; *paideia* and, 30; Paracelsus and, 50–53; Pietism and, 73; *reditus* of creation to God and, 54; responsibility and, 39; Romanticism and, 267–68n53; versus self-formation, 156–57; substantial versus relational view of, 266–67n41; Trinity and, 40–41, 61; virtue and, 41, 267n51
imitation: of Christ, 60, 62, 63–64, 72, 272n27, 282n65; colonial mimesis and, 242; ethical formation and, 240; Herder and, 94–96, 99; social character of Bildung and, 178–79
imperialism and colonialism: Bildung and, 13, 42, 241–42; condemnation of, 88; Hegel and, 218, 223–28, 241; Herder and, 92–93, 94, 249, 283n75
Irenaeus, 266–67n41
Isocrates, 264–65n1

Jacobi, Friedrich Heinrich, 98, 282n61, 300n31
Jacobs, Jürgen, 291n41
Jaeger, Werner, 32–33, 264n9
Jesus Christ: Herder's Christology and, 100–101, 109, 282n65; imago Dei and, 40–41, 44, 48–49, 61–62, 267n51; imitation of, 60, 62, 63–64, 72, 272n27, 282n65; Kant and, 245; saving grace and, 267n51; within the believer, 63
Jews and anti-Semitism, Hegel and, 226–27, 235
Joest, Wilfried, 270n95
Jones, Paul Dafydd, 249
Jung-Stilling, Johann Heinrich, 146–47

Kabbalism, 60
Kahn, Jonathon, 308n5
Kant, Immanuel: adulthood of humankind and, 1; aesthetics and, 112, 125, 126–27, 287n54; austerity of moral theory of, 113; Barth and, 243–46; Bildung and, 244, 245; bureaucracy and, 125; categorical imperative and, 209; colonialism and, 88; Copernican Revolution and, 117; cultivation of feelings and, 258n16; Enlightenment and, 1–2, 4–5, 245, 246; ethical commonwealth and, 87–88; ethical formation and,

292n64; freedom to argue and, 125; Goethe and, 246; Hegel and, 190, 203, 204–5, 210–11, 246, 301n57, 303n82; Herder and, 86, 88, 107–8, 113; human autarchy and, 244; Humboldt and, 117; Jesus Christ and, 245; Jews and anti-Semitism and, 226; limits of Kantian reason and, 5, 245, 246; literary preferences of, 142; metaphysics and, 204–5; morality and moralism and, 12, 206, 210–11, 258n16; as non-Christian thinker, 267–68n53; politics and, 129; problem of evil and, 244–46; proto-anthropology of, 308n11; race and racism and, 13, 38, 87–88, 93, 226, 245, 260n38; realization of humanity and, 86–87; Schiller and, 128; subjective idealism and, 203–4; transcendence and, 231
Kemper, Hans-Georg, 267–68n53, 282n66
Kepnes, Steven, 298n105
Klopstock, Friedrich Gottlieb, 144
Kojève, Alexandre, 305n119
Kontje, Todd, 293n73
Körner, Christian Gottfried, 148
Kreines, James, 301n54
Kristeller, Paul Oskar, 266n39
Kunstreligion. See Religion of Art

Labadists, 69
Larrimore, Mark, 260n38, 281n47
Lavater, Johann Kaspar, 173
Lawrence, D. H., 150
Leibniz, Gottfried Wilhelm, 85, 98, 99, 278n7
Lessing, Gotthold Ephraim, 108, 292n64
Levinas, Emmanuel, 298n104
Lewis, Thomas, 303n93, 304n96
Lincoln, Bruce, 257n7, 281n42

literature: biblical poetry and, 103–4, 283n79; Bildung and, 143; canonical, 137, 144–45, 148, 154; commodification of, 189; of conversion, 78–81; critical public reflection and, 290–91n33; devotional, 144; ethical formation and, 82–83; German, 148; German identity and, 145; humanitas and, 34; introspection in, 31; literary societies and, 291n37; Luther and, 74, 76; market for, 154; Pietism and, 23, 78, 79–80; poetry and drama and, 197–98, 199–200, 230; secular scripture and, 142–43; as surrogate for political action, 288n2; truth and, 184–86, 187, 297–98n99, 298nn104–5; universality and particularity and, 186; *Weltliteratur* and, 143, 290n31; writers as artists and, 142–43. *See also* Bildungsroman; novel, the
Lloyd, Genevieve, 261n40
love: active, 70–71; Christianity and, 216; difference and, 241; in Eckhart's theology, 45; equality and, 46, 47; ethics and, 304n96; *exitusreditus* and, 189; as fruit of faith, 57; Hegel's theology of reconciliation and, 215, 220, 304n96; humanity and, 33, 85; imago Dei and, 12, 83; literature and truth and, 186; as relationship versus melting together, 45–46; transcendence and, 11
Luther, Martin: Adam in theology of, 48–49, 269n83; Augustine and, 50; Bible translation and, 28, 75–76; Bildung and, 30–31, 50; catechisms and, 75; Christ within the soul and, 49, 55, 57, 63; Finnish School and, 270n93; grace and, 63; human depravity and,

Luther, Martin (*continued*)
47–48; imago Dei and, 21, 30–31, 42, 47–50, 61, 63; influences on, 47; justification and, 48, 49–50, 57, 270n93, 270n95; mystical tradition and, 55; worldly phenomena and, 74, 76

MacIntyre, Alasdair, 2, 298n111
Maimonides, 267–68n53
Mann, Thomas, 149
Maritain, Jacques, 280n35
Marrou, Henry, 32–33, 264n8
Martin, Lucinda, 271–72n13
Mathewes, Charles, 260n35
McCarthy, Thomas, 14, 242, 309n14
McCormack, Bruce, 262n67
McDowell, John, 302n58
McGinn, Bernard, 46, 269n78
McKenny, Gerald, 18, 248, 262n65, 310n37
Meinecke, Fredrich, 280n31
Mill, John Stuart, 113
Miller, Richard, 284n105
Montesquieu, 94
Morgenstern, Karl, Bildungsroman and, 148, 150–51, 292n64
Moritz, Karl Philipp, 112, 125–26, 142, 151, 183, 287n54
Mücke, Dorothea von der, 290–91n33
Murdoch, Iris, 260n36, 298n104
Muthu, Sankar, 110, 249, 260n38
mystics and mysticism: Bildung and, 29; birth of Christ within and, 76–77; Christ within the soul and, 49, 55, 57; imago Dei and, 41; influence of, 21; Jakob Boehme and, 64; Luther and, 49, 55; Pietism and, 60, 71, 72–73, 78; union with God and, 44, 46, 60. *See also* Eckhart, Meister

nationalism, 3–4, 36, 91–94, 249, 280n34, 281n42
National Socialism, 13, 36, 130, 149, 281–82n56, 285n5. *See also* fascism
nation-states, versus nationalism, 3
natural law, 89–91, 117
nature and science: Bildung and, 53, 85–86, 188; creation and, 64–65; Hegel and, 202–3, 204, 206, 211, 302n58; heliocentric solar system and, 64; Herder and, 85–86, 100, 101; metamorphosis and, 181, 294n6; in Paracelsus's thought, 52–53; physiognomy and, 299n12; purpose of art and, 158; teleology in, 157–58
Nazis. *See* National Socialism
Neoplatonism: Aquinas and, 39; Eckhart and, 45, 47, 269n78; *exitus* and *reditus* and, 8, 25–26, 39–41, 90, 189, 231; Herder and, 83; influence of, 43; Jakob Boehme and, 64; Paracelsus and, 50, 52; union with God and, 269n78
Novalis, 267–68n53, 308n11
novel, the: aesthetic education and, 134–35; Bible as literary antecedent of, 138–39; Bildung and, 133, 146, 193, 200; commodification of, 132, 155; context for emergence of, 135–40, 289n18; critical public reflection and, 290–91n33; defense of, 147–48; definitions of, 148; dignity of the individual and, 137–40; ethical formation and, 135–36, 144; formal realism and, 153; in Germany, 141–42; Hegel and, 190–93, 198, 200, 300n31; individualism and, 137–38, 144–46; intensive versus extensive reading and, 137; literary excellence and, 143; literary market and, 154; as new genre,

23–24; novelty of, 136–37; objections to, 141, 142, 145–46, 291n41; objectivity and subjectivity and, 230; Pietism and, 80; popularity of, 140–41; reading public and, 144, 152; Religion of Art and, 131–32; as Romantic art, 198; role of, 131–32; as secular scripture, 140–47; spiritual autobiographies and, 147; versus theater, 140; writer as artist and, 158–59. *See also* Bildungsroman

Noyes, John K., 277–78n4, 283n75

Nussbaum, Martha, 3–4, 11–12, 185, 187, 260n36

O'Regan, Cyril, 68, 273n44, 273–74n58, 300n37, 304n96

paideia: competing visions of, 264–65n10; democratized, 23; education as, 30; elitism and, 32–33, 47, 264n9; formation of humanity and, 54; gentility and, 36–37; Greek origins of, 20, 27, 31, 32; human dignity and, 264n9; humanism and, 37–38; humanitas and, 33, 34, 38

Panaetius of Rhodes, 33–34

Paracelsus: entelechy and, 157; epigenesis and, 51–52, 91; God's will and, 52–53; Herder and, 91; imagination and, 52, 58; imago Dei and, 21, 30–31, 42, 50–53; Jakob Boehme and, 64, 66, 68, 273n44; nature and, 22, 50; Neoplatonism and, 50, 52; as non-Christian thinker, 267–68n53; Pietism and, 60

Peirce, Charles Sanders, 301n57

Pelagius, 234

Pfau, Thomas, 2, 263n76, 283n87

Phenomenology of Spirit (Hegel): absolute knowing and, 211–12; Beautiful Soul in, 210; Bildung and, 200–203, 205, 209; Bildungsroman and, 25, 191, 201; consciousness in, 200–203, 205, 207–10, 211–12; historical forms of thought in, 207–8; individual reason in, 208–9; infinite interrelatedness and, 206, 302n60; master-slave relationship in, 207; morality in, 210–11; movements of, 205–14, 303n69; problem of evil and, 250; religion in, 211; sense-certainty in, 206–7; Spirit in, 205, 209, 210; *Wilhelm Meister's Apprenticeship* and, 201–2

Philadelphians, 69

Pico della Mirandola, Giovanni, 50

Pietism: active, practical Christianity and, 57; active love and, 70–71; art and, 31; autobiographies and, 23; autocratic humanism and, 54–58; Barth and, 17–18, 243; Bible study and, 60, 75–76, 78, 133, 144, 189; Bildungsroman and, 135, 155, 156; birth of Christ in the heart and, 57; boundaries of, 59–60; charges of unorthodoxy and, 71, 74, 81; communal practices of, 155; community versus individual and, 57; conversion and, 76–77; definitions of, 59–60; deification and, 73; devotional literature and, 155; divine and human agency and, 21–22, 31, 58, 63–64, 76, 133, 239, 240; domesticated Providence and, 81; Eckhart and, 73–74; election and, 78–79; Enlightenment and, 56, 271n1; Goethe and, 157; human autarchy and, 245; human depravity and, 71; humanism and, 80–81; hymns of, 73, 275nn78–79; imagina-

Pietism (*continued*)
tion and, 54, 58, 70–75; imago Dei and, 73; imitation of Christ and, 72; incomplete Reformation and, 59; individualism and, 79, 81; inner voice and, 59; interiorization of Christianity and, 56–57; introspection and, 22, 24, 58, 76, 79–80; Jakob Boehme and, 69; Johann Arndt and, 71; language of, 79–80; literature and, 78, 80, 133, 137–40, 142; Lutheran, 78; mystical tradition and, 60, 71, 72–73; origins of, 59–60; outer activity and inner passivity and, 72–74, 81; Philipp Jakob Spener and, 70–74; radical, 60; rationalism and, 54, 57, 76–78; Religion of Art and, 80, 155; salvation and, 71, 72; spiritual autobiographies and, 79, 80, 139, 144, 146–47, 175–77; spiritualism and, 60; splinter movements and, 21; union with God and, 60; vocabulary of, 29; vocabulary of Bildung and, 70–75; *Wilhelm Meister's Apprenticeship* and, 162, 164–65, 175–77, 184, 187; works-righteousness and, 71, 74, 81, 133
Pinkard, Terry, 257n4, 258n11, 300n43, 301n49
Pippin, Robert, 258n11, 301n47, 302n58
Plato, 99, 116, 211, 260n36, 264–65n1, 298n104
Platonism, 123
Plotinus, 26, 46, 269n78
pluralism, 110, 284n105
police brutality, 237, 251
postcolonialism, 18–19, 92, 109, 110
providence and providentialism, 9, 13, 105–11, 261n40
Pufendorf, Samuel, 90

Puritanism, Pietism and, 59, 76, 78, 79, 139
Putnam, Hilary, 302n58

race and racism: Bildung and, 13, 38, 93, 225, 241–42; Christianity and, 224, 225; critical race theory and, 109; DuBois and, 237–38, 308n5; German *Volk* and, 94; Hegel and, 218, 223–28, 235, 241, 306n132; Herder and, 85, 93–94, 107, 109, 224, 237–38, 283–84n90, 308n5; Jews and anti-Semitism and, 226, 227; Kant and, 13, 38, 87–88, 93, 245, 260n38; progress and, 83; providence and, 13; voices on the margins and, 251; white supremacy and, 237
Ralph, James, 141
Ramsey, Paul, 266–67n41
rationalism, 54, 76–78, 107–9
reconciliation: Bildung and, 25, 58, 60, 188, 190, 193, 243; as Chalcedonian, 203, 301n46; Christianity and, 15, 54, 58–59, 216–19; the church and, 218; drama and, 199–200; freedom and, 213–14, 197, 200; Hegel and, 59–60, 189–90, 191, 212–19, 230, 232–35, 304n96; Herder and, 232; Jakob Boehme and, 60, 68; love and, 215, 220, 304n96; of objectivity and subjectivity, 230; premature, 246; problem of evil and, 26
Reformation, Protestant, 56, 59, 76
Reign of Terror (France), 4, 5, 210, 229
Reiser, Anton, 170
Reitz, Johann, 78, 79
Religion of Art: authority and, 136; Bildung and, 200, 229–30; versus Christianity, 23, 112; coining of term, 284n1; creation of, 112;

divine versus human agency and, 240; Goethe and, 8, 9, 23, 186–87, 189, 229; Hegel and, 8, 24–25, 189, 191, 196, 211, 229; Herder and, 8; Humboldt and, 8, 9, 23, 112, 113, 121–22, 123, 189, 229; inaugural text of, 286n43; insufficiency of, 194; the novel and, 131–32; ontological ambiguities of, 130; Pietism and, 80, 155; Schiller and, 8, 9, 23, 112, 189, 229; truth and, 186

Richardson, Samuel, 141, 147

Ricoeur, Paul, 298n104

Ritschl, Albrecht, 17, 271n1

Robinette, Nicholas, 277–78n4

Rock, Johann Friedrich, 73

Romanticism: art and aesthetics and, 12, 125–26; Bildung and, 6–7; Herder and, 84; human agency and, 58; imago Dei and, 267–68n53; Jakob Boehme and, 69; Pietism and, 22; Religion of Art and, 121

Rose, Gillian, 250

Rosenberg, Alfred, 281–82n56

Rousseau, Jean-Jacques, 108, 165

Saine, Thomas, 294–95n16

Sammons, Jeffrey, 292n58, 293n69, 299n5

Sartre, Jean-Paul, 227

Schelling, Friedrich Wilhelm Joseph von, 69

Schiller, Friedrich: aesthetic education and, 5, 82, 120, 131, 134, 154, 160, 171, 188, 194, 229; aesthetics and, 124–25, 126–30; Barth and, 130; Bildung and, 7, 29, 33, 131, 134, 183–84, 188–89, 229; Christianity and, 229; *Die Horen* and, 134; as fiction writer, 143; freedom and, 124–25, 126, 128; French Revolution and, 129; Goethe and, 131, 179, 183, 194; Herder and, 131; human drives and, 127; Humboldt and, 114, 116, 124, 127, 131; individualism and, 81; influences on, 60; Kant and, 128; literary canon and, 145, 148; literary preferences of, 142–43; literature in ethical formation and, 82–83; *Menschheit* and, 129; National Socialism and, 130; Neoplatonism and, 83; politics and, 129–30; purpose of art and, 158; Religion of Art and, 8–9, 23, 112–13, 189, 229; theater and, 170; valorization of imagination and, 239–40; virtue and, 128–30, 210; *Wilhelm Meister's Apprenticeship* and, 149, 158–59, 162, 183–84

Schlegel, Friedrich, 69, 134, 151, 153

Schleiermacher, Friedrich: Barth and, 231; Bildungsroman and, 148; ethical formation and, 292n64; Hegel and, 16–17, 300n31; Kant and, 308n11; as non-Christian thinker, 267–68n53; Religion of Art and, 184n1; telos of humanity and, 283–84n90

Schweiker, William, 259n21

Schwenckfeld, Caspar, 64

Scipio Africanus, 33

Selbmann, Rolf, 147, 289n18

Shakespeare, William, 161–62

Shorten, Richard, 281–82n56

Sikka, Sonia, 277–78n4, 279n22

slavery, 13, 207, 212–13, 220, 225, 227, 305n119

Smith, Ted A., 308n10, 311n57

Sophism, 31

Sophocles, 196, 206

Speight, Allen, 300n33

Spencer, Richard, 237–38

Spener, Philipp Jakob, 59–60, 70–75, 78–79

Spinoza, Baruch, and the Spinoza Controversy, 98, 101, 157, 282n61, 282n66
spiritualism, 60
Staël, Madame de, 3
Stahl, Ernest, Herder and, 280n31, 282n62, 282n65
Steiner, George, 144–45, 288n2
Stern, Robert, 301n44, 301n54, 301n57
Stoicism, Christianity versus, 11, 33–34, 89, 99, 207–8
Stout, Jeffrey, 260n36, 305n118
Strauss, David Friedrich, 291n40
Sturm und Drang, cult of genius and, 6–7, 80, 97, 277n1
Swales, Martin, 292n66, 293n67, 293n77

Tacitus, 36, 93–94
Tanner, Kathryn, 263n77, 298n113
Tauler, Johannes, 42, 47, 60, 78
Taylor, Charles, 12, 88–90, 121–22, 187, 277n1
Teerstegen, Gerhard, 72–74
theater: in Bildungsroman, 151–52; cultural authority of, 137; in Germany, 169–70; Goethe's involvement in, 169; moral education and, 143–44; versus the novel, 140, 147; Schiller and, 170; *Wilhelm Meister's Apprenticeship* and, 159–61, 169–74, 180
Thirty Years' War, 68
Thomas à Kempis, 60, 78
Thomas Aquinas, *See* Aquinas
Tonstad, Linn, 273n56
transcendence: Christianity and, 196; conception of the good and, 12, 263n76; contrastive versus noncontrastive, 187; divine versus human agency and, 239, 240; humanity as transcendent ideal and, 109; of ideology, 10; versus immanence of God, 101; immanent, 9–11, 12; Kant and, 231; love and, 11; *Menschheit* and, 116; radical, 12, 25–26; reconciliation and, 217–18; sacred value and, 12, 260n36, 262n68
Trinity: Hegel and, 215–16, 217–18, 304n96; imago Dei and, 40–41, 61; Jakob Boehme and, 65, 273n56; trinitarian life and, 242
Trinkaus, Charles, 266n39
Troeltsch, Ernst, 271n1
truth, Hegel and, 105–6, 203–4, 230, 283n87

Upton, Nicholas, 36–37

Vial, Theodore, 283–84n90
Virgin of Divine Wisdom, 66, 69
virtue: Aristotelian tradition and, 128; critique and, 250; freedom and, 129; grace and, 267n51; humanitas and, 33–35, 38, 265n18; imago Dei and, 41, 267n51; morality and, 128–30
von Hertzberg, Ewald Friedrich, 93–94
Voßkamp, Wilhelm, 293n74

Waugh, Patricia, 152
Wawrykow, Joseph, 267n51
Weeks, Andrew, 273n51
Weigel, Valentin, 64
Weimar Classicism, 6–7
Wellmon, Chad, 278–79n8, 308n11
Wicke, Erhard, 285n4
Wieland, Christoph Martin, 147, 149, 150, 153
Wilhelm Meister's Apprenticeship (Goethe): authentic humanity and, 180, 181–82, 294n11; author as Providence and, 161–62; au-

thor's role and, 159; Beautiful Soul in, 164, 175, 176–77; being versus appearance in, 173–74; Bildung of readers and, 151; Bildungsroman as metafiction and, 293n73; consciousness and, 212; context of writing of, 180; ethical formation and, 161, 193–94; as exemplar of Bildungsroman, 24, 131, 147–48, 149, 155, 193–94, 294–95n16; as falling short of Bildungsroman, 193–94; fate and, 159–64, 167–68, 182–84, 187, 194, 294–95n16; Freemasonry in, 149, 164, 167; Goethe's comments on, 162; Habermas and, 295–96n50; *Hamlet* and, 161; Hegel and, 24–25, 192–93; interpretive key of, 180; life of the soul to neglect of the body and, 176, 296n65; misunderstandings of Bildung and Bildungsroman and, 158, 183–84; narrating Bildung and, 174–78; particularity in, 188; passivity of title character and, 149;
Phenomenology and, 201–2, 212; Pietism and, 162, 164–65, 175–77, 184, 187; problematic of Bildung in, 168; as pseudo-confession, 156; publication of, 134; review of, 153; Schiller and, 158, 159, 162, 183; as secular scripture, 24, 184–87; social character of Bildung and, 178–81; telos of Bildung in, 187; theater and, 151–52, 159–61, 169–74, 180; Tower Society in, 149, 159, 161–63, 164–68; *Wilhelm Meisters Wanderjahre* and, 184

Williams, Bernard, 298n110

Williams, Robert R., 305n119, 306n124, 306n140, 309n29

Williams, Rowan, 302n60, 304n98, 307n163

Wittgenstein, Ludwig, 298n104

Wolff, Christian, 125

Wood, Allen, 201

Woodard-Lehman, Derek, 309n32

World Council of the Alliance of Reformed Churches, 249

World War I, 232, 249

www.ingramcontent.com/pod-product-compliance
Lightning Source LLC
Chambersburg PA
CBHW022031290426
44109CB00014B/818